HOW THE BRAIN WORKS

HOW THE BRAIN WORKS

MICHAEL S.C. THOMAS AND SIMON GREEN

WHAT PSYCHOLOGY STUDENTS NEED TO KNOW

Sage

1 Oliver's Yard
55 City Road
London EC1Y 1SP

2455 Teller Road
Thousand Oaks
California 91320

Unit No. 323–333, Third Floor, F-Block
International Trade Tower
Nehru Place, New Delhi 110 019

8 Marina View Suite 43-053
Asia Square Tower 1
Singapore 018960

Editor: Janka Romero
Assistant editor: Emma Yuan
Production editor: Martin Fox
Copyeditor: Tom Bedford
Proofreader: Jane Fricker
Indexer: Silvia Benvenuto
Artist: Scarlet Forrester
Marketing manager: Camille Richmond
Cover design: Wendy Scott
Typeset by: C&M Digitals (P) Ltd, Chennai, India

Library of Congress Control Number: 2023934178

British Library Cataloguing in Publication data

A catalogue record for this book is available from the British Library

ISBN 978-1-5297-4195-7
ISBN 978-1-5297-4194-0 (pbk)

CONTENTS

DETAILED CONTENTS

ABOUT THE AUTHORS

Michael S.C. Thomas is a Professor of Cognitive Neuroscience at Birkbeck, University of London, and Director of the Centre for Educational Neuroscience. One of his main interests is the translation of research between neuroscience and education. With Cathy Rogers, he recently published the book *Educational Neuroscience: The Basics* (Routledge 2023). The focus of his research laboratory, the Developmental Neurocognition Lab, is to use multi-disciplinary methods to understand the brain and cognitive bases of cognitive variability, including the use of behavioural, brain imaging, computational, and genetic methods. He has published over 150 scientific papers, books, and book chapters, and his work has been cited over 10,000 times. He is a Chartered Psychologist, Fellow of the British Psychological Society, Fellow of the US Association for Psychological Science, and Senior Fellow of the UK Higher Education Academy.

Simon Green was for many years a Senior Lecturer in Psychology at Birkbeck, University of London. Recently retired, he specialised in teaching introductory neuroscience to first year students. Along the way he published several textbooks in the area, including *Principles of Biopsychology*, still in print after 25 years. His research interests include neurotransmitter and hormonal modulation of brain function, the evolutionary background to the modern human brain, and the psychological and biological roots of psychological disorders. He is a Chartered Psychologist and member of the British Psychological Society.

ACKNOWLEDGEMENTS

We would like to acknowledge and thank many individuals who contributed invaluable advice, inspiration, and feedback during the writing of this book: Daniel Ansari, Philip Clapson, Michael Dash, Fred Dick, Iroise Dumontheil, Martin Eimer, Barb Finlay, Gillian Forrester, Neil Forrester, Scarlet Forrester, Ane Goikolea Vives, Jo van Herwegen, Paul Howard-Jones, Mark Johnson, Paul Johns, Annette Karmiloff-Smith, Victoria Knowland, Matt Longo, Denis Mareschal, Jay McClelland, Emma Meaburn, Cathy Price, Cathy Rogers, Angelica Ronald, Gaia Scerif, Helen Stolp, Hugh Lawson-Tancred, Sam Wass, members of the Developmental Neurocognition Laboratory, and members of the Centre for Educational Neuroscience Research Group. We would like to thank Iroise Dumontheil for providing the brain scan images used in Chapters 3 and 8 and Ane Goikolea Vives for the neuron image in Chapter 4. Special thanks to Scarlet for her fantastic illustrations, and to Hugh Lawson-Tancred and Lucy Palmer for combing painstakingly through the final draft. We would also like to thank our editors at Sage for their support and patience, Donna Goddard, Janka Romero, Esmé Carter, and Emma Yuan, as well as the production team. Research for this book was supported by a Wellcome Trust Institutional Strategic Support Fund Career Development grant. The authors would like to thank their families for their love, support, and patience during the writing of the book! MSCT: Sharon, Arthur, and Finbarr. SG: Mandy, Nathan, Jeremy, and Bram.

1
INTRODUCTION (AND SOME PUZZLES)

Here are some puzzles:

- Why can I forget what the capital of Hungary is, but not that I'm afraid of spiders?
- Why do I find I have learned things better after a night's sleep?
- I get seven out of ten in a test – why am I over the moon if I was expecting to get five, but down in the dumps if I was expecting to get nine? A seven is just a seven, isn't it?
- Why as a teenager did I start doing risky things to impress my friends (and getting grumpy with my parents)?
- Why does my mind sometimes go blank when I'm stressed in an exam, or forced to stand up and give a speech in front of people? And why do I vividly remember these experiences?
- Why do I learn a new language so much more easily when I'm five than when I'm 50?
- I was walking down the street the other day and I saw the ghost of Elvis Presley, and he was riding an elephant, and Marilyn Monroe was sat behind him. I'm never going to forget *that*. Why is it really easy to remember something unusual that happened – but then really hard to remember unusual facts, such as how to spell *acquiesce*, or the boiling point of nitrogen?

The answers to these questions – the explanations – lie not in psychology. Psychology is the scientific study of the mind, and it tries to figure out how the mind works by observing behaviour. Psychologists look at what people can do, at the mistakes people make, what they find easy and what they find hard. Psychologists then invoke invisible mechanisms to explain this behaviour: mechanisms like perception, memory, and attention. Based on task analyses and design principles, psychologists come up with a reasonable way that the mind might function. But sometimes, the way we think, the way we remember, just seems odd. Why should we forget memories differently based on their content? Why do we need to sleep?

The answers to these questions lie in the way our brains work. Our brains didn't have to work this way. There are other ways you could do what the brain does – think, sense,

Figure 1.1   You may forget facts but you don't forget you're scared of spiders. Why's that?

control a body – which wouldn't show these odd properties. Brains work in the peculiar way they do because of their biology; and the biology works the way it does because of its evolutionary history.

To emphasise this point, think of it like this. If you were the R&D division of *GAppleZonSoft Inc.* and you were building a robot that learns, it's pretty clear that you could design the robot's central computer so that it didn't have any of these odd properties. The robot could store [Capital-Cities] and [Potentially-Dangerous-Animals] as similar types of memories. It could store information independently of how rare the occurrence or usage was. It need not forget memories (have you heard of back-ups?). There would be no reason to include anything like 'adolescence' in the robot's programming. You could build your robot without emotions like 'stress' or 'anxiety' or 'embarrassment', which on the face of it seem to detract from performance. The central computer could learn without getting dispirited at its failures or cock-a-hoop at its successes. It would simply use adaptive algorithms to maximise objective performance metrics. And, battery life permitting, you could build a robot that didn't need to sleep to achieve efficient learning; or indeed, sleep at all.

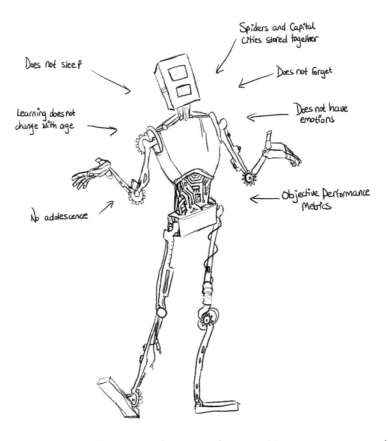

Spiders and Capital Cities stored together

Does not sleep

Does not forget

Learning does not change with age

Does not have emotions

No adolescence

Objective Performance Metrics

Figure 1.2 We now know there are other ways that cognitive systems can work

This book is intended to give you a basic understanding of how the brain works, and why it shows the kinds of properties it does. You might read this book before embarking on a neuroscience course that will then teach you the real nitty gritty – how to distinguish your ionotropic ligand-gated synaptic receptors from your metabotropic ligand-gated receptors, and your gamma frequency neural oscillations from your beta frequency oscillations. On that course, you can discover the array of methods and data that neuroscientists have used to build current theories of brain function. References to relevant research can be found in the bibliography for each chapter. Detailed links to the evidence supporting various assertions about the brain can be found at the website *how-the-brain-works.com*, which also includes additional material and illustrations which didn't make the final cut. Our focus in this book will be on the gist of how the brain works, to provide you with a structure for deeper investigation of the field. As we have already done, we think it's useful to compare the brain to other kinds of information processing devices, to emphasise that the solutions that the brain uses are not the only ones. For this purpose, we'll make frequent reference to the information processing device closest to hand. Your mobile phone.

This book originated from a moment of puzzlement for one of the authors, which he experienced while attending a neuroanatomy course. During a coffee break, the course tutor confessed that 'we understand almost nothing about how the brain works. Maybe in a hundred years, we'll have the answers. But right now?' He shrugged his shoulders. And yet, and yet... the bookshops are full of books about neuroscience and the brain, aren't they? *Fifty Amazing Facts About the Brain. Everything You Wanted to Know About the Brain. The Secret Life of the Brain. Ten Recipes Using the Brain.* There are piles of books out there. So, it certainly seems that we know something about how the brain works, doesn't it?

There's plenty we do know about the brain, even if some mysteries persist. So, let's start by distinguishing what we do know from what we don't know. Roughly, here's what we do know: the broad principles of brain function; that it's made of neurons, with electrical activity and firing rates; that there are lots of connections between neurons, and neurons communicate with each other via neurotransmitters; we know roughly which part of the brain does what, how it's wired together, and how it grows.

Here's what we don't know yet: the detailed circuitry within each part; the dynamic real-time interactions between the circuits that together determine moment-to-moment behaviour, combining the brain's electrical and chemical properties; the exact 'code' in which neurons speak to each other; how the brain handles complex, abstract thought and reasoning, often about itself, and formulates plans deep into the future; and how the physical brain generates the experience of being alive, the feeling that you are you (or I am me, depending on your point of view).

In our opinion, what we do know is enough to give a reasonable sense of how the brain works. That knowledge alone helps answer a bunch of puzzles within psychology, like the ones above. So that's this book.

There are a few things we won't spend much time on. We will only briefly cover the scientific methods used to discover what we know (brain imaging, animal models, single cell recording, and so forth) at the end of Chapter 3. We won't present an exhaustive list of the names of all the structures in the brain, unless the names help us understand how it works (more on that in a moment). We won't be cautious about the limits of knowledge and competing scientific theories – if something is in doubt, we'll make a best guess, and then use words like 'likely' or 'probably' or 'perhaps'. We won't try and impress you with lists of amazing brain facts. For example, we could tell you that each brain contains around 176,000 kilometres of wiring, but we won't. We're also not going to obsess over what makes humans 'special as a species', so special indeed that lots of aliens have to travel to Earth to study us (secretly, of course). We won't portray human brains as 'goofy and irrational' or 'quirky and flawed' just because we sometimes mess up. We won't bedazzle you with 'the mysterious enigma of the human brain, the most complex object in the universe'. Instead, we'll just try to give you a sense of how the thing works.

Not that humans aren't clever – we are pretty clever. However, intelligence is a tricky area. Animals do some pretty clever things, too. Birds can migrate using the Earth's magnetic field. Bees can hover on a windy day. True, the things humans *say* are really clever (there'll be a section on human language later). And human technology is, like, *wow*. But then, what humans end up doing is not necessarily so clever. You know what they say: *Give a man a fish and he'll eat for a day. Teach him how to fish and you get global depletion of fish stocks.* More on the environment and climate change later.

In fact, we'll spend a good part of the book focusing on how brains work in a similar way across most vertebrates, mammals, and primates, because our story will start with the brain's evolutionary origin. Only later will we begin to think about how humans are different, a class apart.

Back to those names. When you pick up a neuroanatomy book, the first thing you'll notice is how many Latin and Greek names there are for all the different parts of the brain. Say we told you that the *retrosplenial cortex* is involved in spatial memory and imagination. What would you take from that? That fashion moves fast in the world of spleens? There's *cortex* and *basal ganglia*, *amygdala* and *hippocampus*, *insula*, *fornix*, and *cerebellum*. It can get confusing. We do need to give names to the parts of the brain so that we can ask questions like *what does x-bit do?* But a list of names of brain structures and the fibres connecting them doesn't necessarily get us closer to understanding how the whole thing works.

Where did these names come from? Well, mostly the names were invented by 18th and 19th century anatomists who were taking human brains apart. The terminology derives from what the structures of the brain resembled when they were dissected. An anatomist might hold up a bit of the brain, and it would go something like this:

'I say, Carruthers, this piece looks like an almond', he'd say.

'That does not sound especially scientific, my dear fellow', his colleague would reply, chidingly. 'An almond, indeed? No right-minded gentlemen would believe that we have nuts in our heads'.

The first anatomist would wipe his hands on his apron and nod thoughtfully: 'True, true, sir. Very well. Let us use a Greek word, or a word of Latinate origin'.

'Latin for almonds… let me see, that would make it amygdala, I believe'.

'Amygdala it is'.

'We have discovered the amygdala. I observe one on each side'.

'Bravo, good fellow, most capital. Let us proceed. Wait, I've found another piece here, just behind it, and this one has the resemblance of a seahorse…'

Names of parts of the brain mainly come from what the structures physically look like. If we were naming them now, they would probably end up with different names. For example, there is a bit of the brain at the front on the left-hand side that looks like a big M. Today we'd probably call it the *Ronaldus McDonaldus* rather than the *inferior frontal gyrus*.

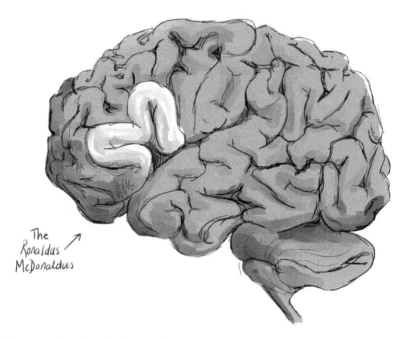

Figure 1.3   A newly identified part of the brain, the Ronaldus McDonaldus

Joking aside, just because there's a bit of the brain that looks distinct enough to get a label does not necessarily mean that the structure has a distinct or single function. Let's use an analogy. The power lead of a computer is a distinct, separable bit (let's be more scientific and give it a Latin name, the *fulminis funiculus* – literally, cord of lightning). But the power lead doesn't turn out to have a separate function in the computer: the *fulminis funiculus* is part of the electrical circuit that contributes to the operation of the whole computer. Focusing on parts by giving them names can divert us from how the whole system operates.

One more thing before we get going: a few words of sympathy for psychologists. Figuring out how the mind is generated by the brain has turned out to be a complicated affair. When we look at human behaviour, what we see is often a fluid, smooth, glistening, dynamic interaction with the world. The mind can seem unified from the outside. It can feel unified from the inside. But when psychologists have taken this outside-looking-in approach, they have constantly run into the same problem. What is one thing in psychology is many things in the brain. For example, although 'keeping something in mind' seems like a single thing, there are many 'working memory' systems in the brain that maintain recent neural activity to influence future behaviour, distributed across control systems and specialised circuits. In this book, we'll come across several concepts in psychology that turn out to be many things in the brain, among them the self, learning, concepts, personality, people, language, and value.

Much of psychology is populated by concepts that are activities of multiple coordinated brain systems, rather than the direct action of individual parts. Activities like 'comprehending' or 'problem solving' or 'drawing' or 'counting' or 'deciding'. In an activity, lots of areas of the brain work together; different subsets work together for different activities; and there is fluid interaction between brain, body, and external world, sometimes including physical and information tools (paper and pen, computer). This complexity isn't always reflected in the simpler terms that psychologists use.

When we 'look inside' our minds, this does not always get us much closer to how the brain works. Take that voice in your head, the one that you use to reason with before you make a decision. 'Should I have that extra slice of cake or not? Well, I only had one slice of toast for breakfast, and I sort of worked out yesterday, so maybe it's okay. I probably deserve the cake'. The voice (psychologists call it the 'phonological loop') is generated in the left side of the brain, in the bit next to the ear. Does the voice give you an insight into how decision making works in the brain? No. That's not the bit of the brain that makes decisions. The bit that makes decisions is the front. When you listen to the voice in your head, you're listening to the commentator, not the decision maker. Looking inside, so-called *introspection*, can mislead.

Introspection tells us that we are conscious, self-aware. Psychologists are rightly concerned with consciousness, the mental life – the 'you' that you experience, your awareness, the thoughts you have about yourself, what it feels like. Here, neuroscience is making progress but still doesn't have definitive answers. We'll take a look at the state of play on this research later in Chapter 9. But broadly, we're still at the stage of lining up which parts of the brain become more active when we have certain experiences, or aren't active when we're unconscious. However, the story seems to be headed in the same general direction: one experience in the mind is produced by lots of bits of the brain interacting with each other. One thing in the mind is many things in the brain.

Nevertheless, there are some areas where psychology has a good story, but neuroscience cannot yet generate useful explanations. These are in more complex areas of cognition: reasoning, abstract thought, imagination, analogies, jokes, metaphors, creativity, planning, sophisticated mental models of the world, scientific theorising. These kinds of complex cognitive processes are inferred by psychologists based on behaviour. As yet, it is not feasible to map patterns of brain activity onto these hypothetical cognitive processes. Building detailed links between psychology and neuroscience is a big challenge and it will take a while. Now, let's get going on the brain.

2
WHERE THE BRAIN COMES FROM: EVOLUTION

Why start here? Shouldn't we be listing how many lobes the brain has or labelling different types of neurons? Back in 1973, a wise person once said that nothing in biology makes sense except in the light of evolution. The same holds for the brain. The brain could have worked differently. Engineers now know that there are other ways to make cognitive systems, for instance to control autonomous robots. The brain works the way it does because of biology, and the biology is the way it is because of evolution. So, we start with evolution.

Figure 2.1   The evolution of *Homo sapiens* (and tools)

Things You Need to Know About Evolution

There are a few things you need to know about evolution. First, many of the basic properties of cells, neurons, and brains are common across a lot of species. They are, in the terminology of the field, 'highly conserved'. When biological changes emerged supporting the survival of cells (either on their own or working together in multi-cellular organisms), these changes were retained and exploited. Because similar mechanisms are found across a range of animals, neuroscientists can discover a lot about the function of neurons by seeing how they work in sea slugs or zebra fish or honeybees – all of which have fewer avenues to complain when their circuits are probed in the lab.

The functions of neurons have taken eons to evolve. The sodium ion channels in the cell walls of neurons that contribute to their electrical activity probably emerged from single cells floating in seas, lakes, and puddles. Those cells needed to regulate their salinity, letting sodium ions in or out, or they risked popping. The chemical receptors that neurons now use to communicate with other neurons probably evolved in single-celled organisms to help them find algae to feed off, by sensing the chemicals those algae exuded. It took a long time to fine-tune and bring together all these properties into cells with the specialised function of neurons, sitting inside complex multi-cellular animals.

Here's the second thing you need to know. When we look across mammals (furry, warm-blooded vertebrates who feed their young with milk), there are no new bits of the brain for new more complex behaviours observed across the various species. The general plan for building a body with a spine and a brain goes back a long way, perhaps 450 million years; the plans for brain cells – neurons, with their connections, electrical properties, and neurotransmitters – still further. Broadly, the growth plan is the same across vertebrate species. You can spot some differences in the split between amphibians, reptiles, and mammals, so that the type of neurons that make up the cortex (the outer layer of the brain) look like a bit of an innovation for mammals. But within mammals, you see similar structures from rats to cats to chimpanzees to humans (in the diagram, front [white], middle [light grey], and back parts [dark grey], or more technically forebrain, midbrain, and hindbrain). What differs is the relative size of the different parts, and the rate at which those parts scale up as the overall size of the brain increases across mammalian species, with the front part becoming progressively larger in larger brains.

The third point is that there are constraints on the changes that evolution can make. It can only improve what was already there. For example, how did we end up with whales, large mammals that swim in the sea? So, evolution might start with a big wading land mammal, something like a hippopotamus. Then it might double-down on the water dwelling angle and make the move to a species like a whale by adding additional air intake and neglecting those legs. The move was: take a large beast that likes wallowing in shallow water and make it *swimmier*. But there is a raft of moves that evolution couldn't make from this point. It couldn't go from a hippopotamus to a moth. It couldn't leap from a hippopotamus to a water boatman. It couldn't transform from a hippopotamus to a mole (unless you were prepared to put up with really big holes in your lawn).

This means evolution can get stuck in dead ends. It means evolution can produce species with gremlins, flaws, and bugs – because of what it had to start with. Humans have their share of gremlins: Using the same tube to breathe through and to eat through, so

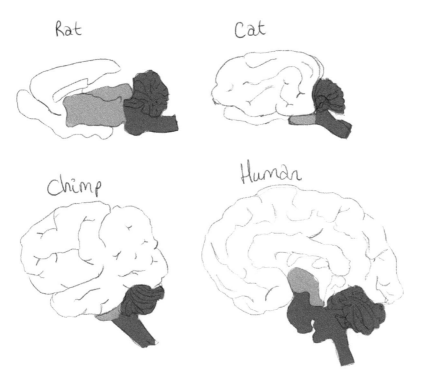

Figure 2.2 Brains for mammalian species all have the same parts, scaled differently

that we can choke. Putting nerves in teeth, so that we can have crippling toothache. There are hiccups, those persistent, uncomfortable muscle spasms of the diaphragm. For the brain, there's déjà vu, the moment of disorientation as you swear you've experienced this exact moment before. Following this principle of make-the-best-of-what-you've-got, it is possible that there are better ways to do cognition than with neurons, but this is the pathway evolution has followed. It adopted cells with certain electrical and chemical properties to sit between cells that sense and cells that move, and now it must make the best of it.

One way of thinking about how evolution is restricted in producing different brains is in terms of a brain-making machine. Let's call it the Brain-Builder-5000. You set the knobs and dials on the machine, and it will grow a brain for you. Depending on how you set the controls, you get different sizes and structures in your brain. Now we let evolution act. For example if, when growing your brain, setting knob #3 to 7 instead of 6 allows you to generate behaviours that lead the organism to produce more offspring, then the next generation will have more individuals in it with knob #3 set to 7. Eventually, some generations later, maybe all members of the species will have knob #3 set to 7 and the poor

6-ers will be long gone. The constraints that evolution must act under are the set of controls on the machine: how many dials and knobs it has. These represent the range of different brains that can be grown using the highly conserved genetic plan.

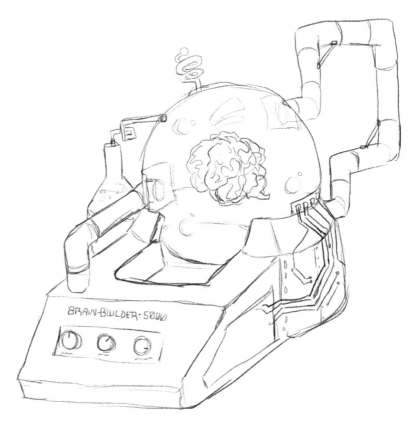

Figure 2.3 One way of thinking about the constraints on evolving brains: The Brain-Builder-5000

Working out how and why the human brain evolved the way it did isn't easy. It's hard to identify long after the fact exactly what it was about setting knob #3 to 7 that gave our ancestors a breeding advantage. There's a lack of direct evidence. It's easy to speculate and come up with plausible stories. For instance, why did humans evolve to walk upright? Was it to run further on the African savannah? Why did humans evolve to use complex language? Was it to complain about how far they had to run on the savannah? We don't know. What we do know is that selection-of-the-fittest only works in terms of the knobs and dials available on the brain-making machine. Those are the choices you can select from. The changes to the *set* of knobs and dials have been few and far between.

In our analogy, the advantage yielded by setting knob #3 to 7 will also alter – and potentially improve – any other behaviour that relies on brain properties set by knob #3. The brains of human ancestors increased in size for perhaps two million years before the emergence of *Homo sapiens*. There must have been some advantage that was making hominin brains bigger. Bigger brains potentially allow you to be more intelligent. Bigger brains support more complex behaviour. We will come back to speculate on how this unfolded in Chapter 9. But right now, just remember that the answers to these questions are mostly speculation.

Sometimes speculation can run into something closer to a party game. In the game, you make up a story about how any given human ability might have been selected for by evolution. You base this on how that ability might conceivably have proffered an advantage on the grassy plains of ancestral Africa. How about humour? *We evolved humour because life was somewhat boring on the savannah, and it would have been attractive to potential mates if you could crack a joke.* How about tidying up? *We evolved the ability to sort objects because our firewood could get lost in the long grass of the savannah, and it was adaptive to keep your patch tidy.* Games are fun. We need to have fun sometimes in these dark days. The key point here is that if there's no knob on the brain-making machine to specifically improve humour or tidiness (which there isn't – see the rest of the book) then evolution *cannot* specifically select for it. Proposals about what was selected for must be couched in terms of what was *selectable*. More broadly, theories of evolution need to be constrained by our understanding of how genes influence brain development.

How Brain Evolution Works

Here are a couple of rules of thumb on how evolution seems to work. *Evolution tends to innovate at the periphery, while the brain is smaller or bigger.* By periphery, we mean changes out in the body, the number of limbs, digits, the musculature and how it works, the set of sensory receptors receiving stimulation from the environment and how they wire up to the central nervous system. The innovations that mark out a new vertebrate species tend to be in the structure and function of its body (including the movements it can perform), its organs, and its sensory equipment. When it comes to the brain, the innovations are less specific. They tend to involve tweaking the general build plan used in this branch of the family tree: some parts of the brain grow bigger, some smaller, but the types of structure are mostly the same. Evolution modifies the existing plan, more here, less there; it doesn't build a new brain piece and add it in to generate a new behaviour.

Take bats. They can navigate in the dark using sound, so-called echolocation. It's a special ability for this mammalian species. But there is no special new part of the bat brain for navigating using sound. The ability to readily emit 'ping' noises, and enhanced hearing to differentiate the echoes that come back, are innovations. The bat brain, however, uses similar types of brain structures to other mammals but develops in these structures the ability to combine sound information to guide flight and avoid bumping into cave walls.

Figure 2.4 Pinging in the dark

What are the specific, peripheral innovations in humans, separate from other similar social primates like monkeys, chimps, and gorillas? We stand upright. We have hands and vocal articulators (lips, tongue, vocal cords) evolved to allow precise movements and speech production. We have rib muscles that allow us to generate a smooth flow of air over the vocal cords to produce speech (this works fine so long as we're not laughing or yawning). Compared to other mammals, humans have an unexpectedly large brain for our body size, and one part of the brain, the cortex, has grown bigger, giving us more thinking power. More on this later. But, in the same way that the bat does not have a new part of the brain for echolocation, don't expect to find a new part of the human brain for human language, or a new part for human rationality.

The second rule of thumb: *When you make a brain bigger, the parts scale up in a predictable way – and some parts get much bigger.* The brain-making machine has a formula for growing brains of different sizes from the common (conserved) basic plan. Look at the graphs on the next page in Figure 2.5. The upper graph plots the size of various parts of the brain against overall brain size, for over 130 species of mammals, from simians (monkeys, apes, humans) to prosimians (such as lemurs) to insectivores (such as anteaters) to chiroptera (bats). Don't worry about the names of the parts just now, and we've moved the lines up and down a bit to separate them, for clarity. The important point here is that the data points across the different species fall on similar lines. In other words, the relative sizes of brain parts are predicted by overall brain size, and this is a relationship that holds across species. It's this consistency across the species, which have potentially very different behaviours, that makes us think that there is a highly conserved plan for growing a mammalian brain, and which is tweaked in a limited number of ways across species. All the species are using the Brain-Builder-5000!

Note that the lines for different brain parts have different gradients. What does that mean? Brains tend to scale with body size (Einstein's brain fits snugly in a jar now possessed by the University Medical Center of Princeton, but a sperm whale's brain would only just fit on the back seat of your car). Bigger bodies need bigger brains because more neurons are required to sense the larger body and to control the greater number of muscle fibres. But if you grow a brain bigger, not all parts will inflate equally. Parts generated later in the sequence during the running of the brain-making programme tend to get disproportionately larger: this is the later-gets-larger rule. The front of the brain (cortex) is generated later in development. Humans have bigger brains than monkeys and chimpanzees. Therefore, according to the formula, this necessarily means that the front of the brain in humans (the so-called 'prefrontal cortex' or PFC, which just means *really* the front of the brain) will be even larger compared to monkeys and chimps. Yes, humans have a really big prefrontal cortex! And this is just what you get when you grow a mammalian brain to that size under the later-gets-larger rule.

The later-gets-larger formula even holds for the variation of brains within a species. So, the lower graph plots both the size of the prefrontal cortex and the size of the rest of the cortex (everything that's not prefrontal!) against overall brain size, for macaque monkeys, chimpanzees, and humans. There sit humans with their bigger brains, on the right of the chart. But crucially, variation *within* each species lies on the same line that links variation across the species. And again, we see a steeper line for the prefrontal cortex than the rest of the cortex, under the later-gets-larger rule.

It takes around 110 to 120 days for the growing human embryo to generate all the neurons that will go into the cortex of the brain; the variations we see from the smallest adult human brain to the largest correspond to letting this neuron-producing programme run for about eight days shorter or longer. So, one of the knobs on the brain-making machine is probably how long the neuron-making programme gets to run, a knob that is set differently between humans and other primate species, but can also vary a little bit even within the human species.

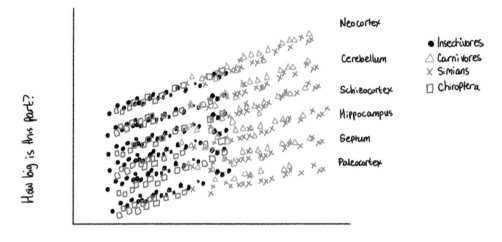

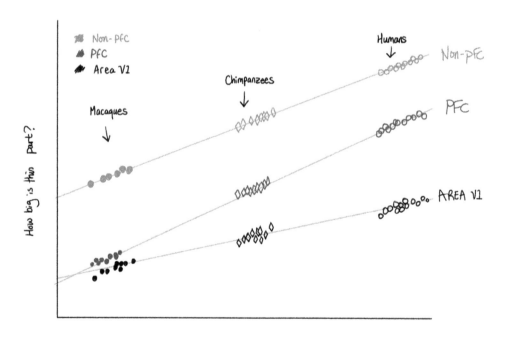

Figure 2.5 The size of different parts of the brain scales up predictably both across and within mammalian species, suggesting a conserved brain-making plan. Data from Charvet and colleagues (2013) (upper) and Donahue and colleagues (2018) (lower). PFC = prefrontal cortex, V1 = the rearmost part of the visual cortex. Axes are log scales.

What, No Banana Detectors?

We call the brain the 'central' nervous system because it brings together lots of information from the senses and drives motor behaviour in a coordinated way. Importantly, the central nervous system is a *generalist*. It organises itself based on the sensory stimulation it receives and the motor systems it must work with, using what's called *plasticity*. On a fine scale, the brain changes its structure to change its subsequent function based on the way it has previously been stimulated. Evolution does not specify which exact functional properties the central nervous system should have in order to fit with the species' environmental niche. In other words, even for monkeys, evolution does not build in banana detectors.

What, no banana detectors? That's exactly the sort of thing you would want in a monkey brain, isn't it… given that monkeys live in a jungle full of bananas, hidden amongst the foliage, and that bananas are so tasty and nutritious? When your monkey visual system offers up yellow curves amongst green shapes, doesn't your monkey brain want some banana detectors to start going off, triggering banana desires and banana-oriented actions like climbing, picking, and eating? Evolution should definitely have evolved banana detectors in the monkey brain, they sound super advantageous.

Here's why built-in banana detectors are a bad idea: if the banana trees in your jungle all catch a disease and disappear, and only orange trees are available to sustain you, you won't be able to detect the oranges. Your species would be finished because your brain-making programme can only build detectors for lovely yellow, curved bananas. A strategy likely to give your species more longevity would be for your brain to use plasticity to develop detectors for whatever fruit you happened to find in your jungle. Be general and then learn from your environment.

Now, we've seen that it's easy to come up with evolutionary stories about what might be advantageous and what might have been selected for, just based on it sounding plausible. Having a general central nervous system that uses plasticity *seems* advantageous. But what is the evidence that the central nervous system really works this way? What is the evidence that evolution has not selected built-in banana detectors?

Okay, let's take a real example. Mouse vision is dichromatic, based on two colours. In the retina of mouse eyes, there are detectors for blue and yellow light, but none for red. However, with modern genetic methods, it's possible to create a new breed of mice which have additional detectors in their retinas for red light. (Genes code for proteins. The proteins in light detectors in the retina vibrate in response to a certain wavelength of light. If you alter the relevant gene, you can change the protein, and this can alter the wavelength of light that will cause it to vibrate.) The brains of these new growing mice are now receiving sensory information about red light that their species has never before received.

Figure 2.6 Evolution does not endow the monkey brain with built-in banana detectors

Can their brains use this sensory information to guide behaviour (to press, as it were, the red button)? If their brain-making machine specifies what objects in the world their sensory systems can detect – things relevant to the survival of the mouse species, cheese, cats, and so forth – then this should not be possible. Red has never been relevant to survival. But it turns out the brains of the red-seeing mice can organise themselves to use the new sensory information just fine. Brains are generalists and will work with whatever sensory information they receive to drive adaptive behaviour.

Here's the Puzzle – Where Do Species-Specific Behaviours Come From if Not From Brain Structure?

This does, though, leave us with a bit of a puzzle. If the brain-making plan is similar across species, with the knobs set just a bit differently, how do you get species-specific behaviours for all the different mammalian species? Where do all their different behaviours come from, if not from the brain-making plan? Why do sheep flock while wolves hunt? Why do moles dig and bats fly? Why do pigs forage for truffles and people post selfies?

The special abilities of each species are likely to come from several sources. First, the sensory and motor periphery impose their form on the central nervous system. The mole's whiskers, the bat's ears, the human's dextrous digits. Second, changes in the chemistry of the brain (neurotransmitters and hormones, which we'll come to) alter the social motivations, desired rewards, and attentional focus of the species – the social or physical environments they want to be in, the experiences they want to have, who they want to hang out with (and what they want to do with them). The wolves hunt, the sheep flock, the humans appreciate views of themselves. Third, the brain is plastic. It dynamically reallocates its neural tissue according to its experiences and motivational preferences. And fourth, as we have seen with the brain-making machine, the size of the brain can change – with more neural real estate, more complex behaviours can be developed.

The final thing you need to know about evolution is that it generally takes *a long time* to make any big changes. The human brain is not much different now from how it was 5,000 or 50,000 years ago (though hopefully healthier and better fed, and certainly more online). If we behave very differently now from how our ancestors behaved all those millennia ago, the answers may not lie in the brain structure that evolution gave us, but in how its function develops in our lifetimes.

Now, let's move on to think about what brains are mainly *for*.

3
WHAT ARE THE BITS OF THE BRAIN AND WHAT DO THEY DO?

When you pick it up in your hands, the human brain has two symmetrical sides, half circles or hemispheres, that are mirror images of each other. On closer inspection, the surface is wrinkly. The hemispheres have some deep crevices that allow you to divide each side into rough parts. These are called lobes and you will find four. Each side has a frontal lobe (so called because it is, um, at the front), the temporal lobe (from the Latin for 'temples of the head' because this part lies beneath the temple), the rear upper part called the parietal lobe (Latin for 'wall of a cavity'), and the rear lower part called the occipital lobe (derived from the Latin for 'back of your head'). If you were to peel the temporal lobe back (we're sure there's a YouTube video on this somewhere), you'd find an extra lobe hiding in there called the insular lobe (Latin for 'island').

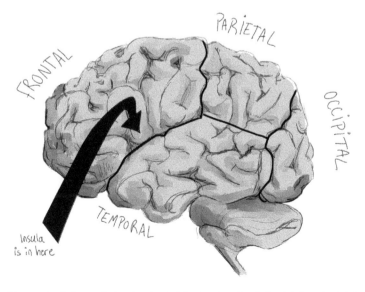

Figure 3.1   The main lobes of the brain (with the insular lobe hiding inside)

What's It All For?

But what's all this brain for? Why in fact do you need a brain? Not all organisms have brains. Jellyfish don't have brains. The main reason for having a brain is for coordinated movement. Sight, sound, and other sensory information is brought together; muscles are controlled to produce coordinated movements of the body in response to perception and to achieve the goals of the organism (e.g., eating, not getting eaten).

Organisms that don't actively move don't need centralised coordination of information. Trees don't move and they have no brains, not even a nervous system. Jellyfish float, gently swim, and stay upright waiting for prey to hit their tentacles. They have a different type of nervous system for this less-demanding repertoire, with separate sets of neurons to synchronise muscle actions in different parts of their bodies. There is no integration in a single central brain. Leeches have bodies with multiple segments, 21 of them, each with its own simple nervous system, and then a mini-brain at each end, one to run the mouth, one to run the bottom. Leeches have a nervous system that is distributed across their bodies, allowing them to swim, latch on, and suck. But no main brain.

Figure 3.2 Not all species have centralised brains

When sea squirts are born, they resemble tadpoles, and these guys do need a tiny brain to coordinate the input coming from their simple eye to wiggle their little tail and swim through the sea. They need a brain for movement. But in tadpole form, sea squirts are unable to feed (well, we said evolution wasn't perfect). Eating must wait until the sea squirt finds an attractive rock to attach to, whereupon its body morphs into a stationary filter-feeder, feeding on plankton floating in the water and probably, these days, small particles of human-produced plastics. At that point, sea squirts no longer need a brain to coordinate sensory information to move. What do they do with it? They simply digest their own brain for food.

The function of our central nervous systems, then, is to control movement: to find food, shelter, a mate, to protect offspring, avoid predators and dangers, and to play Xbox. But even humans don't always need their brains to move. Sometimes, your spine will do the thinking for you. Touch a hot saucepan, and in a split second you will snatch your hand away. Temperature and danger receptors in the skin have rapidly signalled to the spine, where local neurons have already decided to trigger the withdrawal reflex. The arm muscles spring into action – quick, withdraw your hand! It is, as one might say, a real no-brainer. Meantime, the nerves pass on the signal to the brain about that burning sensation, and the brain finds out shortly afterwards why it just saw its hand spring away from the saucepan, and why the hand is now hurting and would prefer to be run under the cold tap.

The nerves in the spine can do more for you than these simple reflexes. In fact, they can carry out highly practised movement sequences like walking, jogging, or running. The spine acts like an autopilot to do the easy bits, so that the pilot can check their email. You know that knee jerk reflex, when you tap just below your kneecap and your leg jerks out? That's part of the autopilot system. The knee jerk is equivalent to a jet airline, on autopilot at cruise altitude, which is buffeted by a crosswind – the autopilot automatically adjusts the plane's control surfaces. In the case of the knee jerk, the spine interprets the signal from your leg as feedback that you are stumbling or tripping, and so extends the leg to avoid falling.

Once you go beyond this limited repertoire of movements – beyond walking to, say, dancing the foxtrot, or making polite conversation – then the autopilot has to be switched off and the pilot must take control. More complex movements are going to involve the brain.

By more complex, we are not just talking dance moves or even making a cup of tea. At the other end of the scale, human actions can be vastly subtle, structured, and sophisticated, aimed towards long-range goals. Studying for a university degree, for example. Or exacting revenge on James Bond for foiling your ambitions for world domination: a dish best served cold. But it is worth remembering the primary function of the brain: making the right movement.

This influence is still discernible in our 'high-level' cognitive skills. Take attention. We focus attention on particular objects in our visual field or on particular sounds around us. The 'attention network' in the brain involves the circuits of the relevant sense (sight, hearing) and two other regions – a system that processes space in the parietal lobe, and a region that controls eye movements in the frontal lobe. In the brain, attention isn't some abstract part of thought, the aspect of the world you choose to focus on and let into consciousness: it is about orienting to objects in space and preparing to make the right movement – including movement of the eyes to look to that region of space to get more information. A child 'paying attention' in the classroom may quite rightly be viewed as exhibiting a high-level cognitive skill, but inside the brain it is about planning for the right movement.

Now we know what the brain is for, it's time to take the tour.

The Tour

Let's do a walk through and see where the main furniture is. A lot of the brain is going to be about sensing and moving – making the right movement for the situation at hand, for your goals and needs. But we'll also see that there are structures involved in processing emotions, structures for deciding what actions to make, and structures for keeping the body running. And remember, per the previous chapter, most of these structures will be found in some form across different mammals.

The brain has a layered structure. You can think of it a bit like the layers of the Earth, from the crust to the mantle, down to the burning, ancient core. The outer layers of the brain process information without caring too much about goals or emotions, just cool, calm calculation. Some call it 'cold cognition'. The inner layers increasingly process information in terms of goals, emotions, and rewards, so-called 'hot cognition'. The innermost layers coordinate with the functioning of the rest of the body. When I see a spider, cold cognition recognises the visual pattern, hot cognition gets worried, the body is informed that its heart should race in preparation for fight-or-flight action, and cold cognition prepares the instructions to jump. The layers work together as an integrated whole.

Here's a photograph of the brain (a magnetic resonance image, see Box 3.2 at the end of the chapter) viewed variously from the side, cut down the middle from ear to ear, and from above. You can divide the brain into grey matter and white matter, which works quite well for a black and white photograph. The grey matter can be seen as the outer wrinkled surface, while the inside is mostly white. The grey matter is made up of neurons, local connections to other neurons, and cells that support the functioning of neurons. The white matter is the long-range cabling that connects neurons in different parts of the brain. From the photograph, it should be apparent that most of the volume of the brain is not neurons, the grey bits, it's the wiring that connects the neurons, the white bits. It's as if you've flipped the lid on your computer and found that it's mostly wiring in there and only a few circuit boards.

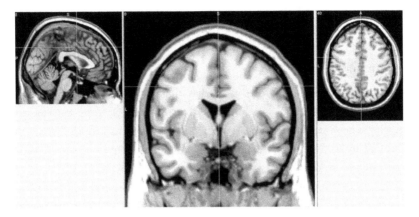

Figure 3.3 A magnetic resonance image of the brain, showing grey and white matter

The cortex

Let's start with the outer layer. This is called the cortex (from the Latin for 'bark' because it looks wrinkled like the bark on a tree trunk). This part is big in humans compared to other animals. The cortex is a sheet of neurons for processing information. It's just a bit smaller than a sheet of A3 paper, about half a centimetre deep, and it needs to be crumpled up to fit it in the skull. It crumples in a reasonably predictable way, so you see similar folds across different people, both in the bulges (gyri, plural of gyrus) and crevices (sulci, plural of sulcus).

The cortex is a general-purpose computational sheet. The sheet processes information without caring too much about the results. Where you are on the sheet doesn't radically change how the information is processed, it just changes what information is processed. The motto is *where you are is what you do*. The back and the front do different things. The back does sensory, while the front does motor.

The back part of the cortex houses regions involved in the senses. Roughly, there is one lobe per sense. The occipital lobe processes sight (vision), the temporal lobe processes hearing (audition), and the parietal lobe processes touch (body surface sensation). That hidden lobe, the insula, is for internal body sensation, gut feelings (so if you're feeling disgusted about anything right now, the insula is responsible). The exception to this pattern is smell (olfaction), which only gets a little bulb, not a whole lobe, and it's snuck in under the frontal lobes because that's where the nose is.

The motor areas of the cortex are towards the front. Further towards the front are areas involved in planning, decision making, and control. As we'll see, these are still *sort of* motor circuits. The motor and sensory areas are separated by a boundary, called the central sulcus, one of the deep crevices. On the sensory side of the crevice, the parietal lobe contains a map of the sensory body, with areas for sensing the hands, feet, lips, tongue, and so on (see Chapter 5 for an illustration of that!). On the motor side, the frontal lobe contains a similar map of the motor body, for moving the hands, feet, lips, tongue, and so on.

Generally, there are two routes to get from the back to front, from sensory to motor: one for recognition and one for action. Think of them as perception-for-later versus perception-for-now. Take vision. One route, called the 'what' pathway, tries to identify what things are (that, my friend, is a cricket ball, it could be useful later if you want to play cricket). The other route, the 'where' pathway, processes where things are in space to directly drive movement (catch that thing flying towards you). You might want to combine these two bits of information: catch a cricket ball (howzat!) but don't catch a snowball (duck!).

These two routes work for audition, too. If you hear a word and you just need to repeat it, you can take a direct route from the sensory temporal cortex over the top to the frontal motor cortex, without needing to understand the word at all. But if you want to understand it, you'll take another route, forward to the tip of the temporal cortex.

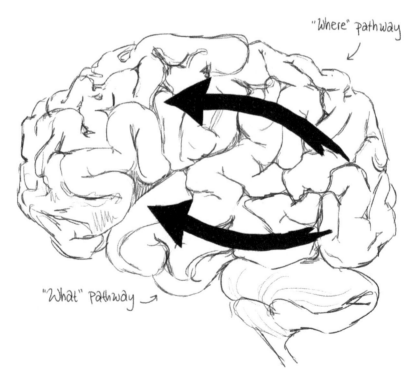

"Where" pathway

"What" pathway

Figure 3.4 Two routes from perception to action

Sensory and motor systems are organised in hierarchies, moving from simple to complex. You can think of these hierarchies as being like a tower with many floors, with a separate tower for each sense. Each floor combines the work done below, and each floor has a wider view than the floor below. The lowest floor spots patterns in sensory informa-tion. The next floor up spots patterns within those patterns. The next floor, patterns within patterns within patterns. Sensory and motor systems are each trying to see patterns within patterns within patterns – and then make connections between the patterns.

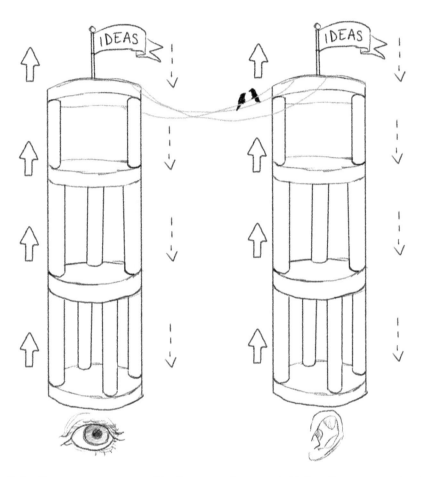

Figure 3.5 Sensory systems are like towers, where each higher floor can spot patterns within the information in the floor below. The tops of the towers are connected to form concepts or ideas

After a while, based on experience, the upper floors of the towers might know a thing or two about what patterns are likely. Based on their knowledge, the upper floors can make suggestions to the lower floors on what they may be perceiving (just to help out, mind, not to insist). The upper floors of the towers for the different senses talk to each other, across cables strung between the upper floors, to see if they can agree what's out there in the world. The upper layers are also connected to the frontal parts of the brain, to pass on conclusions and see if their view fits with expectations. It goes something like this:

In the Visual tower:

Lowest floor: I'm getting light and dark and some coloured pixels.

Lower floor: From that, I'm getting edges and curves.

Middle floor: From that, I'm getting legs and a body.

Upper floor: You know, put those together and you get a spider.

Visual tower to front of brain: Were you expecting a spider?

Front of brain: I wasn't expecting a spider. Are you sure it's a spider, not some fluff?

Top of the Auditory tower: I'm getting scuttling sounds. And someone next to me is screaming. Sounds like a spider to me.

Front of brain: True, that fits with a spider. Wasn't expecting one though.

Visual tower: Definitely looks like a spider. I'm seeing fangs.

Emotions: Eeeeek! It's a spider!

Front of brain: Okay, I think we should do something about this. The emotions don't seem to like spiders.

Emotions: Aargh!

Front of the brain: Motor systems, can we, I don't know, leap up or something? Maybe we should be screaming, too?

What does the sensory tower look like for touch? At the lowest level, basics: pressure, heat, cold, pain. Then we move up to fine sensation, to judgement of texture, to weight, size, and shape. Then up to *touch* objects (i.e., where you close your eyes and try to identify the tarantula that has just been placed on your hands).

The motor system has a hierarchy too, but its higher levels are different. They're about patterns more distant in *time*, integrating the small pieces of movements in the lower levels into more coordinated sequences of actions in higher levels. The lowest levels are about immediate actions, while the higher levels are about more complex sequences of actions, further forward in time. The lowest level says, 'Do it!' (primary motor cortex). The next layer says, 'Prepare to do it' (supplementary motor cortex). The next layer up says, 'You may want to do it sometime in the future' (prefrontal cortex). A complex sequence of motor actions to be carried out at some future point in time can be described as a plan.

While the prefrontal cortex can be viewed as the planning and decision-making part of the brain, it can also be seen as the top of the motor system hierarchy, the highest floor of the tower that looks the furthest forward in time.

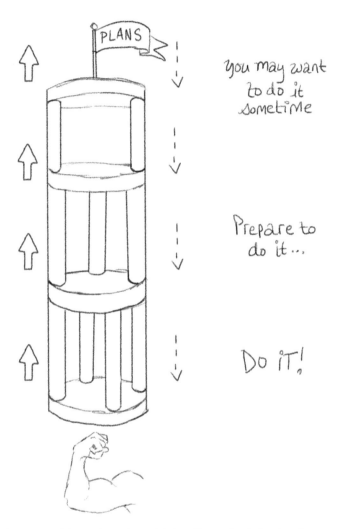

Figure 3.6 The motor hierarchy, where higher floors look further forward in time, building contingent sequences of actions which can be thought of as plans

We saw in the section on evolution that humans have more cortex than many other animals. This means that humans can build their sensory and motor towers higher. In their senses, humans can discern more patterns within patterns, more complicated concepts; and in their motor systems, they can build further forward in time, creating plans into the more distant future.

Deeper layers

We're standing on the cortex, looking down. What lies beneath our feet? Down there are some structures that make up what's called the limbic system, a network of ancient memory systems for emotion and behaviour. There are some balls of neurons involved in action selection, that is, deciding what movement you will make, together called the basal ganglia. There are some fluid-filled cavities, part of an irrigation network called the ventricular system that keeps the brain clean and fed. Finally, at the core, there are some structures that sit at the top of the spine called the midbrain and the brainstem. These are responsible for controlling some of the body's basic functions, like breathing, blood pressure, heart rate, and temperature. These 'sub-cortical' structures form impressive shapes, wrapped around each other, bracketing the brainstem. Let's journey down to take a closer look.

limbic system   ventricular system   basal ganglia

Figure 3.7 The impressive shapes of the limbic system, the fluid-filled ventricular irrigation system, and the basal ganglia, all lying inside the cortex

Cingulate cortex

The first structure we come to under the cortex is called the cingulate (Latin for 'belt' or 'girdle', because it looks like a belt surrounding a big bunch of fibres that connect the two hemispheres). Actually, the cingulate is still part of the cortical sheet, the edge that is folded under in the middle, as the sketch in Figure 3.8 shows (cingulate is in light grey).

Here at the edge of the cortical sheet, this component acts as a broker between the cortex, with its cool calm calculation of motor and sensory information, and the emotion structures below in the limbic system. The cingulate is sometimes added to the limbic system and together they are called the limbic lobe.

The cingulate cortex stretches from the front, underneath the motor areas of the frontal lobe, further back to under the sensory areas of the parietal lobe. The cingulate cortex negotiates between the content of the cortex above and the emotions of the layer below

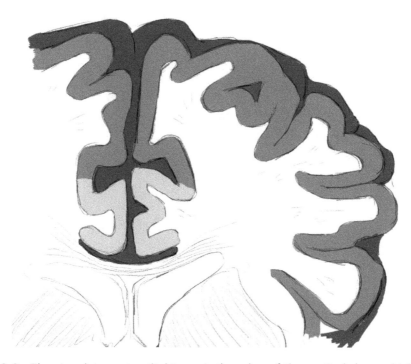

Figure 3.8 The cingulate cortex (light grey), the edge of the cortical sheet which acts as a broker to the limbic emotion systems below

so that in the cingulate cortex, content is now more coloured by emotions and goals. In terms of content, once more *where you are is what you do*. The cingulate cortex under the parietal cortex (processing space) will deal with emotions for space (sense of self in space). The cingulate cortex under the motor cortex will deal with emotions for action (the drive to act). For example, the cingulate cortex underneath the motor cortex controlling facial movements will broker information about emotional facial expressions. The cingulate cortex under the prefrontal cortex will deal with emotions around decision making, the initiation and monitoring of behaviour (Am I doing it right? Is this fun?). However cool the processing of information is in the cortex, it cannot be separated from the emotional dimension that filters through from the limbic system via the cingulate cortex.

The anterior cingulate cortex (we've used the word 'anterior' instead of 'front'! See Box 3.1) plays a prominent role in task performance, processing emotions around decisions. It acts as a monitor, assessing whether performance is progressing towards goals and how hard a task seems to be – as well as how much effort the cortex is putting into achieving it. It acts like a middle manager, not setting goals but monitoring if the workforce is delivering on the goals. If things are not going well, it can act to boost processing in the cortex up above (Try harder! Focus on the things that matter!). If there's an argument, it can

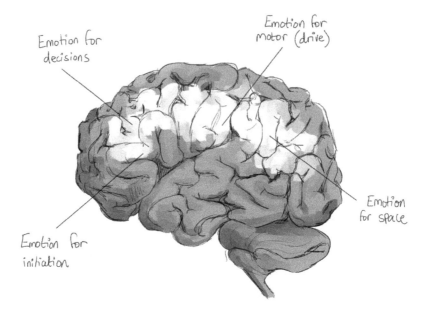

Emotion for decisions

Emotion for motor (drive)

Emotion for space

Emotion for initiation

Figure 3.9 Where you are is what you do: Different regions of the cingulate cortex add emotions to the content in the cortex above

mediate (I don't care if the word says BLUE, you've been told to name the colour of the ink the word is written in, and that's BLACK!!).

The monitoring role of the anterior cingulate extends beyond asking 'Are things going okay?' to 'Is this hurting?' and even 'Is this gonna hurt?' That is, the anterior cingulate also plays a role in the processing of pain and the expectation of pain. When goals are not being met, the anterior cingulate says, 'I don't like how this is going'. When there are sensations of pain, the anterior cingulate says, 'I *really* don't like how this is going'. Indeed, if the anterior cingulate is damaged, you can have the same sensation of pain as before, but not be bothered by it anymore. Go figure. Pain, then, is the most extreme version of the anterior cingulate's general function: to check whether things are or are not working out the way you wanted them to, so that something should be done about it.

━━━━━ **Box 3.1** ━━━━━

Where are we in the brain?

Neuroscientists have a rich vocabulary to describe where in the brain various parts lie. Sometimes too rich. Inferior, medial, lateral, dorsal, ventral, rostral, caudal, anterior, posterior, superior. Here's what these directions mean:

- Inferior = underneath
- Superior = on top

- Medial = in the middle
- Lateral = on the side
- Dorsal = on the back, so kinda on top, if you're lying down
- Ventral = on the belly, so kinda underneath, if you're lying down
- Rostral = the head end, so kinda the front; well, if you're a lizard
- Caudal = the tail end, so kinda the back, if you're still a lizard
- Anterior = front
- Posterior = back
- Left = these are finally getting easier!
- Right = we think you get it

Sometimes neuroscientists identify regions by the folds in the cortex, indicating the gyrus (fold) or sulcus (crease) and the lobe it's in (e.g., the 'inferior frontal gyrus' is one of the frontal lobe's four gyri: superior, middle, inferior, and precentral). Sometimes, neuropsychologists label areas of the brain according to regions where damage produces distinctive behavioural deficits in adults, such as Broca's area (speech production) and Wernicke's area (speech comprehension). Sometimes, neuroanatomists refer to regions according to a historical labelling system. For instance, German neurologist Korbinian Brodmann looked at the cortex under a microscope and found that the cell organisation appeared different in different areas (so-called 'cytoarchitecture'). He used these distinctions to label different areas of the cortex, numbered 1 to 52 on each side, publishing the list of Brodmann areas in 1909. This provides a referencing system still used today.

Sometimes, particularly in brain imaging, neuroscientists use coordinates in three-dimensional space, by an agreed atlas of which bit marks zero, zero, zero. One example of a coordinate system is the Talairach, where zero, zero, zero is the anterior commissure, a large bundle of fibres which connects the olfactory bulb and parts of each hemisphere to the same areas on the opposite side. Sometimes, neuroanatomists, neuroscientists, and neuropsychologists disagree with each other about what a term refers to, for example, disagreeing which part of the frontal cortex counts as 'prefrontal' cortex, or what structures should be included in the limbic lobe.

Lastly, when neuroscientists scan the brain, they like to have special ways to describe which view you're getting of the image: axial (a horizontal slice seen from above or below), sagittal (a vertical slice seen from the left or right side), and coronal (a vertical slice down the middle, seen from the front or back).

The limbic system

Let's continue our journey. The next layer in combines a set of different structures, together called the limbic system. It is so called because the structures together resemble a rim (Latin, limbus) around the bundle of fibres that connect left and right cortical hemispheres. In the limbic system, we are now entering the lava world of the emotions.

Unlike the cortex, which is a fairly uniform sheet for processing sensory and motor information, the limbic system has a set of structures, ancient memory systems with specific functions. This set of structures is similar across primates. In fact, if someone handed you the limbic system of a human and the limbic system of a chimpanzee (casually, perhaps at a party), you would be hard pushed to tell the two apart.

Warning, this paragraph contains a number of brain names. The structures in the limbic system are (roughly) the amygdala, the insula, the septum, the nucleus accumbens, the hippocampus, and the hypothalamus. Latin and Greek names again. Almonds, islands, partitions, leaning against, seahorses, and below-the-bed, respectively. There are two sets of these structures, one in each hemisphere. And the structures themselves can have complex subdivisions within them. The diagram below shows how some of these structures are arranged.

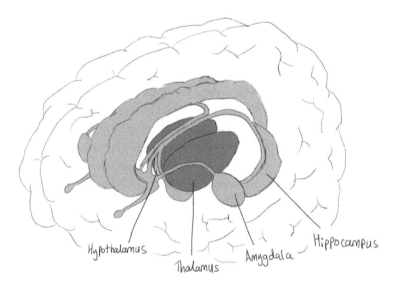

Figure 3.10 Some of the structures making up the limbic system

We said these were ancient memory systems. Now by *ancient*, we don't mean that they are venerable, wise, white-haired, dusty, and so forth. In each of us, our amygdalae and our hippocampi are exactly the same age as the rest of our brains, formed during embryonic development. No, by ancient, we mean these structures are found in a wide range of species, implying that they were present in earlier versions of the brain-build plan, back in the common ancestor of all these species. For example, versions of the amygdala and hippocampus are found not only in other mammals but species as far apart as frogs and sharks. This distant heritage implies that these structures play a key role in an organism's survival.

Here's how to think about what's going on. Emotions are the way that evolution has built long-term goals into the structure of the brain, to give an organism the best chance of surviving and reproducing (two things that evolution especially likes). The structures of the amygdala, insula, nucleus accumbens, and septum are specialised for specific roles in emotion.

The amygdala is responsible for learning and recognising situations, and generating behaviour, relevant to a range of appetites, good and bad. One appetite is to avoid danger! So, the amygdala recognises dangerous situations and generates fear and anxiety. The amygdala also drives aggression, whether to approach or avoid situations, whether to fight or fly or freeze. The amygdala is concerned with novelty and curiosity, and it's also involved in recognising sexual situations. For some of these circumstances, particularly around danger, speed is of the essence. So the amygdala receives low grade sensory information which can drive faster responses, before too much thought has gone into perception up in the cortex. The amygdala also has a hotline from the smell sense (the olfactory bulb), probably a hangover from the brain-build plan of ancestor species for whom smell was really important. Nowadays, this just makes smells especially evocative, like the smell of your old school classroom, the perfume that your first love wore, and the packaging of your first new phone.

For the insula cortex, we heard earlier that this is a cortical sensory system for the perception of internal bodily states, including taste and gustatory sensation. In its role in the limbic system, the insula puts the guts into gut feelings. It does the stomach-rumbling craving for that chocolate cookie. It provides the bodily basis of emotion, what the body wants and what the body needs, the bodily self. When a situation disgusts you to the pit of your stomach, the insula is the structure adding the stomach information to your emotion. It also contributes to empathy, when you feel someone else's pain (particularly watching those epic fail videos on YouTube, where skateboarders land on their tender areas. Ouch!). The insula is sometimes thought of as providing a 'valence map' for concepts stored in the back of the cortex, where valence is the subjective value assigned to an event, an object, or a person. The insula integrates information from multiple emotion and sensory systems to summarise *how the body feels about that*. Your gut emotions tell you what things you like and don't like, adding the *mmm* and *eugh* to ideas. In that sense, the insula is a region that combines information from the limbic system and the cortex to provide emotional value, while also processing more mundane bodily sensations such as pain, hunger, nausea, tickles, and itches.

The septum and nucleus accumbens are two structures involved in pleasure and also, in the case of the nucleus accumbens, reward. Laboratory animals like it very much if these brain structures are directly stimulated, you probably would too. The nucleus accumbens is the kind of system that gets too much of a good thing during addiction. The septum is involved in positive social affiliations and attachments.

These different structures within the limbic system compete for who is going to take control of the body, putting it in a particular state for whichever emotion wins and should launch behaviour. These structures compete to drive another structure called the hypothalamus. The hypothalamus communicates with the distant bodily organs and is responsible for putting them in the correct state to carry out the selected behaviour. It communicates by releasing chemical signals (called hormones) into the bloodstream, which are then picked up by the relevant organs.

Here's how it might go. Eeeek! A spider! The amygdala wins the competition, fear is the order of the day, and it tells the hypothalamus to get the body ready for fight or flight. Cells in the hypothalamus transmit a signal to the pituitary gland. The pituitary gland releases chemical messengers into the bloodstream. When the adrenal glands, down near the kidneys, receive the signal, they respond by releasing adrenaline into the bloodstream. Organs across the body respond to the adrenaline. Heart rate goes up, increasing blood pressure, the air passages of the lungs expand, the pupils in the eyes enlarge, blood is redistributed to the muscles, and the body's metabolism is altered to maximise blood glucose levels, mostly for the brain. The senses are alive, the body is ready for action. Spiders: really, guys, come on, there's nothing to be afraid of. Except the venomous ones, of course. Which are, admittedly, quite hard to tell apart.

A final, but very important structure within the limbic system is the hippocampus. The hippocampus is a memory system of a different sort. It brings together information from all the senses to create snapshot memories of places and events. These memories can be sequences of moments, like short video snippets. And each memory has a date stamp, so you can answer questions like 'What did you do yesterday?', or 'Who did you see last week?' Sensory information comes from the separate lobes of the cortical sheet and is brought together and communicated to the hippocampus via another broker. Like the cingulate, this broker also sits at the edge of the cortical sheet; this time, it's a fold of cortex inside the temporal lobe called the parahippocampal gyrus. The emotion structures such as the amygdala and insula can command the hippocampus to lay down strong memories: 'Remember this situation, it's important, it's where we saw that scary spider!'

The idea that different parts of the limbic system deal with different emotions shouldn't be taken too literally. There is not one limbic structure per emotion, as if a location for each emotion could be found. The limbic system operates as a whole to deliver the most adaptive behaviour, given the evolutionary goals of organisms like you (*eat, drink, and be merry, for tomorrow we die*, as the Old Testament would have it). Rather, emotions are functions carried out by networks. The networks bring together detectors (of particular situations), modulation (of the activity of other brain regions, of the state of bodily organs), and memorisation (of experiences). The emotions themselves are sets of highly variable instances, which depend on the current situation, your own history of experiences, and your response. Fear may revolve around the amygdala as a threat detector, but fear isn't just fear: you can tremble in fear, jump in fear, freeze in fear, scream in fear, gasp in fear, hide in fear, attack in fear, even laugh in the face of fear.

Lastly, the limbic system likes to communicate with the front of the cortex (particularly a bit folded under and sitting over the eyes, called the orbitofrontal cortex). The frontal cortex provides the emotions with some context, and the two are always in dialogue. The limbic system might say, 'Eeeek! A spider! Panic!' and the frontal cortex might say, 'Calm down. The spider you're seeing is on TV. It's crawling on David Attenborough's hand. Should I change the channel for you?' The front of the cortex might intervene to alleviate the physiological effects: deliberately slow the breathing, smile, perhaps conjure an image of a happy place, a sunny beach with the surf up and a warm breeze blowing on your face. But equally, the conversation can go the other way. The frontal cortex, with time on its hands, might start to imagine the public speech that you have to give tomorrow and conjure instead disastrous scenarios: of you forgetting what to say; of you forgetting to put your trousers on that morning. The limbic system will oblige by responding to these nightmare scenarios, setting the heart racing and the stomach churning at the *very thought of it*.

Figure 3.11 The structures of the limbic system compete for who is going to take control of the body via the hypothalamus

The basal ganglia

What are ganglia, and what's so basal about them? Go back and look at the black and white brain scan image in Figure 3.3, and particularly the centre panel showing a cross-section of the brain. We saw that there was a thin layer of grey matter around the outside, the cortex, and inside it white matter, the fibres connecting regions of the cortex. But if you look right in the centre of the head, near the triangular black shapes (those are two of the fluid-filled cavities or ventricles), you'll see *more blobs of grey matter*. There is grey matter on the surface, but there's also deep grey matter, balls of neurons and connections closer to the centre of the brain. These balls are called ganglia or nuclei, and they're called basal because they are deep down. Inside these balls, you'll often find more fine-grained structure, subdivisions that carry out different functions; and there are also various pathways or fibre tracts that link between the nuclei. What does this network of deeper structures do?

The answer is, fortunately, simple. How the basal ganglia carry out their function is, unfortunately, complicated. Up in the cortex, there are lots of competing motor plans for what you should do in the current situation. Say you're in the library, reading a book. Here in the moment are your next motor options: Read the book! Pick up your pen! Scratch your nose! Take a sip of coffee! Check your email! Look up and smile at your neighbour! All plausible, all warranted. Which do you choose? There can be only one. You can't do more than one behaviour at a time. You need a system that resolves this competition, a system to carry out *action selection*, to boost the winner and suppress all the competing motor plans. *Do it or don't do it*. This is the function of the basal ganglia.

The action selection system is also sensitive to outcomes, to rewards. When it chooses one of the competing motor plans in the current situation, is there a good outcome or not? Does your neighbour smile back at you? If so, the basal ganglia make a note to choose the same action in that situation next time. If the outcome is poor – your neighbour glares at you – it makes a note to choose a different action next time. Stick with reading the book. The basal ganglia, then, constitute an action selection system to decide: 'Do it or don't do it!' and then to ask, 'Did it work?' And they're making these selections every few hundred milliseconds.

The basal ganglia select action, but they also select options higher up in the motor hierarchy, including plans of what to do further in the future. In this sense, although the basal ganglia are part of the motor system, they are also part of thought. Now it's: *Have a thought, don't have a thought, did that thought work?*

How the basal ganglia achieve action selection is trickier. It's a hotch-potch of a system linking multiple components, with complex sequences that ultimately deliver one of three outcomes: start motor activity, stop motor activity, or modulate motor activity. Warning: brain names coming up. The basal ganglia comprise lots of parallel loops stretching from different areas of motor cortex down to two input structures, the caudate nucleus and the putamen (together referred to as the striatum), then on to the globus pallidus (which has a subdivision into the internus and the externus globus pallidus), which then link to the motor portions of a structure called the thalamus (the ventral anterior and ventrolateral nuclei sub-parts, specifically), and finally back up to the motor cortex. This is the DO IT!

circuit. There are longer loops that go more indirectly via a structure called the subthalamic nucleus which together make up the DON'T DO IT! circuit, and another set of loops that go via the substantia nigra, to BOOST ALL MOTOR ACTIVITY!

The operation of these loops appears tortuous. So, if you don't like torture, don't read this paragraph or the next. Let's say one of the loops is the winner in the action selection competition, the one for smiling at your neighbour; here's what happens in the basal ganglia: the part of the motor cortex for this action wants to signal the muscles to make the prescribed movement, it wants to DO IT! so it asks the basal ganglia, CAN I DO IT? Now, the thalamus *wants* to signal the motor cortex to do it. It's all in favour of action. But the globus pallidus internus is generally *down on the thalamus*, it wants the thalamus to *shut up* with encouraging actions. The globus pallidus usually gets its way, actions don't normally get permission to DO IT, the brake is normally stuck on. But for the winner of the action selection competition, the cortex signals the striatum (the caudate nucleus and putamen) to *get things going*. The striatum tells the globus pallidus internus that it should *quit being so down on the thalamus*. The global pallidus internus is turned off, and the thalamus is released to encourage the cortex up above to GO! and the cortex gets to signal to the muscles that it's *hammer time*. All this signalling takes a few tens of milliseconds.

What about the other actions, the ones that lost the competition? In the loops where the unwanted actions must be suppressed, an alternative pathway is used: the striatum deactivates the globus pallidus externus, which releases the otherwise suppressed subthalamic nucleus to activate the globus pallidus internus to *turn off* the thalamus, so it can't give permission to the action to happen. And finally, if the substantia nigra gets involved, typically because there are REWARDS in the offing, it can modulate either of these loops to raise the general level of motor activity, using a neurotransmitter called dopamine, which we'll get to.

Big drawing of breath. There is, no doubt, a lot of deep evolutionary history as to why the basal ganglia's operation is so tortuous – of the form 'it could only improve what it started with'. But the whole system does a single job, action selection: Do it, don't do it, did it work? (and if so, making that choice more probable next time).

You can get a sense of what the basal ganglia do when things go wrong with them. Action or plan selections that have been super-rewarded (for instance, sniffing cocaine and getting high; pulling the lever of a slot machine and winning the jackpot) can become powerful enough to win out whatever the situation, and the result is addiction. If the action selection mechanism goes on the blink and can't select any action, the brain will struggle to produce any voluntary actions (as seen in Parkinson's disease). If the competition between action selections isn't strong enough, the system will keep jumping between different winners, and you will get the distractibility seen in attention deficit hyperactivity disorder.

The thalamus

A quick word on the thalamus. It's part of the basal ganglia system, and as such, two of its subdivisions (the nuclei referred to as ventral anterior, that's underneath front, and ventrolateral, that's underneath side) are involved in motor behaviour. But the thalamus also plays an important role in the senses. Other subdivisions of the thalamus serve as staging posts for sensory information as it comes in from the sense organs (eyes, ears) on their way up to the cortex. The thalamus acts as a sort of waystation for sensory information to reach the cortex, but it can also carry out some rudimentary operations, such as fast attentional shifts (involving a subdivision called the pulvinar). For example, if a door slams shut as you're reading this page, your attention snaps from your sight to your hearing. Some neuroscientists even claim that during the development of the foetus, the first glimmers of consciousness begin only when the thalamus grows connections up to the cortex, and the sensory world begins to percolate through to the cortex and activate its neurons (more on that in Chapter 9).

The midbrain, the brainstem

We've journeyed down and we're almost at the centre. We reach the midbrain and the brainstem, at the top of the spinal cord. We'll find more nuclei here, blobs of grey matter, with important, basic functions. We are at the lowest level of the sensory hierarchies, as information trucks its way in from the sensory neurons themselves; we're at the bottom of the motor hierarchies as signals head down the spine to produce muscle movements in the body. There are regions here where basic information for running the head is dealt with: eyes need to swivel, eyelids need to blink, the tongue needs to move (and taste), noses need to itch. There are regions for controlling sleep and wake cycles, for arousal (alertness), for temperature regulation, for controlling involuntary actions of the body such as breathing, swallowing, and the beating of your heart.

We have reached the core. Our journey is at an end. Except for... wait, what's this other thing over here? Oh, there's a whole extra brain. Which contains most of the neurons.

Cerebellum

The cerebellum looks like an extra 'mini' brain, sitting at the back under the occipital lobe, like a petite cauliflower. On psychology courses, you don't always hear about the cerebellum. Psychologists focus on the cortex – that's the thinking part of the brain, right? When psychologists scan brains, they often don't even include the cerebellum in the picture.

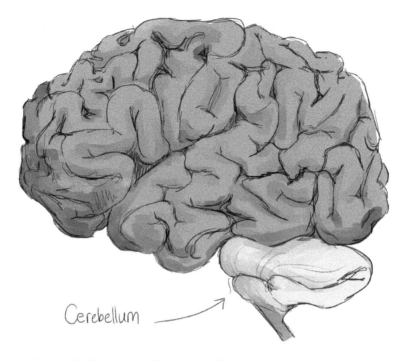

Cerebellum

Figure 3.12 The cerebellum, which has most of the neurons

Although the cerebellum may get less attention from psychologists, somewhat surprisingly, it houses most of the neurons in the brain: 80% of the brain's neurons sit in the cerebellum, four times as many as in the cortex, but they are tightly packed into a smaller structure. If the cortex is wrinkled because it has to be scrunched up to fit inside the skull, the cerebellum is super wrinkled (or to use the technical term, highly convoluted). It is folded in on itself to form a tight ball. If you were to take an adult human cerebellum and unfold it, flatten it out, smooth it perhaps with a steam iron, it would form a strip one metre long and 10 cm wide. By contrast, the cortex is a rounder sheet, 50 cm across.

Across different species, as brains get bigger, the proportion of neurons in the cortex and cerebellum remains the same. This suggests they are controlled by the same knob on the metaphorical brain-making machine. Because humans have a large number of neurons in their large cortex, they have a similarly inflated number of neurons in their cerebellums, but now packed into the smaller structure of the cauliflower.

So, what does this mini brain, of limited interest to psychologists, actually do? The cerebellum is part of the hindbrain (the back part), and a key component of the vertebrate brain plan. The cerebellum is dedicated to the job of coordinating movement and sensation. When the body makes movements, the cerebellum ensures everything hangs together, making movements smooth and coordinated.

Let's say you're thirsty and you want to reach out for a glass of water sitting in front of you. To be honest, your body is already pretty busy. There are muscles holding your posture, keeping you balanced, holding your head up. If you are going to reach out your arm, a limb is a heavy thing, and it's going to change your centre of gravity. You don't want to topple over. To balance, you'll need to lean back a bit, to compensate for the greater weight out in front. This is a subtle, unconscious adjustment made using information from the ear about your balance and acceleration, and information from your eyes on whether you're toppling. A reach of the arm needs to be integrated with everything else, so that overall movement and posture is smooth, so it all flows together. Your cerebellum is also going to estimate how heavy an object is to determine how much force to apply. If the guess is wrong (say, the object is much lighter than expected), sensory feedback must be used to instantly rein in the muscular forces to stop your arm shooting into the air during the lift. These computations take a lot of integration, monitoring of sensory input, and adjusting of motor output. It's heavy-duty number crunching that requires a lot of neurons and connections, and it requires a specialist system.

Figure 3.13 The cerebellum ensures smooth and coordinated motor movements

There are three sections to the cerebellum. The *lateral* cerebellum on each side is involved in motor programming and learning motor sequences. The *intermediate* cerebellum is involved in pattern tuning and correction. The *vestibular* cerebellum is involved in error correction and motor learning for balance – it communicates with the balance system within the inner ear and with visual information to ensure that balance is maintained during movement. The cerebellum communicates with the rest of the brain through its 'peduncles': six peduncles, three on each side, which connect to the midbrain.

The lower (inferior) peduncles bring sensory information into the cerebellum about the actual position of your body parts, including your limbs and your joints. The middle peduncles transmit information about where you want these body parts to be according to the motor plan. The cerebellum crunches the numbers, comparing where the body parts are and where they need to be for the current motor sequence, and then sends commands to adjust the movements out through the upper (superior) peduncles to the midbrain – from there, down the spinal cord to activate or inhibit muscles at the appropriate moments to move your limbs into the desired positions and rapidly execute complex movements. We said the brain was mostly about movement. This is front of house, where it all happens.

You're not aware of this number crunching, of course. The cerebellum is the unsung hero. It can't sing itself because it has no direct connections to the cortex. You only notice what it's doing when things go wrong. When your coffee cup doesn't quite reach your lips and you spill the coffee down your front; when you step off a pavement and misjudge the height of the curb, landing heavily and jarringly – only then do you notice everything the cerebellum has been up to.

One good example of the models that the cerebellum builds of how to move the body is the phenomenon of 'sea legs'. If you spend a week or two on a cruise liner (lucky you), the cerebellum will adjust so that it doesn't trust somatosensory feedback from the feet so much to keep upright (it's the deck pitching, not your body falling, get used to it). Then, when your holiday is done, for an hour or two after you step off the cruise liner, the cerebellum still uses its 'sea legs' model, giving you the sensation that the solid land is moving under you.

The cerebellum is keen to take on more work. As practised actions become less voluntary and more automatic, the cerebellum takes over from cortical commands to deliver movements swiftly and smoothly, building the requisite models of practised movement sequences. When motor movements are highly practised, the cerebellum is thick as thieves with the thalamus and the motor cortex in generating smooth actions. The cerebellum therefore has a key role in motor learning.

The cerebellum doesn't just contribute to movements, but also to some aspects of thought. Instead of movement, the cortex can manipulate images or ideas. When these objects are repeatedly manipulated in the mind, the cerebellum can help make their manipulation smooth and automatic, once more building models of practised sequences. Here are two single digit numbers: 6, 8. Add them together. Adults have years of experience adding single digit numbers. Up pops the answer, '14' you utter, smooth as you like, no thinking required, because the cerebellum has you in cruise control of your number bonds.

It's true that much of the cerebellum's work is too mundane for psychologists. It's just coordinating motor movements and sensory feedback for smooth action. It's just integrating voluntary action with postural control. It's just planning, adjusting, and executing movements of the eyes and the limbs and the body. While this is super heavy duty computationally, if you were a Greek philosopher, this is not the kind of thinking that would get you to closer to the gods. The cerebellum helped Shakespeare hold his pen, but not compose his sonnets. That's why no one cares about it. It's mundane. It just happens to use most of the brain's thinking power.

How's That Gonna Work, Then?

The simple life

We've seen that species which have backbones use similar brain-making plans. Across species, and in evolutionary ancestors, differences in the plans have generally not been about adding new brain parts but about scaling the size of different parts. This alters the balance of their involvement in generating behaviour.

To get a sense of how the scaled-up parts of the human brain alter this balance, it's worth revisiting what earlier versions of brain-making plans would have looked like, such as those found in our distant ancestors or still found in our distant cousins… peering back through evolution to before the mammalian brain, to envision brain-making plans back from when life was simple, when you could just act, without worrying about whether God would be happy with what you're about to do.

Let's start with a simple vertebrate, before the limbic system has scaled up, when the cortex is but a wafer. Something like a frog. Animal behaviour is organised around goals, such as eating, not getting eaten, seeking a mate, resting, and keeping warm. In our simple vertebrate, these goals come from instincts and from homeostatic mechanisms. 'Homeostasis' refers to any self-regulating process through which biological systems maintain their stability, that is, hold things together. When you are thirsty, you need to drink. These are the kinds of mechanisms we saw built into the midbrain and brainstem (see Chapter 6 for more on homeostasis). The simple vertebrate will have a repertoire of behaviours: which behaviour is chosen will be largely determined by the situation the animal is in and its bodily needs; the choice is stimulus-driven and inflexible. When you're hungry and a fly zooms by, shoot out your tongue to capture it, then swallow. Your life as a simple vertebrate is *about the present*.

Who's in charge in this system? Which brain structure manages motor behaviour? It's the basal ganglia, selecting actions from competing options. It's all you need.

Now let's think about a brain-making plan that has scaled-up limbic system structures, although still with only the rudiments of a cortex, like reptiles, or probably how dinosaurs were. Now life is all about emotions and memories. The amygdala is storing memories about situations you've been in that are relevant to your fears and desires, while the hippocampus is storing memories of where this happened: rivals who beat you up, places where predators nearly ate you, nooks where snacks have been found. Behaviour can be modified by these memories. Tremble and run away when you see that nasty guy again; stay under cover where the eagles fly; start foraging when you find yourself in that nook where snacks are to be found. There will still be stimulus-driven moments and homeostatic demands (stop to take a pee, time for a nap), but behaviour can now be informed by memory, *by the past*.

Who's in charge? The basal ganglia will still select actions, but limbic memory systems will contribute to the choice. An integrating structure is needed on top to link basal ganglia and limbic memory systems. In ancestral brain-making plans, this management role may once have fallen to the cingulate cortex. The cingulate has taken over the control function from pure action selection, to coordinate the more complex behavioural repertoire.

Finally, let's think about mammals, where the brain-making plan has been tweaked to scale up the cortex. (Because scaling up the cortex is an evolutionarily new thing, the cortex is sometimes called the 'neocortex', neo = Latin for new; but remember, what's new here is mainly the size of this bit of forebrain.) With a hefty lump of cortex on top, you now have access to the future. With more cool, dispassionate computational power, you can start to carry out complex memory-contingent calculations. You can plan multistep action sequences. You can build internal models of the world, including things that happen, plans that might work according to the models, and steps to deliver outcomes.

Behaviour can be flexible and context sensitive. You can switch between plans. You can inhibit impulses (e.g., to stop yourself from eating a chocolate éclair) to gain larger long-term rewards (e.g., looking ripped on the beach). You can interact with large social groups where you remember each individual, where you modify your behaviours according to whom you are interacting with and your personal history with that person. Social groups can coordinate to deliver complex group behaviour such as hunting or beach volleyball (where you can show off your ripped body). Stimulus-driven behaviour and homeostasis still play a role, and emotions still contribute, and action selection chooses the moment to act. But behaviour can now be driven *by the future*.

Who's in charge? Basal ganglia will carry out action selection. Cingulate cortex, previously the boss overseeing limbic system goals and action selection, is now demoted to a middle management role, just reporting back on progress on the goals set by the new boss up there in the cortex, with its fancy prefrontal plan hierarchies.

This presents a simplistic view of brain evolution. In fact, the most ancient parts of the brain aren't left alone when other parts enlarge but end up co-evolving with them, so that, at least in terms of types of neurons, the brain is a mosaic of old and new across all its parts. And structures that play similar roles – e.g., what serves as the cortex in amphibians (the pallium) and in mammals – may have different evolutionary origins. But overall, we see how scaling up different structures across different versions of the vertebrate brain-making plan leads to the multiple levels of control we see in the human brain – action selection, monitoring, planning – even while the brain's focus remains the generation of movement.

What's Freud got to do with it?

Now, you might be tempted to think (as some have) that evolving a large cortex to control the limbic system is akin to strapping a computer on top of a steam engine: sophisticated control is added to primal urges, willpower is added to override baser instincts, rationality to override impulse. But that would be a mistake: an old-fashioned, early 20th century Freudian view of the mind, dressed in a top hat. The human brain is not a system at war with itself, the ego wrestling the id to the ground as the superego looks on disapprovingly. Instead, the brain is an integrated, adaptive whole, bringing together the lessons of the past, the needs of the present, and the promise of the future to deliver appropriate motor behaviour in the moment.

Sure, impulsivity is a thing. You might be 'unable to stop yourself' eating that chocolate éclair in front of you. Mmm. But that's not a failure of willpower over instinct; it's not a failure of ego over id. All animals make decisions that involve trade-offs between predictable rewards in the present (chocolate) versus less predictable rewards further in the future (admiring glances at your ripped body from the beach volleyball crowd). Impulsivity is a well understood, adaptive component of decision making across animals, where a history of rewards at different time delays sometimes conditions the basal ganglia to override the prefrontal cortex's preferred next motor plan – this kind of *right-in-front-of-you* decision making is particularly useful in an unstable environment, such as where chocolate snacks can suddenly disappear or where beach volleyball games are frequently cancelled. Impulsivity is not a moral failure where human rationality has been overwhelmed by animalistic drives. This modern view of impulsive behaviour is an example of how understanding how the brain works can help us to determine what better psychological theories look like.

The cool thing to say

This brings us to the end of the *parts of the brain and what they do*. So, remember, if some guy comes up to you at a party and says, we know almost nothing about how the brain works, you can reply, yeah, well, it's just some content-specific hierarchical sensory and motor systems; some appetitive and spatial memory systems bothered with survival-relevant behaviour; an action selection system bothered about rewards; a motor-smoothing system; and some bodily homeostasis systems. And then you can move on to a more interesting party guest.

━━━━━━━━ Box 3.2 ━━━━━━━━

Neuroscience methods

About now, you're probably beginning to ask yourself: but how do we know all this stuff about how the brain works? How did we find out? We're not going to focus a great deal on methods in this book, so we'll just cover the basics in this box. But prepare yourself for a blizzard of abbreviations.

Historically, our understanding of how the human brain works was derived from a combination of neuroanatomy (taking apart post-mortem brains), making links between damage to specific areas of the brain and subsequent behavioural deficits (see, e.g., the famous case studies of Phineas Gage on pp. 178–179 and HM on p. 179), and investigating the consequences of drug treatments on behaviour. There were some very limited opportunities to probe human brains directly during medical procedures. These methods then connected with animal work, where non-human central nervous systems were deemed more manipulable and explorable using, for instance, precise damage or stimulation (ethical considerations notwithstanding); and with biology, where the electrical and chemical functioning of individual neurons could be studied in petri dishes (*in vitro* measures).

A big breakthrough in mapping human brain structure and function came with the spread of non-invasive brain scanning technologies in the 1990s, which led to those years being christened the 'Decade of the Brain' by then US President George Bush. Magnetic resonance imaging (MRI) allows neuroscientists to generate three-dimensional images of brain structure and function from individuals lying stationary within a brain scanner. Luckily, some cognitive activities, and a few limited motor activities (wiggle your fingers!), can be done while lying down. Now there was a harmless way to measure brain activity in an awake, behaving human (an *in vivo* measure).

How can you take 3D pictures of the brain when it's hidden inside the skull? The key is that atoms, particularly the nuclei of hydrogen atoms (a single proton), like to align with a strong magnetic field. You can bash them out of that alignment with radio waves. When they then realign to the magnetic field, the atoms emit radiation themselves, which can be measured by surrounding detectors. Ace. But how do you know where the atom is? It turns out the frequency of the emitted radiation will depend on the exact magnetic field applied to the atom. If you can make the field different across the space within the scanner (using what's called a gradient field), then the frequency of the radiation from the atoms will be an index of where they are. This is used to give a 2D image at a given height. You then repeat the exercise moving down, creating a set of 2D slices

(Continued)

to reconstruct the whole 3D brain. For each slice, the strength of the signal detected at a given frequency will tell you something about the tissue at a given 2D location. This is a non-invasive technique because hydrogen atoms carry on doing the job of hydrogen atoms whichever way they are aligned. Hydrogen atoms figure in a lot of the tissue in the brain, and how they are aligned and realigned by the magnetic field depends on the tissue they are in. Therefore, the strength of the signal varies by tissue type. This then allows images of, for example, grey and white matter to be constructed. The early scanners took static images of the brain, which while useful in detecting brain changes in, e.g., schizophrenia, were less useful for studying dynamic cognitive processes. MRI had to be modified to be truly valuable, and so functional MRI (fMRI) was born.

How can fMRI be used to tap into brain function? Unfortunately, it can't detect neural activity directly. However, it has been known since the 1890s that neural activity is closely linked with changes in blood flow and blood oxygenation (known as haemodynamics) as extended neural firing triggers the delivery of increased energy supplies (see Chapter 4). Oxygen is carried in the blood by the haemoglobin molecule within red blood cells. Oxygenated and deoxygenated hae-moglobin have different magnetic properties. This means they show up differently on MRI scans, in the form of a blood-oxygen-level-dependent (or BOLD) signal; and in turn, this signal gives an indirect way to assess which parts of the brain are working harder when performing a given task.

It is worth noting that neural firing takes place at the scale of milliseconds, but it takes 2 seconds for the BOLD signal to change in response to elevated firing in a brain region, not reaching its peak until after 4–6 seconds. Functional MRI is excellent at localising the position of these functional changes in the brain; combined with psychological testing (luckily participants can do a bit more in the scanner than wiggle their fingers, e.g., tests of attention and memory), it has become the dominant method for neuroscientists studying brain organisation. However, the time lag between neural activity and BOLD signal is a problem.

It's also worth noting that there are other related imaging methods valuable for other pur-poses, such as investigating tumours, for example positron emission tomography (PET), where a radioactive tracer is injected into the bloodstream; and magnetic resonance spectroscopy (MRS), which uses different MRI signals to measure the chemical composition of brain structures or regions. And there are different ways that MRI signals can be analysed to investigate separate properties of the brain. For example, diffusion tensor imaging (DTI) focuses on the movement of water molecules to map the white matter fibres (sets of myelinated axons) that connect different parts of the brain, in an approach called tractography. As we are now more aware of the need to study networks rather than individual structures, tractography is becoming increasingly important.

Another non-invasive brain imaging technique with a longer history is electroencephalography (EEG), which dates back to the 1920s. The firing of a neuron involves changes in its electrical properties along the axon, changing the electric field surrounding it. It's a tiny, momentary event. But neurons act in concert, and often the axons of many neurons will be lined up, so their electri-cal fields can add up to produce a detectable signal. For example, the electrical voltage potentials produced by the neural activity of the cortex can be detected by an electrode placed on the overlying scalp. It's not perfect – the technique is not so good for measuring neural activity deeper in the brain; the voltages that are detected are so tiny that they are massively outweighed by the electrical activity in muscles, so try not to twitch your face or blink while thinking! And it's hard to locate exactly which neurons the electrical signals are coming from (for example, two strands of axons running in opposite directions would cancel out each other's voltage potentials).

Nevertheless, using a set of electrodes across the scalp, voltage changes produced by neural activity can be detected with exquisite temporal accuracy, on the level of milliseconds (compared with fMRI, which has good localisation but poor temporal accuracy). If measurement is paired with specific events (e.g., pictures flashed on a screen), the brain's response can be charted millisecond to millisecond, measuring what are called event-related potentials (ERPs). Again, there are related imaging methods with different strengths and weaknesses: with a much more cumbersome detector, one can measure changes in magnetic fields on the scalp instead of voltage potentials: these pass through the scalp with less distortion, so give better localisation (the method is called magnetoencephalography or MEG).

fMRI and EEG are passive methods to measure brain activity when individuals are performing certain tasks. However, neuroscientists sometimes use – with a great deal of care and forethought – active methods to alter brain activity, using electrical or magnetic stimulation from outside on the scalp. The subsequent increase or decrease in the activity of the underlying neurons, and its effect on behaviour, offers a stronger test of the function of specific brain regions. The changes are short lived and leave no lasting effects (although how these electrical interventions produce their neural effects is not necessarily well understood). Methods include transcranial Electrical Stimulation (tES), which comes in two forms, transcranial Direct Current Stimulation (tDCS) and transcranial Alternating Current Stimulation (tACS); and transcranial Magnetic Stimulation (tMS).

There is continuous innovation in neuroscience methods. For example, regarding *in vivo* work, a brain imaging technique that is increasingly popular is functional near-infrared spectroscopy (fNIRs), which shines light into the brain and uses detectors to pick up the light reflected by, or filtered through, neural tissue. The reflected and absorbed wavelengths of light can be used to measure structural and functional properties of the underlying tissue (for instance, oxygenated blood is redder than deoxygenated blood). In animal models, a method called optogenetics introduces genes for light-sensitive proteins into specific types of brain cells, which allows precise monitoring and control of their activity using light signals: neurons literally light up when they become more active, or can be temporally silenced by shining a light onto them. In new *in vitro* methods, induced pluripotent stem cells (iPSs) allow peripheral human cells, such as skin cells or hair follicles, to be reprogrammed to be neurons, which can then be grown in a dish into small patches of neural circuitry, so-called organoids. Organoids are tiny, self-organised, three-dimensional tissue cultures, whose electrical or chemical properties can then be probed in detail.

The main point to take from this constellation of methods is that each one has its flaws (such as the poor temporal resolution of fMRI, or the poor spatial resolution of EEG, where resolution means the level of detail that can be discerned), and all need to be combined to generate a convergent picture of how the brain works, at the multiple different scales at which it can be studied.

Self-test: How many of those abbreviations can you remember? Maximum score is 15.

4

HOW DOES A NEURON WORK?

We've taken a tour of the brain to see what the various parts do. Now we're going to move on to thinking how it works in terms of *computation*. That's the modern way of looking at the brain, as a sort of computer. The brain is made up of neurons. These are the fundamental units that process information in the brain. The brain areas we have talked about are made up of networks of neurons signalling to each other. So, let's look at how a neuron works and build up from there.

The human body contains something like 34 trillion cells. They all have some features in common: for instance, a cell nucleus containing our genetic material in the form of chromosomes, and a cell membrane providing a barrier to the extracellular world. Beyond these basic features, cells can differ dramatically. They can be organised into tissues made up of similar cells, such as the skin, skeletal muscle, and fat tissue. These tissues are made up of cells with particular specialisations; muscle cells for contraction, fat cells for storage and release of lipids (fatty acids which store energy), for instance. Neurons are the cells that make up the nervous system and they are specialised for the conduction of the electrical impulses which represent 'information' flowing through neural pathways.

Computationally, what do neurons do? Nothing as complex as algebra or geometry. They make *mini-decisions*. A given neuron receives stimulation from other neurons (let's call those its *input*). Then it makes a decision on whether it will stimulate the neurons to which it is connected (let's call this its *output*). Neurons act like detectors. They are monitoring the input and asking themselves, 'Is this a situation when I should I get involved? Is this what I'm looking for?' If the answer is yes (let's say the input exceeds the neuron's *threshold*), the neuron becomes more electrically active and propagates this activity on to the neurons to which it is connected. Neurons don't just pass on whatever stimulation they receive to the next neurons like a baton – they only pass it on if their threshold is exceeded, and it is in this way that they make a decision. While the decisions of individual neurons are simple, when you put them together into networks, the whole network can perform complex calculations, like generating the appropriate motor neuron instructions in response to a certain sensory input.

There are two main properties of neuronal cells that give them their information processing functionality: electrical (we'll hear about things like voltage-gated channels and action potentials) and chemical (we'll hear about things like synapses and neurotransmitters). Let's start with the electricity.

Electrical Properties of Neurons

The role of electrical activity in nervous system function (at least in a frog's leg) was first identified in 1791 by Galvani, but the discovery of neurons had to wait until a histochemical stain became available in the 1870s in the work of Golgi. This is a technique that uses a chemical that stains or colours specific cells and allows scientists to identify different types of cells under the microscope. The chemical used by Golgi was selectively taken up by neurons and made them visible under the microscope. Some of the first drawings of neurons such as those by Ramón y Cajal are strikingly beautiful. Cajal's drawings demonstrated a variety of neuronal cell types. However, to explain some of the key specialisations of neurons, we work with the simplest form, shown on the opposite page.

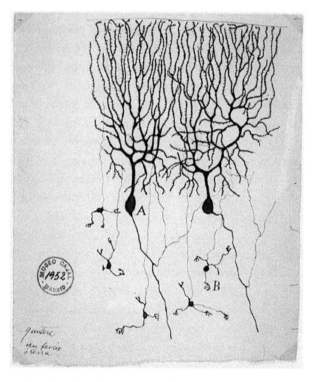

Figure 4.1 One of Ramón y Cajal's drawings of neurons

Source: Public domain

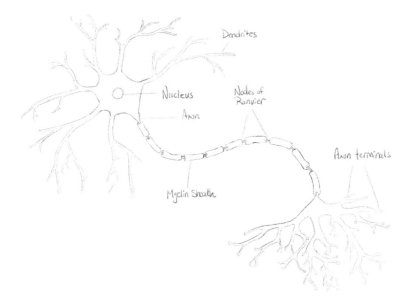

Figure 4.2 Simplest form of a neuron

The neuron is typically elongated. There are extensions from the cell, known as *pro-cesses*. Short processes connect with the cell body on one side, known as *dendrites*, while a single longer process known as the *axon* extends from the other side of the cell body, eventually ending in several branches. Remember that dendrites, cell body, and axon are continuous and elements of the same three-dimensional cell, all filled with the jelly-like cytoplasm.

The neuron is specialised to conduct electrical impulses (nerve impulses or action potentials) from dendrites, across the cell body and along the axon to the axon terminals: input to output. To understand how this happens, we need to look more closely at the chemical environment inside the neuron (intracellular) and outside the neuron (extracellular). This bit is quite complicated, but if it helps, it could be *more* complicated…

The elements sodium, potassium, and chlorine are usually electrically neutral, with the positively charged protons in their nucleus balancing out the negatively charged electrons. If they lose an electron, they become *positively* charged; if they gain an electron, they become *negatively* charged. Charged particles are known as *ions*. The generation of action potentials depends upon the balance of positive (potassium and sodium) and negative (chloride) ions between the intracellular and extracellular worlds. Potassium ions are found mainly inside the neuron, sodium and chloride ions mainly outside the neuron. Organic ions, that is, negatively charged protein molecules, found inside the cell also play a major role.

In the 1940s it was found that there was an electrical or *potential* difference between the inside and outside of the giant squid axon, measured at −70 millivolts (mv). Scientists were playing with the squid axon – which controls part of the squid's water jet propulsion system – simply because the axon is so large: at half a millimetre across, it is easy to study. Given that evolution does not mess with things that work, such as neurons, it is no surprise that mammalian neurons are the same; they too have a *resting potential* of around –70 mv. How can the inside of a neuron be more negatively charged than the outside?

The neuronal cell membrane is made up of two lipid (fat) layers. It is *semi-permeable*, meaning that it allows small particles such as ions to pass through. Negative ions are attracted to positive ions, so theoretically an electrical imbalance between intracellular and extracellular components of the neuron would rapidly disappear as ions pass through the membrane. The electricity leaks out, as it were. So, to maintain a resting potential of –70 mv another mechanism must be at work. This is the *sodium–potassium pump*, a protein molecule embedded in the cell membrane that actively ships sodium ions out of the neuron and moves potassium ions in. Both sodium and potassium ions are positive, but the pump takes more sodium ions out than it allows potassium ions in. This keeps the potential balance between intracellular and extracellular components at –70 mv. It creates the conditions where the neuron is ready to fire, like a cocked pistol.

Besides the sodium–potassium pump, the neuronal cell membrane also contains *ion channels*. These allow the passage of sodium, potassium, and chloride ions in and out of the neuron. These channels are *gated* or controlled, either by electrical forces (*voltage-gated*) or by the action of specific molecules or *ligands* (*ligand-gated*). Ligand-gated channels are opened by the combination of neurotransmitters with their receptors at the synapse (we'll hear about neurotransmitters shortly). This combination opens the channel, allowing ions to enter the cell. If positive sodium ions enter the cell, the resting potential of –70 mv becomes more positive. If it reaches around –55 mv, then the voltage-gated channels get involved: they open and allow sodium ions to flood into the cell. In around a millisecond, the intracellular potential shifts explosively from –55 mv to +40 mv – this is the *action potential*. Almost immediately the sodium channels close and potassium channels open. Potassium ions are moved out of the cell and the intracellular component becomes more negative, dipping down to –80 mv before regaining its resting potential of –70 mv. The whole process, from initial opening of channels to the return to –70 mv, takes about 3–4 milliseconds. (For reference, compare this to the blink of an eye: around 100 milliseconds.) This means the maximum frequency at which action potentials can be generated in a neuron – fire, reset, fire – is around 250 per second.

Neurons are continuously producing action potentials – they represent information in their *firing rate*. Changes in the stimulation of a neuron will increase or decrease its firing rate. Each neuron will have a sporadic or baseline firing rate when not stimulated. Stimulation may increase the rate above this level or decrease the rate below it. This means we need some way of activating neurons and some way of deactivating them.

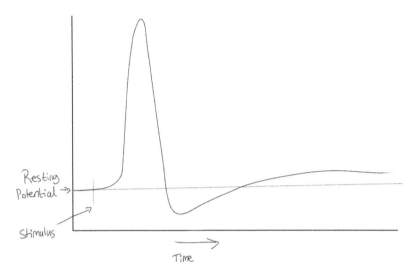

Resting
Potential →

Stimulus

Time

Figure 4.3 An action potential. The plot shows the change of voltage potential (some tens of millivolts) inside the neuron over time (a few milliseconds) as the neuron fires in response to a stimulus

For ligand-gated channels, the combination of neurotransmitters attaching to their receptors opens channels ('ligand-gated') in the neuronal cell membrane that allow positive sodium ions to enter the cell, shifting the membrane potential towards the −55 mv necessary for an action potential to occur. Action potentials are all-or-nothing: either the −55 mv threshold is reached and an action potential is generated, or it isn't, and no action potential occurs. These are *excitatory postsynaptic potentials*, or EPSPs.

But other neurotransmitters can open channels that allow negative chloride ions into the cell. This makes the resting potential more negative and an action potential less likely to occur. These are *inhibitory postsynaptic potentials*, or IPSPs. In other words, signals from other neurons can make a neuron more likely to fire (excite it) or less likely to fire (inhibit it). Changes which make an action potential more likely are referred to as *depolarising* the cell membrane. Changes which make it less likely are referred to as *hyperpolarising* the cell membrane.

The probability of an action potential being triggered is a function of all the inputs to the neuron (you sort of add together the EPSPs and IPSPs, though in reality it depends on where they are landing on the dendrites). The number of inputs from other neurons can number in the order of thousands. So, let's say an action potential has been triggered. This begins at the axon hillock, the small conical region of the neuron where the axon leaves the cell body. At the axon hillock, all the EPSPs and IPSPs from the inputs are integrated. Somehow, this spike in electrical activity then has to be transmitted along the axon to stimulate other neurons. The electrochemical processes behind this transmission are another level of complexity, which luckily are beyond the scope of this book... but one aspect of the neuron we do need to look at is the myelin sheath.

The myelin sheath is a fatty (lipid) covering around the axon (in fact it is formed by outgrowths from non-neuronal cells called oligodendrocytes, which we'll come back to). The covering is not continuous but broken at intervals by 'nodes of Ranvier', where the neuronal cell membrane is exposed. The action potential can jump from node to node (known as *saltatory* – meaning 'jumping' – *conduction*), and so is transmitted along the axon down to the axon terminals. The speed of conduction in myelinated neurons (which includes most neurons in the brain) can reach around 120 metres/sec; in unmyelinated neurons, which make up some pathways of the peripheral nervous system (e.g., those carrying information on pain and temperature), the speed is around 30 metres/sec. As information processing in the brain must be a function of conduction speed, myelination was a critical step in the evolution of neurons, and first seen in vertebrates (animals with a spinal cord, e.g., birds, reptiles, mammals). Our friend the squid doesn't have myelinated axons, even though it's surely important that the squid can fire its water jet pronto to escape from danger. How could it ensure fast transmission in these key axons? The only other way for faster propagation of action potentials down your axon is to make the axon diameter wider. And this is why the squid axon is so giant, and conveniently easy for neuroscientists to study: to make propagation fast without myelination.

Before we get on to chemistry, a note on energy. To keep neurons negatively polarised and ready to fire, ions need to be continuously pumped out of their interiors. This takes energy. It's one of the reasons the brain uses so much energy – perhaps 20% of the body's calorie consumption. When neurons are working hard – lots of action potentials, lots of resetting – calcium ions build up outside the neuron. This creates a signal that is passed on to nearby vessels (by astrocytes – see later!). In turn the vessels dilate and bring in more oxygenated blood, which supports the greater energy consumption. The work-hard => calcium-signal => vessel-dilation process takes a few seconds before a region of the brain can attract the extra blood flow it needs. If, when this occurs, you happen to be lying in a magnetic resonance imaging scanner, doing some thinking, pesky neuroscientists might be measuring this regional change in oxygenated blood flow and discussing with each other what it reveals about your mental processes. And that's one way that functional brain imaging works (see Box 3.2 for more).

Chemical Properties of Neurons

Neurons signal to each other, so that the electrical output of one neuron influences the electrical activity of the neurons to which it is 'connected'. But on closer inspection, there turn out to be tiny gaps between the output of one neuron (its axon terminals) and the input of the next neuron (its dendrites). For the electrical signal to re-ignite on the other side of the gap, chemicals have to be released into the extracellular liquid in which the neurons sit and diffuse across the gap till they reach the neuron at the other side. The chemicals have to latch on to matching receptors on the other side of the gap which, as we saw above, can then trigger changes in the electrical activity in the next neuron. It takes perhaps half a millisecond for these chemicals, called *neurotransmitters*, to cross the gap. The process happens in many tiny structures where the neurons (almost) touch, called *synapses*.

After the discovery of the neuron in the 1870s, already by the end of the 19th century, Sherrington and others had deduced the existence of gaps ('surface of separation' in the words of Sherrington, who introduced the term 'synapse' for these gaps). The deduction was based on their studies of activity in neural pathways and especially the neural control of skeletal muscles. However, direct observation of synapses and their structure would have to wait for the invention of the electron microscope in the 1950s.

Formally, the synapse, or synaptic cleft, is the tiny gap between the axon terminal, or presynaptic membrane, and the following dendritic membrane, or postsynaptic membrane. Although vanishingly small (about one three thousandth of the width of a human hair – it is measured in units called angstroms, one ten billionth of a metre), the synapse represents a physical separation that the action potential reaching the presynaptic axon terminal cannot jump. Ah. This is where neurotransmitters come in. Molecules of these chemicals are packaged in storage 'vesicles' (meaning a small sac or pouch) within the presynaptic axon terminal. When the action potential reaches the axon terminal, another hugely complicated electrochemical process leads to vesicles moving to the presynaptic membrane, where they rupture and release their contents into the synaptic cleft.

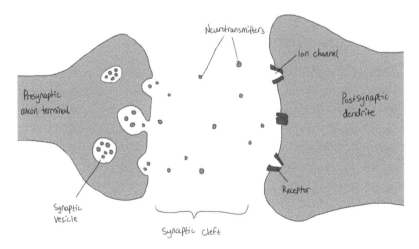

Figure 4.4   The synaptic cleft and neurotransmitters

The synapse is so small that the molecules of the neurotransmitter can diffuse over to the postsynaptic membrane in half a millisecond. Embedded in this membrane are synaptic receptors; these have a molecular structure that matches the neurotransmitter so that the two can combine like a key fitting into a lock. This combination opens those ligand-gated ion channels mentioned previously and disturbs the membrane resting potential. For the moment, we can focus on combinations that lead to EPSPs, making an action potential in the postsynaptic membrane more likely.

A single action potential or nerve impulse arriving at the presynaptic terminal will not release sufficient neurotransmitter to fully depolarise the postsynaptic membrane and will not produce an action potential. So, the information coded by that presynaptic action potential will be lost. To fully depolarise the postsynaptic membrane a burst of impulses reaching the presynaptic terminal is needed, releasing sufficient neurotransmitter to combine simultaneously with postsynaptic receptors. The cumulative effect depolarises the postsynaptic membrane and generates an action potential.

So, we have a filtering system: low frequency impulses travelling down the presynaptic axon do not jump the synapse and that information is lost – a basic form of information processing. But there is a further complication. Synapses are usually on the dendrite and a patch of dendritic membrane can host upwards of a thousand synaptic connections. Some of these use inhibitory neurotransmitters like gamma-aminobutyric acid (GABA); when these combine with receptors they lead to IPSPs and make an action potential less likely. Others use excitatory neurotransmitters like glutamate, which lead to EPSPs and make an action potential more likely. So, the likelihood of an action potential being generated in the postsynaptic neuron is a complex function of inhibitory and excitatory inputs – a more sophisticated form of information processing.

How the Drugs Work

The role of neurotransmitters in synaptic transmission was hinted at in early studies at the start of the 20th century, but it was only in the 1960s that serious progress was made. The major ('classical') neurotransmitters such as serotonin, dopamine, noradrenaline, and acetylcholine (now pretty much household names) were identified, and links made with various aspects of behaviour and cognition. Each neurotransmitter has its own specific receptor, and this allowed some of the actions of drugs on behaviour to be explained. For instance, the antipsychotic drug chlorpromazine, used in the treatment of schizophrenia, was shown to be an *antagonist* at the dopamine receptor, i.e., it blocked the action of dopamine at the synapse, reducing dopamine activity in the brain. It led to the initial simplistic idea that schizophrenia might be caused by too much dopamine in the brain (see Chapter 8 for more on psychiatric disorders and drug treatments).

Figure 4.5 Drugs that reduce symptoms of conditions like schizophrenia work by affecting neurotransmitters

One reason for the focus on the 'classical' neurotransmitters was their organisation into pathways. A pathway consists of a cluster of neuronal cell bodies (as we saw in the previous chapter, this is often referred to as a nucleus), with their axons running together towards their target destination, and clearly identifiable as a pathway. An example is the nigro-striatal pathway in the basal ganglia. This pathway is named from its point of origin in the substantia nigra in the midbrain, running forwards to the corpus striatum in the forebrain basal ganglia, and plays a role in generating reward signals in the action selection system. As with other brain names, the substantia nigra sounds exotic but simply means 'black stuff', as these cells appear darker than neighbouring neurons. The axons of neuronal cell bodies in the substantia nigra run together towards the striatum. It is degeneration of this pathway that leads to the symptoms of Parkinson's disease.

The connection between identifiable pathways and neurotransmitters had to wait for the development of more advanced methods for studying neurotransmission. In the 1960s it was finally established that neurons of the nigro-striatal pathway all release dopamine at their synaptic endings in the striatum, i.e., it was a 'dopamine' pathway. This also explains why in Parkinson's disease drugs that can help reduce symptoms, such as

L-DOPA, serve to increase brain dopamine levels and so help replace the neurotransmitter lost as the pathway degenerates.

Each of the classic neurotransmitters is organised in several identifiable pathways shown in Figure 4.6. These usually run from nuclei in the brainstem or midbrain to forebrain areas. They have been a main focus of research into brain and behaviour. But, in case you are worried that this is too simple, these pathways account for only a minority of synaptic connections in the brain. The majority of synapses use the everyday neurotransmitters, GABA, glycine, and glutamate. GABA and glycine are inhibitory transmitters (leading to IPSPs in the postsynaptic membrane), while glutamate is excitatory. So why are these neurotransmitters less popular?

The main reason is that they are not organised into neat pathways. For instance, GABA neurons are very widespread in the brain, tend to have short axons and form local networks. Their role is likely general inhibitory control of brain activity. For example, epilepsy is a disorder caused by uncontrollable electrical discharges in the brain. One treatment that can be effective is the use of drugs that increase GABA neurotransmission. So, GABA, glycine, and glutamate are as important as their big brothers, regulating neuronal activity throughout the brain. But it is less easy to link these everyday neurotransmitters to specific behaviours and cognitions, which is why they feature less in high-profile research, and hence have a smaller fanbase.

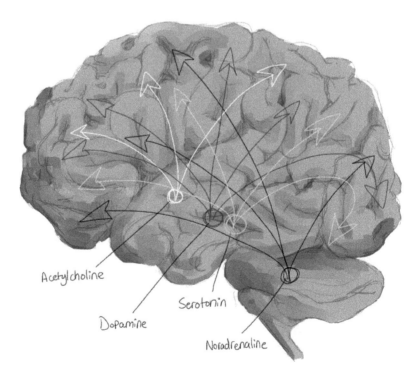

Figure 4.6 Pathways for the most popular neurotransmitters

Yes, but why not just connect the neurons properly?

Stepping back for a moment, we might ask why aren't the neurons in the brain properly connected to each other, so the electrical output of one neuron feeds straight into the next one? Surely that would be much faster and less prone to breakdown? Wired connections are always faster than wireless, right? Well, direct wired connections are found in some places in the brain. Big motor neurons have direct electrical connections, where they need to fire fast and fire strong to get the body moving, especially for defensive reflexes. If direct connections are possible, it is all the more puzzling as to why the rest of the neurons aren't properly connected but instead use neurotransmitters to talk to each other.

Neurons sit in networks where much of what each neuron does only depends on the neurons around it. The neuron receives electrical stimulation and sends electrical stimulation to other neurons. What the neuron does is *local*. It goes about its business oblivious to important issues that may be facing the whole brain.

But let's say you wanted to control the activity of a whole network of neurons at once, or even a whole brain region. There are two ways you could go about this. You could have a bunch of 'control' neurons, which had connections to every single neuron in the region you want to control. Indeed, the brain uses this solution sometimes. As we'll see, you can think of the prefrontal cortex as a sort of modulatory or control system that turns on or turns off relevant parts of specialised systems in the rest of the brain. But there's another way to exert regional control over local neural activity.

First, you sit the electrically signalling network of neurons in a bath of fluid. Next you very slightly separate the neurons, so there are tiny gaps between them. You then make the final bit of communication between the neurons cross those gaps, using chemical communication through the fluid. It's not as fast. It's not as efficient. It may go wrong. But now if you alter the chemicals in the bath of fluid, you can change how communication works in the whole network at once. Instead of your 'control' neurons having to directly connect with every neuron in the brain region they want to control (which would take a lot of connections), the control neurons can simply pump different chemicals into the fluid bath in which that region sits. Those chemicals are the neurotransmitters. And they allow modulation of whole regions of the brain.

Of course, if you take this route, apart from the neurotransmitters that allow this modulation, you're also going to want everyday neurotransmitters, which just do the basics of passing on excitatory or inhibitory stimulation between neurons. As we've seen, the two main everyday neurotransmitters are glutamate, where one neuron wants to stimulate another, and GABA, where one neuron wants to inhibit the activity of another. There are a number of different modulatory neurotransmitters, each issued by their own 'control' neurons. These control systems are wired to different regions, and they serve different roles in modulation. Here are the roles of the four main modulatory neurotransmitter systems.

- *Serotonin* is used in the control system that modulates level of arousal or mood, including sleep or wakefulness. When it's released, the message to the brain region is 'Stay awake! Be happy!' Drugs that alter levels of serotonin have been found to help some mental health conditions that affect mood, such as depression.
- *Noradrenaline* modulates attention, vigilance, and anxiety. It says to the brain region, 'Look lively, this is important!'
- *Acetylcholine* encourages learning and memory, and is particularly used to enhance learning in the hippocampus. It says to the network, 'Remember this!'
- *Dopamine* is more limited in the regions in which it is released, focusing on regions that decide what to do or when to move. It is involved in motivation, and particularly signalling when current behaviour is or isn't getting the expected reward. It says to a region, 'Do this again to get what you want' and then 'Did we get what we wanted?'

Looking Ahead – Neurons and Learning

In Chapter 7, we look at brain systems in relation to different types of memory and learning. To give some background to that section, it is worth having a closer look at communication between neurons, and the phenomenon of long-term potentiation (LTP). As long ago as 1949, Donald Hebb, a legendary pioneer of neuroscience, proposed a theoretical model of learning in the brain. According to Hebb's model, learning takes place within neuronal cell assemblies (circuits) and is grounded in changes in the strength of synaptic connections between neurons. The basic idea was that the more frequently a presynaptic neuron stimulated a postsynaptic neuron, the 'stronger' that synapse would become and the more likely the neuron would be to fire; this could provide the basis for learning in the brain. However, at that time the available technology did not allow the model to be tested in the lab.

In 1973, Bliss and Lomo managed to directly test the idea. Using hippocampal slices from a rat brain (maintained in the lab in solutions of cerebrospinal fluid), they were able to stimulate a key pathway connecting different areas of the hippocampus (for the technically minded, they used the perforant pathway, which connects the entorhinal cortex to the dentate gyrus; presynaptic neurons of the perforant pathway synapse on to dentate gyrus neurons, so the postsynaptic responses of dentate neurons could be recorded. And breathe.). Weak stimulation of the perforant pathway produced, as expected, correlated weak EPSPs (excitatory postsynaptic potentials) in the dentate gyrus. Then the perforant pathway was stimulated with a burst of very high frequency electrical stimuli (but still within normal limits for neurons, around 100 stimuli per second). Following this high frequency stimulation, it was found that the weak stimulation first tested now produced much larger EPSPs in postsynaptic neurons, i.e., the synapses seemed to have become 'stronger' or more sensitive to presynaptic stimulation. This is 'long-term potentiation' – long-term as even in these isolated hippocampal slices, LTP could last for several hours.

Over the following decades research has focused on the hippocampus (understandably, as the hippocampus is a key memory structure), but LTP has also been demonstrated throughout the brain, in intact animals, and across different species. It is likely to be a fundamental characteristic of synaptic activity – repeated high frequency stimulation leading to stronger synapses. This plasticity is an obvious candidate for the basis of learning through repeated experience (and repeated stimulation of the same neuronal circuits). Remember this when we come to Chapter 7!

Although less studied, the opposite phenomenon, long-term depression (LTD) of synaptic activity, has also been demonstrated. Instead of high frequency stimulation of the presynaptic pathway, LTD requires repeated low frequency (1–3 stimuli per second) stimulation. This leads to a long-term depression of postsynaptic EPSP frequency and has obvious implications for models of learning and forgetting, suggesting some low-level basis for the idea of use it or lose it.

Some Complications With Neurotransmitters (and More Drugs)

It was initially thought that a given neuron would only release one neurotransmitter at its synapses (the 'Dale' principle). That would allow us to refer to dopaminergic, serotonergic, cholinergic neurons and so forth. We still do that, though we now know that neurons can release a variety of active neurochemicals into the synapse. In fact, the list of neurotransmitters and neuromodulators (chemicals that influence the release of neurotransmitters) has reached around a hundred. So, life, as always, has become far more complicated.

Next, we've said that neurotransmitters combine with postsynaptic receptors and contribute to the triggering or not of action potentials. What do they do then? If they were just to hang around in the synaptic cleft, they could re-attach to the receptors and trigger more firing, producing continuous activation. To prevent this, after combination with postsynaptic receptors, neurotransmitters are removed from the gap in one of two main ways. Enzymes may break them down into their component parts, or they may be taken back up into the presynaptic terminal for re-use.

Here's one way to think about it. Imagine a cheesy Hollywood movie set in 1950s America, involving teen love. One evening, our hero, let's call him Chad, has snuck into the garden of his true love, Pamela, struck by the urge to see her. Pamela, however, is in her upstairs bedroom, doing her homework. Chad wants to attract Pamela's attention, but he can't call out, for fear that Pamela's strict father will hear. So, Chad collects a handful of pebbles and throws them up at Pamela's window. The pebbles fall back down onto the pathway. The curtains remained closed; Pamela hasn't heard. So, Chad must kneel, collect the pebbles up, and throw again.

In this analogy, the neurotransmitters are the pebbles that are thrown at the window of the postsynaptic neuron (if we may call Pamela that). The pebbles must be collected up to throw again (reuptake), or if Chad turned up with pockets full of pebbles, the fallen pebbles must be swept away to stop them building up (Pamela's father would be on to it). Drugs which disrupt either of these processes can alter the influence of neurotransmitters on neural activity.

For example, dopamine, noradrenaline, and serotonin in the synaptic cleft are broken down by the enzyme monoamine oxidase (MAO). If this enzyme is blocked, transmitter levels remain high and synaptic activity is increased; drugs which do this make up the MAO-inhibitor class of antidepressants. This effectiveness of these drugs is the basis for linking depression to lower levels of serotonin and noradrenaline.

Reuptake into the presynaptic terminal is the other mechanism for removing neurotransmitters from the synapse. This mechanism is located within the membrane of the presynaptic terminal. If this is blocked, the transmitter remains available for use at the postsynaptic membrane, and this is exactly what another class of antidepressant drugs does. The 'specific serotonin reuptake inhibitors' (SSRIs) such as Prozac (chemical name, fluoxetine) block reuptake at serotonin synapses and so increase serotonin synaptic activity. Again, this is the basis for linking the neurotransmitter serotonin with mood.

In our third complication, the membrane of the presynaptic terminal may contain 'autoreceptors'. These are receptors for the same neurotransmitter the neuron releases into the synapse. The transmitter will activate these receptors, and this gives the presynaptic neuron feedback on the level of neurotransmitter activity in the synapse. It's Chad counting how many pebbles he's thrown. As activity increases, autoreceptor activation increases, and transmitter release from the presynaptic terminal will be reduced, i.e., it is a negative feedback system. Chad knows when enough is enough.

In our final complication, neurotransmitters modulate the activity in a range of specialised systems. The contribution of the neurotransmitters to how the brain is working therefore depends on the part of the brain you're looking at. That is, the same neurotransmitter can do different things in different brain systems.

Take dopamine. This influences at least three different functions in three different parts of the brain. It is involved in supporting synchronous firing in working memory areas of the prefrontal cortex. It is involved in reward signals for action selection in the basal ganglia. And it is involved in the motor parts of the thalamus, part of a feedback circuit connecting the motor cortex and cerebellum. So, when the level of dopamine drops in Parkinson's disease, there are potentially a range of symptoms involving cognition (prefrontal cortex), voluntary action selection (basal ganglia), and motor control (thalamus), the latter producing the characteristic tremors. Compare this to the popular notion that dopamine is simply the brain chemical for pleasure! And that's why we're in a 'complications' section…

Hormones Are Also Important

We have looked at synaptic neurotransmitters and how they act across the synapse on their specific receptors. But neurons may also have receptors for other chemicals, in particular hormones. We all know something about hormones – testosterone, cortisol, oxytocin, etc. They are released by endocrine glands in the body into the bloodstream and have a range of physiological effects on the body. For example, testosterone, from the testes, leads to muscle development, growth of body hair and other secondary sexual characteristics in males. Oxytocin, from the pituitary gland (this major gland, secreting many hormones, lies within the cranial cavity and is directly connected to the hypothalamus), controls contractions during childbirth and postnatal milk secretion (see Chapter 6).

In the 1960s, the impressively named research field 'psychoneuroendocrinology' developed. Those guys knew their way round some syllables. Neuroscientists were becoming aware that besides their established effects on the body, hormones could have effects on cognitive, emotional, and social behaviours. How could hormones do this? Over the following decades, it became clear that specific receptors for hormones like testosterone, oxytocin, and cortisol existed in the brain (especially in the limbic system). The receptors are located on neurons, and so hormones in the bloodstream can directly affect activity in neurons and neuronal circuits. Some of these effects are simple regulation – cortisol is released from the adrenal cortex gland (just above the kidney) when we are stressed. Once the stress hopefully disappears, stimulation of cortisol receptors in the hypothalamus acts as part of a negative feedback circuit, eventually reducing high levels of cortisol secretion from the adrenal cortex. We'll come back to stress in Chapter 6.

However, over the last 20 years, it has become clear that these hormones can modulate far more complex human and animal behaviours, particularly related to social interactions, pair bonding, approach/avoidance behaviours, sex, and aggression (see section on oxytocin in Chapter 6). In fact, there are major areas, such as the behavioural and emotional changes associated with adolescence, that could not be explained without reference to changing hormone levels and their effects on the brain.

So, the focus on chemical signalling in the brain may be on 'near' signalling via release of synaptic neurotransmitters from the presynaptic terminal into the synaptic cleft, but the complete picture has to include this 'far' signalling from hormones released from glands in the body and carried in the bloodstream to the brain. Just another fascinating complication…

Now, let's climb back into the brain.

How Many Types of Neurons Are There?

You'll hear about different types of neuron: Purkinje cells, pyramidal cells, granule cells, spindle cells. How many types of neuron are there? We won't go into a lot of detail on this here, other than to say a couple of things. First, if you're looking at the neurons that sit in the spine, that question has an easy answer. There are three types of neuron: sensory neurons, which have some way of receiving stimulation from the world thereby generating action potentials to be sent down their axon; motor neurons, which connect to muscles and cause them to expand or contract; and interneurons, which mediate between sensory and motor neurons and support the processes involved in reflexes. Simple.

If you're in the brain, no one really knows how many types of neuron there are, because there's no agreement on how you count the types. The best way is to think about the different features they have. You can look at their shape – how big or small they are, the shape of their dendrite tree, the length of their axon, the shape of the axon terminal (also sometimes called a tree or arbour), as Cajal did. You can look at the connections – where a neuron receives connections from, or where it sends connections to, tracing pathways. You can look at myelination. You can look at the function of the system in which the neuron lies, along the lines of the brain parts we identified in the previous chapter. Or, following our discussion above, you can look at the types of neurotransmitters they release, such as dopamine or serotonin neurons (but remembering that release of a neurotransmitter into the synapse may involve a host of other neurochemicals) or the types of neurotransmitter receptors they have. The latest approaches consider what genes are expressed in different neurons. It's therefore not possible to say how many types of neurons there are in the brain. But we could make a number up for you, if you'd like. Two hundred and thirty seven.

Wow, I Mean, Literally, Where Did All That Come From?

When you hear that neurons are basic units of information processing in the brain, and that they have (let's admit it) some pretty complex electrical and chemical properties dedicated to supporting this function, one response is, where the heck did all of that come from? It seems miraculous, right? All the action potentials and the ion channels and neurotransmitters and enzymes for breaking down neurotransmitters and so forth. How can this kind of spectacular specialist cellular function have come about through evolution? How can evolution have selected for *computation*? As we heard in Chapter 2, it's hard to answer these kinds of question definitively. You have to look across the shared properties of different species, either in how their brains and bodies work or in the types of genes they have, and contrast more closely and less closely related species to make inferences about what happened in distant ancestors back through evolution.

So, here's the surprising thing: versions of many of the genes and cellular functions involved in what neurons do can be found in *single-celled animals* – for example, genes for properties such as voltage-gated channels and molecules that form synaptic structures. But in this case, there's no brain, no body, just one cell. This means evolution probably co-opted mechanisms that were already present prior to the emergence of multi-cellular animals to produce neurons. A possible selective pressure for specialising some cells for information processing in multi-cellular animals is the requirement to make quick movements to obtain food or to avoid becoming someone else's food, which places a premium on a fast-conducting system that can link sensory cells to motor cells. So, if one of the cell types has properties a bit like that, maybe we can use them.

One possibility for the origin of the chemical properties of neurons (that is, synaptic transmission) is in signalling between unicellular species which aggregate to form colonies. Chemical signalling between the cells – via transmitters and receptors – allows coordinated movements of the whole colony.

What about the origin of the electrical properties of neurons? Voltage-gated channels may have originated in single-celled organisms which used such channels to regulate the salinity of their interior depending on the ocean, lake, or puddle in which they found themselves. Action potentials may have originated in mechanisms for regulating the beating of tails (cilia) or the contraction of muscle cells.

While small animals could have coordinated their behaviour through electrical connections between skin cells, as animals increased in size across evolution, there would be an advantage for having some of these skin cells specialised for rapid conduction (indeed during early development, neurons are mostly generated from the same line of cells in the developing embryo as skin cells, hinting at a common evolutionary origin).

The point here is not that we have definitive answers – the above are speculations – but that an explanation for the evolution of the amazing properties of neurons is feasible and does not require us to *<insert miracle here>*.

Neurons Aren't the Only Cells in the Brain

Neurons get all the glory, and we've given them copious, loving attention here. But there is another class of cells in the brain crucial for supporting the function of neurons. They are, as it were, the dogsbodies, the support team, the guys who hold things together. These are called glial cells (from the Latin for glue because they… hold the neurons together). There is about an equivalent number of these cells in the brain as neurons.

Glial cells make up about half the total volume of the brain and spinal cord. We'll mention three main types here.

Astrocytes look like little stars (astra = star), and these cells support the metabolic function of neurons. They regulate the external chemical environment of neurons and are involved in recycling neurotransmitters released during synaptic transmission. As we heard, astrocytes are also involved in regulating energy supply when they signal the vessels to dilate in response to sustained neural activity, allowing delivery of more oxygenated blood. They also help in repair after damage.

Oligodendrocytes are glial cells that are involved in coating axons with myelin, the fatty substance that insulates the axon to improve the speed at which it can propagate electrical signals. These cells wrap themselves around the axon to generate the myelin coating.

Both astrocytes and oligodendrocytes are called *macroglia*, large glial cells, but there are also *microglia*. These smaller cells are involved in protecting neurons and fighting infection. It's when the microglia are upset that the brain experiences inflammation. As a protection force for neurons, microglia are both mobile and able to multiply when the brain is damaged.

Although this is just a glimpse of what glial cells do, the different glial cells emphasise that while we can look at what the brain is doing in terms of information processing or computation, it is nevertheless a biological organ whose organic and metabolic needs must be supported by a range of other systems. We'll return to that point in Chapter 6.

This completes our detailed consideration of the neuron. Well done for making it through – some hard yards there. As a reward, here is a picture of a happy neuron. We now move on to think about the type of computer that the brain creates.

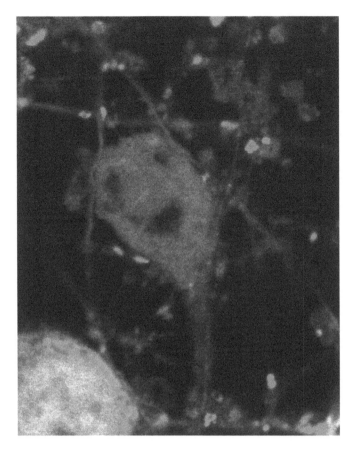

Figure 4.7 The happy neuron. One of our former students was lucky enough to capture a picture of a neuron smiling (centre) while she was trying to image mitochondria in mouse neurons. Maybe it's fun being a neuron

5
THE BRAIN IS A COMPUTER

When neurons change their firing rates, they are making simple decisions about their inputs. But a neuron can't do much on its own. To carry out the complex computations that the brain needs, the neurons must be connected together into networks. In this chapter, we will consider what those computations look like, first at a small scale, then at a global scale. We'll also briefly discuss how a desktop computer works, because this will offer a good counterpoint: brains work *nothing* like this apart from, perhaps, the use of electrical signalling. Then we'll cover some of the tricks the brain uses to carry out its functions. And we'll also take a look at its favoured content: sure, the human brain likes sensory information and motor information, but there's something *else* it could spend all day thinking about.

The Cortical Sheet

We're going to focus on the cortical sheet, the outer grey matter of the brain. That's because humans have a big one. When examined close up, two characteristics of how the neurons are wired together jump out.

First, neurons in the sheet are organised into layers (it's called a laminar structure). There are six layers in the cortex. Some of the evolutionary older parts of the brain (the hippocampus, the cerebellum, the olfactory bulb) only have three layers. That was the old-fashioned way. The six-layer structure is Johnny-come-lately, it's what puts the neo in neocortex. The six layers of the cortex play different roles, in terms of their major inputs and outputs. For example, they differ in whether they have inputs and outputs to/from the thalamus, to/from other areas of the cortical sheet either nearby or far away, whether they receive inputs from the modulatory neurotransmitters systems, or whether they have connections up or down to specific layers.

Second, broadly speaking, the cortical sheet looks the same all over. Sometimes, scientists park the 'neo' bit and start calling it 'iso', isocortex, because it's the same everywhere (iso = same). On the small scale, the neurons are organised into mini-columns that span the six layers, each of around 100 neurons; it's a tiny consistent circuit, which is then repeated millions of times across the cortical sheet. For mammals, evolution has found a robust and flexible fundamental unit of computation that it can use for all sorts of different content. Crucially, what any area of the cortex computes depends on its inputs and outputs: *where you are is what you do*. The mini-column architecture has probably been retained within evolution because it offers the flexibility for the same sheet to process different content by tweaking input and output connectivity. This allows the cortex to respond to evolutionary changes in the periphery (e.g., in sensory equipment, in the body morphology) so that it can use the same brain to control different shaped bodies; or to respond to changes within the lifespan of the individual (e.g., blindness causes the 'visual' occipital cortex to become activated by other sensory systems; teaching children to read causes the underneath of the temporal cortex to become excited by written words rather than visual objects). It was somewhat amazing for neuroscientists to find this consistency across mammalian cortices; that, at the smallest scale, there was little to distinguish a wolf's mini-columns in its motor system from a sheep's mini-columns in its sensory system.

Mini-columns are good at detecting features in their input. This is most obviously seen in sensory systems, where primitive features such as lines are detected in visual input, or transitions between frequencies are detected as sounds in auditory input. The processing in the columns can then be organised into larger areas that combine features to represent sensory or motor objects, which in turn fit into the sensory and motor hierarchies we have already mentioned (and to which we will return).

Although the cortex has the same small-scale neuronal architecture all the way across, regions of the cortex show differences in the distribution, density, shape, and size of cell bodies, collectively known as the cytoarchitecture. When it was viewed under a microscope (and when the tissue was nicely stained to make nerve cells show up), this allowed regions of the cortex to be labelled. At the beginning of the 20th century, the German anatomist Korbinian Brodmann published a set of 52 such areas, assigning each a number. For example, here's one you could drop at a dinner party: Brodmann area 4 is the primary motor cortex. The list of areas has been debated, refined, and renamed since; they may not be fully consistent across individuals; they may not map easily between different species; and other classification systems are available (stand up Constantin von Economo and Georg Koskinas, who published competing systems at the time). But Brodmann areas give you a sense of where you are (for more on this, see Box 3.1); where you are is what you do, and you'll still find Brodmann areas in use in neuroimaging research today.

Different regions of the cortical sheet can carry out different functions using the same fundamental computational units because the strength of the connections between neurons is readily altered, so changing functionality. Such plasticity is the basis of the brain's ability to learn or to form memories. Local neural networks can change their functionality by forming or removing connections, by strengthening or weakening existing connections, or by changing the willingness of neurons to be activated by their input. An important point to take from this is that the knowledge stored in the brain is held within the structure of the neural networks, and that this structure can be altered by how the networks are activated.

The Digital Computer – A Way the Brain Could Have Worked but Doesn't

Let's talk tech. Let's talk about how your computer works, the one that sits on your desktop or inside your phone. For a good period in the latter part of the 20th century, psychologists thought the computer would be an excellent metaphor for how our minds work. There's some irony in this, because the original designers of computers in the 1940s were inspired by a rationalist idealisation of how the mind works – based on reason and logic. Anyhow, the later adoption of the digital computer as a metaphor of the mind followed a trend familiar within the science of the mind. Through the ages, we have tended to use the technological system of the day to understand how the brain works. From water flows to clocks, from steam engines to telephone switching networks, and to the dominant metaphor of the digital computer – our most sophisticated machines have each given us a way to think about the operation of the mind, what's going on inside.

Let's stay with the digital computer for a while. It's worth reminding ourselves how it works, because it's been influential in shaping many ideas in psychology. And because the brain doesn't work this way.

The digital computer has general processing mechanisms, in the sense that the same mechanisms process all the different types of content. There's a hard drive that stores any kind of knowledge. There's a working memory (random access memory or RAM) in which information is held temporarily, then it's fed to the central processing unit (CPU). The CPU is a specialist calculating device. It carries out the calculations and hands back the results to working memory, which can then pass them back to the hard drive for long-term storage, so that the information is still there if you have to turn the computer off and on again.

The CPU can do calculations on any kind of knowledge because of *abstraction*: the details are converted into logical structure. You put all knowledge in a common format and then use the same general-purpose mechanism to process it. To the CPU, the calculations are all the same, whether it is processing images or numbers or the results of keyboard presses or touchscreen swipes or joystick twitches or fruity content glimpsed on the internet.

Because of the way it is constructed, then, a digital computer relies on abstraction and fast movement of knowledge between general-purpose processing mechanisms. If you want a computer that is better at processing photographic images, or a computer that is better at processing music, or a computer that is better at controlling a robot arm, the choice would be the same: go to a shop and buy a digital computer with a CPU that can do more calculations per second, has more working memory, has a faster bus (the communication system that transfers data between components inside the computer), and has a larger hard disk. Do you feel like it's time to upgrade your phone?

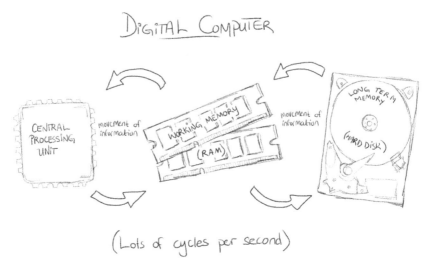

Figure 5.1 How a digital computer works

Maybe this digital way of thinking is better than that managed by the brain. Vertebrate nervous systems long ago committed to thinking with neurons, so it's not been an option for us, only for the tools we have created. Indeed, comparisons between digital computers and human brains are sometimes revealing. Modern digital computer architectures and software can now consistently defeat humans at some of our favourite games like chess, backgammon, and Go. In contrast, our progress in designing machines that can achieve dextrous motor movements integrated with embodied sensory systems has been much more limited.

This gives us a clue that we have probably underestimated how complex it is for the brain to use its sensory equipment to command muscles to deliver fluid and balanced movement; and an explanation for why so many of the brain's neurons are involved in this task (such as the 80% sitting in the cerebellum). Movement, it turns out, is a lot harder than chess – even though in our recent history, chess has been held up as the game not just of kings but of geniuses; for hundreds of years, chess has served as a standard and a symbol for the pinnacles of human intelligence. All along, it turns out that picking up the chess piece, twiddling it in your fingers, absently touching it against your lips in thought, and then placing it lightly on the board, is computationally harder that deciding where on the board to put it.

The operational principle that digital computers use, then, relies on abstraction to turn all knowledge into the same format, and processing all of the knowledge with the same general-purpose mechanisms. But this can't be the way the brain works. Let's see why.

How *Does* the Brain Work, Then?

Here's the problem. Because knowledge is built into the structure of the brain – in the strength of the connections between neurons – it is very hard to move around. This is a stark contrast with the digital computer. The digital computer relies on abstraction and moving knowledge between general-purpose processing mechanisms. How can the brain work if its knowledge is stuck in lots of different networks? It has to work by a different principle.

The brain comprises specialised content systems that handle knowledge specific to their domain. The visual system handles visual information, the auditory system handles auditory information, and so on. These specialised systems store long-term knowledge in their connections. One system stores the shape of a china cup. Another system the sound of the word 'cup' and the sound it makes when you drop one. The specialised systems also process the information they receive. Once activated, they maintain activation states about their current status by passing it around closed circuits (so-called 'recurrent loops': neuron A activates neuron B, which then activates neuron A, which then actives neuron B, and so on). In a way then, each specialised system combines the hard drive (storing knowledge), working memory (keeping it in mind), and CPU (processing) into a single device that is dedicated to handling a specific type of content.

These specialised systems need to be coordinated and controlled. This role is carried out by what we'll call a *modulatory system* (see the illustration on the next page). This system is connected to all the specialised systems and its role is to modulate their activity. It needs to turn on (activate – straight arrows on the illustration) the specialised systems or parts within them that are relevant to the current situation and goals of the individual, and turn off (or inhibit – wiggly arrows) the systems and circuits that are not relevant. It sets up the rest of the brain to do different tasks and switches between different tasks when necessary. It stores the steps required for tasks that have multiple steps and keeps track of which step the brain has reached. It monitors that plans are going as expected and for changes in the current situation that should prompt a change in task.

The modulatory system is at the front of the brain, the prefrontal cortex, while the specialised systems are at the back, the sensory lobes of the cortex. You'll remember that the prefrontal cortex is also connected to the limbic system. This means that emotion is also inputting into which specialised systems are activated or inhibited. And the suite of systems activated or inhibited changes from moment to moment, driving the generation of appropriate behaviour.

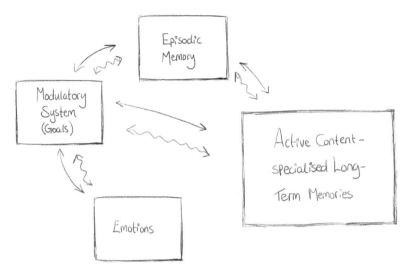

Figure 5.2 How the brain works

Now you might think the modulatory system is a bit like a CPU or a central controller. Psychologists talk about these control processes as 'executive functions'. Perhaps you could see the prefrontal cortex as an executive, but it knows nothing. The executive, stuck in the top office, can't do any of the jobs on the factory floor. It has the specialised role of control – while the content resides in all the specialised sensory and motor systems, stuck in the connections down there. For example, have you ever wandered into a room and forgotten what it was you came in for…? All you are left with is the sensation that you came in for some reason. That is the modulatory system (keeping the plan active), which has lost contact with the information stored in a specialised system (the details of the plan).

A clear demonstration of how hard it is for the brain to move knowledge around can be seen in the case of episodic (or autobiographical) memory. Recall, the brain contains a structure called the hippocampus, which brings together information from all the senses to create snapshot memories, one every few seconds. The hippocampus fills up with memories eventually (a hippocampus can store perhaps 50,000 memories, and you have one hippocampus on each side of your brain). Memories need to be transferred out and stored more permanently elsewhere in the cortex, so making space for new episodic memories (we're assuming you've never had that 'memory full' warning pop up in your brain). In addition to transferring them out, the gist needs to be pulled out of the individual memories. You need to know the capital of France is Paris (as a fact), not remember details of the specific episode or moment when you were told that Paris is the capital of France (it was on a Wednesday, the wind was cold and the sky was grey, you were sitting next to your best friend Ludwig, the teacher was droning on and on about capital cities, and you were leaning back on your chair).

Okay, so now we have a situation where the brain does need to move knowledge around, from the hippocampus to cortex. How does it do it? Here's what happens. The brain must be more or less shut down. It has to be taken offline, detached from voluntarily moving the body. This needs to happen for several hours *each night*. During sleep, the hippocampus spontaneously replays the events of the day, and cortical areas change their connections to store the information (see Chapter 6 for more on sleep). The transfer of memories takes some time – days, weeks. If the hippocampus is damaged in that time, not only is the ability to store new episodic memories lost (called 'anterograde' amnesia – memory going forward), but recent memories are also lost (called 'retrograde' amnesia – loss of previous memories). The lost memories are those yet to be transferred out of the hippocampus, or in the process of being transferred as their strength is gradually built up in the cortex. Full transfer from hippocampus to cortex may take weeks or months. (See more in the later section 'Horses for Courses'.)

Compare this way of working with how the digital computer works. In a digital computer, knowledge is moved between general-purpose devices in a fraction of a second; the faster the movement, the faster the computations. By contrast, the brain activates and deactivates parts of specialised content systems in a fraction of a second, but it takes hours to move knowledge around. These are two very different ways of working.

Hierarchies, Maps, Hubs, and Networks

The constraint that all knowledge must be stored in structure, in the connections determining how neurons are activated by sensory systems or how neurons cause muscles to contract, influences how the whole brain works.

How can you produce abstractions? For instance, in the eye, light falling on the retina excites sensory neurons. How can you tell that the coffee mug you see is the same mug wherever the image happens to fall on your retina, whether seen from the left eye or the right eye, whatever the light illumination in the room, close up or far away, whatever angle you see it from, and whether stationary or moving? And if your goal as a master villain is indeed to take over the world, maybe not today, maybe not tomorrow, but soon and forever, can your master-villainous brain really store that plan as a set of motor codes to move muscles?

The brain's solution to this problem is to build *hierarchies*. We introduced this idea earlier, with the notion of sensory and motor towers. Now you're ready for the real thing. The illustrations on pages 79 and 80 show two of the brain's hierarchies, one for the visual system, one for the motor system (there are others for the touch system, olfactory, auditory, and internal body state). The boxes in the pictures represent content-specialised brain regions (the names of the regions are not particularly important). There are two key ideas that the brain uses to solve the challenge of abstraction.

The first idea is *feature integration*. Lower down in the hierarchy are smaller bits of information, whether they are sensory primitives (edges, corners, bars moving across the retina, a rising frequency in a sound) or shorter bits of motor sequences (flex the fingers). As you go higher up, these features are bound together by neurons in the level above to make larger units of representation, such as objects or complex movements like rotations, and they in turn are bound together in the layer above.

The second idea is *computing invariances*. Invariances are common patterns that hold across lots of instances. The higher levels bind together variable instances of an object or an action which can differ in their individual realisation. So, the different views of a coffee cup may be bound together by neurons in a higher layer so these neurons are always activated by seeing the cup, irrespective of the particular view. In a sense, information higher up the hierarchy is always sensory or motor: it becomes more abstract by sticking more bits of information together, into more complex objects and events across a wider set of contexts, or more extended motor sequences.

The last thing to note about these hierarchies is that information can often flow both up and down them (we didn't use arrows in the diagrams because all the pointing would have gotten confusing). This allows, for instance, expectations to influence sensory systems: if you are expecting to see a girl in a red dress, the red-colour neurons in area V4 can already have their sleeves rolled up ready to go, and the simple-shape neurons in the posterior inferior temporal cortex can already be gunning to spot the triangular shape of her pretty skirt.

So that's the problem of abstraction solved. But we're not in the clear. If knowledge is stored in lots of separate content-specialised systems, how do you bring it all together? Apples are red, taste tangy, fit in your hand, crunch when you bite them. Oranges are, um, orange... they taste acidic and citrusy, they fit in your hand but squelch and squirt when you bite them. How can you have an idea of an apple and an orange when these fragments of information are tucked away in separate brain areas?

This problem comes in two flavours. One is in real time. I see an apple and an orange. My red-colour neurons get excited in the V4 region, and the apple-shape neurons get excited up in the inferior temporal cortex, but the orange-colour neurons are also busy in V4 and the orange-shape neurons are also invigorated up in the inferior temporal cortex. How does the brain know that the red colour goes with the apple shape and the orange colour with the orange shape? This is called the *binding problem*.

One solution the brain uses is to have *maps* (sometimes called topographical maps). In primary sensory and motor cortices, these maps reflect the spatial layout of the receptors.

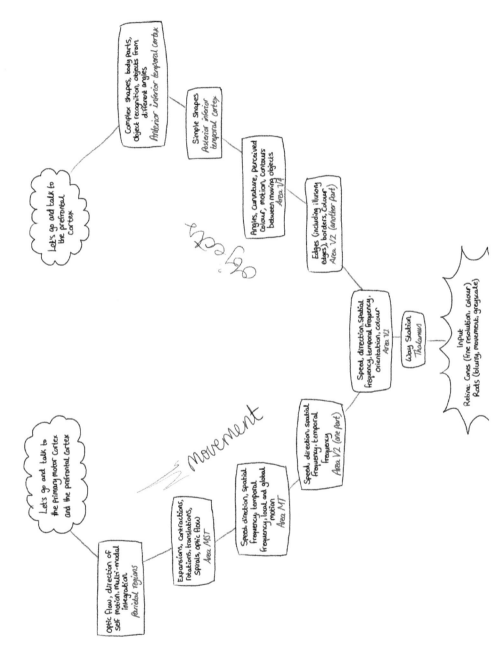

Figure 5.3 The visual sensory hierarchy (MT = middle temporal; MST = medial superior temporal)

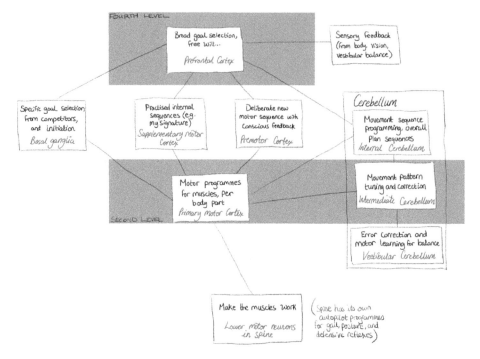

Figure 5.4 The motor hierarchy

In the visual cortex, nearby neurons will be activated by nearby regions of the retina; in the auditory cortex, nearby neurons will be activated by nearby positions along the cochlear hair cell line which vibrate to different sound frequencies; and in the somatosensory cortex, nearby neurons will be activated by nearby locations on the body surface (this map is shown in Figure 5.5 on the opposite page). However, these maps are also retained as you ascend the hierarchies. Nearby neurons in the higher map continue to be activated by nearby neurons in the map below. This gives a way to bind together different features in different systems – because they occur in the same location on the map. The red-colour neurons are activated in the same region of the map as the apple-shape, the orange-colour neurons are activated in the same region as the orange-shape. Maps are also found in the motor cortex, where different regions are responsible for moving muscles in different body parts (this is sometimes called the motor homunculus). Maps may also extend high up into the sensory and motor hierarchies, including language areas and the frontal cortex. They may not, however, be the brain's only solution to the binding problem: a second solution may be to adjust the firing rates of neurons so that those corresponding to features of the same representation fire in synchrony (red-colour, apple-shape). A third solution may be for the neurons in different areas simply to simultaneously increase their firing rates to represent a common object.

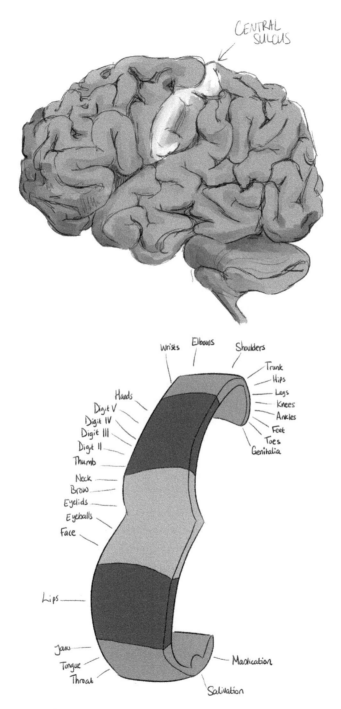

Figure 5.5 The map of the body on the somatosensory strip, showing the strip's positioning just behind the central sulcus, and the map's organisation

Here's the second flavour of the problem of spreading knowledge across different content-specialised systems. How can integrated knowledge be stored across them? How can we learn about apples in general, that they have the juicy, crunchy, tangy properties that we love? How can we recall the memory of the rotten apple we had yesterday, that also featured a worm?

The brain's solution to this problem is to have *hubs*. Hubs are regions where information is brought together and bound into single representations. A hub is therefore a focus of connectivity in the brain's overall network. The brain has several hubs playing this role. One of them is at the front of the temporal lobe (anterior temporal pole). This region sits at the top of the visual sensory hierarchy (on the 'object' side in the illustration) and it is where the brain stores information about word meanings, binding together all the features of individual words, what separates apples from oranges from lemons. The hippocampus is a hub that stores individual episodic memories, binding together information from a range of senses experienced in that moment (or short sequence of moments) and giving them a date stamp (yesterday, when you bit into that apple with the worm, the unexpectedly soft apple, the wriggle of the worm, the exuded whiff of decay). The insular lobe has a hub that integrates sensory information from the cortex with emotion information from the limbic system to give valence (emotional value) to concepts. Another hub is called the posterior association area, where the temporal and parietal lobes meet, a region that brings together the top levels of the visual, auditory, and somatosensory hierarchies. The parietal lobe's preoccupation is with the body and with space, the temporal lobe's with identifying objects and people. Here you can find knowledge about the position of your own and other people's bodies in space; here you can find knowledge about concepts in space, in terms of your own versus other people's perspectives. Artificially stimulate this hub, and you may even experience the sensation of someone else in the room with you. Creepy.

Our final challenge for this section. How do you get complex functionality from lots of content-specialised systems? A digital computer loads a new program into its general-purpose processing mechanisms. The brain instead solves this problem by connecting *networks* of its content-specialised systems together to produce complex behaviours. And it gains flexibility of function by using different combinations of the same content-specialised systems. Here are some of our favourite brain networks:

- The *central executive network* involves part of the modulatory system (the dorsolateral prefrontal cortex) and the specialised content system of the posterior parietal cortex (for space, body) and it dabbles in sustained attention, complex problem solving, and working memory. It supports cognitively demanding tasks, actively maintaining and manipulating information, and making decisions in the context of goal-directed behaviour. It's like: *World, I'm on it.*
- The *default mode network* involves another part of the modulatory system (the medial prefrontal cortex), another part of the posterior content systems (the rear

middle of the parietal cortex), and part of the evaluative system back there, the posterior cingulate cortex. The default mode network powers up when you don't care so much about the outside world, when you're daydreaming, when your mind is wandering to other worlds and other possibilities for yourself and others. When in the early 1980s, the singer Jennifer Warnes warbled these lines:

> Watching all the fishing boats coming
> Lying back in the warm, soft sand
> Seeing you with the sun in your eyes

and then pointed out that this was a place she could go to *any time*, because she was in fact dreaming of a time beyond today ... well, that was her default mode network doing that.

- The *salience network* involves part of the insular cortex and part of the anterior cingulate cortex, with contributions from the limbic system. The insular cortex is interested in what matters, giving bodily emotional value to concepts, while the anterior cingulate is part of the evaluative system monitoring how things are going with respect to goals. The limbic contributions (amygdala, striatum) feed in about appetites and rewards. The salience network has the happy job of switching between the default mode network (*I'm dreaming of a time beyond today...*) and the central executive network (*World, I'm on it!*). It says: *HELLO, HEADS UP, THIS MATTERS, QUIT YER DREAMING*. The salience network integrates sensory and emotional information to trigger the system to pay attention to the world and achieve goals, and let it know when it can have some down time to run mental simulations, consider hypothetical World Cup victories, and spend the money gained from possible future lottery wins.

So, that's what biology makes you do. Because your computer won't let you move information around and because it won't let you use general-purpose machinery, you have to run everything on content-specialised systems and coordinate them with a modulatory system. And to crack the processing problems this poses, you end up needing solutions like hierarchies, maps, hubs, and networks.

Horses for Courses, Structures for Functions

The British have a saying: *horses for courses*. It comes from the world of horse racing, and it means that some horses race better on certain courses than others. Some horses do better when the ground is soft, others when the ground is firm, when the going is good. The phrase is often used metaphorically to mean different people are suited for different jobs. It's a principle the brain uses because different types of tasks require different sorts of computation. Memory provides one example.

We can know facts about the world (the capital of France) and the types of things we encounter in the world (animals, vehicles), so-called semantic memory. And then we can have specific memories of what happened yesterday, or last Wednesday, so-called episodic memory. These two types of memory have very different requirements.

Semantic memory should lay lots of specific experiences on top of each other and pull out general patterns. What dogs look like in general, rather than any specific dog. Such concepts are built from a gradual accumulation of experiences, and they have relationships to each other (dogs are similar to cats, they are both animals). Knowledge needs to be fed in slowly, integrated, and themes extracted. Any one instance shouldn't be too important, it's the overall pattern that matters, so this is a system that should alter gradually with experience.

By contrast, episodic memories must be recorded in a moment; these memories have no relationship to each other, other than the time when they happened; memories must integrate the information from multiple sensory systems, and the memories must be kept separate, not blended. We don't want a sense of the sorts of things that happened yesterday, a general concept of yesterday-ness (other than for Beatles songs). We want to know exactly what happened *yesterday*.

These two types of memory therefore have distinct requirements: {gradual accumulation + extract general theme} versus {instant recording + keep memories separate}. The distinct requirements mean the two types of memory are best handled by two distinct memory systems in the brain. Respectively, they are the cortex (in particular, the temporal lobe) for semantic memory about dogs (and other stuff); and the hippocampus for episodic memory about what happened yesterday (and other days).

As we saw earlier, one of the challenges for the brain is to move knowledge from episodic memory to semantic memory, since the knowledge is stuck in the connections between neurons. Transfer mostly happens while the system is offline, during sleep. Then the dog I saw yesterday can change my knowledge about dogs, and be integrated into my network of knowledge about animals. My knowledge of what happened to *me* can be integrated into my network of knowledge about myself, my identity.

It remains a bit of a puzzle where in the cortex long-term memories are stored when they are shifted out of the hippocampus. We do know that once memories are stored in the cortex, surgeons can reactivate very specific memories with pinpoint stimulation of areas of the cortex during open brain surgery, while the patient is awake. (The brains are not opened for that purpose, but for good medical reasons, often because the individuals have experienced frequent seizures; focal points of epilepsy need to be removed but essential cortex avoided; however, while the brains are open, why not try stimulating them…).

For example, in one case, when the patient's brain was directly stimulated, he said: 'My mother is telling my brother he has got his coat on backwards. I can just hear them.' In another example, the patient said: 'I'm, like, remembering stuff from, like, high school… Why is this suddenly popping in my head?' These vivid episodic memories, brief fleeting reinstatements of past events, are generally triggered by stimulating the temporal cortex, suggesting this is where long-term storage of episodic memories ends up.

This principle of 'horses for courses' is found elsewhere. Take vision, and the recognition of objects. The brain must figure out both what an object is and where it is (perhaps it's moving!), all from light signals registering on the retinas at the back of the eyes. For the brain, the challenge of recognising what an object is stems from the fact that ideally, the visual system should be able to recognise an object whatever angle it is seen from and wherever on the retina the image falls. A coffee cup is still a coffee cup whether you see it upside-down, on the left of your field of view, or on the right. As we've seen, the brain's job here is to extract invariances, in this case 'rotation' and 'translation' invariance.

One way to solve the problem of translation invariance is to have lots of detectors for the coffee cup all over the retina, and to separately store all possible views of the cup. That way, the brain can ignore where the coffee cup is and how it's oriented, and recognise it anyway. This indeed is what the underneath or 'ventral' visual processing channel does in the brain (the 'object' route in our illustration of the visual hierarchy). Sometimes this route is called the 'what' channel, because it's so good at recognising what an object is.

Great. Except that, if you've thrown away information about where in space the object is… how could you reach for it? How could you track its motion? Darn it.

Okay, so the brain is going to need another processing channel, which focuses on movement. It will track motion across the retina, the sequence in which detectors light up at different locations as the image moves across it. This channel won't bother too much about what the object is, just track trajectories, and pass the information to the motor system to prepare for action (move the eyes to follow it, raise a hand to grasp it). This is what the top or 'dorsal' processing channel does in the brain, sometimes called the 'where' or 'how' channel (we labelled it 'movement' in our hierarchy illustration). And so long as the two complementary channels can talk to each other, we'll be catching cricket balls and ducking snowballs to our heart's content.

Another way to look at these two horses-for-courses routes is that there are two ways to link perception to action. The dorsal route over the top involving *perception for now*, to drive immediate motor behaviours (catch the cricket ball), and a ventral route underneath involving *perception for later*, to allow object recognition that may drive future behaviour (I must remember to pack that cricket ball into my bag when I leave). This division is not only found for the visual system but also for the auditory system. For example, for language, if you hear a word, there is a dorsal route that allows you to repeat the word without needing to understand it, and a ventral route that allows you to understand the word, retrieving its meaning and associations.

The computational demands of different functions, therefore, can necessitate different content-specialised systems.

Inside the Executive Suite

The prefrontal cortex is the front part of the frontal lobe. It's the front of the front. It's where the modulatory system is housed. Now we've also talked about the prefrontal cortex as sitting at the top of the motor hierarchy. It lies above supplementary and pre-motor areas. At the lowest level of this hierarchy, in the primary motor cortex, sit patches of neurons for controlling muscle movements in different parts of the body. Ascending the hierarchy, regions combine muscle movements into longer, more complex sequences, further forward in time. Bits of motor sequences are glued together into grander plans, across more contexts, extracting plan invariances. There are plans with contingencies that depend on the outcome of prior movements (e.g., the plan to grind the coffee has a contingency that the beans must first have been put in the machine). The highest levels of the hierarchy contain plans to deliver goals (make coffee).

There are neuroscientists who prefer this view of the frontal cortex, as just a gradient of greater abstraction/invariances, of greater complexity as one travels forward in the brain from the motor cortex. The back of the front (if you will) supports control involving temporally proximate, concrete action representations; the front of the front supports control involving temporally extended, abstract representations of sequences and contingent steps.

However, once you get to the top of the motor hierarchy, to the dizzying heights of the prefrontal cortex, you find something else here. You find a lot of connectivity to other parts of the brain. To the top of the sensory hierarchies in the parietal and temporal lobes. To the hippocampus and its episodic memory system. To structures in the limbic system such as the amygdala (appetites) and the hypothalamus (body regulation). And to the basal ganglia and thalamus (action selection, sensory gateway). The prefrontal cortex also receives input from the brainstem arousal systems. Moreover, its functioning is particularly dependent on its neurochemical environment, such as levels of neurotransmitters like dopamine (reward) and serotonin (mood). This extensive connectivity supports the prefrontal cortex's role in cognitive control, and in integrating between states of arousal, emotions, and plans.

We have called this a modulatory system to distinguish it from the general-purpose processing mechanism of the digital computer, the CPU. The prefrontal cortex has its own specialised content. One might think of these as pointers or markers – links back to the content in the sensory or motor areas. The prefrontal cortex learns computations between the pointers that manipulate the meaning systems sitting in the rest of the brain behind it. These may be sequences of sensory circuits or motor circuits to be activated or inhibited, links between them to be enabled or disabled. The computations may simply involve keeping sensory circuits active when the initial sensory input has gone – keeping the information 'in mind', like the speech sounds of a telephone number you're trying to dial.

One important idea for what the modulatory system does is the *prepotent response*. Actions that are frequently carried out in response to a sensory input can become automatic. For example, the sight of a light switch can trigger the action to flip it on. Think of the brain as containing lots of little agents responsible for performing actions, each agent super keen to spot the right sensory conditions to launch their motor action. This is an efficient way to set up the brain: the actions you need the most are there ready to go. These are called prepotent responses. But there may be circumstances where this action shouldn't be triggered – it's daytime, it's not your house, you know the bulb has blown – and you should use these contexts to inhibit the agent from flipping the light switch. This is a key role for the modulatory system, to ensure behaviour is appropriate to context and goals, despite the best intentions of the agents.

A second important idea is of *task set*. A task set is a way to configure the relationships between sensory inputs and motor outputs that are relevant to a given task: what perceptual information is most important and which motor actions deliver task goals. For example, if you happen to play the (invented) video game, *Zadar Versus the Mind-Munching Zombies from Pluto (Part 2: The Revenge)*, you'll need to watch out for the zombie riders with the green horns and use your middle button to kill them, well, kill sounds bad, let's say, *aggressively rehabilitate* them, using your proton ray gun. But if you get bored of this game and instead decide to play the (equally invented) game *Captain Untenable and the Drag Racers of Doom*, you'll need to tilt your hands to steer your vehicle with the controller and to watch out for the red-outfitted pedestrians, who keep wandering onto the racetrack and whom you would do well to avoid (due to the Lawyers of Doom seeking to sue you for any accidents). Here, you would be switching between two task sets, one that monitors visual input for green features and links these to movements of your middle finger, the other that monitors visual input for red features and links these to movements of your wrists. A key role of the modulatory system is to formulate these task sets and to switch between them according to contexts and goals.

If you ask a psychologist about cognitive control these days, they will talk about *executive functions*. The word 'executive' is metaphorical: it intends the idea of an executive in a company, perhaps sitting in a plush office up on the top floor, making the important decisions, issuing orders to the workers down on the factory floor. Psychologists talk about three main executive functions: updating, inhibiting, and shifting. Updating relates to keeping content systems active in the absence of external sensory cues. Inhibiting refers to preventing the activation of prepotent responses (or indeed, responses prompted by emotional states) that don't fit with current goals or context. Shifting relates to switching between different task sets.

So far, so good. These three functions do leave something out, though. Another key role of the prefrontal cortex is making decisions, deciding what to do. That is why prefrontal cortex is associated with free will. Part of the role of the modulatory system is to

Figure 5.6 The 'executive' function of the modulatory system, on the top floor, is to control the specialised content systems down on the factory floor. We're sure executives work hard really

coordinate with meaning and evaluative brain systems to reason and make judgements to guide future behaviour, be it deciding whether 4 is the cubed root of 64 (hooray, it is!), deciding whether to give money to a homeless person based on your values and their looks (Yes, give some money! that could be me in another life... vs. No! they should get a job), or deciding whether to place a tenner on a particular horse running in the 3.15 race at Kempton Park (worth a punt, we'd say).

So, if we add decision making to the three executive functions favoured by psychologists, we have four main processes going on in the prefrontal cortex. Only, when you look at it, the human prefrontal cortex is very big. Does it really take all that cortex to do just those four functions? Let's put some slightly spurious numbers on that. The prefrontal cortex has been estimated to contain 8% of the neurons in the cortex. That's 1.3 billion. Let's try benchmarking the computational power you get out of a bunch of neurons. It only takes one million neurons to run a honeybee. One million neurons in a bee brain can produce all the flying, navigating, sensing, feeding, and dancing that a honeybee delights in. A single prefrontal cortex has the computational power of a hive of 1,300 bees. What does it do with that immense power?

The mystery deepens when you consider that executive functions are renowned for having a *limited capacity*. People are notoriously bad at performing more than one task that demands cognitive control at a time, and they quickly get befuddled when you ask them to keep too much information in mind, like a telephone number with too many digits. Thirteen hundred bee brains' worth and it's *not enough* – like, how much computational power did you want?

Well, let's enter the executive suite and see what machinery the neuroscientists have found in here. There is, of course, no little guy sitting at a control desk. But there are specialised regions that take on different functions. The room is full of machinery. How do we navigate it? Neuroscientists have been particularly confusing in how they refer to regions in the prefrontal cortex, mixing up spatial location and gyri and Brodmann areas. We'll identify regions by answering three questions: Are you on top or underneath? Are you in the middle or at the sides? Are you right at the front, lying just above the eye sockets (orbits)? We'll call this the Battenberg cake model, because we're feeling hungry.

If you're *on the top at the sides*, the machinery is involved in all the things the psychologists call executive function: deciding what to attend to, which circuits should be activated and which inhibited, what information should be kept in mind, switching between task sets. If you recall the visual hierarchy, it had a 'movement' pathway. The machinery we're looking at here lies at the end of that pathway and is concerned with how to interact with things in the world (or to a neuroscientist, 'stimuli').

If you're *on the bottom at the sides*, you're sitting at the end of the visual hierarchy pathway that identifies objects. This machinery is concerned with information about stimulus characteristics, about their meaning (or 'semantics'). Sitting above motor areas for the speech articulators (lips, tongue), it integrates between motor aspects of speech and semantic aspects, and therefore is involved in language processing: retrieving, controlling, and activating word meanings that link to speech. Other machinery here is involved in re-orienting spatial attention to perceptual events occurring outside the current focus of attention, when things suddenly change in the environment. And there's machinery involved in motor inhibition, in stopping or overriding current activity down in the motor cortex: if you're walking and you decide to stop, perhaps because a thought has struck you, that's this bit overriding the motor plan.

So far, it all sounds very 'controlly', doesn't it, crunching cold numbers like a robot. In the computational view, this type of control is imagined as a tuning process where

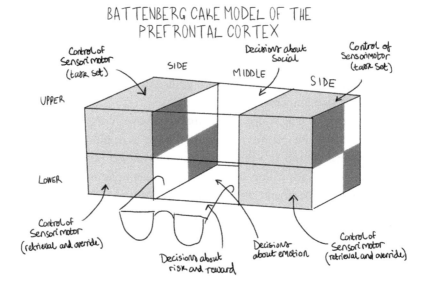

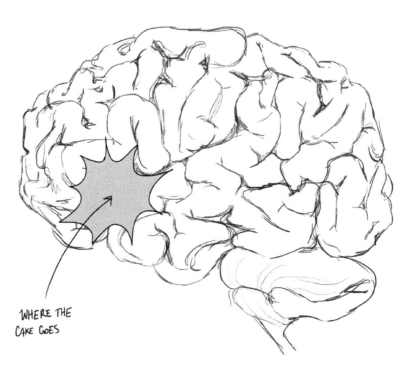

Figure 5.7 The Battenberg cake model of the prefrontal cortex. The front-facing cubes are higher in the motor hierarchy

parameters of processing systems are adjusted to suit current task demands. You'll hear phrases like 'this region enables the brain to split the visual stimulus into parts and only attend to some of them, apply rules, carry out manipulations, while ignoring the other parts'. Very dry. Things get more interesting when we move to the middle of the pre-frontal cortex.

If you're *in the middle on the top*, you are now processing task sets about people and social situations. One of those people is *you*. Your sense of self is here, what you typically do. If you ask someone to roleplay, to act *not like themselves*, you'll see this machinery becoming less active. This is the region making social judgements, how to behave, and coordinating emotional responses to social situations.

If you're *in the middle on the bottom*, you're sitting closer to the limbic system. Now you're less bothered about the social dimension and more about pure emotion regulation. If you're going to display acts of courage to overcome your fears (*Go on, grab the snake*), this machinery will be buzzing away, inhibiting emotions and activating plans. Machinery for moral decision making is also found here, integrating emotional associations with plans and outcomes to make moral decisions. And as we'll see later, here is where you store your currency of value (that is, the units that value will be counted in).

The middle of the prefrontal cortex is also involved in retrieving information from epi-sodic memory down in the hippocampus, and coordinating associations between contexts, plans, emotions, and memories. Indeed, the ability to construct past and future autobio-graphical events depends on interactions between the middle of the prefrontal cortex and the hippocampus, as well as a distributed network of brain regions spanning the parietal and temporal cortices (the latter providing the sensory basis of the content).

Lastly, if you're in the prefrontal cortex *lying just above the orbits (sockets) of the eyes*, the so-called orbitofrontal cortex, well, it's a bit crammed in here. Perhaps this is the broom cupboard of the executive suite. You'll find flavour being processed over in the corner, aromas floating up into the cupboard, because you're close to the olfactory bulbs, smell and taste are being integrated, and you're learning what you like to eat (eventually with age, for example, you may learn that the bitter things that taste so awful to a young child, like coffee and beer, are not so bad after all. That's done in this broom cupboard). But control-wise, here you find the decision making linked to the reward system (stria-tum), storing information about situations that produced good outcomes or bad outcomes in the past (input from the amygdala, insula, and hippocampus).

When you make a decision from the gut, when you make a decision about risk, reward, and danger, when you decide to gamble, it's your orbitofrontal cortex. When you're a character in a Hollywood film (usually a Star Wars film or an Indiana Jones film) and you 'have a real bad feeling about this' as you, for example, explore an apparently abandoned spaceship – that's your orbitofrontal cortex telling you that. In the past, when you've explored abandoned spaceships, bad things have happened, and your orbitofrontal cortex has been keeping track. This new abandoned spaceship is kinda *intuitively* reminding you of that bad stuff. But, if it's a Hollywood film, the plot demands that you decide to push on. (YouTube curators have compiled a video of 35 instances of characters in films having bad feelings about things. Look it up!)

So, broadly, we can see that different regions of the prefrontal cortex are modulating and making decisions with respect to different kinds of content: about sensory and motor information (lateral), about social information (upper middle), about emotional information (lower middle), and about risk (orbitofrontal). These regions are receiving information from and manipulating information in various content-specific systems, and also triggering retrieval of situation-relevant episodic memories.

Why the limited capacity? Maybe it just takes a lot of computation to control all the neurons in those content-specific systems (sensory and motor cortices, limbic system, striatum, and so on). Maybe task sets are Big Things computationally and 1,300 bee brains isn't enough to keep a lot of them going at once. Maybe the circuits are configured in such a way that the same control regions do different things in different tasks, and they can't do two different things at once. No good answer yet.

Still, the prefrontal cortex buys flexibility. It allows behaviour to be differentiated by context, not just triggered by stimuli. It allows plans involving multiple steps towards goals delivered further in the future. Animals with smaller prefrontal cortices and humans with damaged prefrontal lobes show behaviour that is less flexible and more stimulus driven.

Lastly, we hinted that the prefrontal cortex is sitting in a soup of neurotransmitters and is sensitive to the state of the whole system. Is the whole system aroused, is it tired, is it stressed? The modulatory system is vulnerable to suboptimal conditions: the fatigued prefrontal cortex finds itself making mistakes (peevishly reported by the brain's middle manager, the anterior cingulate). The modulatory system might have, say, failed to inhibit a prepotent response. You were tired, you switched on the light even though you knew the bulb was blown. The system might have failed to switch task set. The Manchester United players' brains knew the offside trap wasn't working, but in the 85th minute they were too tired to switch to playing deep.

The prefrontal cortex is also affected by stress: a hotline from the amygdala switches the system to high vigilance, and dials back on working memory and planning, even while other cognitive functions such as rapid learning are actually improved. You remember in vivid detail that time when you turned over your examination paper and your mind went completely blank, failing to retrieve a single relevant concept to answer a question. We will come back to stress in Chapter 6.

So, What Does a Concept Look Like in the Brain?

You may think as adults, we are reasoning, logical, intellectual beings, full of abstract knowledge gleaned from our experiences. Well, we can be like that, but from the brain's point of view, with some reluctance. Although the digital computer relies on abstraction – which allows its gleaming logical calculations to be applied to any content – the brain is reluctant to abstract. Its processing occurs within dedicated sensory and motor systems, configured to identify the physical state of the external world and to prepare the right actions. With its sensory and motor hierarchies, the brain is suited to extracting patterns within patterns tied to the content of the system, and to integrating information across senses to make best guesses about the external world and generate appropriate behaviours.

If the brain utilises content-specific systems, activated and deactivated according to context and goals by a modulatory system, what do concepts look like in the brain? The labels of language, 'dog' for instance, prompt the notion that concepts are unitary wholes. Within the brain's architecture, however, the knowledge about dogs (what their faces look like, what a bark sounds like, the feel of their fur, the actions of stroking the fur, throwing a ball) will be processed in different content-specific systems. And only some parts of this knowledge may be activated in any given context by the interaction of the modulatory system and the current sensory input. The brain is full of partial representations, fragments of knowledge that coalesce, perhaps sometimes uniquely, to provide concepts adapted to circumstances.

The brain *can* do a form of abstraction. This involves making connections between different sensory and motor systems, at the behest of the modulatory system. It requires bringing together different situations, actions, and objects under the same 'abstract' category labels provided by language. Language, as it were, is the unifying context of disparate knowledge.

Take the abstract concept *six*, which children usually learn about between three and five years of age. From the point of view of the brain, *six* is a diverse set of linked situations, involving recognising sounds or visual patterns, and making sequences of actions. There's counting six on fingers. Recognising and writing the number 6 or the word 'six'. Knowing that six is an amount of stuff bigger than, say, three, but not as big as, say, nine. There's forming groups of six items. Placing the number six between five and seven on a number line. Finding ways to split a pile of six sweets among two people, or three people. Splitting a single pizza into six equal parts to give to six people, each getting a sixth. Learning sentences like 'two times six is twelve'. When all these situations are linked together, the child has learned an abstract idea of six – realised across multiple content-specific systems, and coordinated by the modulatory system.

Hierarchical structures lend themselves readily to extracting patterns within patterns – the invariances – in sensory and motor systems. All mammals are likely to do this. The shape of a stable branch that will bear your weight when you jump on it. The difference between ripe fruit and rotten fruit. But learning concepts like 'six' takes time and instruction. It requires exposure to particular situations, and makes use of language to help unify the different situations. Education provides the opportunity for this kind of learning, exposing the child to several years of deliberately structured and linked environments.

Education also provides the environment to learn how to use logic to reason. We'll return to logic in Chapter 9, when we consider why humans in particular seem to be so darned clever. We'll see how logic itself is a fairly recent cultural invention, one that takes special training (and uses the inhibitory skills of the modulatory system) to master. In the meantime, while the brain may not readily abstract, it does develop complex sets of knowledge linking sensory and motor information. For example, it builds knowledge of scenarios – sometimes called schema or scripts. This is information about what tends to happen in the different everyday situations you find yourself in. Making toast. Getting on the bus.

These scripts are probably stored in the same area of the brain that stores meanings of individual words (so-called semantics), the front of the temporal lobe. This is the type of knowledge that babies have yet to develop, so that situations are mostly new and surprising to them. Babies find repetition reassuring because it is an escape from continually not knowing what's likely to happen next. At the other end of life, scripts are one type of knowledge lost in the varieties of dementia that affect the front of the temporal lobe (such as Alzheimer's disease). Here, adults become disoriented in normally familiar surroundings because the scripts can no longer be retrieved. As healthy adults, we can experience what it's like to lose these everyday scripts when we go abroad, and find normal things work in subtly different ways – shops sell different products, doors open differently, people queue up differently. These changes remove the knowledge that supports everyday actions in familiar situations.

By the way that it works, then, the brain loves to spot patterns, make connections between patterns, and predict what patterns are likely to come up. But abstraction and logical reasoning are things it must be taught to do.

The Brain's Favourite Content

Sensory and motor information are the brain's top priority, because its primary role is to use sensory information to move in the world. However, there is another type of content that the human brain especially likes, one that keeps a large number of its regions busy. A lot of what concerns the brain is *other people*.

Humans are social primates. Like gorillas and chimpanzees, we live in groups. There are families, friends, enemies, who's in and who's out, who's the boss. Social primates have the largest cortex relative to their body size across mammals. Across social primates, the larger the social group in which the primate lives, the larger its species' cortex. This suggests the larger cortex may have been an evolutionary response to the computational demands of sociality – to deal with the complications of interacting with the other members of the social group, be they partners, family members, friends, or rivals. *Who did what to whom? Who knows about it? What should I do about that?* Anyone who has spent Christmas with their extended family will be unsurprised by this.

Figure 5.8 Brains are for the people

Of course, we've seen that evolutionary origins are hard to be definite about, and there's also suggestive evidence that a larger brain and cortex across primates correlates with changes in diet. A big brain requires more energy, so perhaps the processing of meat and other foods enabled by tools contributed to subsequent increases in hominin brain size. In other words, human cortical size may be more about Christmas dinner than Christmas intrigue. Who knows?

Many systems contribute to processing 'people' information in the brain. The visual system develops pathways for recognising human faces, including the facial expressions and direction of eye gaze, corresponding to specialised regions within the 'object recognition' visual stream in the temporal lobe. *Are you looking at me?* Eye gaze is particularly important to the brain. It's harder to carry out tasks when we are being watched, whether it's speaking, drawing, or doing a crossword; this tells us that some part of our brain is always monitoring other people's direction of gaze.

The visual system is also tuned to recognise movement that comes from people rather than objects (so-called 'biological' motion) within the movement visual stream, including the gestures people make when they communicate. Multiple aspects of sensory information (form, location, motion) are brought together to allow us to recognise other people and their body parts from different angles, in various places, and while they are in motion. Similarly, the auditory system has specialised pathways for processing human speech sounds separate from other environmental sounds. And the motor system allows us to speak to other people, to hug them, wrestle with them: all social motor actions. The limbic system generates emotions around social interactions, be they the bonding of child to parent, the approach–avoid decisions around possible friends and enemies, attraction, maintenance of personal space, and defence of resources and territory.

More complex systems allow us to verbalise our thoughts, emotions, and intentions, as well as remember factual knowledge of actors in our social group. For example, we saw that the front of the temporal lobe develops social scripts through experience – *Who tends to do what to whom and how does that feel?* And factual knowledge of actors in the social group – *What do I think of Jonny and what does Jonny think of me? How does Jonny tend to behave? Where am I compared to Jonny in the social hierarchy? (Hey, I think I'm way cooler.)*

As we grow up, we create links between different types of knowledge, experiences, and actions. For example, the body sensation system (somatosensory and insular) can detect needs and arousal levels in our bodies, such as thirst and excitement. We link the feeling of thirst to the intention of drinking and the action of picking up a bottle. So, too, in our interaction with other people. We learn social scripts, such as the custom that when you meet a new person, you introduce yourself, try to remember their name, shake their hand, and ask how they are. You're in France, do you greet with a kiss on one cheek or two cheeks? It's awkward when you get that wrong.

Putting these types of knowledge together, we can guess what other people may be feeling and what they will do next, based on our own previous experience. This is called *mindreading* or *mentalising*. If we see someone grabbing a bottle, the neurons that respond to seeing a bottle and those involved in the action of picking up a bottle will become activated in our own brain (some, indeed, call these 'mirror' neurons for mirroring the activity). The neural activation doesn't quite trigger the action itself, but it helps us figure out why the person might be making that action, from what we have associated with that action: they're thirsty.

Similar systems allow us to empathise with the feelings of others. We may link certain actions and facial expressions with, say, sadness in ourselves (crying, walking slowly). When we see others crying, we feel sad. We flinch when we see others in physical pain, courtesy of the insula. But to empathise, the emotional state of the individual must have been recognised from their posture or movement. The supramarginal gyrus, a section of the parietal lobe abutting the temporal lobe, is a part of the somatosensory association cortex involved in the perception of space and limb location, including the postures and gestures of other people. It therefore contributes to accessing emotion states implied by their limb positions.

Even with empathy, frontal brain systems come into play, modulating the activity of these systems according to context. We only feel other people's pain *if we like them*. The frontal cortex applies this rubric to modulate the sensory or emotional pain we experience in sympathy with others. We feel the hurt of other people's misfortunes more *if we take their perspective*. A region at the junction of temporal (facts, scripts) and parietal (space) lobes, the excitingly labelled temporal-parietal junction, plays this role. In its fashion, the brain takes the act of perspective-taking quite literally – it involves spatial computations to see the world from another point of view: to distinguish our view from the other, our self from the other. Finally, the frontal cortex must combine the context, its own goals, and emotional states to select plans and control sensory and motor systems, to behave in the right way in social situations. As we saw in the section on the prefrontal cortex, part of the modulatory system makes decisions about manners. Don't slurp your tea in polite company.

What would life be like without the brain's fixation on other people? Automated driverless cars offer us a clue. Even though the artificial intelligence piloting autonomous cars is extremely sophisticated, what it has cracked is the vision-to-driving-problem: how to control the vehicle in response to information about its current path with respect to the road, landmarks, other vehicles, and pedestrians. It's solved the sensorimotor problem. What it does not possess is a suite of processing mechanisms concerned with the intentions of others and how to infer them based on their body positions, facial expressions, and movements. So, when the car's camera picks up a bystander loitering next to the edge of the pavement, it cannot compute the person's intentions by their gait, posture, and orientation. Will the bystander step into the road or walk on? Is their head down, as if looking at their mobile phone, or is their eye gaze on the approaching vehicle? It is hard to extract the intentions of actors from sensory information unless evolution has endowed you with systems that once developed, are perpetually concerned with using biological motion to generate theories of other people's future actions. Without a social brain plug-in, driverless cars face a daunting computational challenge of trying to achieve safe driving on sensorimotor information alone; this is why in the immediate future, artificial intelligence will likely only augment rather than entirely replace the human driver.

There Are Two Sides to Every Brain

Did we mention the brain has two hemispheres? We can't remember whether we mentioned that. Is it important? Vertebrate bodies are, on the whole, symmetrical. Movement works better if you have the same number of legs on each side; two eyes are better than one for judging distance; and you're deemed prettier if there's one eye on each side of your face (evenly spaced). So, a brain that has two symmetrical sides is in keeping with the overall body plan, not a special feature. The two hemispheres of the brain – two cortices, two amygdalae, two hippocampi, two thalami, and so on – are pretty much mirror images of each other. They are nearly identical both at the large scale and at the level of microstructure. In humans, there's sometimes a minor asymmetry in the temporal lobes, a slight left-side swelling of the superior temporal lobe, but that's about it.

Figure 5.9 Two sides to every brain

Is the fact that the brain has two hemispheres important for how it works? The two sides are connected by a thick bundle of fibres called the corpus callosum, which has around 200 million axons carrying neural signals from one side of the brain to the other, often between equivalent regions. The left and right sides have very similar processing capacities, and mostly work together in generating behaviour. From our current computational perspective, there's an obvious advantage to having two hemispheres: you've got two duplicate computers to start with. If one gets broken early on, you can use the other instead. This is a principle we apply to human-made devices that we really, really want to work, like the James Webb telescope, so you can see why it might have been promoted during evolution. If children have damage to one cortical hemisphere early in development (before the age of around 6) the other hemisphere can develop to take on all the necessary functions.

It would be wrong to think, though, that people differ in how much they favour using their 'left brain' or their 'right brain' or that this produces different cognitive styles or personality types. This is a brain myth. Don't fall for brain myths, unless you happen to be using only 10% of your brain.

And that's it for sides of the brain. Nothing more to see. Move along.

Okay, all right, maybe there are *a couple* of other things to clear up. You may have heard about the importance of the left hemisphere for human language and that this is linked to the majority right-handedness of our populations (the super dexterity of our right hands for manual tasks). You may also have heard that in adults, localised damage to a single hemisphere can produce striking and narrow behavioural impairments – in language for the left hemisphere, in visual attention for the right hemisphere – suggesting that some functions are specialised to individual hemispheres. And you might have found it pretty weird that the left side of the brain controls the right side of the body, while the right side of the brain controls the left side of the body. Where did that come from? Before we *insist* you move along, we'll cover those three points.

We'll start with right-handedness (and apologies to the 10% of readers who are left-handed – guys, take up tennis or fencing, you have a natural advantage!). The characteristic preference for manipulating objects with the right hand isn't just a human characteristic. It is found in other primates too, including monkeys, chimpanzees, and gorillas. So, right-handedness is not a story of human uniqueness linked to language. Rather, it appears to be an exaggeration of a much longer evolutionary trend towards encouraging the two hemispheres to have slightly different functions and to work in parallel. This longer evolutionary strategy involves using the left hemisphere for the control of well-established patterns of behaviour in ordinary, routine situations; and using the right hemisphere to detect and respond to unexpected stimuli in the environment. It is a trend that goes back perhaps 500 million years to the earliest vertebrates. A bias towards the using the left side of the brain in feeding, a routine motor activity, is seen in species as far apart as fishes, reptiles, amphibians, birds, and mammals, pointing to an ancient evolutionary origin. If you have two computers, there is an efficiency gain to run them in parallel. For example, one side of the brain can concentrate on the routine actions required to eat, while the other side scans the environment for danger, linking directly to emotional responses like fight or flight when predators or conspecifics (friends or foes) are detected. In primate communication, the hemispheric bias manifests as a left-side specialisation for routine vocal and non-vocal communication, and a right-side specialisation for highly emotional vocalisation.

What about human language? We'll take up how this species-specialisation works in the brain in Chapter 9, but here we can note that in adult humans, localised damage to the left hemisphere can cause narrow impairments in language production and comprehension, called 'aphasia'. These impairments involve the routine components of language: understanding individual word sounds and meanings; putting them together into sentences. As practised sequences, this fits with the general evolutionary pattern that they would reside in the left hemisphere. By contrast, the right hemisphere is specialised to process the general meaning of the communication in context, as well as the melody (or 'prosody') of speech that spans sentences and conveys emotion. It is the right side that shouts out in surprise. Aphasic patients with left hemisphere damage frequently retain the ability to swear. Adults with right hemisphere damage can retain the ability to comprehend and produce sentences but start talking in a monotone voice like robots and lose the ability to understand jokes. Language processing involves both sides of the brain, then, but specialisation echoes the ancestral routine-versus-emotional difference of the general vertebrate plan.

In adult humans, localised damage to the right parietal lobe can lead to an impairment of visual attention called 'neglect'. Despite being able to see the left side of the world, individuals ignore or neglect it in their behaviour. There is no equivalent impairment following damage to the left parietal lobe. The processing of space in the right hemisphere appears to be more holistic and integrative, perhaps related to the functional specialisation of monitoring the environment for novelty or threat. This may indeed point to the way that tweaks to neural architectures yield the left and right biases. The left hemisphere may be biased to process features and detail, the minutiae of the routine, while the right processes configurations and integrated wholes. Perhaps this is achieved by tweaking the range of connectivity in the neural circuits in each hemisphere, shorter connections in the left, longer in the right. If one added a preferential connection of the right cortical hemisphere to limbic structures such as the amygdala for emotion processing, this could yield the high-level differences in function that we see.

However, it's important to stress that the hemispheric specialisation of function is a developmental outcome. If the left hemisphere is damaged in early childhood in exactly the regions that would cause aphasia in adults, the child can still develop to acquire language skills in the normal range (though perhaps a bit below where they would have been without the damage). Similarly for visual attention in childhood, development allows the undamaged hemisphere to contribute to the acquisition of skills in the normal range. The early brain, then, is closer to the idea of having two duplicate computers, one able to take over from the other if it is damaged. By adulthood, some specialisation of function has occurred yielding parallelisation and efficient use of resources, even though most functions will involve contributions from both hemispheres. The neural biases that steer specialisation, such as those in connectivity suggested above, are initially subtle, so that they can be exaggerated by development when things are going well or ignored and over-ridden when the system experiences damage. Development sounds important. We'll consider it in detail in Chapter 7.

So, that all makes sense, from a computational point of view. Start with duplicated, redundant systems, move towards parallel systems if the going is good. What doesn't make sense, though, is why the left side of the brain should receive inputs from and control the right side of the body, and vice versa. Where does this 'contra-lateral' pattern come from? Well, it's not new: the pattern can be traced back to the dawn of vertebrates and there are no known exceptions throughout the 500 million years of vertebrate evolution. Who takes the blame? Probably some sort of early fish. Here's what may have happened.

Let's say you're a fish that has evolved to twist its body onto its side during embryonic development. This could give you a body shape well adapted to your particular world. Some flat fish still have this feature, bottom dwellers that lie on the seabed camouflaged in the mud, with their bodies twisted so both eyes lie on top. Now let's say your niche has changed, and your species must evolve its way out of that twisted format by altering the embryonic growth plan.

One way forward is not to have the 'twist' stage in the first place, duh. That's the simple option. Remove the twist instruction from the plan. The other option, the one that was ultimately followed, is to undo the twist after it happens. Here's where the snafu may have occurred: when that plan was run, *undo the twist*, the head end of the embryo and the body end of the embryo untwisted in *opposite directions*. Yes, you got your old body plan back, but the head was back-to-front on the body, at least from the perspective of the central nervous system. Oops. Well, then you just have to make the best of a bad lot. You let the wiring up of the nervous system carry on, with the left side of the brain still connected to the right side of the body for its motor control and sensory input, and the right side of the brain still connected to the left side of the body. Still, the organism seems to work okay, so you go with it. As do all your ancestors. We said evolution wasn't perfect.

Now, like we said, left and right, nothing much to see, move along.

Living in the Future, Borrowing From the Past

Our favourite magician does some great tricks. In one, she tosses a coin in the air with her right hand and catches it. She does that a few more times, tossing it up and catching it. Then finally, she tosses it from her right hand over to her left – you see it glitter and flip, arcing through the air to land as her left hand closes around it. Only, when the magician opens her left hand, there is no coin there.

The magician does another trick with balls and it's even better. She throws a little red ball up into the air, once, twice, three times, catching it in her hand each time. We watch it rise and fall. Then she throws it up a fourth time, you watch it rise, and then it simply vanishes in front of your eyes. Holy moly!

Magic tricks give an insight into the way the brain works, the short cuts and assumptions it makes to deliver fast, real-time processing, yet which leave it vulnerable to illusions and deceptions. One of its strategies is a heavy reliance on prediction.

Figure 5.10 The way magic tricks fool us reveals how the brain is always generating sensory predictions

The brain is not a passive system that sits there waiting to respond to events in the world. If anything, it is living in the near future, always predicting what is about to happen, what other people are about to do or say, what good or bad things will happen. Its predictions are built up from previous experience: the sights and sounds that tend to be perceived, and the way objects have tended to move; what actions you have produced in different situations, and the way the world has responded to previous actions; the events that have tended to follow each other, and what you should attend to in different situations; the rewards and otherwise that have tended to accrue from different behaviours; how people tend to behave in certain situations, what goals other people have when they produce certain behaviours, and what are the likely narratives that play out.

The brain's predictions span different time scales: from where a kicked football will be half a second from now (back of the net!), to what ice cream Jonny is likely to choose today (he always likes a raspberry ripple), to what word will pop up next in a sentence ('Jonny ordered raspberry ____'). Multiple parts of the brain are tracking what just happened and what that means for what might happen next. A developed brain has thousands of hours of experience imprinted on its connections. As objects or people move, the brain predicts where they will move next. Each situation will reactivate scripts and prompt goals

('I'm in a restaurant, I need to look at the menu!'). Perceived objects will prompt actions based on their previous use: light switches will prompt the action of turning them on, coffee mugs prompt being lifted to the lips. As we've seen, it's the role of the modulatory system to decide between these options, to select among them according to current goals. When the modulatory system doesn't take command, these behaviours can happen on their own, behaviours borrowed from the past. Idle hands fiddle. Lights get switched on. Coffee mugs get lifted (even if, as you tip it to your lips, you remember that actually you've already had the last sip).

Why would the brain work this way? There are two reasons. First, it makes the brain faster to respond. Time is often of the essence in biological systems. From a standing start, the brain does not work quickly. When you first awake in the morning and open your eyes, it takes a moment to orient to the room around you. However, in its awake state, the brain is always in the game, primed for the most likely next move, predicting what it's likely to see next, getting relevant circuits ready to fire. Second, predictions optimise the brain to learn from situations when its predictions are wrong. Surprise is a powerful teacher. Curiosity and exploration are about playing with the world, poking it, seeing if it responds in the way you expect, and learning when it doesn't.

Some of this prediction is about guiding action. It's hard to make very precise motor movements when the signalling between the brain and the muscles can be noisy, when so many muscles and joints need to be controlled to move a limb, and when the sensory feedback the brain gets about the current position of the body in space is also noisy. One way to achieve smooth accurate movement is by constantly predicting the outcome of any movement from the motor commands given and comparing any mismatch with sensory feedback – when the prediction error is small, the actions will be smooth and accurate. This is the type of prediction carried out by the cerebellum.

Some of this prediction is about anticipating the sensory consequences of your actions on your body. You are much more interested in the effects of the external world on your body than effects produced by the actions you performed – sometimes to the extent that you completely ignore the sensory consequences of your own brain's commands. For example, when you move your eyes round the room, the room seems to stay still. Your sensation is that it's only your eyes that are moving. But movements of the eyeballs cause the image on the retina to lurch all over the place. Fortunately, the frontal eye fields – the region of the frontal cortex responsible for controlling eye movements – let the visual system know the eye movements are coming so it can correct for the consequences. Compare this situation to (gently) poking the upper or lower lid of your eye while it's open, slightly shifting the eyeball (close the other eye for best effect). Now there's no fast signal of predicted sensory changes, and the whole world seems to lurch alarmingly.

Some of the prediction is about guiding learning. Let's say you walk into your very own kitchen. The perceptual input activates a representation of the familiar room, which also generates predictions about the objects you expect to see in your kitchen. Objects that are expected and present aren't very interesting. Familiar objects which are unexpected – which violate predictions – cause learning. Ah, so that's where I left my phone. You update your predictions so that the object is expected next time you enter the room. But if you walk into someone else's kitchen for the first time, you'll have no predictions about what is there, so you won't particularly update your predictions about any novel objects you find (their microwave, their smart speaker), over and above the whole room being novel. Finally, if you step into someone's kitchen for the first time and see *your* phone there – *What's it doing there?* – well, that is unexpected and the association of this object with the novel room will be learned faster than a novel object in that kitchen. As well as triggering some serious conversations with whoever's kitchen it is.

Some of the brain's prediction is about guiding attention, as we'll see shortly when we uncover how the magic tricks work.

What in the brain's structure allows it to use prediction in this powerful way? The answer is the way it is connected. When there is a connection from A to B, there is often a connection back from B to A. Where there is forth, there is back, where there is up, there is down. Recall we talked of the sensory systems as hierarchical towers, with lower floors seeing detail, and each higher floor seeing larger patterns in the detail below, patterns within patterns, until at the top, the system is recognising objects and actions in the world. In the tower, information from the senses is passed upwards. But as the higher floors begin to get a sense of what may be out there in the world, or harbour expectations as to the situation they are in, they pass this information back down again, to help the lower floors make more sense of the basic sensory signal. It is these 'top-down' connections that allow expectations and previous knowledge to influence perception and action, to make the predictions.

Having these back-and-forth connections is not without risk. It allows for the possibility of uncontrolled build-up of activation. A excites B, B excites A, which gets B more excited, which excites A, and so on, until neurons burn out. The brain has to use a lot of damping down to stop such activation build up, using a particular type of inhibitory neuron called interneurons. But even then, there are risks of uncontrolled activation flow, such as that observed in epilepsy. The risks are highest in childhood, when the levels of brain connectivity are at their greatest.

The flow of information up and down the towers also requires a balancing act. On the one hand, if your expectations rule what you perceive, if there's too much prediction, you can miss subtle things changing in the world (sometimes called attentional blindness). You can fall for magic tricks. At worst, if you don't get the balance right, you'll suffer hallucinations: you'll see your ideas and not reality. Neurotransmitters appear to play a role in this balance, modulating the weight given to expectations. When there is too much dopamine in the system – as is sometimes the case in Parkinson's disease when treatment is given to replace missing dopamine – the result can be hallucinations. Too much dopamine has also been implicated in some cases of schizophrenia, where there can also be hallucinations. In Parkinson's disease, the hallucinations are usually visual and non-threatening, involving animals or people: a fleeting glimpse of a furry creature running in the edge of vision, or the sense of someone sitting in the room. The hallucinations are also more likely to occur in low light or low visibility situations, where insufficient perceptual information from the bottom of the sensory tower accentuates the conditions for top-down expectations to overrule sensory input and to spot, as it were, shapes in the mist.

On the other hand, if your perceptions are ruled by the sensory input and are dismissive of previous experience, if there's not enough prediction, the world will look strange and perpetually new, nothing like you expect, all trees and no forest – this is an experience that has sometimes been used to describe perception in autism, and to be associated both with perceptual hypersensitivity and emotional responses. As one individual with autism described it, 'I began to fear all those unknown paths, clothes, shoes, chairs and strange human voices. Each one challenged me by putting me in front of a new situation for me to face and understand.'[1] Notably, the hypersensitivity does not extend to noises that the individual has generated themselves, because these are predictable. As Leo Kanner, known for his landmark work in autism in the 1940s, noted, despite being distressed by external noises or movement, 'the child himself can happily make as great a noise as any that he dreads and move objects about to his heart's content'.[2]

The price of speed, then, and the price of learning from surprise, is to keep the brain in a perpetual balancing act.

So, back to the magic. How do these tricks exploit the predictive brain? Spoiler alert. Look away now if you don't want to know – skip to the next section to preserve the magic. First the coin trick. Of course, for that final throw, from right hand to left hand, the coin is never released from the magician's right hand, it's palmed. But you see it fly through the air! The motion-sensitive areas of the parietal cortex, which represent space, have been tracking the movement of the coin as it's been tossed. In particular, the 'warm-up' tosses have attracted the interest of an area called the lateral intraparietal sulcus. This area is involved in eye movement, and specifically working memory associated with guiding eye movements to track objects through space. Based on the magician's hand movement, this area tracks the predicted trajectory of the coin once released by the right hand. The magician is very careful to time the closing of her left hand to be at exactly the moment when the coin, if it had been released, would have landed there. The closing of the left hand, perceived by the visual stream, and the trajectory predicted by the lateral intraparietal area, together are enough to generate the sensation of perceiving the illusory coin. Your brain added the glittering and flipping as a bit of artistic licence.

What about the magic ball, the one that you actually *see* vanish? The first part of the trick is the same: there are some initial throws so that the predictive tracking system can estimate the trajectory the ball should follow once it's released, and so that the eyes can move to follow its path. The magician increases the effect by following the ball with her own eyes, moving her head up and down to exaggerate the trajectory and to focus your attention. At the final throw, the hand moves but the ball is never released, yet the magician still moves her head and eyes as if the ball were travelling. Here are the two crucial brain properties that allow the illusion. First, the pathways for predictive eye movement and perception operate independently. Second, only the centre of the visual field has high resolution. So, when the ball is supposedly released, and the predicted trajectory momentarily takes the ball outside of the high-res centre of the visual field into the low-res periphery, the brain isn't surprised that it can't be clearly seen. It guesses the ball is there and in motion, provides the illusory percept, and programmes a shift of the eyes to re-position the ball at the centre of the high-res visual field, based on the tracking system's prediction of where the ball is expected to be. When the eyes alight at the predicted location, however, the visual perception system reports that the ball is not there. And so you experience the sensation of it vanishing. Poof!

Well, a non-predictive brain would never fall for any of this nonsense. It would just see what was there. Very slowly.

Keeping Score

Are you happy? Deep down?

Obviously, not right *now*, you're reading a book about the brain. But generally… how have things been going lately?

It is possible to answer questions like this, about your happiness. But how? What information would your brain be accessing? It's not an issue of your momentary state of arousal (curious, sleepy, and so forth). To answer the happiness question, your brain must have computed, stored, and accumulated evidence over some period of time. It's been keeping score, but what scores would it keep?

Perhaps it's just stored how rich you are, your accumulated wealth. Money might not be everything to you, maybe you get your rewards in different ways. But still, happiness might be accumulated rewards, in the bank of the soul.

Partly. The rewards that result from our actions are important, but often, we make decisions about what course of action to take when we can't be sure whether a reward will result. You can't win every game you play. Chance is involved, or outcomes depend on factors not under our control, or on information we don't possess. When we apply for a job, we can't control who else applied. Part of our happiness is whether we can predict what's going to happen, or perhaps more importantly, whether we can accurately predict what size reward we are going to get. A significant part of keeping score of happiness is keeping a tally of our reward prediction *errors* – extra credits get added when the rewards we receive are larger than expected, credits taken away when the rewards are smaller than expected. Previous happiness fades with time, so our more recent reward prediction errors are weighed more heavily.

If your momentary estimate of happiness depends on your recent history of rewards and expectations, mood by contrast tracks general trends, monitoring whether an environment is getting better or worse. You're optimistic if rewards and your ability to predict them are improving, you're gloomy if the world is yielding fewer rewards and they are getting less predictable. Mood is a useful variable for adapting your behaviour to a changing environment.

What parts of the brain are keeping score? Let's take you back to two brain regions. First, the basal ganglia. This is the action selection system, the circuits linking cortex with a chain of sub-cortical structures which choose which of a set of competing action plans to select and execute. The basal ganglia are also sensitive to the outcome of the selection, whether the result was good or bad, to make that selection more or less likely in the future, so-called reinforcement learning. One of these structures, the ventral tegmental area sitting within the midbrain and connected to the ventral striatum, is particularly important for signalling the reward prediction error – if you got a better or worse reward than you were expecting. It is a structure that releases dopamine to modulate the activity of other structures in the basal ganglia, which update to keep score.

Let's say I need to make a tough decision like this: should I complete an extra session at the gym (feel fitter) or eat an extra slice of cake (feel satiated). Both might make me happier, in different ways. Recall, the brain doesn't readily form abstractions, with information held in content-specific systems – in this case, perhaps, in the somatosensory system, in the insula, and in the gustatory system. How could you possibly compare the information in different systems and come to a decision? What we need is a separate system that represents value in a common currency, and then allows value-based decisions to be made with respect to the demands or preferences of different content-specific systems.

This broker is the ventromedial prefrontal cortex. Recall, we partitioned the prefrontal cortex into sides versus middle, and upper versus lower. The middle is involved in control and decision processes around social information (upper) and emotional information (lower). In this case, a small region of the lower (ventro) middle (medial) region is serving as the comparator of different values (it can compare food, money, aesthetic judgements, and even pleasantness). This region can be subdivided into subjective values (the rewards you give yourself for achieving your goals) and external values (the rewards you get from other people for doing what they want).

If you combine these two systems – the ventral striatum (receiving signals from the ventral tegmental area) and the ventromedial prefrontal cortex – you get a system that can return information about your level of happiness right now: the recent history of whether your reward expectations were exceeded across all your value domains.

Figure 5.11 How the brain answers the question 'Am I happy, deep down?' – the ventral tegmental area (VTA) and the ventromedial prefrontal cortex (VMPFC)

Don't be so selfish, this is not all about you. What about other people? What about their happiness? We said that the brain's favourite content was other people, and for sure, we can think about how to add other people into our happiness sum, and even to do something about their (un)happiness, perhaps by giving to charity.

Recall, social cognition brings together a range of brain areas for the bodily basis of empathy (anterior insula), to process social bodily actions and gaze information about other people (posterior superior temporal), to process your own intentions and plans for social movement such as gaze (intraparietal sulcus), to generate emotions about approaching or avoiding them (amygdala), to distinguish yourself from others such as in perspective taking (temporal parietal junction), to store social knowledge such as scripts for situations (anterior temporal).

To count other people in your happiness sum, you have to see their perspective and empathise with their situation, particularly if their lot is worse than yours. So, your happiness sum could include a guilt score, the extent to which your lot is better than theirs. Your happiness might go up if you give them some of your stuff to make life fairer. But the world isn't fair, is it? Sometimes other people have more than you, and refuse to give you their stuff. That would feed into your envy score, the extent to which other people's lot is better than yours. People vary in how much weight they give to their guilt score and their envy score when they add up their happiness totals for the social world, but these aren't closely related: people who experience more guilt do not necessarily experience more envy. Nevertheless, their sums do then predict how much they choose to give to others.

This is something, then, to put on your fridge magnet: *Happiness is... accumulated reward prediction errors.* From the brain's perspective, at least. And if there's sage advice to take from how the brain processes value, it is that the key to happiness in life is to have low expectations which can always be exceeded (but not to have such low expectations that you're miserable).

We are drawing to the end of this chapter that has throughout viewed the brain as a computer. We've seen how the brain may crunch numbers, but it does so in a way that's different from a digital computer, using mechanisms such as hierarchies, maps, hubs, and networks. We talked about the difference between the content-specific systems and the modulatory system that activates and deactivates them according to goals and context. We saw how the brain is always predicting, which makes it gullible, vulnerable to magic tricks, and we saw how it must keep score to tell if it's happy. Now we go on to argue that the brain is not like a computer at all. Because we just can't make our minds up.

━━━━━━━━━ Box 5.1 ━━━━━━━━━

Reductionism – it's all in the brain...

A reductionist approach tries to explain behaviour using the lowest level of explanation, usually the biological level (the concept comes from biology). The more people know about the brain, the more attractive this approach seems to become. So now we don't just feel happy after exercise, but we have a 'dopamine rush'; we aren't just depressed after a bereavement, but we have 'low serotonin levels'. Literally every day new findings come out claiming to have located spirituality, consciousness, love, racist attitudes, criminality, etc., in various parts of the brain; findings are backed up by colourful pictures of brain scans.

But these findings (by the way, most of them are simplistic interpretations and will never be replicated) are simply correlations between brain activity and the chosen measure. All behaviour is correlated with changes in brain activity; in that sense, it is all in the brain, so identifying changes is in itself no big deal – it is exactly what we would expect. But they are not explanations. You may be feeling quite bored with this bit of the book and in theory we could record the brain activity that correlates with that feeling. Does it explain why you are bored? No. That would involve looking at the material, the writing style, your current mood state, the lack of jokes, etc., etc. Do lower levels of serotonin explain depression after bereavement? Again, no. The immediate (proximal) cause is the loss of a loved one.

(Continued)

Explaining behaviour requires investigations at different levels of analysis. A complete picture of depression would require analysis of genetic tendencies, changes in brain activity (ideally, at the levels of synapses, neurons, circuits, and structures), personality and social variables, and life events. It's a complicated business, but neuroscience can give the illusion that it has most of the answers through its reductionist approach; some neuroscientists assume that while the brain is complicated, measuring and understanding behaviour is easy – they could not be more wrong.

Just in case you are bored and it's because of a lack of jokes, here's our favourite reductionist joke: *You can't trust atoms. They make up everything.*

Notes

1   Bogdashina, O. (2004). *Communication Issues in Autism and Asperger Syndrome*. Jessica Kingsley, p. 60.
2   Kanner, L. (1943). Autistic disturbances of affective contact. *Nervous Child*, 2: 217–250, p. 245.

6

THE BRAIN IS A BIOLOGICAL ORGAN, NOT A COMPUTER

As much as it is useful to see the brain as a computer, the brain is, ultimately, a biological entity, shaped by its evolutionary history. For those neurons that are neither sensory (influenced by the external world) nor motor (driving muscles), perhaps we can view their electrical activity in terms of information, mediating between stimulus and response. Perhaps we can see how the processing of that information leads to behaviour more complex than mere reflexes, and perhaps we can view patterns of neural activity in terms of computation. Yet what the brain does is physical, driven by the chemical and electrical activity within and between biological cells, causing changes in the body. Sometimes the idea of computation feels too clunky to capture the diversity of the ways these physical interactions can lead to behaviour.

For example, the jellyfish gives a window onto one of the earliest evolutionary roles of neurons, to ensure muscle activity is coordinated across the body. Evolution found multiple solutions in different jellyfish species to solve this problem. These range from fast propagation of action potentials to carefully tuned attenuation of signals along the triggering axon and local delays at the muscle fibre that depend on the strength of the action potential. A jellyfish can have multiple neural systems based on different propagation chemistries for different behaviours. For example, the moon jelly, *Aurelia aurita,* can propel itself by contracting its bell to expel water. Small clusters of sensory neurons trigger a fast spike of activity in other neurons which spreads quickly, via chemical synapses across the bell causing its coordinated contraction, propelling it forward. The neurons each fire once only, then elasticity brings the bell back to its original shape. But the moon jelly can also steer, for instance to keep away from a rock face. How does it do this? There is another network of neurons that has a much slower pace of signalling. It causes no obvious contraction of the bell but does serve to alter the stiffness of the rim of the bell. Depending on the relative timing of the stiffening of the rim compared to the contraction of the bell, the result is a turning motion to one side or another. A small delay of the slow system compared to the fast system turns one way; a longer delay turns the other. The key to behaviour is the relative timing of two different distributed networks.

A computational view may, then, be insufficient to capture the complexity and diversity of the physical solutions that enable nervous systems to drive behaviour. But computation also fails to give an insight into some of the key functions of the brain that stem from its shaping by evolution – with the inevitable focus on survival, out-competing others to reproduce, and raising offspring. Here we're thinking of behaviours such as parent–child bonding, sexual behaviour, social behaviour, exploratory behaviour, anxiety, stress, and aggression. Under strong selection, behaviours that are key to survival are built into the ancient structures of the limbic system, midbrain, and brainstem. These behaviours are often influenced by levels of hormones, such as testosterone, vasopressin, oxytocin, and cortisol, with widespread modulation and biasing of brain and body systems.

Take sexual behaviour, which we think you'll agree, feels not particularly computational. Out in the body, sexual events for males and females alike involve arousal, erectile tissue engorgement and detumescence, glandular secretion, and contraction of smooth and striated muscles (and you thought we weren't that kind of book). Sexual behaviour is driven by the medial region of the appetitive limbic structure, the amygdala. This region is involved in the regulation of a wide array of social behaviours including aggression, parental behaviour, and sexual behaviour. The structure processes sensory information (sights, sounds, and smells signalling a potential partner in sexual events), as well as information about internal hormonal state (when you might be hot to trot). It influences the reward system in the striatum to encourage successful sexual behaviours in the future (potentially with the same partner!) and the hypothalamus to place the bodily organs in the appropriate state. The fundamental principle here is that the behaviour is driven by the ancient memory structure, which uses sensory cues or hormonal cues as triggers; there is then communication to other brain regions and to the outside body to control the state of relevant organs, as well as hotwiring of the reward system to encourage successful behaviour in the future. (Much of the research here is carried out with animal models, but there is little reason to think humans will greatly differ.)

In the rest of this chapter, we take a deeper dive into four areas of what the brain does that sit less easily with the idea of computation: sleep, circadian rhythms, stress, and the search for love. In each case, watch out for the ancient structures involved; watch out for the role that neurotransmitters play; watch out for the role that hormones play, inside the brain and outside conditioning the body; and watch out for the side effects on the cortex. We may also have to drop in a few more brain structures and pathways. Sorry about that.

Sleepy Yet?

Sleep can seem pretty straightforward. You have a busy day, you feel tired towards evening, you go to bed, if you're lucky you fall asleep quickly, and wake up refreshed in the morning remembering little about the night before apart from maybe a few dreams. If you lived before the invention of electricity, that is, any time before the beginning of the 20th century, night time was also a time when it was difficult to be doing anything else other than sleeping. So sleep was seen as a sort of passive state that the brain fell into when nothing much was happening outside. The fact that you felt better after sleeping was seen as an accidental by-product.

This simple view of sleep has been dismantled by research in the latter half of the 20th century and up to the current day. Just one example: everyone who has a cat or dog knows that animals also sleep. If you happen to keep jellyfish, you might be surprised to know that they also show behaviour that looks quite like sleep. The bell of the jellyfish pulsates at about one pulse per second but this slows down at night time. If you disturb the jellyfish sleep by constantly agitating their tank, it will show reduced activity the following day exactly as you might after a disturbed night's sleep. It's a bit of a stretch to see this as equivalent to human sleep, but it's something we'll pick up later in this section when we look at sleep across the animal kingdom.

Neuroscience is heavily dependent on technological advances (see Box 3.2). Just think of brain scanning techniques and modern methods in behavioural genetics that have transformed our still limited understanding of the brain and behaviour over the last 25 years. But this dependence has always been there. In relation to sleep, the key invention was the electroencephalogram (EEG) developed by Hans Berger in the 1920s. Knowing from previous work that electricity was involved in nervous system functions, he used his son to demonstrate that you could record electrical activity from the brain using electrodes on the surface of the scalp. He was able to describe some basic EEG patterns but did not study sleep, partly because no one thought brain activity during sleep would be very interesting.

This was left to Eugene Aserinsky in 1950, working in Nathaniel Kleitman's pioneering sleep laboratory. He was the first to record an EEG throughout a night's sleep, using his son as a subject (you can see a pattern developing here...). Aserinsky also recorded movements of the eye, as casual observations suggested that during sleep there were occasional periods of eye movements. He found that these periods of eye movements were associated with a highly aroused EEG pattern, and so labelled them 'rapid eye movement' sleep, or REM. A further significant observation was that participants, when awakened from REM sleep, reported dreaming.

REM sleep occurs in episodes during the night. In between episodes, sleep reverts to its other state, non-REM or 'NREM'. But we are jumping ahead...

EEG patterns, stages, and the sleep cycle

The EEG is a continuous recording of the brain's electrical activity, with two basic patterns, synchronised and desynchronised. The synchronised pattern is characterised by recognisable and repeated waves, which can be defined by their frequency (how many waves per second) and amplitude (height). The desynchronised pattern lacks a repeated and identifiable wave form, but spiking is usually of high frequency; this fast desynchronised EEG is characteristic of the aroused waking EEG. As we become drowsy and slip into sleep, so waves become identifiable and as sleep grows deeper the waves become slower and larger.

Stages of sleep

When we are awake but relaxed, the EEG is dominated by alpha waves (the different frequencies of waves are labelled with Greek letters; alpha corresponds to 8–12 waves per second, or hertz, Hz). Then come the four stages of NREM sleep:

- Stage 1 sleep: Theta waves – 4–7 Hz.
- Stage 2 sleep: Theta waves, but with bursts of high frequency oscillations called sleep spindles (12–15 Hz).
- Stage 3 sleep: Delta waves appear – 1–4 Hz, high amplitude, very slow.
- Stage 4 sleep: EEG dominated by delta waves.

The presence of delta waves leads to stages 3 and 4 being referred to as slow wave sleep, SWS, or deep NREM. These four stages of sleep together can be referred to as non-rapid-eye-movement sleep, or NREM, to distinguish them from REM itself. Confusingly, different books and research papers refer to REM and NREM, or to REM and SWS, but they are basically referring to the same phenomena. Then, in addition to the four stages of NREM sleep, we have:

- REM sleep: Fast, desynchronised cortical EEG activity, rapid eye movements, accompanied by loss of muscle tone in the body.

REM sleep and the sleep cycle

When we fall asleep, we descend rapidly into deep NREM of stages 3 and 4. After 30 minutes or so sleep lightens and we move up the sleep gradient into the light sleep of stages 1 and 2. At this point, maybe an hour after sleep onset, we shift into REM. As outlined above, this is signalled by a shift in the EEG to a fast desynchronised pattern, characteristic of waking, though the person is actually in the deepest state of sleep (hardest to awake). We spend about 10–15 minutes in REM, then move back into light sleep and down the sleep gradient to deep NREM. This cycle repeats itself about every 70–90 minutes, so we have around 5–6 cycles each night. As we approach morning, we spend more time in light sleep, and as this seems to trigger periods of REM, we have more REM towards morning. Overall, a night's sleep will consist of roughly 80% NREM and 20% REM (though, as we see later, this varies over the lifespan).

NREM is characterised by other measures. The brain's energy consumption falls to about 20% of waking levels, muscle tone and movement decline, and a general picture of rest for brain and body emerges. (This is linked to parasympathetic dominance, see p. 129.) In contrast, brain energy consumption during REM matches waking levels, skeletal muscles are inhibited so movement is impossible, and a picture of peripheral physiological arousal (sympathetic dominance) emerges. It is also the phase where most dreaming occurs (when woken from REM, about 70–80% of people report dreams, compared with 20–30% during NREM). One possible explanation for the inhibition of skeletal muscle during REM is to prevent 'acting out' dreams.

What else do we need to explain about sleep? Well, how long is a piece of string... at the general level we can investigate the functions of sleep, but we need to look at the evolutionary background (don't forget that states similar to sleep occur across the animal kingdom). More specifically we can investigate the probable separate functions of REM and NREM, both in terms of the body's physiology and their possible involvement in cognition. Then there is the problem of the neural control of sleep: which systems manage the onset of sleep and the REM/NREM cycle, and which systems control the 24-hour circadian rhythm of sleep (see p. 123). From a fairly straightforward picture derived from classic research in the 1950s and 1960s, we now know that the control of sleep and sleep cycles is scarily complex. The stuff of nightmares. We shall try and draw out a few key systems... but firstly, let's get into the possible functions of sleep.

Functions of sleep

We noted earlier that sleep, or states that look like sleep, can be found across the animal kingdom, right down to unicellular organisms, worms, and jellyfish, though at this level sleep simply looks like activity versus rest. However, if deprived of the 'sleep' period even these animals seem to make up for it when allowed to rest, exactly as we do if sleep deprived. But the complex pattern of REM and NREM seems to emerge far later in evolutionary terms with mammals and birds, and most research has focused on these, especially mammals.

So ideally, we need explanations for overall sleep, and then for NREM and REM. These explanations range from the ecological/lifestyle level right down to interactions between brain circuits, so it's best to deal with them separately.

The ecological approach – sleep as adaptation to the environment

Various reviews of sleep across the animal kingdom allow for some generalisations on sleep patterns (though there will always be exceptions):

- *Small animals sleep for longer than larger animals* – rats and cats, for instance, sleep for around 14 hours a day, the horse and the elephant manage on 2–4 hours a day. The sloth is often quoted as an exception, a medium-sized animal sleeping for around 20 hours a day, but it has been pointed out that these observations were done on sloths in zoos. There is evidence that in the wild, where life is more exciting, they sleep only 8–10 hours. Zoos are so boring.
- *Metabolic rate* (the rate at which our cells burn up energy) is positively correlated with sleep time. As small animals have higher metabolic rates than large animals, this means that when they sleep they are conserving proportionately more energy.
- *Trophic position*, a scientist's way of referring to predator/prey status, affects sleep time; prey animals, usually herbivores, sleep less than carnivorous predators.
- *Sleep site* is important. Animals that sleep in exposed sites, say, on the African savannah, sleep less than animals who sleep in safe sites such as caves or nests (and to be safer they may also split sleep into several short periods – 'polyphasic sleep'). The extreme example of a dangerous sleep site is aquatic mammals such as dolphins. They need to come to the surface to breathe, so if they had extended periods of deep NREM they would drown. Evolution has come up with a smart answer – the dolphin sleeps with one half of the brain (left or right hemisphere) at a time, periodically switching hemispheres but maintaining consciousness all the time and staying alive.

These factors interact. For instance, herbivorous prey animals need to graze for far longer than carnivores (and so have less time for sleep) and may have exposed sleep sites, compared to the leopard with its occasional large meals, sleeping safely up in a tree. But there are key observations. The antelope sleeping on the exposed savannah is potentially in great danger; it would be far better not to sleep *at all* but instead to stay vigilant. This reinforces the idea that sleep is essential, and goes against one early but popular idea that sleep was to keep animals safe when grazing and so on was impossible, i.e., at night time for diurnal animals. But if sleep is essential, what is it essential for?

Sleep as restoration

The correlation between animal size, metabolic rate, and extended sleep suggests that sleep in these animals helps in conserving energy. But this is a passive element. Does sleep help in actually restoring brain and body? We know from our own experience that after a night's sleep deprivation we do not feel great. After extended periods of deprivation we feel worse, and tend to sleep for longer when allowed. Early controlled laboratory studies of prolonged sleep deprivation in rats demonstrated that the animals died after 2–3 weeks, although a complicating factor was the stressful procedures used to keep them awake (cold baths…). The most famous human case of prolonged deprivation was Randy Gardner, who set a world record by staying awake for 11 days in 1964 (as part of a high school science project! It is still the record, as similar attempts were banned as being psychologically and physically dangerous). Towards the end, Gardner suffered visual and perceptual disturbances and mild paranoia. When he eventually slept, it was for 15 hours the first night, and over the next few nights he recovered only about 25% of his total sleep loss. What was more interesting was that the recovery concentrated on deep NREM and REM sleep as opposed the lighter stages of NREM.

This fits in with controlled laboratory studies of moderate sleep deprivation in humans. The effects of two or three nights' sleep deprivation can be seen on cognitive processes, including attention, vigilance, and memory. Sleep deprivation leads to an increased drive to sleep ('sleep pressure'), and when allowed to sleep, recovery is concentrated on REM and deep NREM as with Gardner, so maybe these phases are necessary for restoration and maintenance of the brain and its cognitive systems. Deep NREM is also associated with a surge in release of growth hormone, which is vital for various physiological systems in the body, so the stages of sleep, especially NREM and REM, together are crucial in maintaining brain and body.

We can see the physiological consequences of self-imposed sleep deprivation. Regularly sleeping fewer than five hours a night has been associated with diabetes and obesity, hypertension and cardiovascular disease, reduced immune function, and increased mortality (there is also some evidence that regularly sleeping more than nine hours a night is linked to poor health, too. Between seven and nine hours is good…).

Over the last 30 years, the wide impact of sleep on the brain and bodily physiological processes has gradually been documented. It clearly has a role in regulating levels of hormones linked to growth, appetite, immune function, and stress. We have moved way beyond a simple 'sleep as restoration' hypothesis to one where sleep is essential for normal regulation of our physiology. But another area that has taken off over the last 30 years is the role sleep plays in learning and memory.

━━━━━━ Box 6.1 ━━━━━━

Neuroethics

Some classic psychological experiments from the 1950s and 1960s (e.g., Milgram and obedience, Zimbardo and role conformity, Schachter and Singer's work on adrenaline and emotion, the use of cats to study the brain mechanisms of sleep) would not be allowed today as they

(Continued)

would go against current ethical guidelines (luckily for those researchers, but maybe not for their participants, ethical guidelines did not exist back then). The British Psychological Society has a 44-page booklet on ethics in psychological research, covering areas such as informed consent, protection of participants and their data, right to withdraw and debriefing. However the rise of neuroscience over the last 30 years has introduced some broader and more complex ethical and moral issues, and led to the development of the field of 'neuroethics'.

Since the dawn of humanity people have directly interfered with brain function, often by chewing leaves or drinking infusions of psychoactive plants. In the 20th century, the systematic use of drugs to treat psychological disorders began, though at the start we knew as much about their effect in the brain as early humans did about chewing coca leaves; in both cases the effect was more important than the understanding.

We now have an enormous range of methods for visualising, influencing, and recording brain activity, with a range of implications. Not all of these implications are beneficial. New technologies are morally neutral; it is what we do with them that gives them an ethical or moral angle. Nuclear power can provide electricity for millions, or kill millions. The internet has revolutionised information storage and communication, but allows for abuse and scamming. Unfortunately technological evolution is faster than our social and cultural evolution. See Boxes 8.1 and 8.2 for more examples of ethics and neuroscience.

Sleep and learning

It seems obvious that sleep affects learning, as sleep deprivation leads to fatigue and loss of vigilance and attention. But these are general effects. Over the last 30 years a clearer picture has emerged of how sleep is involved in specific aspects of learning and memory. The key was the use of controlled laboratory studies using animals and humans, the application of the new scanning technologies, and the ability to selectively deprive participants of either REM or NREM.

During waking hours, the hippocampus allows for the registering and encoding of new learning and experience. During NREM, consolidation of learning takes place involving interactions between the hippocampus and the neocortex, leading to long-term storage in the neocortex (see the section in Chapter 5 on 'Horses for Courses'). Part of this process is the reactivation of the original learning pattern in the hippocampus during NREM. This has most convincingly been shown in rats, who turn out to have excellent spatial learning and memory. Learning specific locations (using mazes) while awake is reflected in specific patterns of neuronal activity in the hippocampus; these specific patterns are reactivated during NREM, along with correlated activity in the cortex. Parallel studies in humans learning new routes through towns and using PET scans to record brain activity during waking and sleeping show similar results.

NREM allows for a shift in memories from initial registration in the hippocampus to consolidation and long-term storage in the neocortex. In this way the hippocampus is freed up for the continuous registration of daily experiences. There is evidence that memories are also replayed during REM sleep, but not just passively replayed: rather, they are subjected to higher level processing. Our memory systems are complex and interrelated, not separate packets of experience. During REM, rather like a filing system, some newly consolidated memories will be embedded with our previous experiences, while others may be forgotten. In fact, some theories of dream content (remember that dreaming is far more common in REM sleep) link it to the active forgetting or clearing out of unwanted material from memory. Note that this is only one of many theories of dreaming. Some emphasise the tendency of the brain to make narratives out of essentially random activity and conclude that dreams are basically meaningless; others, such as Freud, focus on the symbolic nature of dream imagery.

Sleep over the lifespan – implications

Newborn babies do not arrive with the adult circadian rhythm and REM/NREM patterning. They sleep for about 16 hours a day, mostly at night but with daytime naps (the technical term for this is 'polyphasic sleep'; more than one episode of sleep in 24 hours – some adults have a polyphasic pattern, typically a snooze after lunch); 50% of the infant's sleep is REM (up to 80% in premature babies), slowly reducing to the adult percentage of about 25% by the age of two.

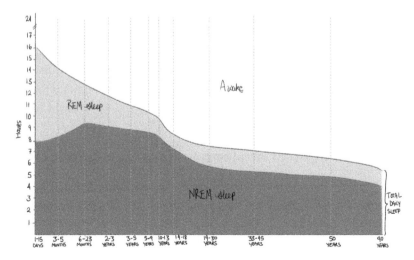

Figure 6.1 The proportion of different types of sleep across the lifespan

This dramatic change has been linked to the rapid brain development of the first two years (see Chapter 7). Although brain development begins early in embryonic life, with over-production and then systematic loss of neurons, at birth the baby's brain has roughly the same number of neurons as the adult brain. However it has far fewer synaptic connections. These increase rapidly during the first postnatal year, reaching a maximum at about eight months. From here there is a progressive reduction in synaptic connectivity to adult levels, reached between 10 and 20 years of age.

These radical changes are occurring along with major life experiences for the baby, beginning with basic sensory and motor development, followed by learning what the world is all about. It is assumed that the high proportion of REM sleep is critical for these neurophysiological and experiential changes, especially the fine-tuning of neuronal networks to the environmental inputs to which the baby is exposed.

There are dramatic changes in sleep patterns during the first two years. From then there are changes, but far more gradual. Deep slow wave sleep reduces from around 24% of total sleep time at age five to around 9% at age 70, while REM falls from 25% total sleep time at age five to 19% at age 70. Total sleep time also reduces over the lifespan, from about eight hours at age five to slightly over six hours at age 70.

The reduction in total sleep time into old age may be highly significant. Over the last ten years there has been a growing awareness of yet another key function of sleep. The ventricles running through the brain (see Figure 3.7) contain cerebrospinal fluid (CSF), while brain neurons are bathed in interstitial fluid (the fluid found in the spaces around cells). There are interchanges between these two fluid compartments, and amongst other functions, this interchange allows for the removal of metabolic waste products from the brain into the CSF system. Why is this critical? Alzheimer's disease, the commonest form of senile dementia, is associated with the accumulation of two proteins in the brain, tau and beta-amyloid. Levels of these proteins are higher during waking, and are increased by sleep deprivation. It has been shown that during slow wave sleep, tau and beta-amyloid are removed from the brain into the ventricular CSF, a critical process in regulating protein levels in the brain. It is a popular idea that the reduction in total sleep time with old age means that protein regulation is upset and leads to the accumulation of tau and beta-amyloid associated with Alzheimer's.

Neurochemical control of sleep – life gets complicated...

The reticular formation (sometimes referred to as the ascending reticular arousal system, ARAS) is a dense network ('reticulum' simply means 'net') of neurons running through the brainstem, from the medulla oblongata to the midbrain. In 1949, Moruzzi and Magoun demonstrated in cats that electrical stimulation of the ARAS produced a cortical EEG pattern of arousal, with high frequency desynchronised activity. This was the first evidence that the ARAS was a key player in controlling sleep and arousal states. Jouvet, in another series of classic studies using cats, demonstrated that different nuclei (collections of neuronal cell bodies embedded in the ARAS, with axons running together towards the forebrain) were involved in the control of REM and NREM sleep. He identified noradrenaline and serotonin as key neurotransmitters in the regulation of sleep states.

So by the 1960s we knew that sleep and its different phases were imposed on the brain, and not just passive states that the brain fell into when not much was happening in the world outside, i.e., night time, or a neuroanatomy lecture. Although this general picture still holds, advances in neuroscience methods have now revealed far more of the daunting complexity of these systems. In fact it is impossible in an introductory text to cover the full details, but we can aim for a reasonable overview…

Sleep mechanisms

The need for sleep increases with time awake – referred to as *sleep homeostasis* – so we need mechanisms to turn sleep on and then mechanisms to wake us up. Within sleep we have oscillations between NREM and REM stages, so we can see immediately that a number of circuits will be involved in the whole process. There will also be overlaps, as some features of REM sleep, for instance, are similar to waking behaviour.

Structures within the ARAS (reminder: ascending reticular activating system, that network of neurons running through the brainstem and midbrain that plays a major role in cortical arousal) have critical functions. For waking behaviour, one pathway runs from the brainstem medulla to the posterior hypothalamus. A second pathway runs from the medulla to the mesopontine nuclei in the midbrain reticular formation, and from there to the thalamus. The thalamocortical projections run to the cortex, modulating cortical arousal. A third component in waking states is the locus coeruleus, made up of nuclei in the brainstem pons region whose connections run to the thalamus, hippocampus, and cortex. It is worth noting that these connections use noradrenaline ('norepinephrine' in the USA) as a neurotransmitter. A final component of these brainstem arousal systems is the raphe nuclei, which project to the preoptic area of the hypothalamus, the suprachiasmatic nucleus (SCN; also in the hypothalamus, see later in this chapter), and the cortex. These SCN pathways give the raphe nuclei a role in the control of circadian rhythms (again, see later in this chapter). Many of the raphe projections use serotonin as a neurotransmitter.

Overall, these brainstem centres are responsible for arousal and waking states, so they need to be inhibited for sleep to be imposed on the brain. NREM sleep has a major control centre in the preoptic area of the hypothalamus. Damage to this area causes insomnia, while stimulation can impose NREM sleep on the brain. It is likely that the preoptic area keeps a check on the duration of wakefulness and then imposes NREM sleep at the appropriate point. It does this via inhibitory pathways running to the brainstem arousal centres, releasing the inhibitory neurotransmitter GABA.

So, with waking states and NREM sleep, we have mutually inhibitory systems involving many pathways and neurotransmitters, modulating cortical arousal from the desynchronised pattern of alert waking behaviour to the synchronised large waves of NREM sleep. But note that these can be overridden by sensory input, either internal (e.g., anxieties) or external (e.g., clubbing).

REM sleep is yet another state. We have an aroused EEG but a behaviourally deep state of sleep. How is that going to be pulled off? So we need some activity in brainstem arousal systems, but these do not include the locus coeruleus or the raphe nuclei, which are inactive during REM. The critical region for REM sleep is in the rostral ('towards the front') reticular formation in the pons of the brainstem – the rostral pontine reticular formation (nobody said that sleep mechanisms were easy...). Damage to this area eliminates REM sleep, while it is normally inhibited by the locus coeruleus and raphe nuclei, and only becomes active as these waking centres are in turn inhibited during NREM sleep; so a phase of REM follows a phase of NREM. One of the key signs of REM sleep is, no surprise, rapid eye movements, and these are also controlled by areas of the pontine reticular formation that connect to the superior colliculi of the midbrain – these structures are central to the control of eye movements during waking and REM sleep. There are also pathways descending from the brainstem and out to skeletal muscles responsible for the loss of muscle tone seen in REM sleep.

Sleep and waking involve many neurotransmitters. In the brief outline above we have mentioned noradrenaline, serotonin, and GABA, but many others are involved. Acetylcholine ('cholinergic') pathways from the brainstem and midbrain contribute to cortical arousal, waking, and REM, while the excitatory neurotransmitter glutamate, widely distributed in the brain, promotes REM sleep. Given this complexity, it is no surprise that many psychoactive drugs (e.g., clinically used drugs such as antidepressants, or so-called drugs of abuse such as amphetamines) affect sleep durations and sleep patterns, and there can be unpleasant side effects.

A final note on mechanisms. There is a condition, narcolepsy, where humans and other animals fall quickly and without warning into a sleep state, moving rapidly into REM. These episodes can occur several times a day, even during daylight hours. Narcolepsy is often associated with cataplexy, a loss of muscle tone that results in physical collapse and is also seen in 'normal' REM sleep. Genetic studies, often in dogs, show that a mutation that eliminates receptors for a neuropeptide called hypocretin (alternative name, orexin) can cause narcolepsy (note that, inevitably, the situation is slightly more complex in humans). Hypocretin neurons in the hypothalamus normally send connections to brainstem arousal centres and play a major part in the complex symphony of waking, NREM, and REM.

Overall the control of waking and sleep states is of impressive complexity as, though hard to believe, the outline above is only scratching the surface. But given that sleep has to fulfil many functions, physiological and psychological, it is no real surprise that its control systems have evolved to such a level of sophistication. But there is more (oh no, we hear you say; stay with it, the next bit is far less technical), as sleep is just one example of our biological rhythms.

Circadian Rhythms

We have had a brief look at the complex regulation of the REM/NREM alternating pattern during a night's sleep. This pattern is an example of an ultradian biological rhythm, one which happens more than once in 24 hours. The human female menstrual cycle and the annual hibernation seen, for instance, in bears and some squirrels are examples of infradian biological rhythms, with less than one cycle every 24 hours. Critical to understanding sleep are circadian rhythms, occurring once every 24 hours.

The Earth rotates every 24 hours, giving us day and night. It also circles the Sun once every year, and as the distance from the Sun varies so we have our different seasons. This has been going on for a long time, around 4 billion years. These various environmental rhythms affect behaviour; diurnal animals are active during the day and rest at night, with nocturnal animals showing the opposite pattern. Hibernating animals begin to lay down extra fat and reduce body temperature as winter approaches, to help them survive times when feeding is difficult. They rouse themselves when spring arrives.

It is possible that these behavioural changes could be triggered directly by the external conditions, but as early as the 18th century we knew this wasn't the case. The heliotrope plant opens its leaves during the day and closes them up at night. In 1729, a French astronomer demonstrated that the heliotrope maintains this pattern when kept in continuous dark conditions. Squirrels kept in constant light and temperature conditions still lay down fat stores at the appropriate time of year, preparing for hibernation.

During those 4 billion years of life on Earth, living organisms have been exposed to these environmental contingencies. It is clear that during evolution, plants and animals have sculpted mechanisms to control a variety of biological rhythms, and do not rely simply on the outside world. Plants, for instance, have photo (light) receptors that feed into a complex genetically controlled internal 'clock', so even the humble daffodil deserves some respect for its time keeping...

Our focus is on animals, because they have brains. The evolution of these internal or endogenous pacemakers, known more simply as 'body clocks', is an excellent example of how the key to evolutionary success is adaptation to and working with the environment. The endogenous system is not perfect; the heliotrope kept in constant dark opens its leaves around every 22 hours rather than 24, so there has to be another factor to keep things synchronised. Clocks can drift and need to be reset.

Much of the early and dramatic evidence for the relative roles of body clocks and the external world in controlling behavioural and physiological rhythms comes from a classic study in 1972. This was a 'free-running study', where the person or animal is isolated from outside influences. Caves play a large part in these... in 1972, Michel Siffre, a French caver and explorer, spent 179 days alone in a cave in Texas. The temperature was kept at a constant 70 degrees Fahrenheit, and Siffre could ask, via a telephone, for the artificial lights to be turned off when he wanted to sleep and put on when he awoke. During his stay, sleep patterns and various physiological measures were recorded.

Given this was 1972, Siffre was unable to use his time in the cave to establish a new highest score on *Call of Duty*. Nevertheless, while Siffre's circadian rhythm of sleep/waking was maintained, it extended from 24 hours to between 25 and 32 hours – his 'days' became longer, so that when he emerged from the cave on day 179, to him it was only day 151. The other key finding was that his body temperature, which also has a circadian pattern (normally it falls in the evening, before sleep, and rises in the morning as we wake) became dislocated, or decoupled, from the sleep rhythm; for Siffre, it did lengthen to around 25 hours, but was far more consistent than his sleep/waking pattern so that eventually the two circadian rhythms were desynchronised. This is strong evidence that we have at least two body clocks controlling these rhythms.

Siffre's cave study was a single case, and however striking the findings it would not be sufficient on its own to establish theories of body clocks – that is not the way science works. However, more controlled free-running studies with more participants have come up with similar findings; both the sleep/waking and body temperature circadian rhythms are maintained but extend beyond 24 hours, with the body temperature rhythm staying more consistent.

The general conclusion is that the body clocks can regulate circadian rhythms in the absence of external environmental influences (technically known as 'external zeitgebers', from the German for 'time-givers', i.e., ways to reset clocks), but with some variation from the 24-hour pattern. To be perfectly attuned to the 24-hour light/dark natural circadian world, some fine-tuning is required, and this involves our key zeitgeber, light.

Body clocks and zeitgebers

The master body clock controlling circadian rhythms is found in the suprachiasmatic nucleus (SCN), part of the hypothalamus in the basal forebrain. This in turn controls body clocks found throughout the body. SCN neurons have one astonishing quality; they have an intrinsic ('inbuilt') circadian firing pattern. When its connections with the rest of the brain are cut, or even when SCN neurons are cultured in the laboratory, they maintain a circadian pattern of activity (more active in daylight hours). Further confirmation comes from transplant studies. When SCN neurons from hamsters with an abnormal 20-hour circadian rhythm are transplanted into hamsters with the standard 24-hour pattern, they impose the 20-hour rhythm onto the recipients. Damaging the SCN abolishes circadian rhythms in sleep (although total sleep time remains the same) and in other physiological processes such as body temperature.

This intrinsic rhythm of SCN neurons is genetic, controlled by a number of 'clock' genes whose detailed description is beyond the scope of this book. Body clocks and their genes are found throughout the body, but the SCN acts as the 'master' clock. However, as we have just seen, left to its own devices in free-running studies the SCN can control circadian rhythms but slightly out of phase with the external world. Under normal circumstances our sleep/waking is in tune with light/dark cycles, so the intrinsic SCN circadian activity has to be synchronised, or 'entrained', with the outside world. To do this, the SCN needs to receive information from the outside world.

The key zeitgeber is light. The retina lining the eye contains layers of cells responsible for visual perception. Most of the output from retinal cells is transmitted through visual pathways to visual processing areas in the occipital, parietal, and temporal cortices. However, a specialised set of retinal ganglion cells respond to light input and send projections directly to the SCN via the *retinohypothalamic tract*. Through this input the SCN activity can be perfectly entrained to light/dark cycles in the outside world. SCN activity increases with light onset, and decreases with darkness.

The SCN is the master body clock, and it needs to be able to regulate the body clocks found throughout the body in tissues such as the liver and adrenal glands. A key player is the hormone melatonin, released from the pineal gland. This tiny structure, the size of a grain of rice, is buried deep within the brain between the thalamus and the brainstem (in birds and reptiles the pineal is close to the surface of the brain and can respond directly to external light passing through the skull). A pathway from the SCN to the pineal allows the SCN to control the secretion of melatonin from the pineal. As light fades away in the evening, SCN activity declines and its inhibitory control of the pineal and melatonin secretion weakens. In this way levels of melatonin rise as darkness falls, reaching a peak around 3–4 am, and then decline gradually with morning and daylight.

Melatonin is distributed around the brain and body, and influences sleep patterns and circadian rhythms of many physiological processes, including body temperature and the release of hormones such as cortisol and testosterone. It plays a central role in allowing the SCN to regulate and synchronise or 'entrain' the body's circadian rhythms.

Circadian rhythms, body clocks, and the genes that control them are found throughout the plant and animal kingdoms, and have evolved over millions of years. They have proved a highly effective way of synchronising brain (where there is a brain…) and body activity with the external world. That doesn't mean that they are perfect. There is natural individual variation, and modern humans have also found a number of ways to interfere with them *reaches for cup of coffee*.

Individual variation

The circadian sleep/waking cycle shows a normal distribution in the sense of when people feel most awake and alert and when they fall asleep (see Figure 8.3 for what a normal distribution looks like). For around 60% of people, the 'chronotype' (when they feel alert and when they feel sleepy) lies somewhere in the middle – feeling alert during the morning and progressively more sleepy during the evening. There are extremes – 'larks' wake early and feel sleepy early in the evening, 'owls' find it hard to wake in the morning but do not sleep until late at night or the early hours of the morning. Extreme larks may suffer from 'advanced sleep phase syndrome', and extreme owls, 'delayed sleep phase syndrome'. Although not common, they represent classes of sleep disorder, as both conditions can disrupt sleep and also desynchronise circadian control of other rhythms, such as body temperature and hormone release.

Chronotypes have a clear genetic basis, but we have already seen that circadian rhythm periodicity also depends on the natural light/dark cycle. So it is no surprise that exposure to artificial light in the evenings can reset the cycle, pushing sleep onset and waking later. So the advice is not to use smartphones and laptops after 6 pm (hard advice to follow…). However, this is not a new problem.

Modern living

Release of melatonin from the pineal is highly sensitive to light, natural or artificial. The invention and wide use of electric lighting at the beginning of the 20th century meant that everyday life, which would normally tail away as the sun went down and darkness descended (most people could not afford candles), could now extend into the evening. This automatically readjusted circadian rhythms, and one clear effect was that we now sleep for less time than we did 100 years go (7.5 as opposed to 9 hours), making sleep deprivation more likely. Given that sleep is essential for cognitive processes such as memory and attention and for physiological regulation, sleep deprivation in the short or long term can have serious effects.

So, in general, we live in a sleep-deprived world, though most of us can adjust to this without suffering too many consequences. But along with electric lighting, we have developed other ways of disrupting circadian rhythms and sleep.

Shift work and jet lag

Electric lighting allows for 24-hour working, whether on factory assembly lines or in the office. Many people work shifts, including doctors, nurses, air traffic controllers, and technicians running nuclear plants. A standard pattern would be eight-hour shifts, 12 midnight to 8 am, 8 am to 4 pm, 4 pm to midnight, with maybe a week on one shift, then a week on another. This has the obvious effect of having people with highly responsible jobs working at times when their biological systems are telling them to sleep. Circadian rhythms can readjust to a new pattern, but only over days or weeks, so the circadian rhythms of shift workers can be in a fairly constant state of desynchronisation with the outside world – in particular, the light/dark cycle.

Flying from the UK to the USA is another excellent way to disrupt our circadian patterns. The flight takes about six hours. Leaving at 12 noon UK time means arriving in the USA at 6 pm UK time but, given the time difference, it is about 1 pm USA time. Your biological clock is telling the body to start preparing to wind down towards sleep, but external zeitgebers such as light and social activity are pushing you to stay awake. This desynchronisation of our body clock and its associated circadian pattern from external zeitgebers is the likely cause of jet lag. When the body clock is ahead of local time (flying east to west) it is termed 'phase delay'; when flying west to east, with the body clock ending up behind local time, it is termed 'phase advance'. Jet lag is usually worse with phase advance than with phase delay, implying that our body clock finds it easier to adjust when it is ahead of local zeitgebers. Incidentally, one solution is to travel by boat, as this gives time for the body clock to slowly adjust to the time difference, and it's much more civilised. Note that flying north to south does not lead to jet lag, as you stay within the same time zone.

Jet lag is annoying, but only rarely a serious problem. However, for workers such as airline pilots and cabin staff, repeatedly exposed to body clock zeitgeber desynchronisation, the effects can be much more serious. Studies have found that aircrew on regular long-distance flights have higher levels of the stress hormone cortisol, perform less well on memory tests, and show damage to the temporal lobes. Similarly, regular shift work has been linked to higher levels of stress and an increased incidence of cancer and heart disease. Anecdotal evidence also suggests that impaired judgement and decision making in the early hours of the morning (when the sleep drive is strongest) lead to an increased likelihood of car accidents and may also have been factors in the nuclear meltdown at Chernobyl and the near meltdown at Three Mile Island.

Stress, Anxiety, Deadlines, and Doom...

Throughout 400 million years of animal evolution, the driving force has been for animals to reproduce and pass on their genes to following generations (modern humans have complicated this process with our rapid social, cultural, and technological advances, but the drive is still there, if not so obvious). To do this, the animal has to survive. Survival means developing systems to detect threat and then to avoid it or deal with it. The problem for modern humans is that we still have these systems, but the nature of the threats has changed.

The zebra on the African savannah (let us call him Marty) needs to be able to detect predators at a distance, then take avoiding action by running as fast as possible in the opposite direction. The zebra needs cortical systems to perceive the situation, threat-evaluation centres in the limbic system (especially the amygdala), then pathways to the body's arousal systems to enable a rapid response. All fairly straightforward when the threats are external and the responses clear cut, e.g., running away… but in today's world, the main threats or stressors do not usually involve lions and cheetahs, and the response of running away as fast as you can, but actual or anticipated internally generated anxieties about finances, relationships, examinations, and global warming, to name but a few potential worries. Unfortunately the conserved threat systems of the brain do not discriminate between different types of threat, but will alert the body's arousal systems regardless of whether there is a cheetah in front of you, whether you are worrying about an exam lying in bed at 3 am in the morning, or whether you are deeply concerned about climate change (see Chapter 10). Before considering the implications of this, we need to look at the arousal systems themselves.

Hypothalamic-pituitary-adrenal axis and the sympathetic-adrenomedullary pathway

If cortico-limbic systems identify threats, either external or internally generated, two major pathways are activated. Both focus on the adrenal glands, found just above the kidneys in the lumbar region of the body. Each adrenal gland is made up of two distinct components, the adrenal cortex and the adrenal medulla.

Hypothalamic-pituitary-adrenal (HPA) axis

The hypothalamus lies at base of the brain. It is connected by a stalk, the infundibulum, to the pituitary gland, which lies just below the brain in the cranial cavity. We can think of the pituitary gland as a sort of 'master gland', because it secretes many hormones into the bloodstream that in turn control other glands and major physiological systems of the body. Neurons in the hypothalamus synthesise corticotropin-releasing factor, a chemical that then passes down the infundibulum to the pituitary gland where it stimulates the release of adrenocorticotropic hormone (ACTH) into the bloodstream.

ACTH is carried to the adrenal gland where it stimulates the adrenal cortex to release a range of steroid hormones, the glucocorticoids and the mineralocorticoids. For the stress response, the key hormone released is the glucocorticoid cortisol (cortisol is closely related to corticosterone, and in fact corticosterone is the main stress hormone in other

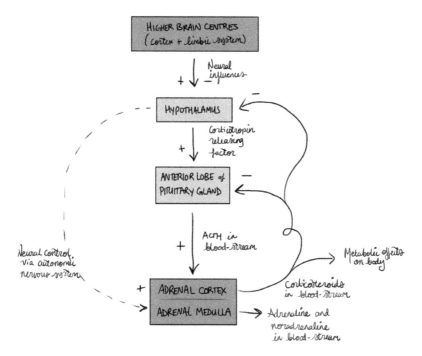

Figure 6.2 The HPA axis

species such as rats, mice, and birds). Cortisol release is associated with a range of effects in the body. The most important are raised blood levels of glucose (to be burnt up in muscular activity) through mobilising energy reserves, and suppression of the immune system. There are also direct actions on brain systems, which we look at later.

Sympathomedullary (SAM) pathway

The autonomic nervous system (ANS) is that part of the nervous system that regulates our internal physiological processes. Through direct connections to internal organs such as the heart, circulatory system, digestive system, and various glands, the ANS controls our internal environment. It has two branches, the sympathetic and the parasympathetic. When the sympathetic branch is dominant, we have a pattern of bodily arousal, with increased heart rate and blood pressure. When the parasympathetic branch is dominant, the pattern is one of relaxation, with decreased heart rate and blood pressure, and increased digestive activity. Control centres ('autonomic nuclei') for the ANS are in the brainstem, with neural pathways running from there down through the spinal cord and spinal nerves to connect with internal organs. The ANS functions largely automatically (we don't have to think about increasing heart rate when running upstairs, it just happens), but it can be recruited or modulated by higher brain centres when necessary.

If threats are detected, signals from higher brain centres activate sympathetic pathways. This leads directly to, for instance, increases in heart rate and blood pressure. Another pathway connects with the adrenal medulla, and stimulates the release of adrenaline and noradrenaline into the bloodstream. The effects of adrenaline in particular are to reinforce the effects of general sympathetic arousal, with its well-known effects in raising heart rate and blood pressure. It also contributes to mobilising energy reserves and increasing blood levels of glucose and free fatty acids.

The big picture

So the picture we end up with when faced by threat or stress is one of preparation for physical action. Blood flow to muscles is increased, providing oxygen for muscular activity, fuelled by raised blood levels of glucose and free fatty acids. Functions we don't need at the time are inhibited. This includes the immune and digestive systems. As we and Marty the zebra both run faster when lighter, urination and defecation are stimulated. The SAM pathway provides a rapid activation of this arousal pattern, which is sustained by the slower acting, hormonally based HPA axis, with cortisol levels peaking at about 20 minutes after the threat is perceived.

Escape from a cheetah is time-limited; either Marty escapes or he doesn't (*tears*). Once a threat is resolved successfully, the stress arousal systems calm down using negative feedback systems. There are receptors ('glucocorticoid receptors') in the frontal cortex and hippocampus that are sensitive to levels of cortisol in the bloodstream. As the levels increase in times of stress, they stimulate these receptors and trigger the negative feedback system that tries to shut down the HPA and so reduce cortisol levels. If the stress persists this negative feedback will be overridden by higher brain centres and high levels will be maintained, but once the stress disappears, negative feedback will return the HPA to normal functioning. It is important to note that the HPA and cortisol secretion are active all the time as cortisol is involved in normal regulation of physiological systems. Cortisol secretion has a regular diurnal rhythm (high levels in the morning) and there is evidence that it has a role in synchronising body clocks and diurnal rhythms generally.

Our stress arousal systems are evolutionarily old, and geared to providing the resources to respond physically and over a short period to time-limited threats and stressors. Returning to the problem outlined earlier, modern life unfortunately does not work like this. Worries and anxieties can last over long periods ('chronic' stress as opposed to 'acute' short-term stress), and if severe enough will lead to extended activation of the HPA and SAM pathways. The pioneer of stress research was Hans Selye, working in the 1930s and 1940s. His initial findings with rats showed that chronic stress led to gastric ulceration and ultimately death, and he produced a simple model – the General

Adaptation Syndrome – of how stress could lead to disease. The first stage is the alarm reaction, when the stressor is first identified and the HPA and SAM systems are activated. The second stage is resistance, when the body's stress systems attempt to cope with the stressor. The third stage is exhaustion, when the body's ability to cope with the situation is overwhelmed, arousal systems are depleted, and stress-related illness may follow. This model has been extremely influential, although in one important aspect it has been shown to be wrong. We never actually run out of cortisol or adrenaline, and it is the prolonged activation of stress systems that leads to illness rather than their depletion.

Long periods of raised blood pressure can mechanically damage the linings of blood vessels. Combined with high levels of fatty acids in the bloodstream, these areas of damage can act as targets for the formation of fatty plaques, or atherosclerosis, which narrow the blood vessels and can lead to blood clots and strokes. Glucocorticoids such as cortisol also suppress the immune system, which in the long term makes the individual more susceptible to disease. So if you do go down with a stress-related illness, we can probably tell you why – and note that stress-related effects are not necessarily physical, as depression is one of the key recognised consequences of long-term stress.

Incidentally, 'allostatic load' is the term used to describe the pressure exerted on the body and brain by chronic stress. It is increased by prolonged periods of stress-related arousal, and reduced by effective coping responses that remove or reduce levels of stress.

Stress and the brain

Cortisol binds to glucocorticoid receptors, which are found widely distributed throughout the brain. We have already seen their role in HPA negative feedback pathways, but their location in frontal cortex, limbic system (hippocampus and amygdala), and brainstem areas suggests a wider involvement in behaviour and cognition. This suggests that stress-related arousal will also be associated with changes in brain systems, and over recent years this has been confirmed.

In general there is a shift from top-down control of behaviour to more bottom-up automatic control to react rapidly to a threatening situation. This is shown by a narrowing of attention (so fewer distractions) and reduced cognitive flexibility (the ability to shift cognitive strategies to cope with different situations). Marty the zebra, faced with the cheetah, does not want to be thinking about where the best grassland is, but needs to concentrate finite physical and cognitive resources on escape. General response inhibition is increased, so actions competing with fight-or-flight are suppressed. Overall the picture is similar to the pattern of stress-related physiological arousal, with all systems geared to coping with the immediate short-term situation. But the chronic stress experienced in modern life also means that prolonged activation of brain systems by cortisol and other stress-linked hormones can increase the allostatic load and lead to pathology.

The hippocampus is a main target for cortisol, but it turns out that repeated exposure to cortisol leads to the death of hippocampal neurons and reduced hippocampal volume. As the hippocampus plays a key role in memory consolidation, it is no great surprise that chronic stress can impair memory. There are also individual differences. Early experience sets up our stress pathways. The work has been mainly done on rats and mice, but there is also evidence from humans that some stress early in life fine-tunes the stress system; however extreme early abuse or deprivation makes our stress response hypersensitive. Adolescents and adults who have suffered such stressors have higher circulating levels of cortisol and a more reactive system generally.

Coping with stress – taking control

Our friend Marty, who has by now escaped the cheetah (phew), is not standing around wondering how to cope with the cheetah problem, not to mention the lions and hyenas. He has used an evolutionarily conserved set of response systems to escape. They have done their job in a reactive and automatic way. Mindfulness and yoga are no help to the zebra, but how about us?

It is hard to define stress in a very specific way, but Lazarus in the 1980s came up with a sensible and useable approach – a state of stress exists when you *perceive* a gap between the demands being made on you and the resources you have to cope with them. The difference between this and earlier approaches was the emphasis on perception and interpretation – cognitive processes.

One student may perceive an upcoming exam as demanding and stressful and their preparation inadequate, another may see the exam as a breeze as they have done at least two hours of work (we hope our sons are reading this). Of course these perceptions may have nothing to do with reality. The first student may be stressed but do brilliantly, the second may not do well but at least hasn't been stressed by it. This is because our perceptions may not be accurate. We may overestimate the demands of stressors, and underestimate our resources. So Lazarus' contribution was to shift the focus from the nature of stressors to our perception and interpretation of them, and to emphasise our ability to reframe experience in different ways. We have inbuilt stress pathways, but even these can be modulated by higher cognitive processes.

There is a whole industry producing books on how to cope with daily stress, but essentially there are only a few basic principles. Perhaps the most important element is control. Uncontrollable events are usually unpredictable and highly stressful. Rats and monkeys given unpredictable mild foot shocks have high levels of cortisol and will develop gastric ulcers if the shocks go on long enough (these studies were done before ethics was a factor in neuroscience. They would not be done today). Give them a lever to press and levels of cortisol decrease, even if the presses don't affect the number of shocks – the illusion of control is very powerful. If the presses enable them to avoid most of the foot shocks, levels decrease even more. In people, the focus has been on a personality variable, *locus of control*: a high internal locus means that you feel in control of most things that happen in your life; a high external locus of control means that you feel at the mercy of life events. A high internal locus is associated with lower stress responses (but don't try and control things that you cannot – dealing with life-threatening illness is usually best left to the medical professionals). Many approaches to coping with stress focus on developing a realistic perspective on the stressors in your life (we have a strong tendency to magnify the pressures on us), and then acquiring skills to improve your control of them. Of course, some major life events such as bereavement cannot be reframed as less than stressful, but an awareness that sadness and mourning are natural reactions can help.

At such times, social support is seen as a valuable resource, and in fact over the last 30 years, research has shown social support to be a critical factor managing stress. Infant monkeys separated from their group show increased stress responses. If reunited with their group, these disappear; but if put in with strange monkeys, responses stay high. Laboratory studies have found that people show a significant stress response when asked to do mental arithmetic, but this is reduced in the presence of a companion, or even their pet dog. Isolation in childhood with little or no physical contact can lead to a more reactive stress system, while social support has been shown to improve the course of and psychological adjustment to serious illness such as cancer.

We are social animals, with brain systems dedicated to monitoring and negotiating our relationships with others (see next section), so it is perhaps no surprise that social support should also be a key element in coping with stress. Evolution of the human social brain has enabled much more top-down control of our reactions to stressful situations, even if it does not always work in the face of our evolutionarily conserved stress arousal systems.

Staying Alive and the Search for Love

We all have a hunger for love. First we'll deal with hunger, then with love.

Ever since life evolved, it has had one basic aim – to survive and reproduce so that your genes continue into the next generation. Of course, humans have managed to complicate things… for Marty the zebra on the African savannah, it remains fairly simple. Find food, water, and mates, and try to ensure you and your kin avoid cheetahs. Zebras do not spend much time planning careers or trying to win the 1,500 metres at the Olympics.

Abraham Maslow, an influential humanist psychologist prominent in the 1960s, produced a pyramidal model of human motivations. At the bottom were physiological needs (food, water, etc.), then safety needs (feeling secure in your life), then love and belonging (self-explanatory), followed by esteem (respect from others), and finally self-actualisation.

This top level, that few people reach, is what we all aspire to. It represents the peak of personal growth and understanding, with high levels of morality, creativity, and respect for others. Maslow's idea was that we cannot move to higher levels until we have satisfied the lower levels of this 'hierarchy of needs'. This seems clearly mistaken. Think of the starving artist in his or her garret, producing wonderful works of art – they seem to have skipped some of Maslow's levels. But the hierarchy does reflect the complexity of human motivations; we feel we are driven by more than just the desire to survive and reproduce.

However, we do need to survive in order to pursue the 'higher' drives, and to fulfil the fundamental evolutionary goal of reproducing. For this, we need to consider the idea of homeostasis.

Homeostasis

The term 'homeostasis' was introduced by Walter Cannon in the 1920s, and refers to the maintenance of a constant internal environment. This means that the body tries to regulate various key processes within relatively narrow limits. The best example is body temperature, which under normal circumstances does not vary much from 98.6 degrees Fahrenheit (37°C), but the term covers a huge number of variables. Another useful concept is 'set-point', the target setting for these variables. For temperature it is 98.6, while other examples are set-points for body weight and fluid balance. A deviation from the set-point triggers a 'drive' to return to the set-point. For body weight it would be hunger, for fluid balance it would be thirst. Once homeostasis has been restored, the drive disappears.

Homeostatic drives are the equivalent of Maslow's physiological needs. Unfortunately, though basic, they are also complex. However, although many hormonal, neural, and biochemical systems are involved, any discussion of homeostatic drives begins with the hypothalamus. This relatively small structure (about the size of the tip of your little finger) at the base of the brain is central to a variety of physiological processes and behaviours linked to basic drives. These include hunger, thirst, temperature control, reproductive behaviour, and aggression. Despite its size, the hypothalamus can be divided into around 15 identifiable nuclei (remember that a nucleus in the central nervous system is a cluster of neuronal cell bodies), some of which we met in relation to sleep.

Using hunger and feeding behaviour as an example, we can gain a sense of how the brain manages these basic drives. Lesions to different hypothalamic nuclei can stop feeding in hungry animals, or maintain feeding in satiated animals. But the brain has no sensory receptors of its own, so it needs feedback from bodily systems to regulate feeding. For short-term regulation of meal size, feedback comes from the presence of food in the mouth and stomach via neural pathways, and release of hormones such as ghrelin from the stomach and small intestine as food passes through. For long-term regulation of body weight, feedback comes from the release of the hormone leptin from the body's fat stores ('adipocytes').

Of course, cognitive factors are also important. You have to find and prepare food. The sight and smell of food can increase or decrease motivation to eat. Taste is crucial – sweet foods are pleasant and in some cases addictive; studies on the Pima Indians of Arizona and Mexico find low levels of obesity and Type 2 diabetes in those in Mexico who largely retained their traditional diet, but extremely high levels of obesity and diabetes in those in Arizona who, through government intervention (however well-intentioned), have diets with high levels of refined carbohydrates such as sugar. The epidemic of obesity in Western societies has been attributed to our highly processed diet, especially rich in sugars and sweeteners such as fructose. Why does this happen if we have sophisticated homeostatic mechanisms to control food intake and body weight?

Well, they are not that sophisticated. They evolved when the priority was to stay alive in environments which were unpredictable in terms of food supply. Carbohydrates, especially sugars, are rich sources of energy and therefore prioritised, i.e., they have high reward value. So any food stimulating our sweet taste receptors on the tongue is prized. We have receptors for a range of tastes (sweet, sour, salty, bitter, and umami, or savoury, linked to meat), which allows us to find a balanced diet while avoiding dangerous foods. Unfortunately the combination of sweet taste and activation of our brain's reward networks can override the need for a balanced diet and lead to obesity. So besides physiological and cognitive factors, we also have to account for social and cultural changes in food availability.

So even a straightforward homeostatic drive such as hunger and feeding behaviour has complex and evolutionarily ancient mechanisms that can be disrupted by social and technological developments. In this sense we have parallels with our stress response systems, and with our sleep networks. They are all struggling with the rapid pace of social and technological change.

Homeostatic drives are interesting up to a point, but other motivations further up Maslow's hierarchy are better illustrations of how the modern human brain has adapted its inherited networks to cope with the complexity of social behaviours and relationships.

Oxytocin and the search for love – cuddle, huddle, or a bit of everything?

The basic aim of life is to keep going, long enough to have offspring to carry your genes on and on through the generations. *Homo sapiens* has made this a little more complicated, with our variety of more complex needs and motivations, but we have built this variety on the back of the fundamental need to reproduce. All animals, from the single-celled amoeba onwards, reproduce, but while the amoeba just divides itself in two (which makes everything much simpler), our evolutionary progression has introduced far more complex genetic, neural, biological, behavioural, and social systems linked to reproduction. Luckily, this is not the place to go into the evolutionary advantages of most of these developments, but a few points are clear.

As we saw in Chapter 5, the evolution of the modern human brain has been linked to our complex human social networks. Even at a basic level we need to keep track of family, friends, enemies, who we trust, who we need to avoid. This requires a lot of cognitive processing – information processing of immediate interactions, such as attention, evaluation, organising responses, remembering practical and emotional consequences. Those group members helped find food, that feels good, stay close and trust them; those group members who did not help but took some of the hunt anyway, not so good, avoid in the future, do not trust. Any social animal has to do this at some level, especially non-human primates, who often embed their social interactions in a hierarchical dominance structure – everyone knows who is boss (more on that in Chapter 9). But below that level, chimpanzees and gorillas still show many complex social interactions, with collaboration, competition, aggression, and, of course, mate selection and reproduction.

But the study of the neuroscience of social behaviour is tricky. It's complicated – what bit of social behaviour do you want to study? In fact what we now know as social neuroscience has only been around for 30 years or so. Historically, neuroscience has tended to focus on the cognitive side of life – attention, memory, perception. These are pretty straightforward to measure and study in the laboratory, whereas social behaviour is difficult to measure and hard to study realistically in a lab setting.

Evolutionary psychologists have always taken the view that human social behaviour, and in particular mate selection (choosing a partner to breed with, to put it bluntly), has its roots in our genetic heritage, the drive to reproduce. So, for instance, it is still a popular view that females, with a limited number of eggs, have a greater investment in mate choice and look for a mate with resources to support them through pregnancy and child-rearing. Males, with a pretty well unlimited supply of sperm, have an evolutionary drive to mate with as many females as possible (spreading their genes far and wide). So, females are choosier than males; though with the introduction of contraception in the 1960s (separating sex from reproduction) and many more females in the workforce with successful careers, the situation is now far more complicated.

But, whatever the long-term aim, we still seek partners, we still need to identify who we trust, we need to recognise our families, and also threats from other group members. This social behaviour has been increasingly studied by neuroscientists, and it has given us a rather different perspective on the scope of neuroscience. Most books on neuroscience and behaviour, including this one, focus on the brain, but we also have physiological systems throughout the body that need to be controlled by and to feed back to the brain.

We have seen how peripheral physiological arousal needs to be coordinated with the body's demands in states of stress, involving the ANS (control centres in the brainstem) and the pituitary-adrenal axis (release of hormones into the bloodstream).

With social behaviour we meet another key hormone, *oxytocin*. Research into the role of oxytocin in social behaviour began in the 1980s, using the prairie vole (a mouse-like mammal), for reasons we will come to soon. Since that beginning, there have been upwards of 25,000 research papers on oxytocin… why this degree of interest? First of all, some background.

Figure 6.3 The prairie vole and oxytocin

Oxytocin – evolutionary origins and functions

Oxytocin is a small peptide hormone (peptides are made up of basic units called amino acids; lots of peptides linked together make up proteins). It consists of nine amino acids, and has a close relation, *vasopressin*, a hormone which only differs by two amino acids from oxytocin. These hormones have been identified in primitive animal groups such as snails, fruit flies, and nematode worms, and are thought to have evolved around 700 million years ago, with the final modern form that is found in humans emerging around 200 million years ago. This is what we call a highly conserved (i.e., hasn't changed much) and ancient evolved system.

Clearly oxytocin has been important for animal behaviour for millions of years. Snails and nematodes are relatively simple animals without complex nervous systems or social behaviour (though they do have some, as even snails and nematodes need to reproduce), but oxytocin systems have continued to evolve and have an enormous and complex range of functions in the mammalian body and brain.

Oxytocin functions in both the brain and the body, acting on oxytocin receptors on brain neurons and on cells of the body. It is initially synthesised within neurons in the supraoptic and paraventricular nuclei of the hypothalamus. An important projection from the paraventricular nucleus (PVN) runs to the pituitary gland (see p. 128), from where oxytocin can be released into the body's circulatory system to act on the body. Other oxytocin pathways run within the brain from the PVN to limbic areas and ANS centres in the brainstem. Important limbic targets include the amygdala, septum, and hippocampus, while other pathways innervate the nucleus accumbens, the caudate nucleus, and cortical regions. So, what you can see immediately is that oxytocin has the potential to affect a wide range of bodily and brain functions. And it does.

It has long been known that oxytocin plays a key role in reproductive behaviour in humans, from sexual receptivity and sperm ejaculation, to uterine contractions during birth and lactation (milk production) in the mother. These are important functions, but research over the last 50 years has shown that oxytocin's role extends to other stages of reproduction – initial partner selection and pair bonding, and maternal bonding with the young. And this is where the humble vole comes in.

There are about 150 species of vole, small rodents related to hamsters. What attracted researchers was the fact that some species are monogamous (one stable mating relationship between a male and a female), and some are polygamous (multiple partners). Pair bonding and maternal bonding can be studied in the laboratory, with oxytocin systematically administered either into the body or the brain. Brain distribution of the peptide or its receptors can also be mapped. In humans, studies are usually restricted to less controlled administration of oxytocin via a nasal spray.

In the monogamous prairie vole, oxytocin is critical in pair bond formation. Administration facilitates partner preferences and pair bonding in female voles, while oxytocin antagonists (which block the action of oxytocin in the brain) prevent pair bonds from forming. Other studies show that partner preferences are linked to increased oxytocin receptors in the nucleus accumbens, a key part of the reward network. Separation from a partner decreases oxytocin synthesis in the hypothalamus, and alters the expression of receptors in the nucleus accumbens. After pups are born, oxytocin supports nurturant behaviour in the mother, and increases aggression to intruder voles. In humans, maternal levels of oxytocin during pregnancy correlate with bonding and affiliative behaviour towards the newborn baby.

Oxytocin has broader roles in social behaviours. Stress early in the prairie vole's life leads to difficulties in forming adult pair bonds, and this is linked to decreased oxytocin receptors in the amygdala. On the other hand, an enriched, stimulating early environment leads to an increase in oxytocin receptors in the prefrontal cortex and amygdala. So the oxytocin system is extremely sensitive to early experience. And if we are talking evolution-ary continuity, and we are, note that the human adult stress system can also be heavily affected by early adversity, though there is no evidence yet that this involves oxytocin. In adult voles, oxytocin is also responsive to stress, in particular separation from the partner. This leads to decreased synthesis in the hypothalamus and a decrease in receptors in the nucleus accumbens.

The montane vole is a closely related species but does not form pair bonds. Whether or not a vole species is monogamous, forming pair bonds or not, is related to ecological factors. Prairie voles live in environments with low food availability, low population density, and high risk of nest predation (losing pups to predators); this combination seems to promote monogamy, with males taking an active part in caring for the young. Given the different lifestyles of monogamous prairie voles and polygamous montane voles (if voles can be said to have lifestyles…), you might expect major differences in oxytocin systems as these are central to pair bonding in prairie voles. However, montane voles have similar levels of brain oxytocin, though there are significant differences in distribution, neuronal release, and the distribution of receptors in the brain. Notably, the brain anatomy of prairie and montane voles is otherwise highly similar. What we are seeing is a differential activation of oxytocin systems (and linked neural circuits) depending on genetic and environmental factors; in this way, social behaviour can be tuned into the particular demands of a species and of indi-viduals. However, note that there are also differences in oxytocin distribution between males and females, and also differences between individuals of the same species.

Oxytocin in humans

The oxytocin system is a highly conserved system central to social behaviours in simple organisms such as nematode worms and more complex ones such as the prairie vole. On the basis of evolutionary continuity we would expect it to be involved in social behaviour in humans, especially given the similarity in oxytocin brain networks across species. Humans are a little more complicated than voles, so precise experimental work is more difficult. The most popular approaches look for changes in salivary or blood plasma levels of oxytocin in response to various factors and challenges. Alternatively, oxytocin is given via an intranasal spray (with little control over absorption and blood/brain levels).

However, given the thousands of studies done, some general conclusions emerge. In studies using judgements of facial expressions, oxytocin increases ratings of trust and decreases ratings of fear (linked to decreased amygdala activity), but significantly more so for faces of similar ethnicity. 'Out-group' faces are seen as less trustworthy and more aggressive. Overall, oxytocin is seen to increase social affiliation to an in-group, but is sensitive to in-group/out-group status; increased plasma levels are associated with per-ceived threat from out-groups. It may seem a bit of a stretch, but given the evolutionary continuity of the oxytocin system this can be seen as similar to oxytocin effects in prairie voles, facilitating pair bonding but also increasing aggression towards intruders.

In game-playing scenarios, oxytocin also increases levels of trust towards opposing players, and generally acts as a social facilitator; though bear in mind the in-group/out-group effects outlined above (see Chapter 10 for more on the neuroscience of trust).

Salivary levels of oxytocin are increased by breast feeding, sexual activity, 'comforting' social relationships, and physical exercise. Together with its effects on trust in others, it seems linked to close emotional relationships, and has become popularly known as the 'love' hormone. However, in view of the clear in-group/out-group effects and evolutionary background, it has been suggested that 'huddle' hormone is a better description – strengthening group relationships and group identity.

Although we have emphasised social behaviour, oxytocin is also involved in other key areas. It has anxiety-reducing properties, with increasing levels linked to coping with stressful situations. It is also an anti-inflammatory, damping down overreactive immune responses, and reduces the perception of pain. In fact a range of bodily processes is modulated by oxytocin, so to reduce it to just the 'love hormone' is really not being fair.

What we have is a highly conserved evolutionary system underlying human social cognition and behaviour. Oxytocin networks distributed throughout the brain evaluate the saliency of social signals; these have become more complex as societies evolve, perhaps driving brain evolution, including the oxytocin network. Species differences in the distribution of neurohormones and their receptors account for differences in social behaviour, from the nematode worm up to modern humans. It is an astonishing story, and not over yet; a very recent paper used genetic techniques to 'knock out' oxytocin receptors in prairie voles, and found that bonding behaviour and maternal care were largely unaffected. This goes against most current models of oxytocin function, and needs to be replicated, but implies that there are alternative networks that can take over if oxytocin systems are non-functional. Perhaps we should not be surprised that redundancy is built into the nervous system: over millions of years, it has had to respond to an ever-changing world, and by and large it has been pretty successful (a shout-out here to all those extinct species in which it hasn't).

A note on vasopressin

As pointed out earlier, vasopressin and oxytocin are closely related peptides with similar evolutionary histories. Attempts are sometimes made to show clear distinctions in their effects, e.g., that vasopressin increases and oxytocin decreases anxiety, or that vasopressin decreases parental investment and cooperation, while oxytocin increases them. However, they have overlapping distributions in the brain and can activate each other's receptors, so at this stage it is difficult experimentally to separate them and perhaps best to see them as two highly entangled systems.

To Compute or Not to Compute?

We will leave it up to you, then, as to whether you think it is useful to view the brain's activities in terms of computations or not. Neural activity seems to resemble a sort of information code to support flexible motor behaviours in response to sensory stimulation. But the communication of the brain to the body occurs both through electrical signalling via the nerves and hormonal signalling through the blood; and many neurons have receptors for those hormones which then modulate brain function and behaviour.

In the next chapter, we will return to the computational perspective and our comparison to the digital computer, in order to answer two questions: how does the brain get to work the way it does, since it has to grow from the humble beginnings of a fertilised egg? And how does it acquire new content – that is, how does it learn?

━━━━━ Box 6.2 ━━━━━

Decoding the brain

If the brain has a computational code, shouldn't we be able to *decode* it? Try imagining two different activities. Imagine first that you are playing tennis (we're sure you hit a mean backhand). Now imagine that you are walking through your home, perhaps looking around your kitchen. It turns out that imagining these two scenarios produces distinct patterns of brain activity. A truly ground-breaking study in 2010 used this distinction to investigate awareness in patients in a persistent vegetative state (PVS). PVS is caused by severe accidental brain damage, and leaves the patient apparently unconscious, comatose, and completely unresponsive to external stimuli. In the study, patients in PVS were asked to imagine the two activities, and astonishingly (though maybe nothing about the brain should astonish us) a few patients (fewer than 10%) could demonstrate the appropriate and distinct brain patterns. When asked to answer some basic questions by using 'playing tennis' as 'yes', and 'walking through their home' as 'no', their brain patterns indicated that these patients were demonstrating understanding and evidence of consciousness.

Since then our ability to 'read' the brain has advanced considerably. Using computer-based artificial intelligence to analyse brain patterns, we are close to actually identifying the content of mental processes (a recent report claimed that such patterns could be used to identify people vulnerable to schizophrenia). On the positive side these techniques are being used to help communication in people who are aphasic after brain damage; on the negative side it is likely that in the next decade or so we may be able to decode 'thoughts' and intentions from patterns of brain activity, a truly scary proposition. However, the scary part is probably inevitable, given that science progresses faster than our ability to handle the moral and ethical issues it raises (see Box 6.1).

7
HOW IT GETS TO WORK THIS WAY: DEVELOPMENT AND LEARNING

So far, we have talked about how the adult brain works. But of course, the brain has to grow from a single fertilised egg floating down a fallopian tube, navigating the stages of embryo and foetus, newborn, infant, toddler, childhood, adolescence, adulthood, and age-ing. There's a big difference between what four-month-olds can do (sucking toes is often enthralling) and what 14-year-olds can do (sophisticated arguments about why it isn't *fair* that they can't stay out late). Has the brain simply learned more facts and skills between these two time points, banked lots of experience, or has it changed the way it works? That will be the principal question of this chapter.

Again, let's start with our comparison to the digital computer. Imagine you unpack your new mobile phone handset and find in the box just a single silicon chip and a sliver of screen, just a flake of chrome housing. 'Don't worry', say the instructions, 'it'll grow into a proper phone, so long as you feed it. And it'll programme itself, so long as you interact with it and treat it right.' 'Oh, um, okay', you say uncertainly, 'but will it end up with the correct version of the latest operating system?' 'Yeah, definitely, sort of', reply the instructions, 'I mean, it depends on what they teach it at phone school.'

No, phones aren't like that. The phone you buy has a fixed way of working, fixed processor speed and memory, fixed screen refresh rate; you change its capability by downloading new software, new information. If you want a phone that works differently, you need to upgrade your handset.

Once the structures of the brain have grown, maybe its way of working is fixed in a similar way and then it just gains more knowledge. Alternatively, because the brain remains plastic throughout life and experience involves changing the connections between neurons (its microstructure), maybe the way it works also changes across life. The structures of the brain certainly grow quickly early on. The brain gets four times bigger from birth to adulthood, but 80% of that growth has already occurred by age two. In fact, put the brains of a three-month-old, a three-year-old, and a 30-year-old side by side, and the three-year-old's brain will look more like the 30-year-old's than the three-month-old's. However, simply measuring growth won't tell us what's going on functionally during development. For example, pretty much all the neurons you're going to get are present in your brain when you're born (only the hippocampus and olfactory bulb can add new neurons as they go). So what is it that's growing? To find out, we have to go back to the start.

Back to the Start

We have a single fertilised egg drifting in a fallopian tube. In its nucleus sit 23 pairs of chromosomes newly assembled from its parents, chromosomes whose DNA contains the instructions to build the body and brain (and heck, a placenta, too; all the instructions have to be in there). How are we going to get a brain? It will be a set of contingent steps, each building on the structures fashioned by the previous ones. Cells multiply and decide – based on sniffing the local chemical environment around them – to do different things, to become different types of cell. They permanently turn off some of their DNA instructions and activate others. A disk of cells forms, with three layers of different cell types. The top layer will one day make up skin cells, the brain, and peripheral nerves (this is called the ectoderm). The middle layer will one day make up muscles, connective tissue, bones and cartilage, blood and blood vessels, the dentine of teeth, and the tissues of the kidneys (this layer is the mesoderm). The bottom layer will one day make up the lungs and digestive tract and other internal organs such as the liver and pancreas (the endoderm). But all this is a long way off.

Let's zoom in on the top layer of the disk, where the cells to make the brain lie. A groove starts to form across the disk. The groove deepens. The sides bend over and close at the top to form a tube. This is the *neural* tube: one end of it will become the brain, the rest the spine. Inside the tube, 'progenitor' cells start dividing until they make a large pool, and then they churn out neurons. The best part of a hundred billion neurons needs to be made for the brain, as well as an equivalent number of glial cells to support their operation. The average rate of generating neurons prenatally is 250,000 a minute.

To get the components of the brain, separate regions of the tube are dosed with chemical signals that make them grow differently. Initially, three blobs form on the end of the tube. The frontmost will be what's called the forebrain – it will include the cortex, the cingulate gyrus, and the underlying limbic structures (amygdala, hippocampus, thalamus, and bits of the basal ganglia). The next blob back will make the midbrain (the substantia nigra, parts of the basal ganglia, low-level sensory systems such as the inferior colliculus for hearing, the superior colliculus for vision and eye movements, the reticular formation for arousal). The third blob will be the hindbrain (the cerebellum, the pons for interfacing with the cortex, the medulla for functions like breathing, heartbeat, and swallowing). Again, subdivisions within each blob will develop by dosing the cells within a given sub-region to get them to grow differently.

Those three blobs of forebrain, midbrain, hindbrain reflect the common brain growth plan across all vertebrates. But the three blobs are in a row and the human brain we know and love has layers, doesn't it? How are we going to get the layered structure from the three blobs? Well, the hindbrain tucks under the midbrain, and then the forebrain just goes crazy, massively expanding all the way under, and back around over the top of the midbrain. Now it begins to look like a real brain!

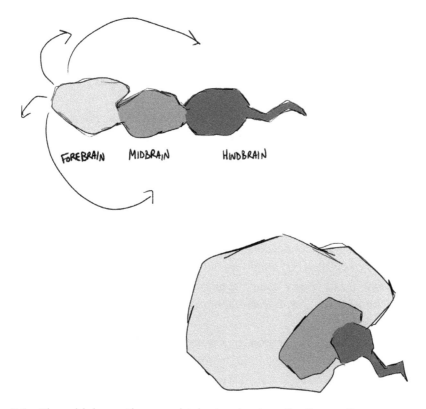

Figure 7.1 Three blobs on the neural tube turning into the 'layered' structure

As the foetus grows, much of brain development involves the production of neurons, moving them to the right place in the brain, differentiating them to be the right sort of neuron for that part of the brain – for example, neurons have to be different depending on which of the six layers of the cortex they find themselves in – and finally, getting the neurons to wire up to each other, both in terms of local networks, and in terms of axons that must navigate the long pathways that connect regions across the brain.

The progenitor cells are turfing out neurons at a hell of a rate. How do these neurons get to where they need to be? When the brain is still small, the distances the neurons must traverse are also small, so that the new neurons can literally reach out, get a hold of where they are supposed to go, and yank themselves over there (it's called somal translocation). When the brain grows bigger, there's further to go. The brain now establishes a system of guide ropes (so-called radial glial guides) which neurons can grab onto and pull themselves along. Typically, this movement is outwards to form layers (bizarrely, the six layers of the cortex form from lowest to highest, so each higher set of neurons must battle through the lower layers to get to the top: evolution... not perfect). The 'moving outward' is called radial migration. Lastly, some new neurons also move sideways along the growing cortex, so-called tangential migration. How do they know where to go? Local regions along the way release guidance molecules, a trail of sweeties to guide the way. The brain uses all sorts of tricks to grow. Indeed, it even builds some transitory scaffolding structures just to get the construction done, which later dissolve away (such as the 'subplate' sitting beneath the ultimate six layers of the cortex).

The next stage is for each neuron to become the neuron they're supposed to be (for that brain region) – to establish their preferred shape, neurotransmitters, and receptors; to connect to the neighbours; and to reach out axons that might have to extend long distances to fashion the long-range connections of the brain. Such architectural manoeuvres depend on chemical signalling of location that demarcates, for example, sensory and motor regions; these chemical gradients are the siren songs that beckon neurons to extend their axons out to distant locations. Neurons also position molecular markers on their surface to encourage connections from any axons (of neurons of the right type) that might touch them, so-called cell adhesion molecules. The reliance on chemical signalling to grow and wire up the brain, using chemical concentrations as markers of location, is one reason why embryos are so vulnerable to toxins or drugs ingested by the mother early in pregnancy.

If you put some embryonic neurons in a warm, friendly petri dish, it's a surprise to see how much they *wriggle*. They reach out to try and find other neurons, probing to connect. It reminds you that these are the distant descendants of single-celled organisms who chose to hang out together to make a bigger organism; and if necessary, to die for each other to keep that bigger organism going. The world of neurons can be brutal: the progenitor cells initially overproduce neurons, and amid this glut, a whole bunch of them will die... lonely neurons which never make enough connections, which aren't activated enough, and which then give up the ghost in a death spiral called 'apoptosis'. Only the well-connected survive.

When, then, does the growing brain come 'online' functionally? If it were your new phone handset, when could you, so to speak, make your first call? It's a much-debated point, because the growth progress is gradual; neurons will have some chemical and electric activity right from the moment they are spawned by the progenitor cells, but we're asking a question about when the whole system *switches on*. One candidate watershed is when the thalamus – the waystation receiving input from the senses and mediating the passage out to motor systems – establishes contact with the growing cortex so these systems can begin a dialogue. These pathways begin to form in the second trimester and are complete by the 26th week of pregnancy. Some argue that the establishment of this connectivity represents the lightbulb moment when the conditions for (some sort of) consciousness emerge. Neurons may have been active beforehand, but now the brain can sense its body, move its limbs, and listen to the faint sounds of music filtering in through to the womb. (If that has set you off thinking about consciousness, don't worry, we'll come back to it later in Chapter 9.)

Self-Organisation

Once it's wired up, how does the operating system upload, how do the parts of the brain gain their function? The potential functionality will have been specified by the major wiring diagram, the chemical signalling that has generated the major pathways from inputs and to outputs and between regions, as well as the local properties of neurons in different regions. But there's not much in the way of content. For that, you need self-organisation. This is a form of self-programming, a process by which neural networks adapt to extract patterns in the activity they receive and to learn useful associations. It's an emergent property whereby regions can develop overall functionality, such as the maps and hubs and hierarchies we saw earlier, from the many local changes happening at the level of each neuron, as it modifies its connections, and how and when it will become active.

For example, the different levels of the sensory and motor hierarchies are part of the broad wiring diagram, but the hierarchy doesn't yet have organisation. If you were to look at the system from a distance, all of it would be working, but none of its activation yet makes a lot of sense. At each level, neurons must decide who is going to do what, and then refine it. Neighbouring neurons strive to do similar things to each other but to do different things from more distant neurons, in a competitive process that leads to the emergence of maps. The bottom level of the hierarchy is the first to make sense of the input; then the next layer up makes sense of what it's hearing from below, then the next layer up, and so forth. Finally, the tops of each hierarchy have meaningful information and can begin to make links to each other. Slowly the functionality grows.

Here are some key points about this process. First, self-organisation depends on how the system is activated. That activity starts prenatally, with dulled senses and restricted motor movements. Some of the brain activity is internally generated and spontaneous – even activity that is no more than internal noise can be enough to trigger self-organisation (e.g., which areas of the lowest hierarchy of the cortical visual system will respond to the input from the right eye and which to input from the left, a separation that is required for the later development of depth perception). From this perspective, birth, though stressful, does not represent a radical change in brain development; instead, it is a radical change in the environment, the patterns of sensory activity that the brain is receiving, and the range of movements it can generate. It is the activity-dependent nature of self-organisation that allows the central nervous system to be a generalist, to adapt to the body it finds itself in and the world that body finds itself in (remember, the brain has no pre-specified banana detectors, see Chapter 2).

Second, the brain isn't some inert object, sitting around like a lemon; it doesn't absorb information passively like a sponge (it is not, in short, a lemon sponge). No, brains generate actions in the body to stimulate new brain activity via the senses. Children are active explorers, they probe and query the world. They test it, they mess around with it, and sometimes they even break it. (Both the authors have twin sons, and we're particularly thinking of you guys here.)

Next, the importance of self-organisation depends in part on how evolutionarily old the structure is. Structures like the amygdala and hippocampus have a longer evolutionary history and there has been time to select more detailed instructions specifying their growth and what sub-regions they will contain. The cortex, and particularly its large size in humans, is a more recent innovation (well, recent in evolutionary terms – the hominid brain has tripled in size over the last two million years). Outside of a few constant landmarks found across all mammals with larger brains, the cortex is mainly just a sheet of general thinking power. These landmarks are the primary sensory regions and the primary motor cortex, areas identified by the connections they receive from the thalamus and the order in which they are arranged. What the cortex will do depends on activity-driven self-organisation. The larger the size of the cortex, the greater the scope for self-organisation to yield refined hierarchical functional regions that can deliver sophisticated capacities like cognitive control. This may be why a big brain can produce behavioural flexibility and intelligence. Lastly, self-organisation needs to be robust to a bit of slipshod finishing in the manufacture. The detail shouldn't matter: the visual system shouldn't collapse if a given brain happens to have grown with only, say, 130 million neurons out of which to fashion the primary visual area in the occipital cortex rather than, say, 210 million. Work with what you've got.

There is a profound point lurking here, which we won't dwell on (because we prefer shinier, more superficial ideas). When it comes to the cortex, there is no destiny, no function that any region of the brain is 'meant to have' that is somehow determined by evolution. The consistent functions we see in the regions of the adult brain are the result of it developing in largely consistent bodies and consistent environments. But in a brain born into a body without certain sensory input, or into a body developing in a world without bananas to detect… but full of books, computer games, and touch screens, brain regions can develop to do different things, so long as the broad neural wiring diagram supports it.

What Grows?

Something doesn't make sense here. You may have spotted it. The brain gets four times bigger from birth to adulthood, but the baby is born with pretty much all the neurons it is going to have. So what grows? Where does all that extra volume come from if it's not more neurons? Part of the growth is in the size and shape of neurons; part is in the local connections (the dendrites and axons), together making up the grey matter; and much of it is in the myelin, the fatty substance that the oligodendrocyte glial cells deposit around the outside of axons to enhance their transmission speed, making up the white matter. This growth means that the cortex, initially smooth in the foetus, begins to wrinkle as it increasingly becomes too big for the skull. Where the cortical sheet is attached – the fibre tracts, the bundles of axons connecting regions – the wrinkling is constrained, so we see reasonably consistent gyri and sulci emerge. That's why neuroanatomists get to talk about 'the inferior frontal gyrus' (or Ronaldus McDonaldus, depending on your preferred naming scheme), because when you look at brains, you often find one.

While brain growth is continuous and smooth through childhood and adolescence and even into early adulthood, there are a few notable points. It is a non-linear growth: it happens faster earlier in development, and then it slows down. Next, growth is strategic. Just as the embryonic brain overproduces neurons and then kills off the ones it doesn't use, the postnatal brain overproduces connectivity (particularly in the form of synapses, but also axons and dendrites) and then cuts back the connections that haven't been used, in a process called pruning. Having lots of connections gives the brain plentiful scope to adapt to the world it finds itself in. But maintaining lots of connections is costly – it requires energy and nutrients. Highly connected brains are also at elevated risk of uncontrolled spread of neural activation, known as epilepsy. In young children, seizures can be induced simply by a fever (febrile convulsions). So eventually the brain moves to optimise – to consolidate the connections that have proved useful by myelinating them to improve efficiency, and to cut away the spare and costly resources (thereby reducing the risk of febrile convulsions – pruning means children can literally 'grow out of them'). Both processes of optimisation will reduce the scope of the system to change in the future – they reduce the brain's plasticity. Structurally, grey matter will therefore start to reduce, while white matter gradually increases across the lifespan.

Lastly, these changes happen at different rates across the brain. Grey matter volume, for example, peaks in the frontal and parietal lobes around 12 years of age after which grey-matter loss occurs, while the peak is around 16 years of age in the temporal lobes. Pruning starts at the bottom of the sensory and motor hierarchies and gradually works its way up. From a distance, it would look like a wave spreading across the brain, from back to front. The last areas to experience the pruning and the linked reduction in grey matter are the prefrontal cortex, as well as the tops of the sensory hierarchies in regions of the temporal and parietal cortex, which occurs in adolescence and early adulthood.

This means that the reduction of plasticity linked to optimisation (sometimes referred to as sensitive periods) is mainly a feature of low-level sensory and motor systems, and not really a feature of high-level concepts or ideas processed at the tops of the sensory hierarchies. Learning a new language as an adult is harder because the sensory systems struggle to master the new sounds and the motor system struggles to produce them. When we're older, we find it hard to learn subtle sounds in a foreign language, or to speak a foreign language without an accent. Sensitive periods don't really affect concepts, ideas, plans, or goals, which are flexible throughout life. And the brain is always plastic to some extent, otherwise you would learn nothing, and never remember what happened yesterday.

The early years are however particularly important for the tuning of emotion and reward systems, and the regulation of emotions. The early years prepare the individual for what kind of world it is. Dangerous or not? Should I crank up my stress response in preparation? When I'm hurt, will someone comfort me? In my interaction with caregivers, are they trustworthy and predictable, or do they sometimes let me down? Is the world going to be generally nice or mean to me? Is it worth holding out patiently for long-term rewards, or do those rewards sometimes not come? Should I just grab what's in front of me? Can I rely on the world, is it predictable, safe, can I take it for granted? Or is the world unpredictable, sometimes dangerous, so that I need to be vigilant, not relax but constantly monitor for threats, at the cost of heightened anxiety? Am I a good person or not? What do I deserve? Such lessons may last a lifetime, and in extreme cases may result in psychological disorders (see Chapter 8).

What Changes in How the Brain Works?

We've grown the brain. Now we're in a position to ask, what changes in its functioning as it gets older? How much is just addition of new information? Let's take a moment to distinguish development (growing the brain) and learning (adding new information). We'll be discussing learning in the second half of this chapter. From the brain's perspective, these two concepts can't be entirely separated since a large part of development and most of learning involves a similar mechanism – changing the strength of the connections between neurons (see Chapter 4).

But one can think of learning and development as concepts that differ over several dimensions. *Development* is slow, general, occurs in all healthy humans, and is usually irreversible. Both your brother's brain and your brain grew in similar ways. *Learning* can be fast, specific to domains, and can be lost through forgetting. You learned Spanish, your brother never did; then you forgot Spanish. *Development* is hard to accelerate (though it can be held back by deprivation) while *learning* can be increased through practice (back to your Spanish vocabulary homework, amigo). The two, of course, overlap: while development is taking place, the infant-toddler-child-adolescent-adult is learning all the time.

Here, then, is our list of what changes in the way the brain works as it develops. Recall the main principles: the brain is a set of content-specialised sensory and motor systems, whose activation is controlled by a goal-oriented modulatory system, which in turn is in conversation with emotion systems with their own appetites, an action selection system sensitive to rewards, and a motor-smoothing system.

First, the detail and resolution of the content-specialised systems increase. They get better at their job. Second, the speed of communication between neurons increases, which is particularly evident in the speed and finesse of motor movements. This is largely due to myelination. Better quality of neural processing improves accuracy, and how much information can be 'kept in mind' from moment to moment. Third, the modulatory system, sitting in the prefrontal cortex at the top of the hierarchy, is slowest to develop. It gradually improves in its ability to control the content-specialised systems, regulate the emotions, to strategically activate the appropriate knowledge and memories in the right contexts, and to stay on task. Fourth, the brain becomes better able to build plans that stretch deeper into the future. Fifth, the brain learns basic lessons about 'what works to get what I want', whether the world is generally a mean or a friendly place, and who are the crucial other people to rely on. Sixth, the dynamic coordination of all the parts of the brain improves, including the interface of plans, emotions, and actions. And the rest is just learning.

But Then the Brain Hits Puberty and Everything Goes Haywire…

You'll sometimes hear that. That the teenage brain is radically rewired, that it undergoes a major period of growth and restructuring. Certainly, there are major behavioural changes following puberty. Just when cognitive skills are reaching a new level of sophistication, adolescents stop wanting to be around their family and want to hang out with friends; the opinions of their peers become much more important, and there's an increase in risky behaviour around, for example, use of alcohol or sexual behaviours. Teenagers can sometimes behave in impulsive, irrational, or dangerous ways, seeming not to think things through, not to fully consider the consequences of their actions. Emotions can run high, in between long lie-ins. And there is increased vulnerability to mental health problems – of development spiralling into negative trajectories, while in others the spiral leads upwards in virtuous circles. That's the press, anyhow.

Figure 7.2 Teenagers are more likely than adults or children to indulge in risky behaviours to impress their friends

Only, when you use brain scanning technology to look at the structure of adolescent brains, as we've already heard, the changes from childhood are smooth, continuous. There is, actually, nothing radical going on in the structure of the teenage brain. All the radical growth happened prenatally and in the first couple of years of life. So, what's going on? How can behaviour be changing so dramatically if brain development is serene, just a smooth wave of maturation with the tops of the hierarchical systems maturing last?

This highlights a broader puzzle that nature has had to solve. One of the advantages of the large-brained great apes is the sophisticated skills they can learn to allow them to adapt to their environments. The downside is that a decent slice of brain development is occurring postnatally when the youngster has limited skills and is very vulnerable. For several years, the infant/child survives under the protection and nurturing of their parents. But then junior is all grown up and needs to make their way in the world – become an independent and responsible adult, figure out who they are, pursue friendships, romantic partners, a career, work out their priorities on family and community, and their fundamental beliefs. Not suck their toes or play *Space Invaders* all day, while their dinner is put on the table for them.

In short, at some point down the line, their behaviour has to radically change. But here's the challenge. *The brain has already been built.* Major rewiring is not an option. It would be like constructing a tractor and then one day insisting it now needs to be a racing car. Your engineer would frown at you. The wheels are wrong. The engine is wrong. How can nature solve this problem, how can it radically change the behavioural repertoires of an organism when it has long since finished sculpting the major structures of the brain?

To answer this, let's take a brief digression to a species where this challenge is writ even larger: the honeybee. (Hey, bear with us!) In the honeybee hive, different bees have different specialisms. There are cleaners, nurses for the hatching larvae, comb builders, guards, and lastly foragers, who head out to secure nectar and pollen from lovely flowers. Only, *these are all the same bee*, at different stages of its life. For instance, foraging flights take over from guarding around 20 days after the bee becomes an adult. This animal model enables a much more precise investigation of what triggers behavioural change and what in the bee brain is responsible, even at the level of gene expression.

The changes are not, for example, just driven by age. If you squish enough foragers (sorry!), the queen will detect insufficient food for its larvae, release a pheromone, and guards will start to prematurely turn into foragers. Brain structures, moreover, seem more closely tied to behaviour than to age (such as the lobes processing sensory information from the antennae). With the bee, nature faces the same problem. How do you turn a guard's brain into a forager's brain, when the bee brain is already built?

Here's what seems to happen. A combination of maturation and the queen's release of pheromones produces changes in the hormones in the bee's brain. These alter its motivation, the environments it wants to put itself in, and the experiences it finds rewarding. For example, one alteration is in the bee's preference to be in the dark or in the light: nurses like to be in the dark, foragers like to be in the light. That same hormonal change then increases the plasticity of the bee's brain so that it can learn new behaviours in the new environments its altered motivations place it in (particularly, in this case, visuospatial navigation). Hormones change motivation and reward; brain plasticity supports learning of new behaviours in new environments.

This is a recurring pattern. We've already seen in Chapter 6 how hormones can alter appetitive behaviours, such as social engagement, simultaneously raising the salience of social cues, the likelihood of initiating social behaviours, and the level of reward for those behaviours across different brain systems. We saw that in prairie and montane voles, two closely related species with almost identical brain structures, differences in the action of hormones such as oxytocin and vasopressin cause very different species-specific behavioural repertoires, from solitary to highly social behaviours.

Something similar, then, appears to happen in adolescence. With puberty, hormonal changes alter the motivations and rewards within the teenage brain. Greater activation is seen in the reward system, including in the nucleus accumbens within the ventral striatum, than is seen in either childhood or adulthood. Teenagers want to be with their peers and the positive opinion of peers becomes extremely rewarding – enough to undertake risky behaviours to impress, without a wider understanding of actual risks (i.e., lacking wisdom). A brain almost identical in structure to that of late childhood now generates modified behaviours, and it undergoes a period of fast learning – particularly in the prefrontal cortex with its extended developmental plasticity – about how to be a responsible (or irresponsible) adult.

The adolescent brain is not off the rails, it is not taking risks due to irrationality, impulsivity, delusions of invulnerability, or faulty calculations; rather, under the recast set of what's rewarding, when it comes to fooling around, in the moment those brains are making the judgement that *it's worth it*; and the bank of common sense has yet to accumulate sufficient credit to intervene. If you're driving a car, that kind of decision can go terribly wrong; if you're deciding to wear a stylish red trilby hat, not so much. But look, despite all this doom and gloom, these days most teenagers are pretty conscientious and hardworking, with all those exams to pass. We're with you, kids, not with all those boring grown-ups (a-hem).

Evolution's solution, to use hormones to manipulate motivation and reward in the initiation of behaviour in adolescence, is not risk-free. It can reveal underlying weaknesses in the dynamics of the system, and this explains the vulnerability to mental health problems observed in adolescence for conditions such as depression, anxiety, obsessive-compulsive disorder, addiction, eating disorders, and dangerous thrill-seeking. These are all maladaptive changes in the *do-it or don't-do-it to change how I feel* network, that is, oscillations between the behavioural initiation system, the limbic system, and the reward system (see Chapter 8 for more on psychiatric conditions). Adolescence is an odyssey, more challenging for some than others.

In Adulthood, It All Calms Down

In adulthood, it all calms down. By age 20, changes in the structure of the brain have stabilised. Grey matter is steady, white matter gently ebbs up across the years, reflecting changes in axons and myelination with continued skill acquisition. Adults are activating less of their brains than children or adolescents, consistent with the elimination of the over-capacity of connections (synapses) and the continuing growth of white matter that serves to tie brain regions together more effectively. It may appear that, in the absence of trauma, disease, or the surreptitious influence of 'lifestyle factors' (like jam donuts), stability reigns. But development is a process that continues across the lifespan, and subtle changes are afoot.

Figure 7.3 Adulthood is a period of relative stability

The 25-year-old brain is sleek, lithe, and optimised. From here, it's like elevators heading in opposite directions. In older adults, on the down elevator stand perceptual abilities, such as visual and auditory acuity. Reaction times slow, memory is poorer, and working memory capacity reduces. But on the up elevator stand general and verbal knowledge, creative problem solving, and wisdom. Experience tells – give older adults a 'Where's Wally' puzzle to spot a visual pattern in a cluttered field, and they will rely much more on attention and top-down strategies, rather than bottom-up detection of visual features. But give older adults a simple task like memorising a list of words while walking, and the requirement to do two things at once causes a decline in memorisation to focus on walking. The young adult can do both tasks at once without any loss of performance. As long as they are not looking at their phone.

Across adulthood, you can see subtle changes in brain structure. There's grey matter loss. This is no longer optimisation. It's probably not death of neurons, either; more likely shrinkage. White matter shows subtle alterations detectable in the fibre tracts linking distant brain regions, probably reflecting mild demyelination and loss of myelinated axons. These changes can be picked up in the pathways linking the two prefrontal lobes (possibly underlying declines in perceptual speed, as well as longer episodic retrieval reaction times, and difficulty retrieving names); in the pathways linking the cortex to the spine (reduced motor function); the output of the hippocampus (poorer episodic memory recall); and pathways linking posterior to anterior lobes of the cortex (poorer performance in cognitive tasks). Ah, we all lose our charms in the end.

It sounds bleak. But crucially, the adult brain retains plasticity. Functional performance can be retained by practice. And under the hood, there is a continuing dance between the processes of growth, maintenance, and the regulation of loss: the modulatory system in the prefrontal cortex is feverishly re-routing processes and bringing in other systems to maintain task performance. The ageing brain shows lower activation in the fading posterior content-specific systems, but greater activation in the prefrontal cortex; there is increased activation of the two hemispheres at once, as all hands are sent to the pump. In healthy ageing, wise old brains can still deliver impressive cognitive skills, before a cup of cocoa and a nap in the afternoon.

Of course, ageing may not proceed healthily. In dementia, neurons can be strangled by the build-up of protein deposits. The tiny blood vessels that feed neurons and glia can become clogged up and the circuits can become starved; blockages and bleeds can cause local regions to die, leading to strokes and the loss of entire abilities, like language. Functional deficits during pathological ageing depend on the regions affected, but the hippocampus (episodic memory, spatial navigation), the temporal pole (semantic knowledge), and the prefrontal cortex (attention, control, working memory) are particularly vulnerable.

It can never end happily. One day your phone is simply too old. It isn't fast enough for the new operating systems and software. It can't cope with modern life. Pop the handset in the back of a drawer and upgrade.

Learning

Now we're onto the easy bit: learning. This is just the insertion of new content, knowledge, and abilities into the brain. We don't have to worry about changing how the brain works, we're just – to use the phone analogy – downloading the latest operating system, downloading the latest apps… Here's *logical reasoning*… Here's *how to play tennis*.

There is a slight whiff of paradox around learning. We've just established that the healthy brain is plastic throughout its lifespan. It's always adapting, predicting, and evaluating rewards to update the value of actions, always laying down new episodic memories, always sleeping on it to distribute these memories into the far reaches of conceptual knowledge. The brain can't help but learn.

And yet, learning is such *hard work*, isn't it, sitting in the classroom, listening to the teacher, paying attention, being asked to think, to read books. *French vocabulary, capital cities of the world, elements of the periodic table, the formula for the distance an object has fallen while accelerating under gravity, books by Charles Dickens, the names of parts of the brain*. It's exhausting. Why? Why bother? Sometimes, learning is too much effort.

And then the dinner bell rings, and already my stomach is rumbling. Oh, oh, right, *some* part of my brain managed to learn the association between the dinner bell and lunch, yet the darned thing won't learn the atomic number for the element krypton. Thirty-six. *Thirty-six*. Colourless noble gas. Krypton, number of electrons per shell: two, eight, eighteen, and eight. *Two, eight, eighteen, and eight*. I wonder what's for lunch.

Perhaps the problem is that we're combining too many things under the umbrella of the word 'learning'. Learning has different meanings depending on whether you're working in education, psychology, or neuroscience. For the teacher, learning is the process by which students acquire new skills and knowledge, new activities they can do in the world. Learning involves a lasting change in pupils' capabilities or understanding. For the psychologist, the focus is on process. Here's one psychological definition of learning: 'a change in the efficiency or use of basic cognitive processes, both conscious and unconscious, that promotes more effective problem solving and performance in the tasks of everyday life'.[1] For neuroscience, we return to a familiar theme. What is one thing in education or psychology is many things in the brain. There are multiple neural systems underpinning learning.

Let's begin by getting a sense of why learning is hard. There's an old science fiction film called *The Matrix*, in which Neo (our hero) discovers his life is actually a simulation in a virtual world. He joins a group of rebels who want to overthrow the simulation and escape into the real world. The rebels have hacked the simulation program: now, in superhero guise, Neo can instantly be given new skills and knowledge to fight the baddies (who are agents of the program, merely seeking to debug coding issues like Neo). For Neo, the acquisition of new skills is just like uploading a new program to a computer: install and go! Need *martial arts*? No problem, install and go. Need to *fly a helicopter*? Install and go. But the brain takes much longer to learn. Why is that?

For the brain to learn, it needs to change the way neurons get activated by situations in the future. Mostly this is done by changing the strength of the connections between neurons; a bit by changing how ready particular neurons are to fire, that is, their 'resting' activity levels (see Chapter 4 on long-term potentiation). There are three reasons why this can't be done instantly like in *The Matrix*. First, for a given skill or piece of knowledge, no one knows what the computer program is to upload or, indeed, a way of uploading it.

The program must be worked out by the brain from the situations it is exposed to, and couched in a form sympathetic to the way that each individual brain has wired itself up over development. Second, mostly, learning isn't about memorising specific moments. What needs to be learned are often skills or concepts that have to be flexibly applied. It takes time to experience the range of situations to which the new knowledge is to be applied. Third, depending on the neural learning system involved, the connections change at different rates, some more slowly than others.

Most of what the brain experiences, however, it forgets. Information to be learned must be sustained in the brain and must be relevant to brain concerns. Famously, the brain can be blind to information entering the senses which is not the focus of attention (because it is engaged on another task). This is so-called inattentional blindness: for example, failing to notice a person in a black gorilla costume walking through a visual scene of white-jerseyed basketball players making passes, when the viewer has been assigned the task of counting how many passes the players make (check out this work at www.theinvisiblego-rilla.com/videos.html). Little will be learned about gorillas under these circumstances. Learning almost always requires multiple exposures, repetition. Although the brain can and does record snapshot memories, these are more often for reward-salient situations (be it pleasure or peril). Most learning is incremental and proceeds via repeated exposure.

There are, depending on how you count them, at least eight different neural systems underlying learning.

1   *Conceptual.* The brain learns associations between knowledge, between perceptual information and motor responses. It spots complex patterns within this knowledge, so-called concepts: of objects, categories, people, situations, and actions and action plans. These can be assigned emotional value or valence. This happens within and between sensory and motor hierarchies of the cortex, where changing connections can take hours.

2   *Control.* The modulatory system in the prefrontal cortex learns how to activate and deactivate the appropriate content-specific systems in the back of the brain to carry out tasks (it constructs the task schema); it learns how to negotiate with the limbic system so that emotions can be integrated with plans and goals.

3   *Procedural.* The procedural learning system learns activities that we perform frequently and often unconsciously, such as tying shoelaces, reading, reciting times tables, or driving a car. These automatic skills can take tens or hundreds of hours to learn through practice – repeating the complex activity repeatedly until all the relevant neural systems work together to deliver fluent performance, whether it's a motor skill or a thinking activity. The structures involved are the looping outer-to-inner circuits connecting the cortex through the basal ganglia to the thalamus and back again, as well as the cerebellum, a specialist in programming smooth motor sequences.

4   *Episodic*. This is the system for memorising specific moments, which produces your so-called episodic or autobiographical memory (e.g., what happened yesterday). This is the hippocampus and the structures around it. This system can change its connections in just seconds to record snapshots, particularly under situations of high reward value (good or bad).

5   *Emotional*. The amygdala is a structure that learns about situations linked to appetite and aversion, identifying the perceptual cues that signal them and driving the requisite behavioural responses, such as fight, flight, freeze, forage, feed, fascination, and other things beginning with *f* (the only letter the amygdala knows). As we've seen, hormones can influence the amygdala's preference for which type of behaviour it wants to initiate (today, are you a lover or fighter?). The amygdala is in close cahoots with the hippocampus to get it to record the places, spaces, and faces of situations where emotion-relevant events occurred and might occur again.

6   *Conditioning*. The dinner bell goes and your tummy rumbles expectantly. This is called classical conditioning, much studied in dogs who enjoy a bell and a snack (a nod there to Ivan Pavlov). A cue that reliably anticipates an event becomes associated with the event through repetition. It is an 'unconscious' form of learning, involving a deep grey matter structure (ball of neurons) sitting under the front of the brain called the nucleus basalis. When some salient event occurs (the snack), the amygdala signals the nucleus basalis, which disperses acetylcholine into the cortex. Recall, this is the neurotransmitter that says 'remember this', serving to increase plasticity and enhance learning. In the cortex, plasticity increases in the sensory systems to learn associations between perceptual information (the bell sound) and its consequences (being fed, experiencing pain).

7   *Reward-based*. This is the action selection system, the basal ganglia, which selects an action from the range of options proposed by the cortex (co-activated plans), and then pays close attention to whether the outcome was rewarding or not (so to bias the decision next time around) using the dopamine neurotransmitter system. When neuroscientists talk about the reward system, you'll often hear them using the term ventral striatum, the part of the basal ganglia that is dosed by dopamine (see Chapter 3).

8   *Mental effort*. It turns out that mental effort costs, and *the brain doesn't like paying*. This is unlike physical effort, where part of getting fit is to learn how hard you can push yourself. People tend to avoid mental effort and the brain tries to find ways to do that. It's continuously running the numbers about how much effort is likely to be involved to achieve an outcome, how likely success is, and how rewarding success will be. Is it worth the effort? Just to learn French vocabulary? The ventral striatum (see above) learns the potential rewards and their likelihood, the anterior cingulate (the middle manager who monitors progress) indicates how much the effort is hurting, and the ventromedial prefrontal cortex contains the currency of value upon

which French/no-French decisions are made (see Chapter 5, the section 'Keeping Score'). Why should mental effort cost? One idea is that extended use of the modulatory system in the prefrontal cortex (for cognitive control, avoiding distractions, and so forth) leads to build-up of toxic neurotransmitter metabolites (e.g., glutamate) from all that excited neural firing, and this is the accumulating 'cost' of mental effort. The amount of sustained activity must be limited to avoid damage, and balanced with the restorative rest that can clear these metabolites from the system. This creates a need for the brain to learn how to spend its mental effort budget effectively. The mental effort required of classroom learning is the explanation for why it seems such hard work, despite the brain's plasticity.

Eight interacting mechanisms of learning, then. And each has a preferred diet of experience that will optimise how abilities and knowledge change. The slow-changing systems have a limit to how much they can alter themselves in any one session (as students know, ten one-hour lectures spread over ten weeks are generally more effective for acquiring knowledge than one ten-hour lecture). Changes in cortical systems require consolidation during sleep. Preferred regimes may be more or less intense, either benefiting more from repetition (perhaps blocked, perhaps spaced out) or more from variety of examples.

The preferences of the learning mechanisms can be quite opposed. For example, concept learning benefits from interleaving material, mixing it up, which can serve to highlight the salient features of each concept. Procedural learning is messed up by interleaving. If you are learning the foxtrot, it is better not to interleave odd lessons on the tango, it will interfere. Instead, learn the foxtrot thoroughly, then extend to the tango by showing which parts are the same and which are different to the foxtrot.

Another example: novelty. Episodic memory loves novel situations, particularly affecting ones, like seeing the ghost of Elvis Presley riding an elephant down the street (see our puzzles at the very beginning of the book). The hippocampus gets all fired up. Conceptual memory, by contrast, finds it harder to learn information that is inconsistent with its previous knowledge, as the new information does not fit comfortably into the established networks of knowledge. Consistent knowledge can enter the content-specific systems with just a little help from the modulatory system. But inconsistent knowledge is a struggle and needs help from the instance-specific hippocampus.

Against the background of this multiplicity of mechanisms, the brain also has an overarching principle: Try to make all processes automatic, so they occur quickly, smoothly, and without need for cognitive effort or even awareness. As we've seen, mental effort costs (and the brain doesn't like paying). Ideally, in generating behaviour, there should be no involvement of the modulatory system controlling which bits do what and when, because this is slow, the modulatory system gets tired, and it can get distracted if it has to do other tasks at the same time.

The more knowledge/skills are used, the more they will become *automatic*. When it's automatic, you can do other tasks that require attention simultaneously (e.g., talking to a passenger while driving). Automaticity is achieved by a gradual shift in the brain systems that are used for producing the behaviour. Initially, performance relies on back-and-forth circuits between the modulatory system in the prefrontal cortex and the basal ganglia (the so-called *executive loop*), which then instruct motor areas. The outcome is slow, goal-driven, but flexible. Progressively, with practice, there is a shift to circuits linking the motor areas themselves and the basal ganglia (the so-called *motor loop*), along with increasing engagement of the cerebellum which has computed the relevant motor programmes. The outcome is fast, inflexible behaviour, driven by the situation, and a modulatory system now freed up to be engaged in other activities. Automaticity is not merely a goal for motor skills, but perceptual and cognitive operations as well, as part of the general push to reduce mental effort.

By the same token, the less that knowledge/skills are used, the more they are likely to be lost. Forgetting happens differently in different learning systems. In the limbic system, the amygdala doesn't readily forget what situations it finds threatening. The memories are stubborn for a reason – they are there to help you survive. The only way to get rid of this information is to actively overwrite it using therapies like progressive desensitisation. Fear of spiders: play with lots of cuddly toy spiders – look, they aren't so bad after all! Here's a real live one, put it on your hand. There, that's not so bad, is it? As we saw earlier, the hippocampus fills up with episodic memories every three months and memories must be shipped out to the cortex for more permanent storage. After three months, if it's not in the cortex, it's gone. The cortex itself is use-dependent, and over time, if unused, the details

Figure 7.4 The spider has not gone away (or at least, its memory)

of knowledge will blur. The capital of Hungary? Of Romania? Umm. Equally, repeating the learning experience later helps to preserve the knowledge. Procedural learning, by contrast, is hard won. Skills take extensive practice to acquire but decline slowly and are readily retrained, as if with the passing of time, the programmes in the cerebellum have merely become detuned. Twenty years after you last tried it, you can still ride a bike; after a few wobbles, and a little cerebellar retuning, it comes 'straight back'.

Knowledge can be put into the brain, but does it always come out when you need it? Part of learning is establishing strategies for retrieving the knowledge in the right situations (like recalling facts to answer an exam question). Activating the appropriate knowledge in context is the job of the modulatory system (the prefrontal cortex), in particular the part of it that has connections to the hippocampus, the medial prefrontal cortex (see Chapter 5, the section on the 'Executive Suite'). Learning activities that build stronger pathways between the medial prefrontal cortex, the hippocampus, and the content-specific systems in the rear of the brain improve access to knowledge. These are activities familiar to teachers, such as retrieval practice, elaborating or organising knowledge, or explaining the ideas to others.

As well as the suite of learning mechanisms, whole brain networks can also be harnessed to learn new skills. One example is *observation*. The brain can take advantage of its widespread circuits for perceiving and understanding other people to learn skills by observation, so-called 'modelling'. Michael Jackson, the American singer, songwriter, and dancer once dubbed the 'King of Pop', pioneered a dance called moonwalking – appearing to walk forward whilst sliding backwards, as if less encumbered both by gravity and a sense of direction. TikTok still shows proponents of this art, including moonwalks performed on road crossings, on ceilings, underwater, and whilst wearing baggy trousers. Let's say you want to learn how to moonwalk (which regrettably, one of the author's hips won't allow). Watch the video clips. When you do that, areas of your parietal and temporal lobes will recognise motions of the body parts and link these to motor commands to produce similar actions in your own body (the so-called 'mirror neuron' system). If you look at yourself in a real mirror, you can progressively make your actions more and more similar to what you see on the video.

Another strategy is for the brain to take advantage of its widespread circuits for comprehending language (see Chapter 9). Skills can be learned through *instruction*. Rudimentary instructions can be used to produce motor building blocks, which can then be honed through practice and feedback. Admittedly, moonwalking gleaned from instructions won't look identical to that from copying TikTok, but there might still be some lesser degree of kudos.

Instructions for moonwalking:

Step 1: Start with your feet together.

Step 2: Raise your right heel so that you're standing on the ball of your right foot.

Step 3: Shift your weight onto that still-raised right foot so that the left one feels weightless.

Step 4: Slide the left foot backwards.

Step 5: Drop the right foot flat and raise your left heel in a snap motion.

Step 6. Repeat on the other side.

The older you get, the less likely you are to learn to moonwalk. But also, the less learning has to start from scratch. In young infants, toddlers, and children, a lot of learning is figuring out the basics, what objects look like, what movements are useful, what is fun, how social situations work. But from late childhood onwards, more of learning is understanding how a new situation is similar to ones you've seen before, so that previous knowledge can be adapted. Say you start playing a new computer game – images appear, you must respond in some way. Then you figure out, *ah, I see, this game is a bit like Tetris*. Then the modulatory system can activate the task set for *Tetris*, enhancing the relevant perceptual information that is going to be useful (shapes, rotational movement) and priming motor actions (button presses to achieve shape alignment). After that, improvement on the game will be about fine-tuning this template to the new game. If you spot the similarity to *Tetris*, or someone is kind enough to point it out to you, this forms another type of learning: *by analogy*.

Figure 7.5 Some of the multiple interacting neural systems that underpin 'learning'

Let's wrap this up. In this chapter, we've separated development, as the brain takes shape and changes how it works, from learning, as the brain loads up its content. But of course, both are happening at the same time. Children are learning as they are developing. Placed in the classroom, all the learning mechanisms are in action, laying down memories, practising procedures, gauging effort and tracking rewards, updating information about the teacher, learning concepts, automating, observing, following instructions, associating cues that predict lunch; all systems interacting, while age brings with it gradual and sometimes abrupt changes in how the whole brain works. So, we say to the teacher standing in the front of the class of 30 students… good luck with that. (Perhaps that is too pessimistic. We have, after all, written another book on how to use knowledge of how the brain works to help with teaching, called *Educational Neuroscience: The Basics*!)

Note

1   OECD. (2007). *Understanding the Brain: The Birth of a Learning Science*. Organisation for Economic Co-operation and Development, p. 212.

8

WORKING BETTER, WORKING WORSE, WORKING DIFFERENT

Think of your phone. So long as you remembered to charge it, how well it works depends on the model – how much processing power it has, how much memory it has, its peripherals, how good the camera is, and the quality of the touchscreen. It also depends on the software, the sophistication of the programs it's running, the 'OS' or operating system. And those two have to match up: if you run the latest sophisticated operating system on an old phone, it will labour. The software has to fit the hardware. What about brains, do some work differently to others, do some work better, and some worse? Are there differences in processing power, or in software? Might some have disorders, might some be gifted, might some have the 'pro' version, the 'max' size?

Not everyone is comfortable talking about differences. But people do differ, both physically and cognitively: tall and short, fat and thin, fast and slow, smart and daft, placid and prickly. Let's address that discomfort first. There are physical differences between people; there are cognitive differences between people; but all people are intrinsically equally valuable. It is people's actions that determine their value. Now we're going to talk about differences.

The main difference between brains is their size. The average size of a human brain is around 1,350 cm³. Male brains are around 11% bigger than female brains, in line with differences in the sizes of male and female bodies – brains tend to scale with body size (we'll come back to sex differences in a bit). But in both sexes, there's wide variation: in one study, brains varied from 1,053 cm³ to 1,499 cm³ in males, and 975 cm³ to 1,398 cm³ in females. Does size matter? Does a plus-size model give any better functionality? Well, a bit.

Let's remind ourselves once more of the main functionality of the brain. There are some content-specific hierarchical sensory and motor systems; a modulatory system determining which parts of the content-specific systems should be active given the goals (that's the cortex); some appetitive and spatial memory systems driving survival-relevant behaviour

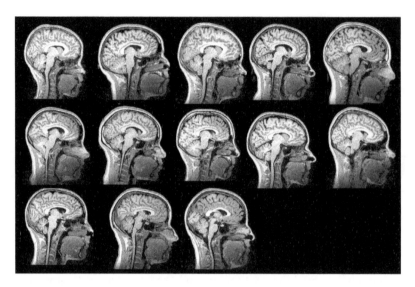

Figure 8.1 Some brains of different sizes and shapes (MRI scans)

(the limbic system); an action selection system bothered about rewards (basal ganglia); a motor-smoothing system (cerebellum); and some bodily homeostasis systems to keep the biology within its tolerance limits such as its working temperature range (midbrain, brainstem). There are two main dimensions across which brain function differs. The first is what psychologists call *intelligence*. The second is what psychologists call *personality*. They seem to be largely independent sorts of variation.

Intelligence refers to general mental ability to reason, think abstractly, learn quickly from experience, and comprehend complex ideas; it also refers to planning and the ability to nest sequences of actions to achieve sub-goals that lead to longer-term goals. The 'general' part in that sentence is one of the biggest empirical findings in the history of psychology – that when individuals are good at one kind of cognitive test, they tend to be good at another type of cognitive test. Intelligence looks like it is a property of the cortex, affecting the speed of sensory and motor processing, the levels of abstraction (invariances, nested sequences) achieved in the sensory and motor hierarchies, and the resolution of the control that the modulatory system can exert over the content-specific systems.

Some argue that 'general' cognitive ability comes from a 'general' mechanism. In the brain's parlance, this must be a *finger-in-every-pie* general system, one that has its own specialised function but the facility to influence lots of other systems, since there is no *jack-of-all-trades* general system in the brain able to carry out lots of different functions, in the manner of the CPU in a digital computer (as we saw in Chapter 5). The mechanism producing general intelligence would therefore have to be the modulatory system and its interactions with the content-specific systems (you might hear of phrases like 'the multiple-demand network' or the 'parietal-frontal integration theory' as species of this type of story). But the generality may not come from a single mechanism. It could come just by having better processing of information, and better learning, right across the cortical sheet.

Having a bigger brain explains about 10% of the variation in intelligence, so maybe just having more cortical neurons does the job. But genetic research also points to the contribution of many different low-level properties, from neurogenesis (number of neurons produced), to neuron differentiation (neurons in different regions specialising in the processing they have to do there), to the synapse (local communication and plasticity), and to oligodendrocyte differentiation (the support cells that help with myelination, again pointing to local communication and plasticity). In the analogy of your phone, intelligence is closest to variations in processing power and memory, but because the brain self-organises its detailed functioning, it is also equivalent to more sophisticated software. The more intelligent cortex learns more higher-order invariances and associations in content-specific systems and controls them better.

The second sort of variation is personality. For a psychologist, personality refers to a set of characteristics or traits that drive differences in how people tend to behave – who you are, what has happened to you, what you believe, what you desire. Who you are is, in part, a consequence of your previous experiences, and the experiences you have had depend in part on the situations you have chosen to put yourself in. These tendencies can be traced back to another way in which brains can work differently. This stems from differences in the systems processing reward, motivation, and aversive experiences – the limbic system and the basal ganglia – as well as the interaction of the limbic system with the prefrontal cortex. As we saw in our discussion of differences between species, motivations and rewards may be influenced by levels of hormones (e.g., vasopressin, oxytocin) and neurotransmitters (e.g., dopamine, serotonin, noradrenaline), including the amount expressed, and the number and distribution of receptors. Differences may also depend on the size of structures such as the amygdala or the nuclei within the basal ganglia, and connections between them. The result is different tuning across individuals for approach and avoidance behaviour, arousal, novelty seeking, threat detection, sociality, territorial defence, and sensitivity to rewards.

Studies of humans tend to distinguish personality dimensions of extraversion, neuroticism, agreeableness, conscientiousness, and openness. Similar dimensions of behaviour are seen in other social primates such as chimpanzees, where the dimensions of dominance (aggression) and level of activity are also sometimes added. Extraversion represents greater sensitivity to rewards, frequently sought from interactions with other people or through achieving social status. Agreeableness involves greater empathy and pro-social decision making. Openness is a calibration to approach new situations, while conscientiousness is a tendency to inhibit impulses to pursue non-immediate goals, and to follow rules. Neuroticism represents a combination of greater sensitivity to threat and punishment, and less emotional regulation. Aggression is a tendency to react to threat or stress with approach behaviour (not of a nice kind).

Exactly how the tuning of different sub-cortical structures produces personality types is still being figured out. Tuning may involve multiple systems. The monogamy of the prairie vole over the polygamy of the otherwise highly similar montane vole involves more receptors for oxytocin both in the amygdala (to increase the detection of social cues) and in the striatum (to find social situations more rewarding). It's likely to be a similar explanation for the variation between humans. So the tuning that represents different personality types will likely involve a range of the systems we have encountered before: for detecting social, threat, or curiosity-driven situations and triggering relevant behaviours (the amygdala); systems involved in the prediction of reward or punishment such as the basal ganglia (especially the striatum) and the nucleus accumbens (for the pleasure part); systems for social attachment (septum); systems for processing own and others' body states for empathy and the tendency to experience disgust (insula); systems for monitoring current behaviour against goals and expectations (cingulate cortex); systems for recognising situations associated with past rewards or punishments, or for detecting novel situations (hippocampus). And then there will be various prefrontal decision-making mechanisms around reward-relevant situations (orbito-frontal cortex), emotion regulation (middle lower prefrontal cortex), social situations (middle upper prefrontal cortex), and control of plans (upper side prefrontal cortex).

As you alter the tuning of these various systems, you will get a whole brain which chooses actions that are more or less likely to lead to certain kinds of rewards or experiences; a brain more or less likely to approach or avoid certain situations; more or less likely to make decisions based on emotional states versus plans and goals; and more or less likely to respond to other people in convivial ways. On the next page is an illustration of the systems involved, in case you're getting frustrated with all these words and frankly want to move on (some of you, by contrast, will appreciate this sort of detail).

Do phones have personalities? This is where our analogy to digital computers is not so hot, because limbic and reward systems are particularly biological, representing the long history of evolution that has tailored brain structures to meet the survival needs of organisms, and accepted (maybe even promoted) variation in these systems within populations, whereas phones are inert and disposable (poor things). At best, there are phones with user friendly or user hostile interfaces, reflecting the personalities and distant priorities of the programmers who created the phone software.

Nature or Nurture?

If there are differences in how the brain works, where do they come from? Are they genetic, inherited, passed down through families, and perhaps selected for by evolution?

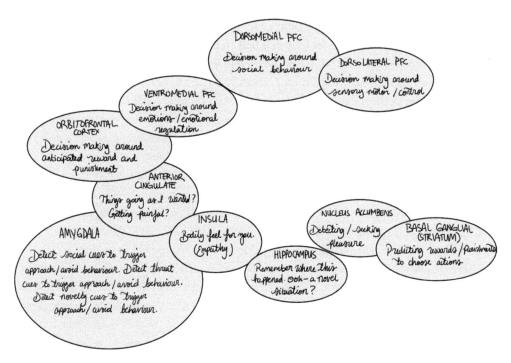

Figure 8.2 Brain systems which, when tuned differently, contribute to differences in personality

Or are they a product of the environments we are raised in, the experiences, rewards, and disappointments we receive, the product of parenting, teaching, and peer interactions, the result of life experiences? Yeah, dunno.

Look, that's a really complicated question for a number of reasons. First, from a biological point of view, everything is genetic and everything is environmental. Our DNA sits in the nucleus of each of our cells, generating the proteins that support cellular function. All that a cell can do depends on its DNA. But the DNA is a set of instructions that is only able to make proteins due to the machinery of the cell, the machinery that reads the instructions and fabricates the proteins. This is the environment of the cell. That same environment helps regulate which proteins are going to be made at any given time (what DNA instructions are 'read off' at any given moment). And the environment of the cell is influenced by the local environment in which it sits: the other neighbouring cells signalling to it, and the chemicals in the surrounding fluid, which are ultimately influenced by the rest of the body and the outside world. Genes and environments can't be pulled apart.

Second, let's say that of the tenth of a percentage point of DNA that varies between humans (the rest making you, respectively, a multi-cellular organism, a vertebrate, a mammal, and a human in particular), let's say some of this tenth was giving your brain different properties – in how it grows, or the functioning of its neurons, or in the tuning of its emotional and reward systems – and let's say that had an effect on your behaviour. But behaviour itself comes from a long chain of interactions with the world as you develop – your early physical environment, your nutrition and health, your interactions with your parents, your friends. And some of these experiences are likely to be correlated with your genetic variation – if you have better DNA to learn language, it will have come from your parents, who because their language is better, will talk to you more, so you have richer language input as a baby. If you're an introvert, you will likely form a peer group of friends who share your more contemplative preferences. Trying to pick apart the notional contributions of genetic variation and environmental variation to, say, the level of conversation an 18-year-old has with their friends, or to the grades they achieve in their A-levels, when these contributions are so heavily entwined is, possibly, futile – even if specific bits of genetic variation, altered proteins, and their functional biological consequences can be identified.

There are a few things we can say, though. If genetic variation is important, it should make people whose genetics are more *similar* behave more *similarly* (or grow to more similar heights or have similarly coloured eyes). We can use studies that measure the genetic similarity between people to see how much it predicts the similarity in their behaviour (or brain function or brain structure). This gives a sort of summary of all the genetic effects combined. The level of genetic similarity between people can be estimated simply based on how closely related they are (say, identical twins versus non-identical twins, or siblings versus cousins). Or it can be identified by directly measuring the similarity of DNA between lots of pairs of unrelated people. When you calculate this summary of all genetic effects, you find that genetic similarity explains about half the variation in intelligence (maybe a little bit higher) and about half the variation in personality (maybe a little bit lower). The variation in large-scale brain structure seems somewhat higher, with perhaps 80% linked to genetic similarity; but then it's the detailed circuitry that delivers the function, not the volume of grey matter, and genetic similarity only predicts around 40% of the similarity in brain function. So, from this summary, we can conclude that the differences between people in how their brains work are about half due to nature (genetics) and half due to nurture (environment).

We don't know quite where one goes with this finding; 50% – is that what you were expecting? If we accept that genes influence attributes like height, eye colour, and health, how could they possibly not also influence intelligence and behaviour? Anything to do with the brain requires neuronal communication, which requires proteins, which are encoded by genes. And we do kind of *need* behaviour to be influenced by genetics somehow, otherwise the theory of evolution doesn't work. Behavioural variation must be related to genetic variation (to some extent) so that gene variants can be selected for, to produce the diversity of behaviours that we see across species, such as the lovely voles. We know from farming and domestication that we can breed selectively for certain behaviours in animals, such as aggressive guard dogs and loving lap dogs.

Indeed, in experiments, when we deliberately try to breed for certain behaviours in mice – say, the tendency for a mouse to run under a cupboard versus explore out in the open – we find that these selected-for behaviours increase only gradually over many generations. There is an incremental change as more of the relevant DNA variations are directed into the next generation via selective breeding. This points to one of the major findings in the genetics of human behaviour – that variation in behaviour is associated with variations in many, many bits of DNA. That's both in genes and in the regions of DNA between them, which can influence how genes are read off to produce proteins. If you're counting genes and their variants, hundreds, perhaps thousands contribute to variability in behaviour (including disorders, see later this chapter). Many of those variants will be fairly common in the population and each will add only a tiny fraction of variation to the outcome. This is called *polygenicity*. It's what you'd expect if genetic variation alters many different low-level properties of brain development, neural functioning, neurotransmitter functions, hormone levels, signalling, and plasticity.

This modern understanding contrasts with the old-fashioned view that major chunks of behaviour, such as intelligence or the symptoms of schizophrenia, were caused by variation in single genes producing large effects, and it represents a major shift in thinking. Polygenicity is probably the reason we see variations in cognitive ability that are in the shape of a 'bell' curve shown in Figure 8.3 below (most people around average, fewer very low or very high). There's a theorem in statistics which stipulates that simply by adding together lots of small effects, you end up with this type of distribution (the so-called Central Limit theorem). It's unusual to end up with *all* the good versions of the genetic variants, and it's unusual to end up with *all* the bad versions of the genetic variants, but it's common to end up with a mix of good and bad variants.

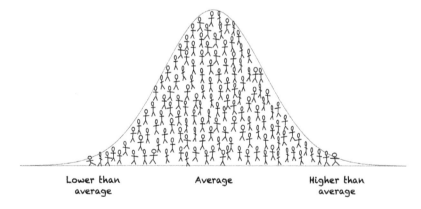

Lower than average   Average   Higher than average

Figure 8.3 The bell curve or normal distribution, seen in traits such as intelligence that are the result of combining many small differences in the low-level properties of the brain

The last thing we should say about genetics is that because genetic similarity partly predicts behavioural variation – so that we can call behaviour somewhat 'heritable' – this is only a summary of what's happening *right now* in a given population, with a given set of DNA variants, raised in a given range of environments, in a given society. Should the range of environments change (say get much poorer, nutritionally or cognitively, or more dangerous), genetic differences may be less important in outcomes (because the environment would now act as a limiting factor). If a country improves its education system and healthcare, the average level of intelligence can appear to rise from generation to generation, as it did in many countries in the 20th century (known as the Flynn effect). So, it doesn't look like intelligence is being held back by genetics, does it? And yet, in a world of improving environments, genetic differences may conversely become more important for predicting variation: if everyone is getting the best education possible, genetic differences will be the only distinguishing factor in achievement.

In other words, heritability doesn't mean destiny. Genes don't control your future. You are free to act as you want. You've inherited red hair. Dye your hair blue. And if you don't like the direction your genes are taking you with respect to behaviour, if you don't like the option that your limbic system is urging you to take, you can always choose to do something completely different. That's free will for you. Only when you make that choice, you may not enjoy the outcome. That's genetics for you.

Back to Sex for a Moment, It's on Our Minds

Back to sex for a moment. It's on our minds because there is a puzzle lurking here that is both curious and reassuring. We have seen that having a bigger brain with more neurons is associated with having slightly higher intelligence. We've also seen that brain size scales with body size (this is a general observation across species – as we've heard, a bigger body requires more sensory processing for its surface area and more motor innervation for its muscles). And we've seen that in line with their generally smaller bodies, female humans tend to have smaller brains than males (11% smaller on average). Should we not then expect female intelligence to be mildly lower on average? Misogyny and sexism alarms are going off all over our computers as we even type this question. But rest assured, on average, there is NO DIFFERENCE between adult female and male intelligence (even though, within each sex, the same weak association is seen – bigger brain, slightly higher intelligence).

How can this add up? It tells us that female and male brains have slightly different ways of working. There are likely multiple aspects of the brain's structure, function, and connectivity that allow the two sexes to produce on average similar levels of cognitive functioning with different sized brains. These may be quite detailed differences, because at the large scale, apart from the overall differences in size (which has some scaling consequences on the relative size of particular structures), there's almost no difference between male and female brains. However, viewed under a microscope in a petri dish, sex differences can be seen in neurons. For example, neurons from male and female mice look a little different in the structure of their axons and dendrites, likely because embryonic neuron growth is influenced by sex hormones like testosterone. Some neurons even have receptors for sex hormones; when they detect the hormones, it can alter their functioning (for instance, inhibitory GABAergic neurons have receptors for oestrogen and progesterone). Sex differences in brain functioning are therefore likely to be low level. Of course, if males and females end up acquiring different skills in a given society for whatever reason, functional differences might also be observed. But as one group of scientists recently concluded, overall size aside, human male/female brain differences appear trivial and population specific.[1]

When Variations Are Larger

Let's move on. We've discussed variation in terms of intelligence and personality, but sometimes variation can be more extreme. Sometimes it can cause challenges for individuals or societies, and in the case of associated disabilities, we use the label 'disorder' and refer to 'deficits' (in the absence of disabilities, greater variations are otherwise referred to simply as 'differences'). Sometimes extremely high levels of intelligence are labelled 'giftedness'. We'll stress again before we get into this: there are physical differences between people, there are cognitive differences between people, but all people are intrinsically equally valuable. Now let's ask, in these cases of greater variation, what kinds of differences are we seeing in how the brain works?

We'll start with disorders. There are two ways that differences can end up being extreme. The first is by an extension of the type of variation we see in the usual case, due to lots of small genetic or environmental influences adding up. Let's say there are 1,000 genes whose variants contribute to intelligence, each of which has better or worse versions. In some family lineages, the number of worse versions may accumulate by chance, increasing the probability of low intelligence. Or many small environmental influences on early brain development, or early experiences, may combine to restrict cognitive development. The effects may be general across cognitive abilities, or uneven, with particular impact on, say, verbal or non-verbal abilities, or on behavioural regulation, or on motor skills.

The second way to extreme variation is through a genetic mutation or a sledgehammer environmental event. Mutations include recurring genetic syndromes such as Down syndrome, Fragile X syndrome, and Williams syndrome, though one-off new mutations can also occur. Major environmental events may include early viral infection, birth complications, severe malnutrition, mistreatment, or deprivation (such as that experienced by children placed in Romanian orphanages in the 1980s and early 1990s). In both genetic syndromes and major environmental events, multiple body and brain systems may be affected.

For genetic mutations, it's often possible to see their effects on brain development, such as differences in overall brain size or of particular lobes, as well as down in the chemistry of neuronal functioning. For example, in Down syndrome, the overall brain size is often smaller, especially the frontal lobes and the cerebellum, while volumes of temporal and parietal lobes are less affected. In infants and toddlers with Fragile X, some regions of the brain appear to be larger than in typical development. In Williams syndrome, overall brain size is smaller, but the back of the brain (parietal and occipital lobes) is less affected, as is the cerebellum. All these disorders are characterised by learning disability.

By contrast, developmental conditions caused by multiple small influences are often not reflected at the whole brain level (apart from the general weak association we've seen between brain size and intelligence). For conditions like autism, attention deficit hyperactivity disorder (ADHD), or dyslexia, it's not generally possible to make a diagnosis from a structural brain scan: there's nothing large scale to see.

For both of the two broad types of disorder, however, brains work in pretty much the same way. There are cortical hierarchical motor and sensory systems in the front and back of the brain respectively, a modulatory system right at the front, deeper limbic structures mediating emotions and episodic/spatial memory, the basal ganglia action selection system, the cerebellar motor-smoothing system, and midbrain and brainstem structures for body regulation and basic sensory processing.

Why don't you get any radically different ways for the brain to work in disorders? The reason is that the build-plan for developing vertebrate/mammalian/primate brains cannot be disrupted too much by genetic mutations or environmental events and still produce a viable embryo or foetus able to survive to term. For example, Down syndrome is caused by having three copies instead of the usual two of chromosome 21, so-called 'trisomy'. Apart from the sex chromosomes (X and Y), humans have 22 pairs of chromosomes. Mutations can occur such that a fertilised egg can have three copies of *any* of these 22 chromosomes. But in 16 out of these 22 instances, having three copies means the foetus can never survive to term. For five more trisomies, the foetus rarely survives to term. Only trisomy of chromosome 21 allows a foetus that can survive to term and, barring other complications, have a normal expected lifespan. In short, we generally only see a subset of the possible disorders in children and adults, those that have brains that develop fairly closely to the usual way of functioning.

So where do the disorders come from? A little like our previous discussion, it can be hard to unpick exact causes of the behavioural differences we see in developmental disorders, mainly because a lot of development has taken place before we see, say, a lack of attentional control or problems with learning to read. A range of low-level differences could impact on development, including the number and organisation of neurons in different brain regions, how they wire up locally or via long range pathways, the dynamics of local neural activity, the mechanisms of plasticity, or the balance of neurotransmitters and distributions of receptors.

Because the central nervous system is plastic, it will develop and self-organise to optimise performance whatever these initial limitations, including brain areas compensating for one another. In genetic syndromes, multiple brain systems may be affected. And the presence of an initial brain difference can also alter the world the child experiences and how people respond to them. We might not therefore expect the differences to be highly specific to functions or brain regions. However, we can think of developmental disorders broadly in terms of the systems they affect – cortex, limbic system, basal ganglia, cerebellum, midbrain. (Note, for reasons of space, we're not going to consider sensory impairments, such as blindness or deafness, or congenital growth problems with the body or its peripheral nervous system.)

Starting with the cortex, we've seen that this is about intelligence. Most of the variation in cortical development is likely to be general across the cortical sheet, so that the greater variation manifests as generally low intelligence. We would expect sensory and motor hierarchies to develop less complex representations, less abstract concepts (sensory) or less sophisticated plans (motor). We would expect the modulatory system to have less detailed control over the content-specific systems, less ability to maintain information or manipulate task sets.

However, there must be some regional differences in how the cortex is impacted to produce uneven cognitive profiles, where there appear to be greater problems in certain skills. For example, if the temporal lobe is more affected, there might be greater impact on language (developmental language disorder, dyslexia, problems with music); or if the parietal lobe is more affected, there may be greater impact on visuospatial skills (dyscalculia); or if the frontal areas are more affected, there may be greater impact on motor skills (developmental coordination disorder); or if the prefrontal areas are more affected, there may be greater impact on cognitive control skills like maintaining attention and task set (ADHD).

We've seen that the limbic system is linked to personality, and greater variation in tuning the responses of structures like the amygdala and the insula may link to disorders around anxiety (e.g., generalised anxiety disorder), social approach or avoidance behaviour (autism), or empathy (callous and unemotional traits). Variation affecting the interaction of the limbic system with the modulatory system, such as the orbitofrontal region, may impact emotion regulation (conduct disorder).

The basal ganglia are involved in reward-based action selection. Greater variation here may be reflected in difficulties with controlling and selecting actions and routines, manifested in disorders like stuttering, obsessive-compulsive disorder, and Tourette's syndrome. The cerebellum is involved in learning automated motor routines and delivering smooth action. Extreme variation here may produce clumsiness in motor skills and balance (developmental coordination disorder).

Disorders affecting the midbrain and brainstem are perhaps rarer because these are more fundamental systems for survival, but such conditions are also found. They tend to affect basic sensory systems, for instance impairing hearing, or the nerves for sensing the face or controlling eye movements, or autonomic nervous system functions which regulate involuntary physiologic processes including heart rate, blood pressure, respiration, digestion, and sexual arousal.

This system-by-system approach makes it sound like we'll see lots of clearly differentiated disorders, but disruptions to early developmental processes may impact multiple systems at once. This is particularly seen in genetic syndromes, but for many behaviourally defined disorders too, multiple problems ('comorbidity') are the rule rather than the exception. And where motivation and reward systems are involved, these may then alter the environments that the child prefers to place themselves in, and therefore the experiences that help shape the self-organisation of the cortex.

Environmental disruptions to early development can also affect multiple systems. For an environmental 'sledgehammer' event, take the example of the Romanian orphans who experienced extreme physical and social deprivation. The children showed significantly decreased activity in the orbital frontal gyrus, parts of the prefrontal cortex, the temporal cortex, the hippocampus, the amygdala, and the brainstem. The dysfunction in these brain regions may have resulted from the stress of early global deprivation and be involved in the long-term cognitive and behavioural deficits displayed by some Romanian orphans.

In typical variation, we saw that differences in intelligence aren't closely tied to differences in personality. Likewise for greater variation, there could be differences stemming from the limbic system (say, lack of motivation to approach social situations) that could either occur with typical development of the cortex, so the result would be usual levels of intelligence but something like an extreme personality trait; or social differences could occur alongside developmental limitations in the cortex, where the result would be social disengagement and a learning disability, more clearly a disorder.

Let's turn to extreme variation in the other direction – giftedness. Here we find a slightly different situation: while there are many ways that development can go awry to produce deficits, there's only one way it can go right to produce top performance according to society's current cognitive metrics. Everything has to line up. Giftedness is only produced by extremes of typical variation, an accumulation of many genetic variants all making brain function better, combined with a rich and stimulating physical, social, and educational environment for a child to thrive within. Giftedness does not arise through mutations; it's not a mirror image to genetic syndromes. Significant mutations almost always make development worse.

Again, we might distinguish between independent dimensions of intelligence and personality. A cortex with large computational capacity would produce faster learning of sensory and motor hierarchies with greater scope for complex concepts and sophisticated plans, along with a modulatory system with detailed control and flexibility. Precocity in intelligence is linked with early mastery of technical, bounded conceptual domains and motor skills, like mathematics or playing musical instruments. But for giftedness to lead to societal success, variation in personality also has to line up, providing motivation, conscientiousness, hard work, the dedication to practise skills or to read books, the inquisitiveness to pursue information, and the trait to find praise rewarding. Intellectual capacity aligned with laziness does not yield giftedness; conceptual prowess with deficits in empathy yields, at best, tech entrepreneurs, and at worst criminal masterminds.

Let's Break One We Made Earlier

By the time we are looking at the adult brain, regions of the content-specific systems and regions of the modulatory system have become quite specialised in what they do, through the process of developmental self-organisation. For the cortex especially, *where you are is what you do*. There is different content in different regions. If the adult brain then experiences damage to a specific area, this can result in quite specific loss of behaviour.

Of course, brain damage is capricious, it may impact multiple structures depending on the nature of the accident, be it a blow, a loss of oxygen, pressure through inflammation, growth of a tumour, surgery, a bleed, blockage to blood flow, or a boxing match with neural twisting and sheering events. Moreover, the effects of damage on behaviour can reduce or spread afterwards. For example, during recovery, the brain may harness other ways of performing tasks, so-called compensation, or reorganise to utilise regions just next to the area of damage; by the same token, regions connected to or next to areas of damage can in turn experience decline or atrophy. Nevertheless, neuropsychologists have tended to focus on the cases where specific behaviours are lost following damage to discrete areas as a way to understand which structures are involved in generating which behaviours.

First, let's think about damage to the content-specific systems, the hierarchies in the sensory lobes, and the hierarchy of the motor system. If you knock out bits of sensory and motor hierarchies, you get perceptual problems or problems in generating actions. It depends on how low down or high up the hierarchy you damage it. For example: low in the system, perceptual deficits (blindness); higher in the system, conceptual deficits (faces, objects, written words); if it's in regions where the tops of the sensory hierarchies communicate, such as temporal-parietal areas, you will knock out conceptual knowledge that spans sensory modalities.

The patterns of behavioural deficit can be quite specific, and show right–left differences, reflecting the history of specialisation of function to narrower areas of the cortex. One example is the temporal-parietal areas in the left hemisphere that are involved in the comprehension of language – taking the auditory or visual information of spoken or written language and turning it into the literal message (see Chapter 9 for more detail on the language system). If this region, so-called Wernicke's area, is selectively damaged, the adult can experience loss of the ability to understand language – but may still be able to produce language (perhaps without the most meaningful content). That's because production involves a specialised part of the motor hierarchy in the frontal area in the left hemisphere, so-called Broca's area (the names reflect the esteemed neurologists of the 19th century who linked the patterns of brain damage to the loss of behaviour). Damage to Broca's area produces a loss of the ability to produce language, even while comprehension may be unimpaired. These are called, respectively, Wernicke's and Broca's aphasia (aphasia = acquired language loss).

Another part of the sensory hierarchy that produces characteristic patterns of behavioural deficit following damage is the system that deals with space in the parietal lobe. Recall, at the bottom of the sensory hierarchy of the parietal lobe is sensation of the body surface. At the bottom of the sensory hierarchy of the occipital lobe is raw visual information. Where the tops of these hierarchies meet is the representation of space out in the world, the position of the body in that space, and how the body should generate motor actions to orient itself in that space, such as where to look with your eyes. (We don't want to leave auditory information and the temporal lobe out of it – if you hear someone creeping up behind you, for sure you may want to turn around.) But if you damage this high-up spatial region in the parietal cortex, you get something called *neglect*. Damage to the right hemisphere gives the most obvious deficits because it is specialised to deal with holistic, large-scale properties of space (the left hemisphere more with detail). In neglect, following right parietal damage, adults show a lack of attention to or awareness for the left-hand side of the world (remember, the brain does this contralateral thing, see the section 'There Are Two Sides to Every Brain' in Chapter 5). The individual can perceive the world, but the brain doesn't care about the left of the world – it seems not to generate the relevant actions.

Let's move from the sensory and motor hierarchies to the modulatory system. If there is selective damage here, there can be problems in controlling behaviour; in sustaining activation in content-specific circuits (keeping information 'in mind'); or for those regions talking to limbic emotion systems and reward-sensitive action selection systems, changes in personality, moral behaviour, or decision making around risk, which brings us to Phineas Gage.

One of the most influential studies in neuroscience was one of the earliest. In 1848, Phineas Gage was working on the railways in the USA. His job was to pack explosives into holes drilled in rocks obstructing the railroad and blow them up. For some reason he was using a metal tamping iron (a thin rod about 28 cm long) to pack the dynamite down. A spark ignited the explosive and blew the tamping iron through his left eye socket and out through the top of his head. Despite massive brain damage he did not lose consciousness (!) but walked some distance to seek help. After a few days of coma and delirium, he gradually recovered, with intact memory and intelligence, so that some months later he could do light work. Anecdotal accounts indicated that he became 'coarse and profane in company', unreliable and obstinate, and was 'no longer Phineas Gage'. This case study was influential in suggesting the frontal cortex was involved in behavioural control, emotional regulation, and personality. However, later accounts were more positive: Gage worked in Chile for several years as a stagecoach driver, a job demanding both skill (managing six horses) and reliability, almost up to his death in 1860.

In the 1990s, scanning studies on his preserved skull showed severe damage but limited to the left frontal lobe. Despite this damage, he survived and demonstrated an amazing recovery. What does this show? That the brain is plastic, that recovery systems, perhaps involving alternative pathways or axonal and synaptic regrowth, can in some cases compensate for tissue loss. Unfortunately, this is not common. Specific damage and cognitive loss, such as aphasic (language) deficits after left hemisphere stroke, or HM's amnesia (see below), can be permanent.

The deeper structures, such as the limbic system and basal ganglia, are less commonly selectively impaired. The hippocampus has sometimes been linked to the generation of severe and intractable epilepsy and therefore has been the target of selective surgery. For example, one patient, HM, had both left and right hippocampi removed for this reason. The result was a particular deficit in episodic memory. Recall, memories in this system are gradually shipped out to the cortex, but it takes a while. So, if you remove both hippocampi, you'll lose the ability to lay down new episodic memories (so-called anterograde amnesia), but you'll also lose your last three months of memories too (so-called retrograde amnesia). However, other learning, such as gradual learning of procedural abilities (of the shoelace tying variety) is still possible in the motor hierarchy.

Deep structures can also be differentially impacted in some neurodegenerative diseases. For example, the action selection system of the basal ganglia particularly relies on certain neurotransmitters to work. If the neurons that provide dopamine to this system die back, as is seen in Parkinson's disease, the action selection system loses function. It becomes less able to decide on which action to produce from the cortical plans in play, so a deficit emerges in initiating voluntary action (though as we saw in Chapter 4, dopamine plays different roles in different brain systems, so a loss of dopamine produces multiple deficits).

The brain functions via the interaction of its content-specific systems, modulatory systems, and deeper structures, so sometimes the effects of damage produce unexpected effects, such as *alien hand syndrome* – where a person experiences their limbs acting seemingly on their own, as if the person doesn't have conscious control over a limb's actions – or *believing one's spouse has been replaced by an identical imposter or robot* (which even the individual will admit is extremely unlikely... while insisting it has nevertheless happened). These odd circumstances represent situations where the brain is trying to interpret unusual perceptual or emotional states caused by damage.

For example, in alien hand syndrome, following damage, the lowest part of the cortical motor hierarchy that controls hand movement, the primary motor area, starts to operate in isolation of the level above it which normally generates the plan, the premotor cortex. The primary motor area might instead be activated by sensory input (e.g., a pencil on the table activating a motor plan to pick it up). The sequence for generating an action should normally proceed down the hierarchy, from supplemental motor area through premotor down to primary motor cortex. But importantly, the mid-levels also send information along to the parietal system which processes the sensation of the hand moving, about what sensory input to expect. It is this generate-movement-then-sense-movement loop that produces a feeling of agency: that it was 'you' who produced the action. But if the sensory prediction is not sent to the parietal cortex by the mid-levels of the motor hierarchy, when the movement of the hand is perceived, the brain interprets the movement as being generated by someone else (see p. 187 for a similar delusion in schizophrenia).

When a person insists that a loved one has been replaced by an imposter, called Capgras delusion, this is a disconnection of the ability to recognise a face (in the visual sensory hierarchy in the underneath of the temporal lobe) from the retrieval of the emotional response linked with that face (stored in the amygdala). Once more, the brain must find a way to interpret the anomalous state, now of recognising a highly familiar person's face but having no sensation of an accompanying emotion. Those computations end up spitting out a delusional belief – possibly the best explanation, however strange it seems – that the loved one has been substituted by an identical imposter.

Damage does reveal one interesting fact about how brains differ when they are working normally. Let's say we ask a group of adults to perform a task where they are shown sets of pictures, say of a violin, a tennis racket, and a piano, and they have to say which two go together. It's the violin and the piano, right? They are both musical instruments. It's a semantic relationship. Now, put this group of adults in a brain scanner while they are doing this task. When you look across the group, you'll see *five* areas of the cortex involved in doing this task: these are the areas that consistently demand more oxygenated blood when deciding that it's the violin and piano that go together.

Here's the intriguing part. If you now look at another group of adults who, according to brain scans, have suffered various patterns of brain damage impacting one or more of these five areas, you can nevertheless find individuals who are performing with 100% accuracy on the task. What's going on? The explanation for this finding is twofold. First, it means not all the five areas are essential to do this visual recognition + meaning retrieval

+ categorisation + motor response task. You can clearly get away with just using subsets of the five. Second, it likely means that, before the damage, the brains of these individuals had developed to perform this kind of task using different strategies, different subsets of mechanisms. (For example, one brain might take a more visual approach, another a more meaning-based approach; one might focus more on visual features, another on global forms; one might access other sensory information rather than just visual shape, such as the names of the objects or actions linked to each object, or the sounds they make; one might rely more on the perception-for-now route than the perception-for-later route.) How our brains normally do cognitive tasks may differ across adults, a difference we are blind to until the brain is damaged.

Damage has different effects when it happens in the developing brain, which is still in the process of self-organising its functional circuits. Children are both more vulnerable to damage than adults and more robust in recovering from damage, depending on the type of damage. If damage is widespread, such as in the case of traumatic head injury, development itself may be derailed and the outcome poorer than in adults (who already have knowledge and skills in place, and can adapt what remains). If damage is localised, for example just to one hemisphere, children's brains can self-organise to use other brain areas to deliver the same function (often the equivalent areas in the undamaged hemisphere). For example, if the same left-hemisphere areas which cause Broca's or Wernicke's aphasia in an adult are damaged in a young child, while the child's language development will be affected, he or she usually recovers to exhibit language skills in the normal range.

Disrupting the Dynamics

As we saw in the last section, physical damage to the brain can have dramatic effects. We can all be a little forgetful, but nothing like the disabling amnesia seen in HM. There is no doubt that for him, something had gone profoundly wrong.

With psychiatric diagnoses the behavioural changes are often less dramatic. Before looking at these issues we need to be clear on terminology. In psychology, we usually refer to these psychiatric conditions as 'psychological disorders'. Psychiatry is embedded in medical science, as psychiatrists complete a medical degree before specialising. Psychologists do not, but come through a training programme in clinical psychology. Psychologists cannot prescribe drugs, but use psychological therapies. Treatment of disorders has been long dominated by psychiatry and drug therapies, but over the last 20 years problems with drug therapy (e.g., they do not always work, and can have issues of side effects, dependence, and withdrawal) have led to more focus on psychological therapies such as cognitive behavioural therapy. Unfortunately, access to these psychological therapies on the NHS is limited, and drugs are still the main treatment for many disorders.

Anyway, back to the main theme. We tend to diagnose psychiatric disorders based on behavioural symptoms. The most popular diagnostic system used in psychiatry, the *Diagnostic and Statistical Manual of Mental Disorders* (DSM), lists around 17 categories of disorder (e.g., anxiety disorders, mood disorders, schizophrenia spectrum disorders, personality disorders) and hundreds of specific conditions. The aim is to allow practitioners to clearly identify a disorder, which then leads to (hopefully) successful treatment. However, it has become increasingly clear that the brain does not cooperate. Underlying these conditions are disruptions and biases which affect the dynamics of brain systems, including arousal, motivation, identification of and response to rewards, self-cognition, and perception of the surrounding social world. The DSM approach assumes that disorders are categorical and clearly distinguishable, but clinically, schizophrenia and bipolar disorder can share symptoms such as hallucinations, while eating disorders are often combined with high levels of anxiety and depression ('comorbidity'). Behavioural genetics has been instrumental in identifying common genetic influences in, for instance, schizophrenia, bipolar disorder, and major depression. That is not to say that specific disorders do not have core features, but that a strict categorical approach is not justified, and we cannot ignore overlaps between disorders. The brain operates through complex networks of interacting systems, and disruptions will not necessarily produce the neat classifications of the DSM.

In the next sections, we'll take a look at the examples of schizophrenia, depression, and anxiety disorders, before finishing the chapter with a puzzle – how do psychiatric disorders, sometimes showing a partial genetic basis, fit into an evolutionary context?

Schizophrenia

In the 1950s, a popular distinction was made between neuroses and psychoses. Neuroses were conditions such as anxiety and depression, which seemed to be on a continuum with 'normal' behaviour – unless you are very lucky, everyone has been anxious or depressed at some time, so clinical depression would be an extreme version of everyday experience. By contrast, psychoses, such as schizophrenia, involve a loss of insight and a separation from reality. They are often associated with hallucinations (e.g., hearing voices) and delusions (e.g., paranoia, the sense that the world is out to get you, or grandiosity, the sense that you were put on this world for a special purpose). Psychoses, with their loss of insight, were seen as beyond normal experience and more severe and disabling than neuroses.

Schizophrenia was first formally described by Emil Kraepelin in the late 19th century (he labelled the condition as 'dementia praecox' – early onset dementia) and was elaborated by Eugene Bleuler in the early 20th century. Bleuler introduced the term 'schizophrenia' in 1908, and over the following years provided more detailed accounts of the symptoms. 'Schizophrenia' means 'splitting of the mind', by which Bleuler meant a disconnection between brain systems controlling perception, cognition, and emotion – as we shall see, Bleuler was well ahead of his time.

Bleuler was also the first to categorise the symptoms as either positive – unique additions to everyday behaviour such as hallucinations and delusions – or negative – loss of everyday functions, leading to a lack of emotional responsiveness ('flattened affect'), reduced speech content ('speech poverty'), and loss of motivation ('avolition'). This constellation of symptoms still provides the backdrop to research into schizophrenia but is also a persistent conceptual and research problem as different people may have different combinations of symptoms.

The DSM system was introduced in the 1950s and is periodically revised in line with research into different disorders and sociocultural developments. So homosexuality was removed from the DSM in the 1960s, while eating disorders, substance abuse disorders, and autism were later additions. In the early versions of the DSM, schizophrenia could be diagnosed based on a single auditory hallucination. It then became clear that a significant proportion of people experiencing a single hallucination would never go on to have another one; recent surveys suggest that around 5% of the non-clinical population have experienced at least one psychotic episode, usually auditory hallucinations – another observation that blurs the distinction between psychosis and 'normal' experience.

In response to these findings, in the 1970s the DSM changed the diagnostic criteria for schizophrenia to one requiring active symptoms for at least one month and signs of disturbance for at least six months. So schizophrenia became a 'chronic' or long-lasting disorder, which fits with Bleuler's original model viewing the condition as essentially lifelong and incurable. The diagnosis also required the presence of two symptoms, either positive or negative. The current version of the DSM (DSM V) specifies that at least one of the symptoms must be positive (e.g., hallucinations or delusions), and does not include the earlier subtypes such as paranoid, catatonic, or disorganised. This was in the light of observations that the subtypes, though descriptively useful, did not correlate with response to drug therapy, progression of the disorder, or any causative factors, i.e., they were not very useful…

Despite the inconsistencies and variability in diagnosis (note that even today, two people diagnosed with schizophrenia may have no symptoms in common), the idea of 'schizophrenia' has retained an honoured position in psychiatry – in fact, the anti-psychiatrist Thomas Szasz referred to schizophrenia as 'the sacred symbol of psychiatry'.[2] On the plus side, this focus has generated an enormous amount of research into the condition, with several research journals devoted just to this one disorder. What have we found?

Explanations – neurotransmitters

Antipsychotic drugs were introduced in the early 1950s, and one, chlorpromazine, was found to be reasonably effective in around 50% of patients with schizophrenia. This was a major breakthrough, as previous non-drug treatments such as insulin-coma therapy and the legendary frontal lobotomy were largely ineffective, as well as being barbaric. Drugs rapidly took over, with a range of compounds being available by the 1960s. Simultaneously, neuropharmacology had finally begun to unravel the role of neurotransmitters and their pathways in behaviour. It turned out that all drugs effective against schizophrenia were potent antagonists at dopamine receptors (antagonist = blocks the receptors so dopamine can't bind onto them); that is, they reduced dopamine neurotransmission in the brain. Using what we now see as rather simple-minded logic, it was theorised that schizophrenia must therefore be caused by *overactivity in dopamine pathways*. This dopamine hypothesis then dominated the field for the next 30 years – the simple idea that the system disruption underlying schizophrenia was rooted in biased dopamine pathways.

There were always problems with the dopamine hypothesis: 30–40% of patients were resistant to drugs, while efforts to find consistent changes in, e.g., dopamine levels or dopamine receptors were unsuccessful. Specific and more powerful dopamine (DA) antagonists were not necessarily more effective as antipsychotics. There was some indirect supporting evidence: amphetamine and other drugs which release DA in the brain can lead to hallucinations and paranoid delusions similar to the symptoms of schizophrenia.

Then a new generation of drugs (second-generation or atypical antipsychotics) were introduced in the 1990s. These drugs were less potent DA antagonists, but had actions on a broader range of neurotransmitters, such as serotonin. Early signs were that these compounds were significantly more effective against schizophrenia, but this was premature. Although one drug in particular, clozapine, seems to be more potent against negative symptoms, in general there are few clear differences in effectiveness between first- and second-generation drugs. More recently, third-generation drugs have been introduced, which also have a range of actions on different neurotransmitters but are not significantly more effective than previous antipsychotics. So why do we keep introducing new compounds? Well, we would like to find one that works better than previous ones, but failing that, it is important to find drugs that have less severe side effects and are better tolerated by patients. What we call 'patient non-compliance', where the side effects of drugs prevent the patient continuing treatment, is a real issue in drug therapy for schizophrenia. We have never had drugs specific enough to target only the disturbed brain systems.

As neuropharmacology unpacks the detailed functions and interactions of neurotransmitters such as DA, serotonin, acetylcholine, glutamate, GABA, etc., so models of schizophrenia shift. For instance, DA overactivity in the striatum (the action selection and reward system) has been linked to positive symptoms, while underactivity in the mesocortical DA pathway, leading to reduced frontal cortical activity (affecting the modulatory system), might be linked to negative symptoms. Restoring the balance between sub-cortical and cortical activity by targeting DA, serotonin, glutamate, and cholinergic networks is a current goal of drug research. But it is difficult…

When drugs do work, the therapeutic effect, damping down positive symptoms, takes some days or weeks to develop. As the drug's pharmacological action on receptors is immediate, this implies that what we are seeing is a readjustment of circuits downstream from the drug's primary target (e.g., DA receptors). This also explains why 'messier' drugs, acting on several neurotransmitter targets, are more effective than 'purer' compounds. The symptoms of schizophrenia can involve sensory and motor functions, cognitive domains such as attention and language, and our emotion circuits, so it is no surprise that multiple brain systems need to be targeted. The specific pattern of symptoms will vary from patient to patient (this heterogeneity is why research into schizophrenia is so difficult and why progress is so slow), which explains why no single drug is consistently effective across patients and why there is such a high proportion of treatment-resistant patients.

Explanations – genetics, neuropathology, and neurodevelopment

It has been known for 60 years that schizophrenia has a high genetic loading. Twin studies, looking at the incidence of schizophrenia in monozygotic (identical genes) and dizygotic (born at the same time from two different eggs, so not genetically identical) twin pairs, demonstrated conclusively that the concordance rate (the chance that if one twin has the disorder, the other has it) was much higher in monozygotic twins than in dizygotic twins. This was backed up by family and adoption studies, which showed that the closer the genetic relationship to someone with schizophrenia the greater the chance of developing the disorder. However, the concordance rate in monozygotic twins was nowhere near 100% (it's around 40–50%), as it should be if schizophrenia was 100% genetic, meaning that environmental factors are also involved.

However, the high genetic loading (of all the psychological disorders, only bipolar disorder has a higher genetic component) did lead to a search for the 'schizophrenia gene'. Did they find one? No. There were early claims for one or two 'schizophrenia genes', but these were soon dismissed. Consistent with the notion of polygenicity, which we came across in the 'Nature or nurture?' section, the revolution in genetic research over the last 20 years has conclusively shown that there are over a hundred genetic factors involved in schizophrenia. These are not major mutations, but slight alterations in the makeup of particular genes (e.g., differences in single letters of the DNA code, so-called single nucleotide polymorphisms or SNPs) or in mechanisms of gene expression. Although different studies come up with different arrays of these factors, what is noticeable is that many of the genes affected are involved in brain growth and development. Chapter 7 reviewed some of the complexities of brain (and behaviour) development and their interactions with the environment. It is easy to see how even minor perturbations in these processes might lead to imbalances between the various brain systems reviewed throughout this book, and a range of cognitive and emotional symptoms.

The view that schizophrenia is a neurodevelopmental disorder is becoming more prevalent. Although classic symptoms emerge in the late teens and twenties, studies have found minor movement abnormalities in children who go on to develop the full schizophrenia profile. Research has also found brain pathology (loss of brain tissue) in a significant number of people with schizophrenia. In common with virtually every aspect of schizophrenia, there are inconsistencies in findings, though the temporal lobe and frontal areas are often implicated. This pathology can already be found in first diagnosis, drug-naïve patients, so it is not due to long-term drug therapy, but may be the result of problems during early brain development.

If schizophrenia is not entirely determined by genetics, what are the contributing environmental factors? Those with links to schizophrenia include birth complications (which may lead to oxygen deprivation and consequent brain damage), prenatal infections in the mother, early postnatal stress, e.g., physical or emotional abuse, and being born in the spring months (the latter linked to the greater risk of maternal infections during a winter pregnancy). Additionally, chronic cannabis abuse in early adulthood has been identified as a trigger factor for the onset of schizophrenia. Note that the contribution of any one of these environmental factors is small compared to the genetic contribution, but they may interact with genetic factors to produce slight perturbations in the development of brain circuits that lead eventually to schizophrenia.

Most research into schizophrenia (and there are hundreds of research papers annually) takes this biomedical approach, trying to identify, through brain scanning and genetics in particular, brain abnormalities. Psychologists often take an alternative approach, focusing on cognitive deficits in schizophrenia and building models of the processing impairments underlying the disorder.

Schizophrenia – cognitive processing

People with schizophrenia show a range of cognitive deficits, so much so that cognitive impairment has been proposed as a potential diagnostic criterion for the disorder. Studies have shown deficits in basic processing speed, attention, working memory, verbal and visual learning and memory, reasoning, and social cognition. (Note that these deficits will vary from person to person, a variability that unfortunately applies to most areas of schizophrenia research, psychological and biological.) More severe deficits do seem to be linked to poorer response to drug therapy and worse outcomes.

Given the range of cognitive loss it is difficult to imagine overall integrative models. The most plausible accounts see the impairment as a global deficit rather than a set of localised problems, so they can focus on broader brain systems. The focus has been on the prefrontal cortex and its sub-areas that impose top-down modulatory control on many other systems, i.e., in the dynamics by which the modulatory system controls the content-specific systems. In particular, executive processes and attention would be severely affected by prefrontal dysfunction. This could come about by imbalanced inputs from striatal dopamine hyperactivity, and cortical dopamine hypoactivity (as outlined earlier). There may also be local imbalances in cortical microcircuits, involving neurotransmitters such as GABA and glutamate. The loss of top-down control would affect most cognitive functions, including attention, perception, and language processes. It would explain bizarre interpretations of sensory input (e.g., auditory hallucinations), and dysfunctions in the use of memory, knowledge, expectations, and emotion to interpret input.

Some of these effects are linked to the idea of self- and source monitoring, the fact that we normally predict the sensory consequences of our own actions (see Chapter 5, the section on 'Living in the Future', and the discussion of 'alien hand', p. 180). We've seen that anomalies in predicted sensory consequences of actions and predicted associations between information arriving from different brain systems can lead to delusional beliefs, in the examples of alien hand and Capgras syndromes. This also applies, for example, to inner speech and our thoughts. Top-down executive control allows us to recognise their origin, but if this is lacking then inner speech may be experienced as auditory hallucinations, while thoughts can be attributed to other 'alien' sources (in people with schizophrenia, their thoughts are sometimes interpreted as being inserted by other people, often celebrities…).

One even broader approach is through social cognition and the computations about other people's intentions (mentalising). This idea covers our ability to put ourselves in another's place, and understand their motivations, actions, thoughts, and emotions, and is seen as the basis for empathy and cooperation. Psychologists call this 'theory of mind', a model introduced in the 1990s to help explain the symptoms of autism. We have seen that there are many systems in the brain that process information about other people (see 'The Brain's Favourite Content' in Chapter 5 for more detail on our social brain). In theory of mind tasks, participants might be shown a scenario and asked to predict the behaviour and moods of the people involved. Over the last 20 years, deficits on these tasks have been demonstrated in people with schizophrenia.

Schizophrenia is in part a profound breakdown in conscious self-awareness, and unfortunately, we do not have simple models of consciousness (see Chapter 9 for more on this). Approaches almost always take too simple a view, such as looking for localised deficits or single neurotransmitters. This made sense in the past. An analogy for this is when you lose your keys on a street with occasional lamp posts; the keys probably aren't under the occasional lamps, but it makes sense to start looking there before exploring the whole street, because that's where the light is. With schizophrenia, we now need to be looking in the rest of the street. We still hope there are some keys out there.

We have spent a long time on schizophrenia. That's because it is among the most serious and disabling of the psychological disorders, and still responsible for the highest proportion of institutionalised patients. People with schizophrenia have shorter lives and most are not in employment. Although they can occur in a small proportion of non-clinical people, the dramatic positive symptoms (hallucinations and delusions) and loss of insight represent an apparent qualitative shift from normal experience. Despite 70 years of intensive research, we still do not know exactly what causes it, and advances in drug therapy have been grindingly slow. We have some general models of brain systems, but little in the way of consistent and specific findings. All very frustrating.

On a more positive note, we'll take a much shorter look at clinical depression, or major depressive disorder.

Major depressive disorder (MDD)

MDD seems clearly on a continuum with normal experiences of low mood, though far more severe. There is no loss of insight, and diagnosis is relatively straightforward; for a minimum period of two weeks there needs to be occurrence of at least five symptoms, such as sad mood, significant changes in sleeping patterns or appetite, loss of energy, feelings of guilt, and thoughts of death and suicide. A key difference with schizophrenia is that people with depression will often self-refer for treatment, as it interferes with daily life, and they are aware they need help.

Studies find a genetic loading in depression of 30–40%, significantly less than in schizophrenia. It's more about bad things happening out there. There is also evidence that this varies with type of depression, with the genetic contribution being higher for endogenous melancholic depression than for depression clearly linked to major life events ('reactive' depression). In line with schizophrenia, at least 100 genes have been identified as possibly being involved in depression.

Depression – neurotransmitters

Driven by the effectiveness of antidepressant drugs, the serotonin model of depression has dominated the medical approach in the same way the dopamine hypothesis dominated schizophrenia research and therapy. Although different antidepressant drug groups work in different ways (e.g., by increasing synaptic release, blocking enzymatic breakdown in the synapse, or preventing reuptake into the presynaptic terminal) it is assumed that they all increase serotonin neurotransmission in the brain. As we saw in our back-of-an-envelope introduction to neurotransmitters in Chapter 4, serotonin is the mood neurotransmitter.

However, there is a current controversy over the lack of direct evidence for changes in the brain serotonin system in depression, e.g., reduced serotonin release, or variations in receptor numbers or distribution. This follows a similar controversy over the actual effectiveness of antidepressant drugs. As in schizophrenia, a significant number of people with depression do not respond to drug therapy, while effectiveness studies always find a substantial placebo effect – i.e., the antidepressant action of an inert substance is sometimes close to the effectiveness of active antidepressants; drugs may help in around 50% of cases, while the placebo effect may be of the order of 30–40%. An extreme view is that only for the most severe cases of depression is there reliable evidence that drugs work (but note that even if drugs are only working through a placebo effect, they can still bring relief to the depressed person). In our section on 'Keeping Score' (Chapter 5), we saw the importance of accumulated reward prediction errors in estimating current happiness, so an information processing explanation that takes into account expectations may explain some aspects of the placebo effect.

As with all our behaviour, depression will be correlated with changes in the brain. This book has implied all the way through that isolating individual systems is not the way to study the brain. All complex behaviour will involve dynamic interacting systems, and focusing on single neurotransmitters was never likely to provide a comprehensive answer. fMRI studies (comparing resting state brain activity in people with depression compared with neurotypical controls) implicate a range of neural circuits: in particular, connections between frontal cortical areas, striatum, limbic areas including the amygdala and the anterior cingulate, and the angular gyrus. Given that depression involves major shifts in mood, motivation, and cognition it is no surprise that a range of structures and pathways is implicated. It also follows that numerous neurotransmitters and neuromodulators will have a role in the brain state we call depression. It is vanishingly unlikely that modulating levels of single neurotransmitters will restore the balance between several dynamic systems.

One interesting recent development in treatment is the use of cortical stimulation using electrical or magnetic pulses through external electrodes (transcranial magnetic or direct current stimulation, see Box 3.2); this has had some promising results in people with depression, though it does not help localise antidepressant action to specific circuits or neurotransmitters.

Depression – cognitive processing

Studies comparing drug therapy for depression with a variety of psychological therapies, including Freudian psychotherapy and cognitive behaviour therapy (CBT), consistently show comparable levels of effectiveness (unlike schizophrenia, where many studies of

CBT show only small and inconsistent effects that are highly dependent on individual differences). One obvious reason for this is that in depression we have a fairly coherent cognitive profile that can be addressed through psychological approaches. This is summarised in Beck's influential model of cognition in depression, the 'negative triad'. According to this, the depressed person is in a habitual cognitive state made up of negative views of the world, themselves, and the future. The goal of, for example, CBT is to challenge these beliefs; for instance, can it be really true that nothing good has ever happened to you, or that you have never achieved anything worthwhile in your life? It sounds easy, but these negative thoughts are often based in early experience of abuse, separation, or loss. They become embedded as these early stresses lead to differential tuning of those brain systems underlying personality (see earlier in the chapter). Early biasing of our value, trust, decision, and reward systems can lead to the depressive personality. Change through therapy is possible but difficult, as the adult with depression has lived with this personality for many years. As anyone who has tried to break straightforward bad habits (cigarettes, cake) will testify, shifting behaviour is hard. Time for some cigarettes and cake... but first:

A note on anxiety disorders

A number of disorders are listed under the category of 'anxiety'. These include generalised anxiety disorder, phobias, panic disorder, social anxiety disorder, agoraphobia, post-traumatic stress disorder (PTSD), and obsessive-compulsive disorder (OCD). Each has its own specific symptoms, but what they have in common is a pervasive sense of perceived threat, that the world is a dangerous place. The extreme levels of anxiety drastically affect everyday behaviour, with some sufferers finding it difficult to even leave the house.

Anxiety disorders have some genetic influence but have also been strongly linked to adversity in early life – physical and emotional abuse, separation from primary carers, socioeconomic deprivation. We know from animal work that our stress response (see Chapter 6) is primed by early stress: in general, moderate levels of stress in the early years produces stress arousal systems adapted to the world we live in – we need to respond to environmental threats. Too little or too much early stress produces maladapted stress responses. High levels produce systems that are constantly vigilant and produce exaggerated physiological and cognitive responses to any perceived threat, preparing for fight, flight, or freezing. As with depression, we see early experience, perhaps combined with genetic influences, altering the dynamics and biases between brain systems.

Of course, other factors may be involved. Direct traumatic events can lead to PTSD or, say, a phobia of dogs after being bitten (though notably, spider phobias are rarely linked to traumatic spider experiences...). Overpowering experiences, especially threats to survival, may lead to overactivity and 'burn out' of key structures such as the amygdala (fear and threat) and hippocampus (emotional memory). There may be biological factors – some cases of OCD, with their obsession with hygiene, cleanliness, and infection, have been linked to a prior infection with streptococcus bacteria (perhaps through the autoimmune response to the infection then affecting brain systems). Phobias can have a learning basis through modelling – you see your carers overreacting to spiders, so you guess these things must be very dangerous (the same thing happens with young chimpanzees and fear of snakes; if mum is scared, I'm scared); relearning appropriate responses through systematic desensitisation can be very effective for simple phobias, but as we have seen, left to its own devices, the amygdala does not forget.

Brain circuits in anxiety disorders include the limbic system, especially the amygdala and its role in vigilance and the detection of threat, leading to an exaggerated state of 'fear'. Also critical are connections between the amygdala, the hypothalamus and brainstem centres involved in the stress arousal pathways (see the section on the HPA axis in Chapter 6) and organisation of defensive behaviours. Of course, cognitive appraisal of threat and decisions on appropriate responses will involve forebrain systems, especially frontal cortical areas and basal ganglia. Otherwise, there would be no place for horror films or bungee jumping.

So the overall picture for anxiety is similar to those for schizophrenia and depression. It involves many brain circuits and their associated neurotransmitters. One difference is that apart from the moderate effectiveness of antianxiety drugs in generalised anxiety, there is no consistently effective drug therapy for anxiety disorders such as PTSD, OCD, and phobias. There is therefore no drug-based evidence that these conditions involve just one or two neurotransmitters. As argued above, this is to be expected with complex disorders involving cognition, emotion, and motivation, and their associated brain circuitry. Until models of these disorders are built around the interaction of multiple brain circuits, there will be little progress in understanding them or developing new therapies.

Psychological disorders – an evolutionary conundrum?

We'll finish this chapter with an evolutionary conundrum. Schizophrenia is associated with lower life expectancy and lower fertility. In its classic form it is seriously disabling. It also has a significant genetic component. According to classic evolutionary theory, based around selective advantage, schizophrenia should have been eliminated from the human genome, given the substantial disadvantages it comes with. Why is it still around? Why are DNA variants that increase its risk still circulating in human populations?

Throughout this book we have emphasised the evolutionary continuity between the modern human brain and behaviour, and our ancestors throughout primate evolution. One argument for the persistence of schizophrenia is that it must be associated with some advantageous characteristics. The current evidence that its genetic background involves over a hundred genes makes this more likely. The suggestion is that some combinations of these genes result in characteristics that would be advantageous in small hunter-gatherer groups. These might include imagination, creativity, magical thinking, and leadership, but fall short of producing the full schizophrenia syndrome. Evidence that some of the key 'schizophrenia genes' seem to have appeared as late as 100,000 years ago also supports ideas that they are linked to the rapid cognitive evolution (e.g., language, self-awareness) that we see in *Homo sapiens* between 100,000 and 50,000 years ago. These rather controversial views (i.e., speculations) see schizophrenia as an unfortunate by-product of the evolution of the complex modern human brain. Perhaps there are more risks of dysregulated dynamics in trying to control a bigger cortex. Going back to earlier discussions, it is the full complement of schizophrenia risk DNA variants that leads to a disruption of typical brain development, leading to dynamic imbalances between brain circuits, and the classic symptoms.

There are, as you might guess, evolutionary approaches to depression and anxiety. The behavioural inertia, lack of energy, and social withdrawal associated with depression has been linked to submission behaviour seen in primate groups. In monkey and ape colonies there is a dominance hierarchy, reinforced by conflict (more on this in the next chapter). Submission gestures are common (also seen in dogs and cats, if you look closely), and function to reduce physical aggression between protagonists and leave both animals alive. Primates isolated from their peer groups show behaviour that looks very like human depression, reinforcing the idea that human depression is an evolutionary hangover, albeit overlaid with all the complexities of human social and cultural evolution. Other speculations are less convincing, e.g., that the depressed hunter-gatherer found it hard to generate the energy to leave the home cave, so was less likely to be squashed by a mammoth (this is a genuine published idea, apart from the mammoths, which we have added for colour).

With phobias, speculation is more straightforward. Simple phobias usually involve clear situations of threat and danger – dogs, spiders, alligators, heights, darkness, balloons, being trapped in a small space. No one (and we have checked the literature) has a phobia of tulips or tennis racquets, so we are dealing with situations that would always have been a potential threat, from the first moment a hominid ancestor inflated a pig's bladder to bursting point. So it makes sense that throughout evolution we have developed brain circuitry to detect them and avoid them – this is referred to as 'biological preparedness'. But note, these will be systems to develop detectors for threat, not built-in banana detectors (see Chapter 2; in this context, detectors for dangerous bananas). Bias these systems in early development, and the developmental outcome may be a phobia. With OCD there is a focus on hygiene and cleanliness (avoidance of infection), so a similar argument would apply.

It is hard to imagine the sort of evidence that would test these evolutionary hypotheses (which is why speculation is rife) and the acid test for them is as dilute as mere plausibility. Genetics is likely to be the key battleground. This would depend on the genetic architecture of a disorder being identified and its effects on brain systems clarified. It could be tracked back to the genomes of archaic homo species – one of the most dramatic breakthroughs in genetics in recent years has been the ability to screen ancient genomes, e.g., of Neanderthals – so we would then have a convincing model of underlying brain dysfunction in, e.g., schizophrenia, and a picture of its evolutionary origins. Genetic studies have shown that *Homo sapiens* interbred with Neanderthals and outside of Africa (Neanderthals evolved outside the African continent) we all carry some Neanderthal DNA (up to around 3%). A fascinating recent study found that schizophrenia risk and the severity of schizophrenia symptoms in those with a diagnosis was found to be lower in those with a greater proportion of Neanderthal DNA; moreover, more Neanderthal DNA was associated with lower dopamine synthesis capacity in the striatum and pons (less dopamine!). This supports the notion that schizophrenia may be specific to modern humans.

━━━━━ Box 8.1 ━━━━━

Predicting and changing behaviour

Psychopathy (antisocial personality disorder) is a syndrome characterised by self-interest, a lack of empathy for others, and a lack of remorse for actions that hurt others. It is often associated with antisocial and criminal behaviour. It could be seen as a bad thing... There is also evidence that incarcerated psychopaths or people scoring highly on psychopathy scales have specific abnormalities in brain function (you may think this is obvious, given their behaviour). It has been claimed that potential psychopaths can therefore be identified from brain scans; if so, what should we do? Incarcerate them in case they act out their psychopathic tendencies ('pre-emptive custody')? Or wait and see what happens – not all people with this brain pattern show psychopathic behaviour... these are tricky problems, involving balancing individual liberty against protecting society. And let's not forget free will – already in the United States defendants have used arguments that their criminal behaviour is due to (or 'determined by') genetic tendencies or brain abnormalities. So (argue their lawyers) they are not technically responsible for their actions.

At some point we may have the clear data and means to correct these brain abnormalities. We already do this; drugs effective against schizophrenia or depression act to restore neurotransmitter

(Continued)

balances and we see this as unambiguously good (leaving aside issues of side effects), allowing people to live better lives. Lithium is a drug used to stabilise mood in people with bipolar disorder. Formerly known as manic-depression, this syndrome has episodes of mania and hyperactivity, followed by episodes of depression. However, the episodes of mania are often associated with creativity and imagination, and some people prefer not to take the drug but live with the mood instability, as the drug removes this vital part of their personality.

Deep brain stimulation (DBS) of areas of the basal ganglia via implanted electrodes is sometimes used to help restore voluntary movement in people with Parkinson's disease, a movement disorder characterised by uncontrolled tremors and eventual loss of movement. However, a few patients suffer serious changes in mood and personality after DBS, so much so that they have to be institutionalised – in these cases, is the cost–benefit of the intervention worthwhile?

Box 8.2

Neuromanipulation – do it yourself?

Drugs and electrical stimulation have been used by professionals over the last century to alter behaviour in what they hope are systematic ways. In recent years, a new technique, transcranial magnetic or electrical stimulation (tMS or tES; see Box 3.2 for more detail) has been used in investigations of cortical function or for treatment of depression. Electrodes on the side of the skull are used to pass small magnetic or electrical pulses across the cortex, stimulating or inhibiting various areas of the cortex and perhaps the limbic system. Understanding of how these techniques work is limited, but they have shown some benefit in treating depression (probably linked to the established effects of electroconvulsive therapy in depression), and in improving aspects of cognition. Neurons are electrical entities which use chemical signalling, so an effect of electrical stimulation on neurotransmitter-linked differences in neural activity is not beyond the bounds of imagination.

Kits for tES are actually available on the internet, allowing for unregulated use of tES by individuals for whatever reason. Side effects of tES can include facial twitches, headache, episodes of mania, and, in rare cases, seizures, so it should not be used by non-professionals. However, the appeal of lifting depression or improving cognitive skills is likely to overcome any worries over side effects, while official regulation of this area is largely absent.

Over the last decade drug use by healthy people to improve learning and memory has increased rapidly. Ritalin (methylphenidate) is used clinically as a treatment for ADHD. Related to amphetamine, and probably working through dopamine systems, Ritalin can also improve concentration and memory in some healthy individuals (though it is unlikely to increase intelligence); it is the most common of the 'smart pills', 'cognitive enhancers', or 'nootropic' drugs. Nootropics are proving popular with students at exam time regardless of potential side effects such as nausea, increased anxiety, and even psychosis, while evidence suggests cognitive improvement is variable across individuals and is in many cases absent. Supply of nootropics, like tES, is largely unregulated. Ritalin is a prescribed drug but finds its way routinely into the general population. Coffee, on the other hand, is available at the local corner store.

Notes

1   Eliot, L., Ahmed, A., Khan, H. & Patel, J. (2021). Dump the 'dimorphism': Comprehensive synthesis of human brain studies reveals few male-female differences beyond size. *Neuroscience & Biobehavioral Reviews*, 125: 667–697. https;//doi.org/10.1016/j.neubiorev.2021.02.026

2   Szasz, T.S. (1976). *Schizophrenia: The Sacred Symbol of Psychiatry*. Basic Books.

9
HUMANS APART

In much of what we have covered so far, we have focused on how brains work in a similar way across most vertebrates, mammals, and social primates. That's because the way the brain works is rooted in its evolutionary origin and evolution has been conservative in the range of mechanisms it has deployed. And we did say at the outset that we weren't going to obsess about what makes humans fantastic and better as a species. After all, humans don't have the biggest brains – that's elephants and whales. And while humans have a high proportion of cortex in our brains, it's on a par with chimpanzees, horses, and short-finned whales. Sure, humans have quite a lot of brain for our body size, but amongst primates, this proportion isn't strongly linked with thinking ability. We do have a decent number of neurons: over twice as many as gorillas. But even then, not close to the number that dolphins have. And to be honest, we probably have the same number of neurons as our ancestors in the wider archaic homo family tree, including Neanderthals.

But this has left us feeling a little sad. Surely there is something special about humans? Bats have their echolocation, moles are great at digging, whales sing a mean song, and orangutans shine at climbing and clinging to trees. What's our thing? Humans may not sit above other species in a hierarchy, we can accept that, but we'll have some species-typical behaviours, right? So, that's what this chapter is about: what it is that humans do that makes them human (and not pingers or diggers or singers or clingers).

Let's start with a couple of easy wins. *Language*. Undoubtedly, the ability to share ideas through language is our species' signature cognitive skill. And *consciousness*. Yes, other animals are probably conscious to some extent, but surely we are the apogee of sentience, full of self-awareness and lived experience, sensation and emotion, reflection and intro-spection, bearers of an existential loneliness that has us staring to the starry skies wondering if there is any other sentient life out there. No other species spends as long looking in the mirror as humans.

Language in the Brain

We've skirted around language so far in this book – only mentioning it here and there. That's because language is *big* for humans, and we wanted to save it up. Language is a truly beautiful artefact, capable of infinite expression, the medium of some of our greatest

WINNER OF THE "BEST AT BEING A HUMAN" CONTEST:

HUMANS!

Figure 9.1 What humans are best at... being humans

works of art. And some poems. It has a unique syntactic recipe that allows a limited vocabulary of words to be recombined into a boundless variety of sentences. We needed to do all the biological groundwork first, so we could do it justice. But we're here now. The stage is set. Let's do it.

The psychology of language distinguishes different elements: sounds (phonemes), words (the lexicon), meanings (semantics), grammar (syntax), the emotional melody of spoken sentences (prosody), intended meanings (pragmatics), and the symbols of written words (orthography). How do these work in the brain? Based on our groundwork, let's review how we might expect language to work in the brain and how we're going to pin down its evolutionary origin.

First, language as a species-specific skill is unlikely to involve a special additional part of the brain, in the same way that bats haven't evolved a special new part of the brain that supports their echolocation. It will be a new use of the existing brain structures.

Second, it's going to be hard to be definitive about evolutionary origins, although we can speculate. We've seen that evolution tends to innovate at the periphery (out in the shape and function of the body, or in the sensory organs) rather than in the central nervous system. Mammalian brains are limited variants of a basic plan, involving differential scaling up of structures and some tweaks of wiring and neurons. The brain is large but predictably scaled up in humans (including more at the front of the cortex).

Third, the central nervous system is a generalist and doesn't (evolutionarily) commit in advance to very specific computations (no built-in banana detectors). Neurons adapt during development to their neural neighbourhood, the body they find themselves in, and the experiences that the body has. We may, therefore, not find built-in grammar detectors.

Fourth, species-typical behaviours likely arise from the brain in three ways: from tuning attention and motivation through hormones and neurotransmitters, which generates different experiences to learn from; from plasticity, the ability to self-organise and learn from experiences; and from differences in computational power through bigger brains, providing more scope to acquire sophisticated behaviour and planning abilities.

Fifth, because the brain doesn't like abstraction, a lot of language will likely involve sensory and motor hierarchies and the links between them. For perception to link to action, the brain has two main routes, a dorsal route over the top involving perception for now (to drive immediate motor behaviours) and a ventral route underneath involving perception for later (object recognition). Although the left and the right hemispheres are largely the same, the left tends to specialise towards habitual or routine behaviours while the right tends to specialise towards vigilance and emotion.

Sixth, the brain works by prediction, by a continuous crosstalk between sensory and motor systems (what will I sense when I do this action, what action would produce this sensation) and comparison to actual outcomes.

Lastly, the brain basis of language will inevitably involve a historical legacy of strange names for bits of the brain based on the endeavours of pioneering neuroanatomists.

This is the framework we'll need to fit language into. Let's get the history out of the way first. Franciscus Sylvius was a Dutch scientist and anatomist who in the 17th century observed the presence of a deep fissure or cleft on each side of the brain that separates the frontal and parietal lobes from the temporal lobes. This became known as the Sylvian fissure. The key language areas of the brain lie around this fissure on the left-hand side, in the so-called perisylvian region (in true neuroanatomy style, this area is also called the lateral sulcus and the lateral fissure; it's almost like they don't want you to understand it).

Next, in the 19th century Pierre Broca, a French scientist and anatomist, observed that several patients who, post-mortem evidence revealed, had experienced localised damage to a particular brain region then showed impairments in producing language, particularly in forming sentences. The syndrome was thereafter called Broca's aphasia. The frontal cortex has three main gyri (folds): the superior (upper), middle, and inferior (lower). The key region was towards the back of the inferior frontal gyrus on the left-hand side (a region that sits, coincidentally, just above the primary motor areas for articulating the lips, tongue, and larynx in the motor hierarchy). This region became known as Broca's area.

Carl Wernicke was a 19th-century German physician and anatomist who was a fan of Broca's work. He observed that several patients who had experienced localised damage to a different brain region then showed impairments in comprehending language; while they could still produce speech with a natural-sounding rhythm and a relatively normal syntax, it was empty of meaning, often with invented words and expressions. The syndrome was thereafter called Wernicke's aphasia. The temporal cortex has three main gyri: the superior, middle, and inferior (there are two others, the fusiform gyrus and the parahippocampal gyrus). The key region was towards the back of the superior temporal gyrus on the left-hand side (a region that sits, coincidentally, where the tops of the sensory hierarchies for sound, vision, and body/space meet). This region became known as Wernicke's area. There is a major white matter fibre tract (communication superhighway) linking Wernicke's and Broca's areas called the arcuate fasciculus. This tract is ideally positioned if you wanted to use sensory information about meaning and concepts to drive sequences of motor actions of articulators like the tongue, lips, and voice box.

Now let's get into the nitty gritty of how language works in the brain. When you are listening to someone say 'The referee blew the whistle', the perceptual information enters the bottom of the sensory hierarchy in the primary auditory cortex in both temporal lobes next to the ears. Moving up the sensory hierarchy, the next steps occur in the left temporal lobe, combining information from both sides of the brain. Patterns are spotted in the auditory signal that correspond to speech sounds, the consonants and vowels that make up the phonology of the language, and this allows the recognition of individual words.

Now that you have recognised a spoken word like 'whistle' from the *whur* and the *iss* and the *ull*, there are three directions you can head. First, there's the perception-for-now dorsal route, allowing repetition of the speech without accessing meaning (you say 'whistle', I say 'whistle' too). This route connects the superior temporal lobe to the premotor cortices in the frontal lobe via the arcuate fasciculus and superior longitudinal fascicle (another superhighway). The perception-for-later route by contrast involves connecting the sounds of words with two different stores of meaning, which work in partnership. One store sits right at the front of the temporal lobe, at the very top of the visual object recognition sensory hierarchy (the anterior temporal lobe). This is a hub that connects all the sensory and motor features of objects across modalities (e.g., the shape of a whistle, the colour of a whistle, the sound of a whistle, what actions are associated with a whistle). Accessing the meaning of words often reactivates the systems that encode these dimensions – for example, motor systems for verbs, sensory systems for nouns (visual for shape, somatosensory for touch, etc.). This hub recognises objects irrespective of the sensory context in which they are encountered. The other store of meaning sits at the back of the superior temporal gyrus, integrating information across the sensory modalities (audition, vision, body, and space). It processes meaning in context, the actual emerging understanding as you process the words in a sentence (a referee blowing a whistle at a particular point in the football game). Yes, you guessed it, the meaning-in-context system lies in Wernicke's area, and your language comprehension will be stuffed if this area is damaged (though if it's any help, you can still pass 20-questions type tests about word meanings using the context-independent store of definitions at the front of the temporal lobe).

Let's say you want to produce a sentence yourself ('I disagree with the referee's decision at this critical point in the match'). Once the message is formulated in the meaning-in-context system, this must be communicated to the motor hierarchy in the front of the brain. The principal communication is via the arcuate fasciculus. The motor hierarchy has multiple levels, from the primary motor areas that will drive the expulsion of air, the tension of the vocal cords, and the position of tongue and lips, to the higher levels that will be required to plan the complex sequence of motor movements that make up a sentence. These higher levels of the motor hierarchy lie further forward in the frontal cortex and include Broca's area. However, the motor hierarchy also involves systems for initiating voluntary action in the basal ganglia, and for executing automatic motor programmes in the cerebellum, so language isn't all in the cortex.

Language comprehension and production are tightly linked activities. You learn to produce your native language as a baby by shaping your speech production from burbling so it increasingly sounds like the words you hear other people saying. It is a continuous crosstalk of motor production and sensory evaluation, in which the brain makes predictions of what motor commands should produce what sounds. This tight coupling is maintained throughout language processing, so, for example, Broca's area is involved in language comprehension. The brain also uses a predictive model of what word is going to be perceived next in an unfolding sentence to help build its understanding. If I were saying this sentence, the system speculates, what would I say next?

Language production also involves control processes that select which words to retrieve and which to ignore (e.g., in choosing how to describe the referee, you may wish to inhibit certain more colourful vocabulary items when in polite company). A lot of language production is about selection, of particular words (*friend* or *mate* or *colleague*? *dog* or *chien* or *Hund*?) or sequences (*the dog chased the cat*, or *the cat was chased by the dog*? – depends on who the story is about!). Selection is determined by the context, audience, and intended message, and is particularly tricky when the best choice is the one you least frequently use. Selection requires the involvement of parts of the modulatory system in the prefrontal cortex, including those sitting at the top of the ventral stream, to boost the activation of certain parts of the semantic and phonological systems and inhibit others. You can feel it hurting when you are asked to give a list of animals: *dog, cat, horse, pig, cow*, um, *zebra, lion, giraffe*, um, um. The further you go, the more the modulatory system is inhibiting your previous selections so you don't produce them again, which eventually leaves your lexicon drenched in a sea of inhibition and unable to offer anything more.

At the heart of the language system, however, lie Broca's and Wernicke's areas, which are each involved in both language perception and production tasks. These likely function as hubs that receive and send signals to all the other areas involved in perceiving and producing speech.

The special bit

Plenty of animals communicate, don't they? Other primates have whoops and shrieks, facial expressions and hand gestures. What is unique about human language is syntax, the grammatical rules that allow recombination of words to make an infinite number of sentences, rules that specify which words in a sequence link to which other ones to create the correct meaning. However, it's hard to find any part of the brain's language system that just processes syntax and not a word's meaning. Any region bothered about syntactic information also seems to be bothered about individual word meanings. Syntax may be a special human power, but it's hard to spot inside the brain. Instead, brain systems are equally wedded to meaning, as if the main goal of language were communication, with most of our knowledge of language dedicated to lexical semantics (word meanings) and comparatively less knowledge required on how words should be combined.

Language systems are still content-specific. Broca's area processes complex motor sequences over articulators, but this is not a jack-of-all-trades processor for any skill involving rules. Although other domains are underpinned by rules that resemble grammars, such as arithmetic, music, and action observation/planning, these skills don't employ the same regions within Broca's area. Moreover, the content-specific systems involved in language are also involved in other non-linguistic tasks that use this content (for example, Wernicke's area and the anterior temporal lobe are involved with making semantic decisions about pictures; the primary motor areas for moving the tongue and lips are equally used to make a click or blow a kiss). The 'language system', then, is the online functional integration of these content-specific systems in the service of language tasks.

Broca's and Wernicke's aphasia only occur after left-sided damage and therefore demonstrate that some skills are specialised to one side of the brain. However, not all of language is specialised to the left hemisphere: it is the small-scale structural parts – recognising speech sounds, words, and sentences to construct sentence-level meaning. Other parts of language processing are specialised to the right hemisphere – emotional vocabulary such as swear words; recognising the melody or prosody of how a sentence is spoken, often signifying its emotional intention; understanding non-literal aspects of language, such as humour, irony, or sarcasm ('Oh, *very* good decision, referee'). These pragmatic skills require wider integration of the sentence-level meaning with the context and with what is known about the speaker, and utilise circuits for processing situational scripts, social intentions, and agents. Overall, the pattern of left–right specialisation fits with the pattern observed across species: parallelisation, with specialisation of habitual or routine behaviours to the left side, and vigilance to new situations and emotional responses to the right side. The hemispheric specialisation of language is a developmental outcome but not inevitable; early damage to the left hemisphere can lead to all aspects of language – phonology, lexical semantics, syntax, prosody, pragmatics – developing in the right hemisphere.

In short, while language and particularly grammar look special from the outside, when we go inside the brain, we see the usual suspects in operation: sensory and motor hierarchies, control, action selection, and motor-smoothing systems. The special brain structures aren't there.

The evolution of language

But look, cheer up, language is special from the outside. We don't have to quote you a Shakespeare sonnet to prove that (we particularly like the one with the roses). And it's fair to say that language *is* a species-typical behaviour for humans. There are no sonnets comprising whoops and shrieks. So how did it come about? Why do we have language but not other social primates?

Identifying selective pressures and evolutionary advantages of certain behaviours is, as we've said, like spotting shapes in the mist: very hard to do reliably. One of our favourite speculations is that the evolution of language was linked to the evolution of tool use. Social primates today use gestural communication as well as vocalisations. Perhaps an increasing reliance on tool use meant that humans needed their hands for tools and were pushed to channel communication through vocalisations (though to this day, a residue of gestural communication remains in humans). The combined demand to manipulate tools and to produce complex vocalisations might have offered reproductive advantages to those with more dextrous hands and more flexible vocal articulators. But that is speculation.

We can identify our broad evolutionary principles in action, however. Evolution can only improve what it already has – there is no new brain area for sophisticated language, just altered use of the sensorimotor association cortex. Evolution operates mainly on the periphery. The predominant modifications are in the articulation of our tongue and lips, the position of our larynx, the musculature controlling airflow (observe how you can't talk if you are extremely out of breath after a tough workout; if you're yawning; or if you've collapsed in fits of laughter – evolutionarily, laughter takes precedence over language as a primate-wide form of vocalised panting that supports social bonding, so go with it).

If you compare the structure of the vocal cords, these look different in humans compared to monkeys. But if you compare the arcuate fasciculus, connecting Broca's and Wernicke's areas, it looks similar in humans and monkeys. The central nervous system remains a generalist, ready to adapt. Indeed, it is sufficiently flexible that it can use the hands to produce language and vision to perceive language, using similar sensorimotor association cortex, in the form of sign language. There's no prior commitment to particular auditory computations for language. No built-in banana detectors.

Very likely, two further changes were important to evolve language. One was the increase in brain size, to provide the computational power necessary to learn the complex invariances (abstractions) in motor sequences required to produce language, as well as the conceptual power to generate and understand meanings in social contexts. The second was a change in motivation to make humans more social and less aggressive. Most social primates live in small or medium-sized groups of related individuals and are aggressive to out-group members. Humans live together in much larger groups of unrelated individuals, who specialise in different skills to contribute to the success of the group. Reduced aggression and larger group size provide the conditions for language to be advantageous in coordinating group activities. Tweaking motivations through hormonal influences on the limbic system and the reward system are likely important elements in creating species members who want to communicate and cooperate with each other, rather than fight.

Why don't other primates have our kind of language? Could they learn a language like ours, since they have similar brain anatomies (if a little bit smaller)? Maybe other primates like chimpanzees and gorillas don't have grammatical language only because they *never thought of it*? Well, if bribed with enough bananas, if trained from an early age when their brains are most plastic, if allowed to use clumsy hand signals rather than non-optimal vocal articulators, you can indeed get other great apes to learn language of a sort. A few hundred signs, some simple combinations.

But other primates *just don't care*. They are not interested in grammatical language. It's not their thing and they wouldn't choose to do it spontaneously. You might as well dress them in clown outfits to test how human-like they are. This lack of interest in grammatical language in other social primates is likely analogous to the difference in mating behaviour between prairie voles (monogamous) and montane voles (polygamous), when the species have otherwise identical brain structures. That is, the species-typical behaviour is partly created by different distributions of hormonal receptors in limbic and reward systems, altering the salience and reward value of certain social behaviours which drive the sensorimotor systems to acquire certain skills (provided those systems have the requisite conceptual power). Social motivations are therefore likely to be a key element to the distinctiveness of human language.

And then we invented reading

So, we evolved language and that's all working nicely and then, boom, 5,000 years ago, humans invented reading. Perhaps only a few hundred years ago, most of the world's population was illiterate. Is reading at odds with an evolutionary perspective? Not really. Per our theme, the central nervous system is a generalist, it has not made a commitment that language can only have auditory input; it's plastic and will adapt to experience. That's how it works (again, no built-in banana detectors).

Granted, when you try to learn to read as a five-year-old, your visual system has already had five years of tuning itself to recognise visual objects, shaping the development of its neurons, receptor densities, and patterns of connectivity, so there are likely to be teething difficulties when you ask it to recognise letters or symbols. For example, the visual system has worked terribly hard to master rotation and orientation invariance, so it can recognise objects whichever way they are facing, like a coffee cup with its handle facing to the left or to the right. Same coffee cup. And then an English learner is required to learn that p, b, d, and q are not the same object (a circle connected to a line) oriented differently, but actually different symbols to be linked to different speech sounds. That'll be confusing for a while.

And by five years of age, the high-resolution pattern recognition system in the visual hierarchy (the bit of the fusiform gyrus on the underneath of the temporal lobe that processes input from the fovea, the centre of the retina) has started to specialise to recognise faces. Now a new expertise is required, to learn sets of symbols. The two hemispheres divide and conquer. The left kicks out face processing and comes to focus on recognising written words (at which point it gets to be called the *visual word form area*) while the right focuses on recognising faces (and gets to be called the *fusiform face area*). It takes some time for the reorganisation to be complete and for the brain to become literate (and still recognise faces). But literacy is delivered via the same broad principles – experience and plasticity allow new content-specific circuits to become part of the language system through the functional integration of visual processing with articulation and semantics.

Consciousness

In this section, we consider consciousness and how the brain generates it. We include consciousness in this chapter not because we think other animals don't experience something similar, but because humans are the ones bragging about it. We're the ones taking the selfies. Our theories about the degree of consciousness in other animals feed into our moral views on how we should treat other species: what rights they should have to be free, who or what should be open to exploitation, and which ones we feel comfortable eating. Consciousness feels important.

By consciousness, we mean our subjective experience of reality, the sights, the sounds, the thoughts, and the feelings that make up our mental life. We did consider being poetic to emphasise this point, perhaps mentioning the sulphurous spritz of the sea air and the sensation of sand between your toes as you stroll along a beach at sunset, or the waft of bluebells and evening primrose as you brush through the long grass of a meadow in late spring, but we decided against it. This is neuroscience, people.

Somehow, the *whomp whomp whomp* of neural processing – the cycle of nerve stimulation arriving at the sensory lobes of the cortex via the thalamus, the massive parallel computations within the higher cortical areas and sub-cortical memory structures, the action selection in the basal ganglia, the activation of programmes within the motor cortex and their calibration in the cerebellum to generate the next motor response back through the thalamus – somehow this cycle generates the moment-to-moment sensation of experience.

Our approach in this book so far has been to give the current, consensus view on how the brain works (or make reasonable guesses where there's still some uncertainty). This is more difficult when it comes to consciousness because there is still a great deal of debate – on how physical matter could possibly generate subjective awareness; on what the function of consciousness is; on which parts of the brain are involved in that function; on how consciousness might have evolved and what other species (or devices or substances) might also possess it. Some view consciousness as the greatest current mystery in science. Others slice up the problem, identifying the easy part (the biological processes that underlie mental functions, like perception, memory, and attention) and the hard part (explaining subjective experience, why the operation of these biological processes should feel like anything – why when you stub your toe, it *hurts*).

Figure 9.2 A key element of consciousness. Stubbing your toe not only hurts, it hurts *in your toe*

In this section, we'll do three things. We'll draw out the territory of possible explanations – you can pick your favourite. We'll make a couple of distinctions that we think are important to explain consciousness, such as between phenomenal experience (hard to explain) and the self (easier but not what you expect). And then we'll outline how we think the greatest mystery in science will eventually be solved, so you'll recognise it when it happens. By way of illustration, we'll even give a possible solution to the hard problem of how the brain produces subjective experience that fits pretty well with the current evidence. You couldn't ask for more.

First, the territory. If you don't think consciousness is something magical, there are four kinds of ways you could explain it. They are shown in the diagram below. Consciousness could be a property of biology, or it could be a universal property of matter. It could be a consequence of performing a certain kind of function, achievable by a range of devices. Or it could be an overlap – when biology performs a certain kind of function. What might the function be? There have been various propositions. Perhaps it is some kind of function of integrating and sharing information, or of monitoring, or of meta-representation (i.e., having thoughts about thoughts, so-called higher-order thoughts, where the mind builds a model of itself).

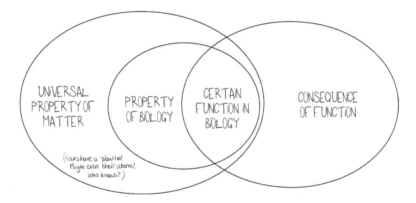

Figure 9.3 The territory of possible explanations of consciousness

What might consciousness be if it is not just biology but instead an intrinsic property of matter? Perhaps it is something analogous to the way the flow of electrons generates a magnetic field. Perhaps it is a fiddley quantum effect down at the atomic level. Beyond the four kinds of explanation, there is another, nuclear option for researchers: deny consciousness exists. It's just some sort of introspective illusion reflecting the limited access we have to our own mental processes. For these guys, the job is to explain why we are so deluded as to believe we are conscious. Huh… Well, when current explanations span all the way from everything is conscious (panpsychism) to nothing is conscious (eliminativism), you know there's still plenty for neuroscientists to play for.

If we were going to guess, we'd say consciousness is probably *a certain function in biology*. So, something to do with neurons, but not *all* neurons, only those involved in a certain function. The cerebellum contains 80% of the brain's neurons and doesn't seem to contribute to consciousness – for us, that's a big clue that consciousness is not just about neural activity per se. But we don't know.

Second, let's make a couple of distinctions. There may be properties of the brain that enable consciousness to come about but don't generate it. These enabling systems are targeted by anaesthetics and compromised in coma. For example, the reticular activating system that we came across in Chapter 6 changes the arousal state of the cortex, toggling down activation during sleep. The thalamus coordinates signalling across the cortex and damage to some parts of the thalamus can lead to coma. We are probably more interested in the bits of the brain that generate consciousness rather than just enable it. Next, there could be cortical activation which doesn't contribute to experience but anticipates it or is triggered by it: processes that precede or follow the experience might be things such as selective attention, expectation, self-monitoring, unconscious stimulus processing, task planning, and reporting. It takes clever experiments to distinguish just those brain processes that tightly associate with consciousness, with so much else happening across the central nervous system, even with all the tools of brain imaging at our disposal. Lastly, we should distinguish between *experience* and the *self*. *Experience* is subjective and hard to explain, while the *self* is a concept and therefore falls in the easy part of the problem.

Because the *self* is a concept, we should be able to link it to brain processes. However, the *self* is an idea that comes from psychology. How the *self* works follows the general rule throughout this book: what is one thing in psychology is many things in the brain. There are multiple brain systems that process aspects of the self. Among them are, variously: the dorsal medial (upper middle) part of the prefrontal cortex which processes your self-identity, your goals and task schema for your typical behaviours; the somatosensory cortex that processes the external bodily sensation of self; the insular cortex processing the internal sensation of self, the inside of your body and the gut feel of your emotions; the parietal cortex processing your body's position in space, and a part of this lobe called the precuneus which is involved in mental imagery involving the self; the temporal parietal junction processing yours versus others' perspectives; the motor decision self with the free will to initiate voluntary actions in the basal ganglia; the commentator self in the phonological loop – your internal voice; the autobiographical self that unifies sensory experiences as memories and date-stamps them in the hippocampus; the anterior cingulate monitoring self that checks how well things are going for you against your goals. The self, then, fragments into many neural shards.

Finally, let's sketch how we think the greatest mystery in science will eventually be solved, so you'll recognise it when it happens. We think it will come in three parts: reconceptualisation, explanation, and speculation. The hard problem of consciousness only seems so hard because of the way the question has been asked (a bit like posing, 'Why are ducks invisible?'). At some point, a neuro-philosopher will reformulate the question so that it's answerable, changing our very conception of what consciousness is. No doubt this will scramble our brains and turn our worlds upside-down, until we have to pay the electricity bill. Minimally, this reconceptualisation will do away with our intuition that there's a little 'us' inside our heads spectating as our life unfolds. After reconceptualisation will come explanation, figuring out which parts of the brain are involved in this new conception and what they are doing. Lastly will come speculation: pursuing questions about how we might change our consciousness, whether robots could be conscious, whether we can upload our consciousnesses to the internet, how much that would cost, and so forth. These will involve speculation because they will be hard to answer definitively – how could you tell if a robot was conscious or not? Google *says* its chatbot isn't sentient, but how do we tell... Nevertheless, an explanatory account will provide a more solid ground on which to speculate.

Figure 9.4 To explain consciousness, the first step will be a reconceptualisation of the problem to get away from ideas like this

Okay, let's illustrate this reconceptualise–explain–speculate cycle by using a possible explanation of consciousness, one that fits reasonably well with what we know about the associations between brain activity and conscious experience. The evidence suggests that consciousness is primarily associated with activity in the higher levels of the sensory hierarchies in the back of the brain, and not with activity in the frontal cortex, sub-cortical structures, or cerebellum. We'll call this illustrative proposal the *sensory render theory* of consciousness.

First, the *reconceptualisation* phase. Here's the old view: there's you, inside your head, looking out of your eyes at the world, walking along beaches and smelling the sea. As you look out of the window of your eyes, there's even a bit of nose in the corner of your field of vision. There's you, using your free will to move your body around in the world and *oof*, you stub your toe on a piece of driftwood, and that *hurts*.

Let's change that conceptualisation: your brain has no direct contact with the external world or indeed your body. It's isolated in the skull. All it has is patterns of stimulation arriving from various sensory neurons, from organs such as the eyes, ears, or nose, or from neurons sensing states of your body. From this nervous stimulation, the brain must construct a model of the world out there and your body in it. Ask yourself, why does it feel like the pain of stubbing your toe happens *out there in your toe*? The neural activation for the pain is in the somatosensory cortex, with the anterior cingulate flagging how much it does not like this. The experience feels like it's *out there* because the brain has formulated a three-dimensional model of your body from sensory information. Similarly, there is no external world out there that a 'you' can look at, sitting there inside your head. The world *out there* is a three-dimensional construction assembled by the brain from the sensory information it receives. Consciousness is the brain's generation of the three-dimensional model of your-body-in-the-world. It is a condition required for a brain to send signals so that its supposed *body out there* can successfully interact with a supposed external *world out there*, both suppositions constructed from sensory information. The role of consciousness is to guide behaviour by generating a version of the world it can do something with.

Next, the *explanation*. In video games that create photorealistic 3D worlds, the program generates the photorealistic images by a process called rendering or image synthesis, whereby information about surfaces and lighting are painted onto a wireframe three-dimensional model of the world. If you're in a shoot-em-up game, your body may also be rendered, holding your proton ray gun out in front of you to zap the aliens.

Evidence of the external world and the state of your body is delivered to your brain via sensory information arriving along axons from the relevant sensory neurons. The external world, the place of your body in it, and the body's internal state are reconstructed by the brain based on that sensory information, using similar 3D models. Because sensory information is often partial and ambiguous, it's necessary to integrate information across senses, as well as to make reasonable guesses based on experience. (If the model guesses wrong, that produces an illusion.) The brain paints sensory information onto models of the world and your body in it.

This function gives the brain the sensation that it is inside a body placed in an external physical world, and that you're looking out from behind your eyes – even though both world and body are the brain's 3D constructions based on sensory information. The function of this render is to plan and execute actions as if that external world were real. Given the predictive preferences of the brain, there is a tight coupling between sensory and motor processing, so that motor actions should produce direct sensory consequences, and indeed conscious experience (your sense of agency) is disrupted when those consequences don't occur.

Which parts of the brain are involved in this new conception and what are they doing? The function of 3D model construction is realised by the upper levels of the sensory hierarchies and their interaction with each other. Behaviour can sometimes be driven by perceptual information not in the 3D render, from lower levels in sensory hierarchies, such as fast adaptive orienting to danger, enabled by direct connections from the bottom of the sensory hierarchies to limbic structures such as the amygdala or links between thalamus and motor cortex. In that sense, the bottoms of sensory hierarchies are not conscious because they haven't been integrated into the 3D models.

In this illustrative proposal, most brain activity is not conscious. The prefrontal cortex planning, the motor cortex commanding muscles, the activity of limbic systems like the amygdala and hippocampus, the reward systems, the action selection systems of the basal ganglia, the motor smoothing of the cerebellum, the midbrain ensuring homeostatic body conditions – none of that is conscious. However, these systems may contribute content to the sensory render. For instance, the prefrontal cortex may contribute contextual expectations to sensory cortices that alter what is perceived: attention will influence consciousness by altering the acuity of some parts of the 3D model. The limbic system activity may produce the sensation of a fast-beating heart and cold sweat, sensory information delivered from bodily organs modulated by limbic activity. Decisions may involve the insula, which associates valence (emotional value judgements) with memories of past situations, but as the insula is also a disgust processing system, this can produce sensations in the gut. Cerebellar control over balance may involve lurching feelings. Hippocampal episodic recall may reactivate sensory circuits producing sensory mental images. Neural activity in these other brain systems isn't, in this account, different by virtue of being unconscious; conscious awareness is just one function among many – the production of the sensory render, the world you feel you're in.

Once you get to a point where you have a concrete proposal like this that identifies a clear function of consciousness and the structures responsible for it, other questions then become easier to answer. So for the illustrative sensory render theory, the answer to when consciousness develops in babies would be: once the baby's brain has matured enough to bring together sensory information to build a 3D sensory render in the cortex (probably prenatally shortly after the thalamus can innervate the cortex, but the nature of consciousness would change rapidly over the first few months as the model is constructed, and the senses mature and couple more tightly to motor responses).

The answer to why consciousness evolved would be: there is a selective advantage of generating behaviour in response to a model of the presumed external world rather than reflexively in direct response to sensory stimulation. The answer to how it evolved would be: increases in central nervous complexity intervening between sensory and motor systems began to allow the self-organised development of 3D sensory models which could drive behaviour. The answer to what consciousness is like in other animals would be: it depends on three things, the suite of sensory information about their bodies and the external world that their brains receive, the conceptual power to develop complex 3D sensory render models, and the complexity of the actions that can be performed on that world. Life that involves reflexive responses to direct sensory stimulation is not conscious. So, ethically, if consciousness is your benchmark, this is the sort of life you can eat. With ketchup, if you'd like.

Third, *speculation*. Let's try a wild one. Could we *alter* the 3D model of our bodies? Could we extend the consciousness of our bodies to include tools? Or prosthetic limbs? Or exoskeletons?… so that these inert objects actually felt like parts of our body, that we sensed as out there in space? The answer would be probably yes, since the out-there-in-space of the body is a rendered 3D model constructed in the somatosensory cortex from sensory information (the insula does the internal body). We know that the 3D model of the body is flexible. For example, the 'bored' bit of the 3D model that is left after limb amputation can get up to mischief and cause phantom limb sensations. But it can be manipulated and reshaped via therapeutic techniques, allowing the phantom limb to seem to move. The perception of our bodies can even be instantly distorted through multisensory illusions, anaesthesia, or virtual reality. For example, we can be made to feel that we have extra body parts, such as a sixth finger; or even given a robot sixth finger to control.

The key to altering our conscious bodies would be to replicate the brain's usual multisensory integration, the tight link in time between motor commands and returning sensory information from touch and vision. If you wanted a tool to act like a limb, to feel like it was part of you, the tool would need to move precisely when instructed by the brain and, assuming it contained sensors, it would need to yield in return the changed perceptual states expected based on that movement. Then it would be accommodated into the sensory render. The limiting factor in expanding the conscious body would be the interface of the tool with the motor nervous system and sensory nervous system (hacking your brain). But if you could pull that off, if you could deliver swift predictable tool movement in response to motor commands, feed sensory information from the tool back into the nervous system, and deliver the tight timing of sensory motor integration, your conscious body could likely be extended in all sorts of ways (according to the sensory render theory, at least): to an exoskeleton, to an invented body in virtual reality, maybe even to a virtual body quite different to your own. Perhaps in a video game, oh dragon lord, you could even feel your dragon scales. Solving the mystery of bodily awareness could one day produce some really neat gameplay. But that's speculation.

We'll touch very briefly on another speculation: the perennial 'Could computers ever be conscious?' That's a question of whether a sufficiently accurate simulation could ever become in all respects what it is simulating. Is a perfect model of a phenomenon necessarily equivalent to a real instantiation of that phenomenon? Would a computer model of the motion of water molecules ever become truly wet? Would a computer model of the sensory render be truly conscious? If we're merely talking about a computer program that has a data structure which stores information about the program itself (a meta-representation), in our view that's probably not enough for a computer to be conscious. But if we're talking about an embodied robot system with a tight sensorimotor coupling between action and a constructed 3D sensory model of body-in-the-world, maybe. Either way, this question is entirely speculative because it would not be possible to verify.

The final explanation of consciousness may very well differ from the sensory type of account we have outlined here. It might rely on other functions such as higher-order representations or information sharing. But we think solutions are likely to fall within the territory we have identified. And if they involve a function, identifying the function of consciousness will point to the brain structures involved, their functional development, and their evolutionary origins.

More Gizmos

Let's look at some other specialisms of humans, the gizmos that mark out our species, and make us winners in the 'best at being human' contest.

Tool use

An obvious gizmo is tool use. One thing humans do exceptionally well is to build and use tools, to shape and interact with our physical world. Think saws and shovels, plumblines and spirit levels, screwdrivers and hammers, tape measures. Think needles and threads. Think Rubik's cubes. What does tool use require in the brain? As we saw with language, evolution tends to innovate at the periphery, out in the body, rather than the central nervous system. We have dextrous hands and opposable thumbs, and we don't (usually) use our hands to walk on. But tool use also requires that we have a central nervous system able to develop the fine motor control and coordinated movements to use tools, problem-solving skills to know when to use them, and learning ability to learn how to use them.

More power

Both complex language and tool use are enabled by having a more powerful brain. What marks humans out is more conceptual power, which comes from larger brain size (when this extra power is not used up by running a very big body). The increase in brain size in hominids began at least by the time of *Homo habilis* around 2 million years ago, increasing from the 600 cm³ of archaic humans, through the homo genus to the 1,300 cm³ of modern humans. Brain sizes are smaller in other contemporary primates: chimpanzees have brains around 400 cm³ and gorillas 500 cm³. (To be awkward, *Homo neanderthalensis* likely had a brain that was 150 to 200 cm³ larger than modern humans but oops, somehow they got extinct. Size isn't everything.) Across species, greater brain size tends to be associated with several correlated properties, including toolmaking and innovation, greater success in moving into new territories, and longer lifespan. It is also associated with better cognitive control. For example, one study of primates found that the time an individual would wait for a preferred reward was correlated with absolute brain size. The human brain has a particularly large prefrontal cortex, a predictable consequence of the brain-making programme – if you let it run longer, the cortex (especially its front) and the cerebellum get disproportionately larger. For the cortex, the result is more association cortex (the parts of the cortical sheet that sit between sensory and motor areas). Association cortex takes longer to develop, and this is also a particular feature of the human brain: it is slow to develop its functionality. Because its development is slow, there is a greater opportunity for postnatal experience to shape the circuits of the brain.

The evolutionary reasons for the increase in brain size in humans are murky. Evolution didn't single out the cortex to inflate, it selected for a bigger brain as a whole: the relatively greater increases in cortical and cerebellar volume in the human brain are the predictable result of an overall increase in brain size. Simply extending the duration of generating neurons during brain development may be the cause of human brain expansion – applied to all brain regions but with different consequences on the scaling of the structures, depending on how long during the brain-making programme the neurons for each part are generated. Perhaps the selective advantage for humans was the enabling of language, perhaps it was the enabling of tool use, perhaps it supported greater group coordination among bipedal savannah hunters, perhaps it supported extra social cognition to deal with life in larger less-aggressive groups (e.g., keeping track of who likes whom, who did what to whom, what each individual wants, who tends to be honest and who a liar, etc.). Maybe all these things at once, which nicely deliver more offspring for the individuals with genes for bigger brains.

The greater amount of association cortex in the larger brain offers more conceptual power, so that more complex ideas can be developed. Sensory and motor hierarchies can be built higher, more patterns within patterns. Sensory systems can see deeper patterns of meaning in what they perceive, motor systems can plan motor sequences that reach farther and more contingently into the future, with greater flexibility to achieve goals.

The deeper patterns of meaning include mental models of how the physical world works. This can include invoking invisible forces to explain physical events (gods, ghosts, germs, electrons). In the social world, it can include more sophisticated knowledge of social scripts, episodes, situations, and motivations. Invented social categories can become as real as physical objects (so that you must be equally careful not to break teapots and the rules). While our basic emotions may be similar to other social primates, we can attach these to more complex social scripts and causal models (*W* does *X* under *Y* circumstances and feels *Z*; Sophie snubs Bill at the party but then feels guilty). The mixing of limbic activity with concepts and social scripts in the cortex creates a wider palette of emotions, like pride, hubris, dignity, honour, schadenfreude, admiration, and FOMO.

Our mental models can include ideas about ourselves, so-called meta-cognition or self-awareness, where the brain forms a model about how the individual behaves and uses this knowledge to alter future behaviour. More prefrontal cortex, where the modulatory system lies, also gives the modulatory system more precise control over the content-specific meaning systems in the back of the brain. It can separately manipulate bits of ideas. I'll have *this* bit of the idea, but not *that* bit. I'll look at a red square and focus on the shape of the square but not its colour. More conceptual power allows for thinking about 'what-if' counterfactuals, about hypothetical situations. What if the moon were made of cheese? What would it be like? How smelly?

A clutch

One advantage of more precise internal control is that it allows the brain to have a *clutch*. For those only familiar with automatic cars, a clutch is a mechanism for connecting and disconnecting an engine from the transmission system, so that when disconnected, the engine can run in isolation without producing any drive. One part of the modulatory system (sitting in the middle lower prefrontal cortex) plays just this role. Brain activity can be decoupled from perception and turned to internally focused thought. You hear a sad story, and it makes you *think about life*. When disengaged from the present moment, the brain can run mental simulations, fantasise, and imagine. It can retrieve memories of past experiences to envision future events, alternative perspectives, and scenarios, conceive the perspective of others, simulate the navigation of social interactions, ruminate, generate and manipulate mental images, decide on moral dilemmas. We run decision experiments to imagine what the consequences of different choices might be and weigh the costs and benefits; we run emotion experiments to imagine how different outcomes would feel. All these things we can do when we sit and think rather than perceive and respond to our immediate environments. The brain can even disengage while it carries out automatic activities. We can daydream about winning the lottery while we do the washing up, and cause faint images of Hawaiian beaches to flicker in our minds. When the clutch is pressed down and the engine is isolated, as it revs, we have the opportunity to learn not from the world but from our imaginations.

Niche construction

The final gizmo builds on the previous human specialisms: tool use, the social coordination enabled by language, and the planning and imagining of other worlds enabled by greater conceptual power: *niche construction*. A niche is the particular environment that a species lives in, and to which it is adapted. Niche construction is the modification of components of the environment through an organism's activities. Unusually, the human species can be found across a very wide range of environments, almost anywhere in the world in fact. Jungles, swamps, savannahs, mountains, deserts, tropics, icy wastes, Birmingham. Humans use their gizmos to prosper in all these environments through constructing their own niches, altering the environments in diverse ways to fit our biology, wearing different types of clothes, building dwellings, employing different modes of transport, methods of hunting, varieties of farming equipment, and fancy umbrellas. Human niche construction acquires a special potency by its combined reliance on learning, plasticity, and culture.

So, there you have it. Without being particularly biologically special, humans have skills and gizmos that set them apart. Take a breath. Because... unfortunately, these gizmos aren't enough to explain how the modern human brain works. And that's because you can't explain how the modern human brain works just by looking inside it. Which may be a little disappointing to hear, having got this far in the book. Let's complain about it some more in the next section.

No, This Is Simply *Not* Good Enough

Sure, we can have all this evolutionary evidence that human brains lie on a continuum with other mammals; that they use the same biological mechanisms with no special parts. Perhaps it's reassuring to see how humans fit into the fabric of the natural world.

But sorry, this argument is just *nuts*. It's not good enough. We are *completely* different from other animals. Look at what we've done to the world. Jet planes, men on the moon, skyscrapers, TV, the internet, the Metaverse, Dolly Parton, *a lot* of plastic. Global warming. Astrophysics. Astrology. Charles Dickens, Monty Python, Agatha Christie. The Marvel universe. We just do things other animals don't do. If we are so similar to gorillas and chimpanzees, why don't other apes have legal contracts, sports teams, fashion shows, and awards ceremonies?

Figure 9.5 Top banana. What sets us apart from other social primates: Award ceremonies

This brings us to a puzzle. If we look back to the origins of modern humans, if we follow the evolutionary path from tree-dwelling rainforest primates to grassland-ranging savannah hominins of 5 million years ago – through *Australopiths*, *Homo habilis*, *Erectus*, *Ergaster*, *Heidelbergensis*, to *Homo sapiens* over those millions of years – we see a gradual increase in brain size. It increased from the size of an orange to the size of a melon. If we follow the evolution of culture, based on the archaeology of tools, we see increasing complexity. Stones were used for cutting 3.4 million years ago by *Australopithecus afarensis*, who also evidenced group hunting; stone tools were found from 2.5 million years ago with *Homo habilis*; 1.5 million years ago, *Erectus* and *Heidelbergensis* had developed large cutting tools. From 800,000 years ago, the first hearths appeared, then 600,000 years ago, evidence of ritual defleshing of skulls and 400,000 years ago, stone flake production routines. There is evidence of a similar increase in the complexity of group social activities, cultural artefacts, and cave paintings.

But the rate of change of brain size and culture don't match up. There were long periods in the archaeological record where tool technology appeared to plateau or stagnate, sometimes for as long as half a million years. *Homo sapiens* appeared 150,000 to 195,000 years ago, but for the first 50,000 years, the record shows little evidence of cultural variation in tool behaviour. The gradual increase in brain size – conveying the potential advantages we talked about in the previous section – took 2–3 million years, while most of the increase in cultural complexity has occurred in the last 100,000 years, with an exponential increase in the last 8,000 years.

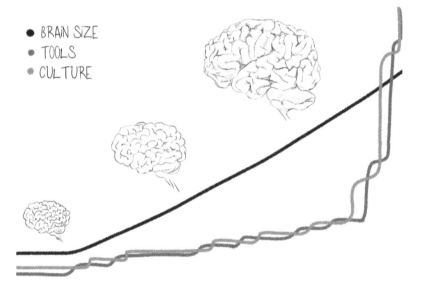

Figure 9.6 The mismatch in the evolutionary increase in hominin brain size and the increase in cultural complexity

To sense that acceleration, think of your smartphone. Humans started to count perhaps 50,000 years ago. Calculating devices were invented around 2500 BC. Mechanical calculators were invented in the 1800s. Digital computers were invented in the 1940s, the internet in the 1970s, touchscreens shortly after. Smartphones sit atop these inventions. Now, there are innovations to phone models every year, with the addition of cameras, GPS, health sensors, calls from remote regions that can bounce off satellites. And over this period of history, human brain size has hardly changed. (Some have even noted a possible *decrease* in human brain size since the end of the last Ice Age, perhaps because highly coordinated group-level behaviour places less pressure on the cognitive abilities of the individual.) We can only conclude that big brains are necessary for tool use and culture, but are not enough to drive them.

Where do the innovations come from, then? We need to understand two ideas: *cultural evolution* and *circumstances*. In cultural evolution, innovations in cognitive development are passed between generations not by genes but by social learning. Ideas are transmitted through social processes such as conversation, storytelling, turn-taking, demonstrating, and teaching. It usually involves adults structuring the developmental environment that children experience. Cultural innovations undergo selection just as in biological evolution, but the behaviours, beliefs, tools, and techniques that spread through human populations stem not from the individuals who have the most babies, but from the teachers who have the most students.

Cultural evolution is not free from biology – transmitted skills need to be consistent with the brain's basic sensorimotor mode of functioning. The brain is not infinitely flexible because it is limited by its embodiment, its initial genetically programmed sensorimotor wiring, its emotion and reward preferences, and the potential conceptual power of any given brain. Nevertheless, given the plasticity of the central nervous system, there is a good deal of scope for variation in culturally acquired skills – witness the range of written scripts humans have adopted for the visual encoding of language. The scripts all fit within biological constraints: they are all about the same size to fit within the central field of the retina, they all use similar lines and junctions consistent with the contours the brain uses to recognise objects. But within these limits, there is a vast diversity of written scripts that have sprung up and spread throughout history (or died out to remain only on the odd piece of pottery) – from pictograms to logograms to alphabets, from cuneiform to hieroglyphs.

The origin of cultural innovations is not obvious, and evidence of long periods of cultural stagnation across deep human history suggests innovation is not inevitable. Likely, innovation is triggered by particular circumstances. This means the origin of the modern human mind is as much about history as evolution. A chance combination of conditions. Let's consider an innovation that is possibly the most important cause of the explosion in cultural complexity of the last 8,000 years: the invention of *information tools*.

Information tools are artefacts that can convey knowledge between individuals. They rely on *symbolism*, the notion that some artefact can stand for some state of affairs in the world. This has been described as the association of culturally shared fictions with facts. Information tools, from simple markings to pictures to written numbers and words, allow information to be propagated across time and space. They both allow for knowledge to be accurately transmitted and create the conditions for knowledge to accumulate across generations; crucially, these conditions permit the gradual improvement of knowledge, skills, and technologies.

It works a bit like this: John figures out a plan for making bricks as a platform to build his fire on. John's son, John-son, looks at the plan years later and realises that with bricks you can build a wall. His son, John-son-son has the insight that if you combine the walls with a roof, you can make a single-storey building. John-son-son-son figures out that with stronger bricks and crossbeam supports, you can make a two-storey building. And so on. Each generation can improve on the plans of earlier generations (so long as the plans are not lost). This virtuous circle of accumulation depends on information tools. Of course, things would have probably gone more quickly if John had had daughters.

What are the circumstances that led to symbolism and to the invention of information tools? We have to speculate, but it likely involved the confluence of several factors. These could have included: humans starting to live together in larger groups, in villages and towns, perhaps enabled by the invention of agriculture that produces enough surplus food to support larger groups; specialisation of roles and the emergence of a bartering system for the exchange of excess produce for goods or services provided by specialists. Against this background, the use of tokens in transactions becomes advantageous, since quantities can be accurately tracked. Simple tokens, a number of beads or marks on a piece of clay, can be expanded to signify not just how many but also what, where, when, and how. A symbol for 'how many' can become distinguished from 'of what', in turn producing systems of number. The stage is set for the adoption of physical systems as information tools, that ultimately leads from the invention of numeracy to the invention of written forms of language and to reading, which followed some thousands of years later.

Although there is evidence of symbolically mediated behaviour in humans as far back as 100,000 years ago, the uninterrupted accumulation of cultural innovations did not begin until around 20,000 years ago, when the record shows a continuous accumulation of non-utilitarian objects (for worship, for decoration, for fun). This is suggestive of a step change in the cultural transmission of knowledge, but more broadly, points to the importance of circumstances rather than just cognitive abilities in driving innovation. Through history, those conditions may have been met (and lost) in multiple populations or even species – Neanderthals show some evidence of the symbolic use of red ochre colouring and feathers from 100,000 years ago until their extinction 30,000 years ago. Local conditions, therefore, may have been important in both the appearance and disappearance of symbolic behaviour in human populations, the accumulation of knowledge spiralling upwards or sputtering out in different cultures. Brain-wise, it could have been Neanderthals on the moon. Instead, *Homo sapiens* got lucky.

Where Does Your Mind Stop?

To change the topic slightly, one of the author's phones recently filled up with applications, songs, photos, and videos. It started getting all *laggy*, running unbearably slowly and crashing. The internet imparted the following advice: 'If your phone accepts external storage, try buying a micro-SD memory card for it. That will give you an instant boost, and it's a relatively cheap method of expanding your phone's capacity.'

Sage advice, indeed. Add extra memory to the phone to boost its functionality, to make it work again, to make it smarter. So, here's the question. Is the memory card part of the phone or not? Is it part of the phone's computations? Probably. It makes it work better.

We ask because when people use a notebook, they are often much better at arithmetic. When they no longer have to keep all the numbers in mind, people are much quicker and less error prone when, say, multiplying 35 by 17. They can jot down the sum on a pad and follow simple procedures on the columns of written numbers. When we do this, is the notebook part of our mind or not? Likewise, when we complete a crossword or a Sudoku, we often find ourselves scribbling ideas and partial answers in the margin of the newspaper. Is the newspaper part of the mind or not? People are certainly more effective at these kinds of complex reasoning tasks when using external information tools.

The use of information tools in performing tasks is sometimes called cognitive off-loading, and it makes us cleverer. It can involve multiple artefacts that range from physical notebooks to computers, to satnavs and calendars, to diaries and alarm clocks, to photo reels and blogsites, to Facebook and Instagram pages. So powerful are information tools that smartphones have even been pioneered as a strategy to support the everyday living skills of people who have experienced damage to their hippocampi and can no longer form new episodic memories: the smartphone has stepped in to replace the hippocampus.

If it's reasonable to argue that the micro-SD card becomes a part of our phone by virtue of enhancing its functionality, it is only a small step to think that information tools become part of the mind – an extended mind which has spread its tendrils out into the world. What, then, marks the new boundaries of the mind? This is a question for philosophers. Since in this book, we're just neuroscientists, things are more straightforward. These tools are not part of the brain because information about the state of the tool needs to enter the brain via perception, and the state of the tool is then altered when the brain instructs the motor systems to make the body act on it.

However, the existence of an information tool changes what the brain must learn to perform a task. Take our mental calculation, to multiply 35 by 17. If we carry this out in our heads, we must embark on an extended sequence: form a plan that breaks up the problem into stages, store the results of each, and combine them together. Something like, well, 17 can be split into 10 and 7, so that's 35 times 10, which is 350, remember that; and then 35 times 7; and 35 times 7 is 30 times 7, 210, remember that, plus 5 times 7, which is 35; then I need to add the 350 and 210 and 35, which is 560 plus 35, which is 595, done. Since precise numbers are encoded in language, this will involve the interactions between language circuits, fact retrieval about the times tables, and a heavy load on the modulatory system to track the stage in the plan and keep certain phonological representations active (350, 210) before triggering the final procedure to combine them as the last step. Contrast this with the same calculation done with pencil and paper. Now the key operations are writing symbols in the correct spatial location (columns) and carrying out simpler proce-dures (put 0 in the rightmost column, multiply 35 by 1, write 35 next to the 0 and so on) that can be largely driven by the current state of the sum on the paper: much less engage-ment of the modulatory system and phonology, more use of visuospatial representations and motor circuits (though you still gotta know your times tables, people).

We can get more sophisticated, however. We can form an internal mental model of the information tool in our brains. We can visualise a piece of paper and writing the sum on it. For some, this may be easier than performing the calculation using number sentences encoded in language, allowing alternative cognitive strategies. Internalising mental models can be taken to extremes. Abacuses are information tools that allow complex calculations to be performed quickly and effortlessly (such as 256,371 + 528,813). But expert abacus users can also form a mental model of their abacus and use the model to carry out these calculations swiftly in their heads. When they do so, brain imaging shows that they are using interactions between the frontal modulatory system and the parietal visuospatial system while non-abacus-expert participants set the same problems used a language-related brain network including Broca's area. The answer was 785,184, by the way, if you were wondering. We know you were wondering.

The important point is that interactions with information tools both make the brain more powerful in the behaviours it can support and crucially change what it needs to learn. It can give up on mental maps to navigate to the pub, it can give up on a rich episodic memory for who was at your birthday party. Instead, the brain acquires sensorimotor procedures that fluidly mesh with and rely on information tools as part of producing the final behaviour: follow the instructions of your satnav, access your photo reel to recall who was at the party. The more complicated and powerful human information tools become, the smarter humans become in what they can achieve. The internet. Tablets. Virtual reality. In a sense, we become as clever as the machines we create. In turn, new machines enable the creation of more complex machines. Culture spirals up and the brain adapts.

We raise our children in the cultural environment of the current set of tools. This changes how their brains develop – albeit in ways limited by the flexibility of the under-lying biology. When we learn to read – through arduous practice – the experience modifies parts of the visual system, causing a part of the brain to specialise in recognis-ing print. When we learn mathematics, multiple brain areas must be encouraged to work together to integrate number symbols, quantities, object relations, scales, quantities, calculation, spatial formats, and all the links between perceptual information and motor procedures that go with them. Tools change the brain processes we use to complete tasks: the availability of Google and chatbots may lessen educational pressure on mem-orising and retrieving facts, and the brain structures that this employs, while necessitating new expertise on plans and procedures for using the 'Google' tool to unearth information on the internet and check its veracity. For old people, this may mark the collapse of society and the cultural decay of the youth of today who can't, apparently, pay attention to anything for very long; but to the central nervous system, this adaptation is simply par for the course.

Upgrade Your Operating System

Part of the problem with our troublesome phone, why it jammed up, was that overnight it tried to download a new operating system. This was supposed to give it new features, new widgets. It was supposed to make it cleverer. Culture can do the same sort of thing to brains. Culture can invent new modes of thought and use education to train the brains of the next generation to give them new powers.

Logic is a good example. Deductive logic is an invention of culture that occurred only 2,500 years ago. Deductive logic involves working out which arguments are valid, such as *If A then B; A, therefore B*. So: *All men are mortal; Socrates is a man, therefore Socrates is mortal*. The cultural innovation was to deliberately separate logic from rhetoric, rhetoric being the use of argument to persuade people. This distinction was made by Aristotle in ancient Greece. While other forms of argumentation existed in ancient India and in ancient China, these forms were used for persuasion. No ancient culture ever investigated valid argumentation before the Greeks. Indeed, it is even more singular: every study of logical validity comes from Aristotle or his subsequent readers.

How did Aristotle come up with the idea that reasoning in logic should be separate from argument in rhetoric? What were the circumstances? Cultural innovations can have obscure or chance origins. The inspiration for drawing the distinction probably arose from the particular sociocultural and political conditions in ancient Greece at that time, which led the Greeks to be interested not just in whether an argument is valid (which is helpful when trying to persuade) but also in how it works: the structural features that make a logical argument valid. Innovation is rare, sporadic, but once it occurs, information tools allow it to spread.

The normal mode of operation of the brain is not logical and deductive. It doesn't like to abstract; it likes to be based in the concrete, the sensorimotor; it is influenced by what's familiar and what's likely to happen; its ideas are painted in shades of grey, not black and white categories and rules, shades influenced by context, settings, and goals; it is a social and emotional device that is prone to give in to peer pressure (what most people believe) and to place trust in authority figures; it is influenced by anticipated rewards and losses; it gets tired and it gets irritable. And it interrupts long lists to say now is a good time for a cup of tea.

For the brain to perform logical reasoning, the modulatory system must be trained to focus on the structural elements of sentences rather than their contents, in order to follow the procedures for logical inference. Indeed, the modulatory system may need to inhibit the semantic content of sentences about what is likely to be true in the world. For example, in one study, participants were asked to derive valid deductive inferences for problems that stipulated erroneous facts about the world, while their brains were scanned. In other words, they had to judge the validity of problems even when the logical validity of the conclusion might conflict with their beliefs about the world. Here's one example: using the same logical form as above (called *modus ponens*), participants might be asked to judge whether this is a valid argument: *No mammals are dogs, all German Shepherds are mammals, therefore no German Shepherds are dogs.* Which is valid but nonsense. When the researchers ran this study, they found heightened activation of a region of the modulatory system involved in inhibiting prepotent responses (or heuristics): the right inferior frontal gyrus. In another study, when transcranial magnetic stimulation was used to temporarily disrupt the functioning of this region, the participants struggled to reason about these belief-conflicting logical problems.

The logical mode of thought is the result of educational training within a given culture. To show a contrast, here's an example of reasoning from an adult who had not experienced such training. It is taken from Alexander Luria's 1976 book on the social foundations of cognitive development and reports a discussion between an 'educated' human, taught to reason logically, and a peasant from a remote area of the Soviet Union, who is prompted to use formal, abstract logical reasoning:

> *Question*: All bears are white where there is always snow. In Novaya Zemlya, there is always snow. What colour are the bears there?
>
> *Answer*: I have seen only black bears and I do not talk of what I have not seen.
>
> *Question*: But what do my words imply?
>
> *Answer*: If a person has not been there he cannot say anything on the basis of words. If a man was 60 or 80 and had seen a white bear there and told me about it, he could be believed.[1]

Inhibitory control processes from the modulatory system may be involved whenever we have to learn and manipulate information that does not fit with our everyday sensorimotor experience: for example, when children are asked to learn the culturally acquired and propagated knowledge that the world is a sphere, even though they have spent several years of playing football in the park on apparently flat pitches.

Language may be a key enabler in allowing different modes of thought to culturally evolve, since it separates knowledge acquisition from direct experience. Language permits learning through instruction. It supports building abstract concepts using language labels to unify diverse sensory situations and sets of procedures. For example, the label 'six' can be used to bring together all the different situations involving the invented notion of six-ness: an Arabic numeral, a group of six things, an object split into six parts, a sequence of numbers where 6 falls between 5 and 7 on a number line, a pile of sweets bigger than 3 but smaller than 20, a length of six units. A diverse range of sensorimotor procedures can then be linked: grouping, combining, matching, classification, comparison, ordering by size, counting, and measuring.

Language can be used to bring to mind knowledge that is not automatically elicited by the current situation, through the use of verbal analogies (e.g., *this football match is like David vs. Goliath; electricity is like the flow of water along a pipe*). The language of metaphor, contingent on the high resolution of cognitive control provided by the prefrontal cortex, allows the selection of only some dimensions of concrete concepts to support the construction of abstract concepts. For example, difficulties can be conceived of as physical containers (*we're in this thing together; we're in hot water; he's in it up to his neck*); progress in a relationship can be conceived of as physical forward motion (*Romeo and Juliet are at a crossroads in their relationship; their fling isn't going anywhere; they're in a dead-end marriage*).

There are other examples we could give to show how cultures can innovate new modes of thought. The cultural evolutionary psychologist Cecilia Heyes wrote a book which laid out a range of such innovations, which she referred to as *cognitive gadgets*. But our main point here is that, while the modern human brain may have taken millions of years to evolve, its current detailed functioning is shaped by the educational environments, tool sets, and social customs in which we develop – environments that have been generated by mere millennia of cultural accumulation.

For The Cool Kids, The Basic, The Noobs, The Geeks, The Neeks, and The Nerds: How Humans Do Hierarchies

Let's look at another phenomenon found across a range of social mammals where humans sometimes do it differently: social hierarchies. Most social species organise themselves into dominance hierarchies. This is a ranking system that establishes unequal access to limited resources: who gets first dibs on the best food, access to the choicest mates and the nicest places to hang out. Hierarchies offer benefits in reducing aggression and conserving energy – to those in the highest ranks, the benefits are obvious; to those lower down, the benefit is merely in choosing fights that they stand a chance of winning.

Hierarchies differ across species in how graduated they are (an alpha and the rest, or a full ladder of positions); whether there are separate hierarchies for males and females; how high rank is attained (by inheritance among high-ranking families, or through the outcomes of challenges and fights); and how stable they are (in the frequency of revolutions).

Animals are extremely interested in information about social rank, monitoring for social cues about dominance and the status of high-ranking individuals. Life for lower ranking members can be miserable and stressful, with limited access to resources, the risk of being bullied, and little control over their destinies – a misery ameliorated only when there is a grooming partner with whom to share their woes, or someone lower ranking on whom to take out their frustrations (at least for baboons – see Robert Sapolsky's excellent work on this). But it is not all plain sailing for the higher ranking either, who must constantly look over their shoulders for challenges and form allegiances to defend their status. It is particularly stressful to be high ranking when there is a whiff of revolution in the air, and indeed, this can unsettle everyone in the hierarchy.

For humans, too, perceiving social rank is an important skill which we employ in our everyday lives. We consciously or unconsciously adapt our behaviours at school, at work, or at home according to the social status of the partners we are interacting with. If we ignore or challenge social rankings – talk back to the teacher, shout at the boss – it can lead to sanctions, such as being expelled temporarily or permanently from the social group (sent to your room, detention, expulsion, getting fired). A promotion, by contrast, can leave us feeling on top of the world.

Where is social rank processed in the brain? Let's start with mice, who are another species that like a pecking order. One ingenious study traced the encoding of social rank to the mouse's medial (middle) prefrontal cortex. Here's what they did. Mice were housed in groups of four, and after a while, each group formed their own dominance hierarchy. Then the mice were entered into a round-robin competition: pairs of mice from the four were let into a cage and allowed to compete for a liquid reward. Usually, the more dominant mouse got more rewards, spent more time hanging round the juice dispenser, and displaced the less dominant mouse if they happened to be there. The more dominant mouse won the competition more often – but not always. When neural activity was recorded directly from the mouse medial prefrontal cortex during the competition, the activity could predict a mouse's social rank. That's where its status appeared to be stored. But here are two interesting follow-ups: activity from this region could also predict the mouse's rank even when it was on its own. Social rank was a badge the mouse carried round with it (or a chip it carried on its shoulder). The medial prefrontal cortex was storing the mouse's social identity. Second, occasionally, it was the subordinate mouse that would win the competition for the juice, and the likelihood of this 'upset' could also be predicted from a nearby population of neurons in the medial prefrontal cortex. This nearby population appeared to encode a *winning mindset* – a desperation for the food reward sufficient to attempt to overcome the social dominance order. Sometimes you're hungry enough to barge in front of the boss in the line at the canteen, blow the consequences. Lastly, this study showed that the mouse medial prefrontal cortex has a hotline to the hypothalamus, the limbic structure that signals to the body to put it in the right fight-or-flight condition for the planned behaviour. Rank matters for the whole body.

What about the human brain? Social dominance is equally salient to humans. Infants can detect it by their second year – they are surprised if a bigger character is defeated by a smaller character in a cartoon. We've already seen in our tour of the prefrontal cortex that the upper middle part of the prefrontal cortex is involved in processing social schemas about the self (the kinds of things you do) and this is likely where information about your self-perceived social rank is stored (and next to it, whether today you have a winning mindset!). A range of other areas are also involved in social dominance behaviour.

We saw in the section on 'Keeping Score' (Chapter 5) that the lower middle part of the prefrontal cortex (ventromedial) is involved in computing a common currency of value (in that case, in cahoots with the ventral striatum with its tracking of reward prediction errors, to track how well life is going). This system is likely the place where social rank is played off against other demands in the system: where the decision is made that hunger overwhelms social dominance when you push in front of your boss in the canteen line.

A dominance hierarchy is a set of social norms that guide behaviour according to status. This means that an individual needs to control their behaviour according to the context of social partners to deliver compliance. It therefore implies that other parts of the prefrontal cortex are going to be involved, the lateral parts that deploy inhibitory control so that, for example, you may eat sloppily when it's just you and your siblings, but not when your parents are watching. Sensory systems will be involved in monitoring cues about social dominance, such as the interest of the inferior temporal gyrus in faces and eye gaze, and the superior temporal gyrus in body posture. Direct gaze is a sign of dominance, as are open arms revealing the torso, while subordination is signalled by averted gaze and a rounded posture hiding the torso. Parietal attentional systems will also be tracking the positions of high-status individuals in space.

Several limbic structures will take a role. The amygdala is involved in learning or challenging social hierarchy, becoming particularly interested in detecting elevated threat (or opportunity) when the social hierarchy is unstable. The striatum will process the rewards and aversive experiences of actions that accord to or do not accord to the dominance hierarchy (how much did it pay to please the boss?). There may be motivational differences when the social competition is against a higher ranked individual than a lower ranked: it's a huge win if you take down the number 1. But a big humiliation to be sent out of a classroom (unless your prefrontal cortex reappraises the experience as confirming your teen rebel status). The hippocampus will be recording and date stamping pertinent events for interactions with respect to people at different levels in the hierarchy. Neurotransmitters will also be colouring the system. Apart from the dopamine released in the striatum to flag unexpected rewards or punishments in social competitions, a burst of testosterone marks a victory in a conflict (Come on! Get in!). With higher social rank, you feel big about yourself, which is reflected in higher serotonin levels when you are among your people.

All of this is similar to other mammals and to social primates like chimpanzees and baboons. Where do human social dominance hierarchies differ? There are obviously some cosmetic differences. Where baboons monitor behavioural cues for information about the status of high-ranking individuals, we gossip about celebrities and politicians. Where chimpanzees groom and tickle to reduce stress, we chat and joke. But there are three ways we clearly distinguish ourselves. The most salient difference is that for other animals, there is a single hierarchy that spans all domains of behaviour, while for humans, our self-identities contain multiple dimensions, and each dimension can have a hierarchy. What is our status in the family? What is our status in the workplace? What is our status in the sports team? As an online gamer? A YouTuber? At music? At fashion? Across these many dimensions, we tend to subjectively identify with the hierarchy in which we figure highest (and downplay the importance of the others). Our vocabulary is peppered with these different status terms. (For the uninitiated, a *cool kid* is someone who is popular and a trendsetter worthy of emulation for their fashion sense; a person who is *basic* is unoriginal, unexceptional, and mainstream; a *noob* is a person who is inexperienced in a particular sphere or activity, especially computing or gaming; a *geek* is someone who is obsessively interested in and knowledgeable about a technical subject; a *nerd* is a person who is extremely enthusiastic about a niche subject; a *neek* is a combination of a geek *and* a nerd; and out of politeness, we didn't mention *losers*, individuals who seldom experience success at jobs or personal relationships.)

Second, across different human cultures, almost all have entrenched gradients of socioeconomic status. Social structures and norms create and perpetuate unequal access to economic resources, with widespread correlated differences in health, diet, money, quality of housing, quality of air, quality of education, and opportunities for employment. These impact the individual from the time of development in the womb – is that a place of good nutrition, low stress hormones, and free from environmental toxins, or the opposite? The gradient of socioeconomic status differences varies across human cultures, as does the absolute level of resources (from poverty that affects physical growth and infant mortality, to poverty that merely restricts opportunity). We won't editorialise here, other than to note that social dominance hierarchies have been writ large through human cultural evolution.

The third human difference is that we have leaders. In other social primates, the highest-ranking individual does not lead, on foraging or defence of the troop, nor do they model behaviours which others should follow. They merely have first dibs on all the best stuff. Humans on the other hand have leaders who (if all goes well) intend to act on behalf of all for the common good, and who set an example for others to copy (or are castigated as hypocrites). People often show loyalty not just to an individual but to a role – to the *President* or the *Prime Minister*, whoever it should be; they are showing loyalty to a concept. Leaders deploy language to negotiate, and to communicate plans (visions of possible worlds) to persuade others to follow. In some cultures, people even get to select their leaders through organised social processes like voting. The people, of course, weigh the intellectual arguments when deciding who to cast their vote for, which vision of the future is most likely to serve the common good. But they also tend to vote for more beautiful leaders and those with faces that look trustworthy…

In fact, around 40% of the differences we see in political leaning are heritable (gauged by the greater similarity in political views between identical twins compared to fraternal twins). Of course, it's comforting that 60% is left to be determined by the strength of the arguments, but what biological mechanisms could explain the genetic transmission of political ideologies – whether you are a right-leaning conservative or a left-leaning liberal? These are likely the same mechanisms that we saw underlying differences in personality, involving the limbic system. They include the liability of the insula to signal disgust (moral disgust is handled similarly in the brain to rancid food); the likelihood that the cingulate cortex and the insula will promote empathy for suffering; and the readiness of the amygdala to detect threat (from conceptual entities like 'foreigners' or 'criminals', or in the dangerous future versus the comforting past), threats which can be more readily mitigated by authoritarian rule. Suppressing these intuitions to focus 'on the arguments' may be better achieved by a stronger prefrontal cortex, and more cortical power may permit more sophisticated mental models for solutions to problems and abstract ideas of justice and fairness. Or just vote for the politician who has a nice smile and looks good in a suit.

In sum, social dominance hierarchies are prevalent in social mammals, but we do them differently mainly because of our larger cortex, which affords us more conceptual power. It gives us greater facility for distinguishing multiple dimensions of meaning in our self-identities; it provides the clutch to disengage from our surroundings and imagine possible worlds to guide our choices; and the facility to construct plans reaching far into the future. Our large cortex provides the foundation to change behaviour through language-mediated negotiation and persuasion; for the cultural construction of social abstractions that are treated as if they were real barriers in the world; and for the propagation of ideas through information tools. But the conceptual power that has been used to sculpt cultural edifices such as democracy does not free us from our biological ancestry, manifested in the biases we show (often springing from our limbic system) in the way we treat the democratic opportunities that human societies have fought for. That's got us feeling passionate. In the next chapter, let's save the world.

Box 9.1

Cognitive enhancement – who should get it?

Our lives already include techniques for cognitive enhancement and mood elevation, such as caffeine, exercise, vitamin supplements, increased sleep, etc. Should we treat newer techniques differently? If transcranial electrical stimulation or nootropics ever become reliable, safe, and effective methods for improving attention, memory, and learning, should we make them widely available? Public views are inconsistent. We think use of nootropics is generally okay, but think less of people who achieve through their use than we do of those who achieve through their own efforts (so it seems to sort of fall under cheating). Should they be available only to those struggling in the education system? England, for instance, is notorious for its wide gap between the poor and the better off in terms of academic achievement; if neuromodulation leading to improved cognitive skills reduces this gap, in the interest of fairness should we not support its use? There is also a cultural angle. Use of new techniques is bound to be concentrated in advanced societies, widening the gap between rich and poor countries.

Box 9.2

Neuroethics – the big questions

We have previously encountered several ethical and moral issues in neuroscience, but provided no answers. That is largely because, as yet, there aren't any. The notion that explanations for human behaviour require analysis at all levels seems unarguable, but brain scans are far more persuasive than a complex mix of genetics, neurotransmitters, and sociocultural factors. Regulation of new techniques for recording mental processes and for neuromodulation proceeds, if at all, at a snail's pace (that would be between 2 and 3 metres per hour), while the very big questions – what is personality, implications for free will and our personal identity – lie in the realms of philosophy, so don't expect any answers soon.

It is truly fascinating that the evolved human brain can produce such extraordinary technological advances (neuroscience over the last 50 years is an excellent example), but sociocultural institutions take so long to catch up with the ethical issues they present. It is not that neuroscience is easy and ethical issues are difficult, but that the sheer attraction of knowing how the brain works is a far more powerful motivation than the need to cope with the social and ethical challenges it presents.

Note

1   Luria, A.R. (1976). *Cognitive Development: Its Cultural and Social Foundations.* Harvard University Press, pp. 108–109.

10
SAVING THE PLANET

Let's see if we can start to pull together what we've learned and apply it to something that will be topical for a few years to come: climate change. This example will give us a framework to consider how the various structures of the brain combine to produce behaviour, and in this case, make decisions about how to alter future behaviour. We will assume, for the purposes of this chapter, that we are in the *Anthropocene* geological epoch when human activity has started to have a significant impact on the planet's climate and ecosystems. In a sense, the impact of *Homo sapiens* is a mark of its success: when you can find ozone-eating hydrochlorofluorocarbon gases in the heights of the stratosphere, and microplastics in the depths of the Mariana Trench, as a species, you know you've made it. We'll also assume that humans may want to change their behaviour in coordinated ways to address the negative environmental impact of the species. But look, if you're a climate change sceptic who is merely enjoying the warm weather, feel free to substitute some other threat to the species that requires coordinated social action to address. It'll work just as well.

Figure 10.1 Using neuroscience to address climate change

Climate Change: Should We Beat Ourselves Up About It?

There are now a lot of humans on the planet, our increase in numbers propelled by the very characteristics that distinguish our species: niche construction, conceptual power, and technology. We can live everywhere (we're even lining up Mars). We use technology to fashion the local environments to our needs. Because of the resources we consume and because of the by-products of our technology, our large population numbers have undermined the ability of ecosystems to support us in long-term sustainable ways.

But then, this is fairly usual in evolutionary terms. Most species have no plan; their numbers increase whenever environmental resources and an absence of predation and disease permit. It is not unprecedented for species to destroy the environments that support them, leading to population crashes. Elephants, for example, have a reputation for damaging their local ecosystems in ways that then seriously impact on their population numbers. Moreover, the particular cocktail of abilities found in *Homo sapiens* was the direction that evolution was headed with primates anyway. One study compared 62 different primate species and measured ecologically relevant cognitive abilities across multiple domains. It found that the traits of behavioural innovation, social learning, tool use, extractive foraging, and tactical deception were strongly correlated across the species. This suggests that social, technical, and ecological abilities have evolved together in primates, to yield both general intelligence and cultural intelligence. There is no inevitability in evolution, and ultimately it took the organisation and technological innovation of *Homo sapiens* to have a global impact on the environment. But one could see human culture as just more primate evolution down the same track. We shouldn't, then, beat ourselves up too much about it, or hate ourselves and imagine the planet would be better off without us.

That doesn't mean we shouldn't be worried. At least six different *Homo* species have populated the world over the last 3 million years. Short, small-brained ones; strong, stocky, big-brained ones; tall, rangy, big-brained ones. The *Homo* family tree is complex, with populations splitting, remixing, seducing, or dominating each other, rather than falling into a simple linear sequence. But the stark fact is that only one *Homo* species remains. It's possible to look back over geological climate records and match these to the fossil records to understand the range of climate conditions in which each *Homo* species existed. Like *sapiens*, several of them showed cultural innovations and were found across distant geographical locations, using stone tool technology and control of fire to survive in a range of climate conditions. When researchers ran this climate vs. fossil analysis, they found that for all the *Homo* species that went extinct, just before the extinction the species was restricted to territories with unfavourable climatic conditions. For example, the extinction of *Homo erectus* took place during the last glacial period, which was the coldest period the species had ever experienced. While some extinctions are caused by competition with other species that are fighting to occupy the same niche, this mostly wasn't the case for *Homo* (with the possible exception of *Homo neanderthalensis*, who may have experienced some competition from *Homo sapiens*). There is strong evidence that climate change was a common factor in the extinction of all our ancestors. Be warned.

But there's also good news. The high rates of population growth and technology-related encroachment on the planet's resources have only occurred in the last 10,000 years, and so have little to do with our evolutionary past. The environmental impact is instead a product of the modern human brain, shaped by its accumulated cultural practices. Therefore, the relevant behaviours are, in principle, amenable to change. The very conceptual powers that have driven our encroachment enable us to anticipate the consequences of our actions and do something about it. If the rest of the brain is willing.

Decision Making: What Have Emotions Got to Do With It?

Our human brain can entertain complex concepts and models of causal processes in the world. When we do this, we are often more comfortable anchoring our concepts and models on concrete sensorimotor underpinnings (e.g., for climate change, via metaphors like 'the world is on fire' or 'about to fall off a cliff'). We can, nevertheless, use language to index abstract and invisible causes that might be producing the outcomes we observe – for example to entertain the possibility that invisible 'greenhouse gases' are linked to the baking temperatures outside our window or to the pictures flashing up on our news feed of children wading through their flooded villages in far-off lands. Through cultural accumulation of knowledge, information tools, and direct communication, we can learn which of our specific behaviours are contributing to the problems, be it burning fossil fuels or burying plastic in the ground. We can therefore use our beliefs and our causal models to change our behaviours. Should be simple. End of chapter.

Except, the brain is not tailored to work this way. Its fundamental operation is about delivering adaptive motor behaviour in response to sensory input in the moment. As we saw in Chapter 5, it even has a direct, dorsal perception-for-now pathway to link senses to action without any intermediate understanding of what those senses mean. When we are being asked to make decisions about the environmental impact of our behaviour, the outcomes are often abstract, distant, probabilistic, and affect other people. The impact may be as nebulous as possible negative outcomes for future unborn generations. By contrast, the brain is fine-tuned to make decisions about what affects us personally, in the current time and place, and for outcomes that will definitely happen.

No worries. When push comes to shove and governments need people to change their behaviour, they can always scare them. They can start talking about 'tipping points' and 'final wake-up calls' to save the planet, so inspiring quick and decisive action to turn off lights, turn down thermostats, think twice about driving the car or eating meat. However, inducing fear, engaging the amygdala, does not always have predictable results. While it may produce the desired 'fight' behaviour in some – adjusting the thermostat – in others it may produce 'flight' as people disengage from the topic, or 'freeze' as people bury their heads in the sand and ignore the doomsday messaging; or even 'fight' in the form of aggression towards the senders of a message intended to manipulate behaviour.

Moreover, unless there are very clear actions that individuals can take to address the induced threat and give them a sense of control, then as we saw in Chapter 6, people may experience chronic anxiety, or even a sense of defeat that it is too late to do anything about climate change (it's irreversible, it's inevitable…). A sense of danger will only be effective in changing behaviour when the threat feels personal and when the solutions to the problem are concrete, achievable, and make sense in removing the threat.

The field of neuroeconomics has investigated how the brain makes decisions about questions of value, albeit in that field, mostly concerned with consumer behaviour and economic transactions. Two findings stand out. The first is that people are short-sighted about weighing the immediate versus future benefits of their actions. Should you buy a fuel-efficient car that is slightly more expensive? Should you invest in solar panels to cut energy bills? Consumers systematically discount future benefits, how much they will save in the future, instead focusing more on immediate costs and rewards (but this gas-guzzling car has stripes and goes faster!). The imbalance reflects the tuning of our reward-learning system to downplay the value of (vague) future outcomes about rewards, although we seem to discount less for future possible losses. The second finding is that consumer behaviour – whether an advertisement will lead you to buy a chocolate bar – can be predicted by how much the advert lights up the nucleus accumbens, the part of the basal ganglia action selection system that encodes and predicts positive rewards. Anticipated positive rewards are the strongest driver of consumer behaviour.

Sub-cortical structures like the limbic system and the basal ganglia play a surprisingly influential role in making decisions about value, such as when we make moral judgements. In contrast, beliefs about what is right and wrong seem insufficient to drive behavioural change – indeed, sometimes it looks like the sub-cortical structures are driving actions and then the beliefs are playing catch-up to offer justifications. The illustration opposite depicts how the brain processes value. Following our common theme, value is many things in the brain. But the illustration allows us to edge closer to answering the question, if you care about the planet, which parts of your brain are doing the caring?

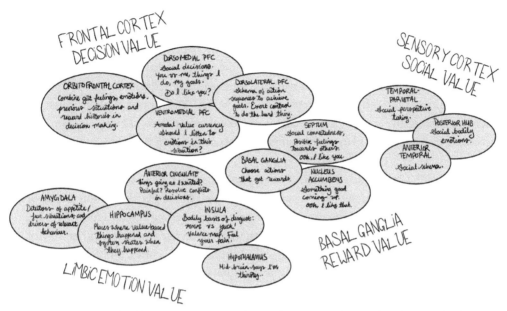

Figure 10.2 How the brain represents value – if you care about the planet, which parts are doing the caring?

Let's have a look at what the structures contribute. In the limbic system, the amygdala detects threats and opportunities for appetitive behaviours (such as curiosity) and drives decisions to avoid danger. The anterior insula is the bodily basis of emotion and particularly deals with negative responses towards losses, risks, and situations that are aversive both physiologically and morally; it deals in gut intuitions and choices that might disgust, be it the rotten cheese or the rotten politician. The insula is also involved in (bodily) feeling the pain of others and therefore in empathy. It motivates choices driven by pity. The septum is involved in value around positive social affiliations; it is more activated, for instance, when you choose to make a charitable donation. The hippocampus stores snapshots of the situations where value-based events happened, in case you find yourself back there again. The anterior cingulate cortex is a broker between the limbic system and cortical decision-making mechanisms, monitoring progress against goals, and also resolving conflicts between competing processes and options – in the current context, it helps resolve quandaries. And as we've seen, the nucleus accumbens within the basal ganglia is a marker of anticipating positive rewards as the outcome of decisions – based on stored histories of what kinds of action selections were met with positive outcomes in the past.

Moving to the cortex, the front has the business of actually making the decisions. Two neighbouring regions in the bottom middle of the prefrontal cortex play important roles: the orbitofrontal (combining gut feelings, emotions, and reward information from previous situations to judge risk) and ventromedial (weighting emotional input and running the cost–benefit analysis to make the decision). As we saw in Chapter 5 where we considered how you decide if you are happy (really, deep down), the ventromedial prefrontal cortex is where the amodal currency of value sits enabling the brain to make judgements between the competing demands of different content-specific systems. The upper outside parts of the prefrontal cortex, the dorsolateral, moderate the responses of these risk and emotion systems according to context and plans, and then pull the sensorimotor levers to make things happen once the decision is made.

Recall that in Chapter 8, we talked about how brains differ. One of those dimensions was personality, and we discussed how it could be thought of in terms of different tuning of the limbic system. In Chapter 9, we saw how differently tuned limbic systems may percolate up to influence political leanings and voting behaviour. Differences included the liability of the insula to signal moral disgust, the likelihood of the cingulate cortex and the insula to flag empathy for suffering, the readiness of the amygdala to detect threat, and the strength of the prefrontal cortex to suppress the intuitions that disagree with current plans.

If people's limbic systems are tuned differently, and the limbic system is involved in value-based decision making around climate change, then people's responses to the challenge of climate change will differ. Since the challenge is a conceptual one (what we understand to be going on, as communicated to us through language: the world is metaphorically on fire) rather than a perceived situation (something we can see is physically on fire – grab a bucket), this means that the same message will produce divergent responses. Solutions to climate change may need to be framed to fit with the preferences of those different limbic systems.

Let's take two examples. On the one hand, if we have a more fearful, disgust-sensitive, uncertainty-aversive limbic system, we may prefer to hear about *a concrete plan to secure old-fashioned neighbourhood conservation against climate threats*. On the other hand, if we have a more empathetic, uncertainty-tolerant, prefrontally dominated limbic system, we may like to be told about *an ambitious plan to achieve a future of global environmental balance through international cooperation and justice*. When we need to engage with entire populations to address the challenge facing us all, we need to embrace not just how the brain works (including the involvement of emotion and reward systems in decision making) but also how brains can work differently.

Decision Making in Favour of Other People

These are all decisions made based on self-interest: what will reward me, how will I protect myself? But decisions about climate change involve everyone, they involve doing the right thing to *favour other people* rather than just me. They involve what is called the *prosocial* brain. How does that work?

As we discussed in Chapters 5 and 9, a lot of the brain is interested in processing other people, both their physical attributes (what their faces look like, where they are looking, how their bodies are positioned), their social status (more attention is paid to higher status individuals), and what this physical information suggests about their immediate future actions, as well as their long-term future actions related to their thoughts and beliefs. This information is processed in the sensory hierarchies in the back of the brain, including temporal cortex and parietal areas, together processing faces, bodies, and space. The parietal cortex also processes your bodily self and abstract properties of your self (what one might call reflective self-awareness). The precuneus, a wedge of parietal cortex sitting above the occipital visual cortex, is particularly into this stuff. This bodily self communicates with the limbic system via the posterior cingulate cortex, the broker to the emotions, to check how it is doing. The junction of parietal and temporal regions is involved in perspective taking, as your 'view' and your knowledge can be spatially transformed into someone else's. The brain stores social scripts, how people usually behave in different situations, in its repository of knowledge in the anterior temporal lobe. These scripts also contain standards, how you should behave. If you force yourself to go against these standards (not, for instance, recycling your waste), the 'control' regions of the prefrontal cortex (dorsolateral) will enable you to do this, but the anterior cingulate will start to light up with the internal conflict you are causing, and the limbic structures will be ablaze with self-evaluative emotions, guilt and shame, as the amygdala flags social threat, the insula registers self-disgust, and the posterior cingulate cortex updates the reflective self in the precuneus that you have been a bad boy/girl.

Prosocial behaviour, acting in favour of other people, generally involves the reward system (the nucleus accumbens signalling positive rewards, the ventral tegmental area pumping dopamine into the basal ganglia action selection system to signify when rewards were even better than expected). As authors, we find this reassuring: most people are rewarded by being good citizens. But this isn't blind do-gooding: the brain needs to run the relevant calculations to compare social welfare and individual benefits, and solve any conflicts to produce prosocial behaviours (it is, after all, a lot of mental effort to sort through your rubbish to fish out all the plastics, isn't it? As we saw in Chapter 7, the brain is keeping track of mental effort).

These calculations must be run during various kinds of social interactions, and mostly involve limbic structures and reward structures pitching in, with the lower middle part of the prefrontal cortex (ventromedial) running the numbers to make the decisions. For example, in choosing to give to charity, the insula and anterior cingulate are involved in empathy, feeling others' pain, and the temporal-parietal junction in taking others' perspective, while regions of the basal ganglia and the ventral tegmental area are excited by giving an anonymous donation to a charitable organisation (the same regions that like receiving money yourself).

In interactions with others, we value fairness. If the ventromedial prefrontal cortex spits out the conclusion that, according to the numbers, the outcome of an interaction was *not fair*, the amygdala starts to get bothered that there is a social threat underway. Under these circumstances, and indeed when social norms are violated by others, we do like to punish offenders. In fact, we will go to some effort to do so, and when punishment is meted out, our reward circuits light up again. (So, do check on that plastics recycling.)

Cooperating with others in social interactions is complex. It requires a lot of those social brain circuits to be running a simulation of the person you are trying to cooperate with. But when cooperation works, the reward areas are activated by successful cooperative interactions (the kind of hit you get working with a person rather than working with a computer). But that amygdala is going to flare again if someone screws you over.

Perhaps one of the most important questions for our topic is how the brain processes *trust*. Climate change is mostly an idea and not a consequence of direct experience. We must trust the word of others that our actions are linked to certain environmental outcomes and that certain actions will reduce the distant risk of those outcomes; that our tossing the empty plastic Coke bottle in the trash may lead to microplastics in the ocean which build up in fish, and that placing the bottle in a recycling bin will reduce that risk because it will be disposed of safely. Trust is built through histories of interactions with others and understanding their intentions, so partly a job for the social brain and partly a job for the reward system to compile a record of outcomes linked to each individual.

However, it is worth distinguishing between two types of trust: *conditional trust* is built up solely via this system of recording rewards from previous interactions. Is it worth trusting this individual? By contrast, *unconditional trust* depends more on the limbic system, particularly the septum, which is involved in social affiliation and attachment. We are more likely to trust people (or organisations) to which we are attached. We can see the hand of the limbic system in trust decisions by manipulating levels of hormones (in Chapters 4 and 8, we saw how hormones play a role in tuning the limbic system to be more or less fearful, more or less friendly). If we give the limbic system a puff of oxytocin, this promotes friendliness (at least for the in-group), and the individual will become more trusting. If we give the limbic system a puff of testosterone, the amygdala is more likely to become socially vigilant to the threat of untrustworthy faces (more trustworthy faces tend to have higher inner eyebrows and pronounced cheekbones, and be symmetrical, while less trustworthy faces tend to have lower inner eyebrows and shallower cheekbones, and be asymmetrical).

Lastly, we saw in Chapter 9 how the brain is also bothered about social hierarchies, keeping a record of ranks in the prefrontal cortex. On the whole, we are more likely to trust individuals higher in the social hierarchy (although not if in your own personal past, they have undermined that right through a bad record of behaviour, stored in your reward system). How high up your hierarchy are politicians? Climate scientists?

Celebrities? And as a conceptual species, we saw how loyalty can be to roles rather than to individual people. Similarly for ethical responsibilities: is your sense of responsibility aimed at the world at large (a concept), your country, the local community, or your family (where the bonds become more about social attachment)?

How Can We Use Neuroscience to Save the (People on the) Planet?

All our hominin ancestors went extinct because of climate change. But they didn't influence the climate, they were merely its victims. The human facility for niche construction suggests that in response to our current *Anthropocene* climate change, we can use tools and technology to either resist its effects (that'll be air conditioning) or change the environment itself (carbon capture, seeding cloud cover to refreeze the polar icecaps, big stuff). Okay, so we would have preferred human decision making in this sphere to be fact-based and reflective, deliberative, as if determined by a mental spreadsheet with causal models and cost–benefit analyses. Ideally, we should need to do no more than make the argument. But no, people get all emotional about things and want to know what's in it for them. So how can emotions and rewards be leveraged appropriately and responsibly to shift populations to the sustainable use of environmental resources?

Here are half a dozen lessons from neuroscience. First, people will respond to what other people are doing. Social learning and social norms are effective in shaping behaviour. The limbic system has the twin sticks of shame and guilt to keep us in line. We'll behave a certain way because everyone else is doing it. Second, fear messaging can have unpredictable results, spurring behaviour change but also disengagement from the issues. Moreover, in the absence of a sense of control, it can produce anxiety. Therefore, any use of fear messaging needs to be accompanied by detailed, immediate, and relevant action plans that lessen the threat (for instance, how practically to use an electric car with a range of 120 miles to go on holiday next Thursday on a trip of 130 miles between London and Wells-next-the-Sea).

Third, we need to consider the brain's biases in the way it processes future rewards and losses. We tend to discount future gains (£10 today feels better than £100 in ten years' time). So, the future gains need to be emphasised more heavily (for instance through pervasive eco-labelling); or individuals need to be given an advance on future gains to bring them closer in time (a grant to insulate your house). We have less of a tendency to discount future losses (in terms of misery, a forest dying next week doesn't feel that different to the same forest being dead in ten years' time); so better decisions may be made when the future is presented in terms of potential losses.

Those negative outcomes we're being asked to make decisions about are also proba-bilistic, diffuse, and far away; our own contribution to them may be tiny. It's easier to make decisions about issues that will 100% affect us, personally and immediately. For this, we need to emphasise personal consequences; emphasise the trustworthiness of the causal models; and establish the authority of the evidence and those who communicate it. Trustworthiness is more effective through institutions or individuals to which people have a social attachment.

Fourth, the strongest lever to alter choices in decision making is to elicit positive emo-tions around environmental issues and the fate of other people. Cooperation and charity can elicit positive rewards as much as our own gains. Visualisation of the people whom the decisions will help (those cute future generations of children) can elicit empathy, as can a view of the planet from their perspective; visualisation of bad outcomes (that drown-ing polar bear) can elicit disgust; both will influence decision making.

Lastly, communication around climate change is speaking to a diverse audience. Messages need to be tailored to those with differently tuned limbic systems (level of fear, pro-sociality); to those who more or less heavily discount the value of future rewards; and to those with different reward histories, and therefore trust of, authority.

If this all sounds like a recipe to manipulate people, yes, we have been rather taking it for granted that people's behaviour needs to change to address climate change, and that we need to overcome the brain's limitations in responding to an existential threat. But if you are more cynical, we think we've helped, because now it's going to be easier to spot when you're being manipulated – by those government grants to install solar panels or to buy electric cars which aim to offset your over-discounting of future ben-efits, and by those vivid images of swimming polar bears with no ice left to climb on to which intend to engage your insula and generate disgust. You'll know what's going on. We agree, reader, don't be manipulated, make your own minds up based on the argu-ments and the facts.

Isn't climate change a moral issue, a political issue, you might ask? Should neuroscien-tists really be playing in this sandbox? No, no they shouldn't. Speak to your local representative. Pressure the United Nations. It is, however, helpful to know what features of the brain will make it easier or harder to change human behaviour.

I Don't Buy it

And if you don't buy any of this climate change nonsense – perhaps you're content to wait for the conspiracy to blow over, or for the next ice age to come along – we did encourage you to imagine an alternative, hypothetical species-threatening scenario, which would serve the purposes of this chapter equally as well, like a giant asteroid hurtling towards Earth. As we speak, we expect your thoughts are running to how to persuade government representatives to send adapted space shuttles to intercept and destroy the asteroid, how to convince other citizens that the asteroid threat is real and not a media hoax, and that they should refrain from panic-buying tins of soup – all based on your new understanding of the contributions of emotion, reward, and risk to decision making. In which case, good work, reader.

━━━━━ **Box 10.1** ━━

Self-test

The strange names of the bits of the brain can prove a barrier to understanding how it works. Here's a self-test you can take to see how you're doing.

What are the putamen, the pulvinar, and the precuneus?

One of the authors of this book admits that he has, on occasions, momentarily got these mixed these up. They seem arbitrary names full of p-sounds and u-sounds. (They are, as it turns out, derived from Latin, based merely on what the bits look like, as we discussed in Chapter 1. Putamen – shape of a nutshell; pulvinar – shape of a cushion; precuneus – found in front of the cuneus; cuneus: the shape of a wedge.) Do these terms seem at all familiar?

Let's start with putamen. Remember, the brain has an action selection system, called the basal ganglia: lots of parallel loops going from motor and frontal areas of the cortex down to sub-cortical lumps of neurons (nuclei) and back up again. In any situation, the cortex may have several actions it might want to perform, or several thoughts it might want to have (plans, task sets) but only one can win. The basal ganglia loops have lots of components trying to turn each other on and off, some bits particularly interested in when action selection yields rewards, but together, they allow the brain to select one of many possibilities of things to think or do in the moment. The putamen is one of the components of these loops, a bit that receives input from the cortex (as well as the caudate nucleus, another part of the bigger structure called the striatum). You pass the test if you remembered *action selection*.

Now, the pulvinar. Recall, sensory information from the eyes and ears comes into the brain via a waystation, the thalamus, before being processed and pored over in the cortex. The thalamus has a chunk called the pulvinar which is involved in talking to the sensory parts of the cortex about what to focus on. Given prompting from the cortex, it will help with filtering or suppressing irrelevant information in a cluttered visual display. It will also deliver fast automatic switching between visual and auditory information – say if a door slams while you're reading a book. So, the pulvinar is involved in rudimentary, low-level aspects of sensory attention. You pass the test if you remembered the brain has a *waystation* that sensory information comes in via.

(Continued)

Last, the precuneus. The precuneus is just a part of the parietal lobe, one of the sensory content systems of the cortex. It sits in the inside surface of each hemisphere, in front of a part of the occipital lobe called the cuneus (wedge) which is involved in processing visual information. Remember, the parietal lobe is the sensory lobe for sensing the body and for generating representations of space. Further away from sensory input from the body, but sitting next to the occipital lobe, the precuneus is running computations around space and vision involving the body. Some of these are high-level computations, involving mental imagery, retrieval of relevant images from episodic memory (with the help of the hippocampus) and even body awareness (seeping into the realm of consciousness!). If you got *cortex* or *content-specific system* in the back of the brain, you pass.

How did you do in the self-test? If you recognised *waystation*, *action selection*, and *content-specific system*, you're doing well – you're getting a gist of how the brain works. If you recognised and didn't mix up the words putamen, pulvinar, and precuneus, you're doing better than at least one of the authors.

———————————————————————————————————

11
CONCLUSION (AND ANSWERS TO THOSE PUZZLES)

We're back at the party. The guy has come up to us and told us that scientists know almost nothing about how the brain works, it's far too complex, the most complicated thing in the universe. And that scientists don't have the *first clue* about how consciousness works.

We've sent him on his way, telling him how the brain is just some content-specific hierarchical sensory and motor systems modulated by a control system, some appetitive and spatial memory systems bothered with survival-relevant behaviour, an action selection system bothered about rewards, a motor-smoothing system, and some bodily homeostasis systems. And we've told him that consciousness is probably a 3D sensory model of the body-in-the-world created by the isolated brain to guide action. We take a sip of our drink and count ourselves lucky. We could have been stuck in the corner with one of those climate change bores.

We remember, too, that there's stuff we didn't tell him, the parts that indeed remain mysterious. The detailed circuitry within each brain region. The dynamic real-time interactions between the circuits that together determine moment-to-moment behaviour, combining the brain's electrical and chemical properties, the dynamics that can go wrong in psychiatric disorders. The exact 'code' in which neurons speak to each other. How the brain handles complex, abstract thought and reasoning, often about itself. And until scientists and philosophers reconceptualise the mind-and-brain, quite how the biology of the central nervous system generates the experience of being alive. The vast majority of what the brain does, for instance, doesn't seem to figure in consciousness, such as the 80% of the brain's neurons in the cerebellum, crunching motor control information.

Let's leave the party behind and start to pull out some of the themes that have emerged through the book.

First, a tough part of neuroscience is naming bits of the brain, which is generally confusing because so many different terms are used, both in parts (regions of lobes or gyri/sulci or Brodmann areas) and in orienting (rostral-caudal; anterior-posterior; inferior-middle-superior; ventral-dorsal). Names of parts turned out largely to have originated from 19th-century anatomists based on what bits of the brain looked like (translated conveniently into Latin or Greek). We helpfully suggested they could add the *Ronaldus McDonaldus*. We also noted that naming bits of the brain can sometimes lead us astray, because it encourages us to think in terms of certain bits having certain functions. But the central nervous system is plastic and can adapt to have different functions – e.g., the 'primary visual cortex (V1)' processes other sensory information in the blind. And parts may have functions that depend on the networks of connected regions into which they are integrated.

Next, we saw how the way the brain works only makes sense in light of its biology, and its biology only makes sense in the light of evolution. The brain could have worked differently – we now have digital computers, artificial intelligence, machine learning, robots. These tell us there are other ways that thinking and learning devices can work. There may be side effects of having to think with neurons – the need for sleep being one of them – but evolution likes neurons because they are flexible enough to do all sorts of computations in the brain. We saw a common computational unit, the mini-column, comprising around 100 neurons wired together in a characteristic configuration, and then replicated millions of times across the cortex, processing many different varieties of information in different regions.

We saw that the brain is mainly a sensorimotor device, not readily given to abstraction. This is a slightly tricky point that bears repeating. What the brain is *not* good at doing is the type of abstraction that involves separating the structure of an idea or problem from its specific contents (e.g., that 'dog' and 'cat' are both nouns), and then doing thinking based only on these structures using general-purpose devices. This is how a digital computer operates. Humans can manage this type of logical thinking but have to fake it using the crutch of symbolic language. What the brain *is* good at is computing a type of abstraction called *invariances*. Invariances are common patterns that hold across lots of instances. It extracts these invariances in the higher levels of sensory and motor hierarchies. The higher levels bind together variable instances of an object or action which can differ in their individual realisation, so for instance, the different views of a coffee cup may be bound together by neurons in a higher layer, so these neurons are always activated by seeing the cup, irrespective of the particular view. Information within the hierarchy is always sensory or motor: it becomes more abstract by sticking more bits of information together, into more complex objects and events across a wider set of contexts, or more extended motor sequences.

This turned out to be important, because it means knowledge is stuck in the content-specific systems in which it is stored. It led to the principle *Where you are is what you do.* To run the central nervous system with this limitation, the brain must use devices like hubs, maps, and dynamically configured networks of regions. It needs a modulatory system to control the prepotent responses (imagine mini agents desperately wanting to launch well-practised actions when they see the right sensory conditions); the modulatory system must select only the agent appropriate to the current goal. The modulatory system has its own specific content, which includes task sets. These configure the sensory systems to look out for certain inputs and prepare the motor systems to produce certain actions in response, to achieve the selected task. The modulatory system primarily makes decisions, including decisions about sensorimotor processing, social situations, emotional situations, and situations involving risk.

We thought of the brain as a computer – sometimes this worked for us, sometimes it didn't (it didn't work so well when we had to focus on the biology of the body, its hormonal signalling, and phenomena like stress and, er-hmm, romance). We spent a lot of time comparing the brain to a mobile phone. We sympathised with psychologists, because oftentimes we found that *what is one thing in psychology is many things in the brain*. Examples included the self, learning, concepts, people, language, and value. The psychologist's job is to find simple concepts like these to explain how the mind works, but the concepts do not map in any nice way to all the brain regions involved in producing the relevant behaviours.

The skills we teach in schools, literacy, numeracy, science, art, all the great ideas of civilisation, are mostly activities of the cortex. The cortex is big in humans, so big that it wraps around the rest of the brain structures during the development of the foetus. But the human cortex is just the size you'd expect according to the conserved brain-making plan that is shared across mammals. If you scale a brain to the size of a human brain, that's how big the cortex will be (and according to the plan, the cerebellum gets big too). Scale the brain up even more, say to the size of a dolphin, and you get even more cortex and cerebellum. Brain size is clearly important: *Homo sapiens* has a big brain for its body size, making it the crafty hominin. But brain size isn't everything. Somehow, *Homo sapiens* competed (and/or seduced) the Neanderthals out of existence, even though Neanderthals had bigger brains than *Homo sapiens*. *Sapiens* may have had some help from climate change in dislodging Neanderthals, which is ironic.

If all mammals use a similar programme for growing their brains, that makes it more complex to understand where species-specific skills come from. There's no new part in the bat brain for echolocation, no new part in the human brain for language. The answer lay in a combination of innovations in the periphery (changes in sensory equipment, body shape and movement options), different motivations and attention, a plastic central nervous system which learns from the experiences generated by its motivations, and changes in conceptual power (how much can be learnt). Evolution doesn't commit to high-level computational solutions in the central nervous system, these are the outcome of self-organisation. We saw that *evolution does not pre-specify banana detectors* – because a species that could only detect bananas in its visual system would be extinct if bananas died out. Instead, fruit detectors are the outcomes of self-organisation depending on the fruit available in the environment where the organism is developing.

We never could raise much excitement from the brain having two sides – they are mainly mirror images, with the facility to take on similar functions. There was some deep evolutionary evidence for a division of labour (left hemisphere: habitual or routine actions; right hemisphere: monitoring for danger or novelty) which might explain some of the left–right specialisations we see in the developmental outcomes of adults (such as in language functions). We got a little bit excited by the question of why the brain should be twisted round, so the left side controls the right side of the body, and the right side of the brain the left side of the body. That's weird, right, putting the brain on back to front? We thought it had something to do with fish.

The cortex may be where human civilisation lies, but for the brain, it's only one game in town. Indeed, if you want to switch focus, you can see the cortex as a sort of strap-on problem-solving device that crunches the numbers to deliver the goals mandated by the limbic system and to act out the behaviours selected by the reward system. We saw that variations in the tuning of the limbic system across people (in how fearful or friendly it is) are manifested in behaviour such as different personalities and even in supposedly intellectual activities such as how we exercise our right to vote in democracies.

After lots of hard work, we then discovered that we can't understand how the *modern* human brain works just by looking inside it – its circuits are fashioned by the cultural niches we have constructed for ourselves through cultural evolution. Hominin brain sizes have been increasing for millions of years, but the sophistication of our tool use has increased more slowly and sporadically, only accelerating exponentially in the last few thousand years. This is likely due to the invention of information tools that allow cultural knowledge to be accumulated, refined, and spread. The sporadic nature of tool innovation suggests that the origin of modern *Homo sapiens* may be partly due to biological evolution but also partly due to history and circumstance, unfolding in cultural evolution that takes advantage of the plasticity of the central nervous system to allow us to develop cognitive gizmos and gadgets, like logical reasoning.

Finally, back to those puzzles. We promised we'd tell you the answers as to why the brain seems to work in various odd ways. Here you go:

Why do I forget what the capital of Hungary is, but not that I'm afraid of spiders? Because they are stored in different memory systems in the brain. Cortical knowledge of facts decays gently if not used; memory of things you're scared of is stored in the amygdala, part of the limbic system, and it does not forget (that's its job, to protect you).

Why do I find I have learnt things better after a night's sleep? One function of sleep is to consolidate knowledge learned during the day, strengthening the changes in brain connectivity, integrating it with existing knowledge, forgetting details, and extracting themes.

I get 7/10 in a test – why am I delighted if I was expecting to get 5, demoralised if I was expecting to get 9? Humans are most sensitive to their predictions about the rewards they will get, rather than the absolute size of the reward. People respond most if those predictions are violated. A key principle of brain function is that it is predictive, guessing what's going to happen next, what it's going to experience next, how much fun it's going to have next, and learning from when its guesses are wrong. Doing better than expected is much more rewarding than achieving the same level of performance when you were expecting it.

Why as a teenager did I start doing risky things to impress my friends (and getting grumpy with my parents)? The changes in brain function that occur following puberty include altered motivations – to want to spend time with friends instead of family – and an increased sensitivity to the rewards of peer group approval. This increased weighting of 'what your friends think' and relatively poor knowledge of actual long-term risks and rewards of decisions can lead to making choices that are risky. The teenage brain hasn't gone wrong, it needs to find its place in the adult world.

Why does my mind sometimes go blank when I'm stressed in an exam, or forced to stand up and give a speech in front of people? And I why do I vividly remember these experiences? The thinking part of the brain, the cortex, is closely connected and in dialogue with the emotion structures in the limbic system, including the amygdala and hippocampus. If a situation is deemed threatening, the limbic system can trigger the fight-or-flight response. The cortex changes to restrict mental flexibility and long-term knowledge recall (both needed to answer exam questions), and to activate habitual plans to escape the situation (usually not needed to answer exam questions). The fight-or-flight state increases the performance of the memory system, the hippocampus, which likes to record where danger happened. So, you'll remember every agonising moment of forgetting everything.

Why do I learn a new language so much more easily when I'm five than when I'm 50? Adults are actually pretty good learners in the classroom – they pay attention, they follow instructions, they don't mess around in the back row. But their perceptual and motor systems have long specialised to the speech sounds of their own languages. This interferes with their ability to process the sounds in the new language, slowing down both comprehension and production. Adults may also need to practise more than children to make skills automatic, due to structural changes in their brains (pruning, myelination). The goal of learning a new language is often to achieve fluency, and that can be harder for adults to get to.

Why is it easy to remember something unusual that happened (seeing the ghost of Elvis Presley riding an elephant down the street, with Marilyn Monroe sat behind him) but hard to remember unusual facts (how to spell 'acquiesce', the boiling point of nitrogen). These bits of information are stored in different memory systems: experiences are stored in the hippocampus, where novelty makes the strongest memories. Facts are stored in the cortex, in an integrated network. It is easier to learn information that is consistent with what is already in the network, as the new memory is supported by lots of similar knowledge. Knowledge that stands out or is different takes more effort to learn and decays more easily in the absence of practice. The boiling point of nitrogen is minus 195.8 degrees centigrade, but we don't know how to spell acquiesce. If it is spelled correctly here, we thank the publishers.

BIBLIOGRAPHY

Chapter 1

Johns, P. (2014). *Clinical Neuroscience: An Illustrated Colour Text*. Churchill Livingstone.

Marner, L. (2021). Communication among neurons: Quantitative measures in aging and disease. *Danish Medical Journal*, 59(4), Article B4427.

Martin, R.C. (2021). The critical role of semantic working memory in language comprehension and production. *Current Directions in Psychological Science*, 30(4), 283–291. https://doi.org/10.1177/096372142199517

Poldrack, R.A. (2010). Mapping mental function to brain structure: How can cognitive neuro-imaging succeed? *Perspectives on Psychological Science*, 5(6), 753–761. https://doi.org/10.1177/1745691610388777

Price, C.J. & Friston, K.J. (2005). Functional ontologies for cognition: The systematic definition of structure and function. *Cognitive Neuropsychology*, 22(3), 262–275. https://doi.org/10.1080/02643290442000095

Chapter 2

Cesario, J., Johnson, D.J. & Eisthen, H.L. (2020). Your brain is not an onion with a tiny reptile inside. *Current Directions in Psychological Science*, 29(3), 255–260. https://doi.org/10.1177/0963721420917687

Charvet, C.J., Darlington, R.B. & Finlay, B.L. (2013). Variation in human brains may facilitate evolutionary change toward a limited range of phenotypes. *Brain, Behavior and Evolution*, 81(2). https://doi.org/10.1159/000345940

Costanzo, M., et al. (2016). A global genetic interaction network maps a wiring diagram of cellular function. *Science,* 353(6306), Article 1420. https://doi.org/10.1126/science.aaf1420

Donahue, C.J., Glasser, M.F., Preuss, T.M., Rilling, J.K. & Van Essen, D.C. (2018). Quantitative assessment of prefrontal cortex in humans relative to nonhuman primates. *Proceedings of the National Academy of Sciences USA*, 115(22). https://doi.org/10.1073/pnas.1721653115

Finlay, B.L. (2019). Generic *Homo sapiens* and unique *Mus musculus*: Establishing the typicality of the modeled and the model species. *Brain, Behavior and Evolution*, 93(2–3), 1–15. https://doi.org/10.1159/000500111

Finlay, B.L., Hinz, F. & Darlington, R.B. (2011). Mapping behavioural evolution onto brain evolution: The strategic roles of conserved organization in individuals and species. *Philosophical Transactions of the Royal Society, B*, 366, 2111–2123. https://doi.org/10.1098/rstb.2010.0344

Jacobs, G.H., Williams, G.A., Cahill, H. & Nathans, J. (2007). Emergence of novel color vision in mice engineered to express a human cone photopigment. *Science*, 315, 1723–1725. https://doi.org/10.1126/science.1138838

Kristan, W.B. (2016). Early evolution of neurons. *Current Biology*, 26, R949–R954. https://doi.org/10.1016/j.cub.2016.05.030

Moss, C.F. & Sinha, S.R. (2003). Neurobiology of echolocation in bats. *Current Opinion in Neurobiology*, 13(6), 751–758. https://doi.org/10.1016/j.conb.2003.10.016

van Eijk, L., Zhu, D., Couvy-Duchesne, B., Strike, L.T., Lee, A.J., Hansell, N.K., Thompson, P.M., de Zubicaray, G.I., McMahon, K.L., Wright, M.J. & Zietsch, B.P. (2021). Are sex differences in human brain structure associated with sex differences in behavior? *Psychological Sciences*, 32(8), 1183–1197. https://doi.org/10.1177/0956797621996664

Vuoksimaa, E., Panizzon, M.S., Franz, C.E., Fennema-Notestine, C., Hagler, D.J. Jr, Lyons, M.J., Dale, A.M. & Kremen, W.S. (2018). Brain structure mediates the association between height and cognitive ability. *Brain Structure and Function*, 223(7), 3487–3494. https://doi.org/10.1007/s00429-018-1675-4

Woych, J., Ortega Gurrola, A., Deryckere, A., Jaeger, E.C.B., Gumnit, E., Merello, G., Gu, J., Joven Araus, A., Leigh, N.D., Yun, M., Simon, A. & Tosches, M.A. (2022). Cell-type profiling in salamanders identifies innovations in vertebrate forebrain evolution. *Science*, 377(6610), eabp9186. https://doi.org/10.1126/science.abp9186

Chapter 3

Allen, T.A. & Fortin, N.J. (2013). The evolution of episodic memory. *Proceedings of the National Academy of Sciences USA*, 110 (Suppl 2), 10379–10386. https://doi.org/10.1073/pnas.1301199110

Amthor, F. (2016). *Neuroscience for Dummies*. John Wiley & Sons.

Barrett, L.F. (2017). *How Emotions Are Made*. Macmillan.

Cesario, J., Johnson, D.J. & Eisthen, H.L. (2020). Your brain is not an onion with a tiny reptile inside. *Current Directions in Psychological Science*, 29(3), 255–260. https://doi.org/10.1177/0963721420917687

Finlay, B.L. & Uchiyama, R. (2014). Developmental mechanisms channeling evolution. *Trends in Neurosciences*, 38(2), 69–76. http://dx.doi.org/10.1016/j.tins.2014.11.004

Hain, D., Gallego-Flores, T., Klinkmann, M., Macias, A., Ciirdaeva, E., Arends, A., Thum, C., Tushev, G., Kretchmer, F., Tosches, M.A. & Laurent, G. (2022). Molecular diversity and evolution of neuron types in the amniote brain. *Science*, 377(6610). https://doi.org/10.1126/science.abp8202

Hain, T.C. & Helminski, J.O. (2007). Mal de debarquement. In S. Herdman (Ed.), *Vestibular Rehabilitation* (2nd edn). F.A. Davis Publishers.

Herculano-Houzel, S. (2010). Coordinated scaling of cortical and cerebellar numbers of neurons. *Frontiers in Neuroanatomy*, 4, Article 12. https://doi.org/10.3389/fnana.2010.00012

Koch, C., Massimini, M., Boly, M. & Tononi, G. (2016). Neural correlates of consciousness: Progress and problems. *Nature Reviews Neuroscience*, 17(5), 307–321. https://doi.org/10.1038/nrn.2016.22

Kristan, W.B. Jr., Calabrese, R.L. & Friesen, W.O. (2005). Neuronal control of leech behavior. *Progress in Neurobiology*, 76(5), 279–327. https://doi.org/10.1016/j.pneurobio.2005.09.004

Laberge, F., Mühlenbrock-Lenter, S., Grunwald, W. & Roth, G. (2006). Evolution of the amygdala: New insights from studies in amphibians. *Brain, Behavior and Evolution*, 67(4), 177–187. https://doi.org/10.1159/000091119

Lee, S.J., Ralston, H.J.P., Drey, E.A., Partridge, J.C. & Rosen, M.A. (2005). Fetal pain: A systematic multidisciplinary review of the evidence. *JAMA*, 294(8), 947–954. https://doi.org/10.1001/jama.294.8.947

Lindroos, R., Dorst, M.C., Du, K., Filipovic, M., Keller, D., Ketzef, M., Kozlov, A.K., Kumar, A., Lindahl, M., Nair, A.G., Pérez-Fernández, J., Grillner, S., Silberberg, G. & Hellgren Kotaleski, J. (2018). Basal ganglia neuromodulation over multiple temporal and structural scales – simulations of direct pathway MSNs investigate the fast onset of dopaminergic effects and predict the role of Kv4.2. *Frontiers in Neural Circuits*, 12, Article 3. https://doi.org/10.3389/fncir.2018.00003

Muday, G.K. & Brown-Harding, H. (2018). Nervous system-like signaling in plant defense. *Science*, 361(6407), 1068–1069. https://doi.org/10.1126/science.aau9813

Pabba, M. (2013). Evolutionary development of the amygdaloid complex. *Frontiers in Neuroanatomy*, 28(7), Article 27. https://doi.org/10.3389/fnana.2013.00027

Reddy, L., Zoefel, B., Possel, J.K., Peters, J., Dijksterhuis, D.E., Poncet, M., van Straaten, E.C.W., Baayen, J.C., Idema, S. & Self, M.W. (2021). Human hippocampal neurons track moments in a sequence of events. *Journal of Neuroscience*, 41(31), 6714–6725. https://doi.org/10.1523/jneurosci.3157-20.2021

Sereno, M., Diedrichsen, J., Tachrount, M., Testa-Silva, G., d'Arceuil, H. & De Zeeuw, C. (2020). The human cerebellum has almost 80% of the surface area of the neocortex. *Proceedings of the National Academy of Sciences*, 117(32), 19538–19543. https://doi.org/10.1073/pnas.2002896117

Woych, J., Ortega Gurrola, A., Deryckere, A., Jaeger, E.C.B., Gumnit, E., Merello, G., Gu, J., Joven Araus, A., Leigh, N.D., Yun, M., Simon, A. & Tosches, M.A. (2022). Cell-type profiling in salamanders identifies innovations in vertebrate forebrain evolution. *Science*, 377(6610), eabp9186. https://doi.org/10.1126/science.abp9186

Xiao, X. & Zhang, Y-Q. (2018). A new perspective on the anterior cingulate cortex and affective pain. *Neuroscience & Biobehavioral Reviews*, 90, 200–211. https://doi.org/10.1016/j.neubiorev.2018.03.022

Chapter 4

Bliss, T.V.P. & Lomo, T. (1973). Long-lasting potentiation of synaptic transmission in the dentate area of the anaesthetized rabbit following stimulation of the perforant path. *Journal of Physiology*, 232(2), 331–356. https://doi.org/10.1113/jphysiol.1973.sp010273

Dudek, S.M. & Bear, M.F. (1993). Bidirectional long-term modification of synaptic effectiveness in the adult and immature hippocampus. *Journal of Neuroscience*, 13(7), 2910–2918.

Kristan, W.B. (2016). Early evolution of neurons. *Current Biology*, 26, R937–R980. https://doi.org/10.1016/j.cub.2016.05.030

Purves, D., Augustine, G.J., Fitzpatrick, D., Hall, W.C., Lamantia, A-S., Mooney, R.D., Platt, M.L. & White, L.E. (Eds). (2018). *Neuroscience*. Oxford University Press.

Chapter 5

Andersen, B.P. (2022). Autistic-like traits and positive schizotypy as diametric specializations of the predictive mind. *Perspectives on Psychological Science*, July. https://doi.org/10.1177/17456916221075252

Arnsten, A.F. (2009). Stress signalling pathways that impair prefrontal cortex structure and function. *Nature Reviews Neuroscience*, 10(6), 410–422. https://doi.org/10.1038/nrn2648

Badre, D. (2008). Cognitive control, hierarchy, and the rostro-caudal organization of the frontal lobes. *Trends in Cognitive Science*, 12(5), 193–200. https://doi.org/10.1016/j.tics.2008.02.004

Bates, E., Reilly, J., Wulfeck, B., Dronkers, N., Opie, M., Fenson, J., Kriz, S., Jeffries, R., Miller, L. & Herbst, K. (2001). Differential effects of unilateral lesions on language production in children and adults. *Brain & Language*, 79(2), 223–265. https://doi.org/10.1006/brln.2001.2482

Blain, B. & Rutledge, R.B. (2020). Momentary subjective well-being depends on learning and not reward. *Elife*, 9, e57977. https://doi.org/10.7554/eLife.57977

Blakemore, S.J., Wolpert, D. & Frith, C. (2000). Why can't you tickle yourself? *Neuroreport*, 11(11), R11–R16. https://doi.org/10.1097/00001756-200008030-00002

Bogdashina, O. (2004). *Communication Issues in Autism and Asperger Syndrome*. Jessica Kingsley.

Botvinick, M.M. & Cohen, J.D. (2014). The computational and neural basis of cognitive control: Charted territory and new frontiers. *Cognitive Science*, 38, 1249–1285. https://doi.org/10.1111/cogs.12126.

Brown, S., Cockett, P. & Yuan, Y. (2019). The neuroscience of Romeo and Juliet: An fMRI study of acting. *Royal Society Open Science*, 6(3), Article 181908. https://doi.org/10.1098/rsos.181908.

Cassidy, C.M., Balsam, P.D., Weinstein, J.J., Rosengard, R.J., Slifstein, M., Daw, N.D., Abi-Dargham, A. & Horga, G.A. (2018). Perceptual inference mechanism for hallucinations linked to striatal dopamine. *Current Biology*, 28(4), 503–514. https://doi.org/10.1016/j.cub.2017.12.059

Cevoli, B., Watkins, C. & Rastle, K. (2022). Prediction as a basis for skilled reading: Insights from modern language models. *Royal Society Open Science*, 9, Article 211837. https://doi.org/10.1098/rsos.211837

Chew, B., Blain, B., Dolan, R.J. & Rutledge, R.B. (2021). A neurocomputational model for intrinsic reward. *Journal of Neuroscience*, 41(43), 8963–8971. https://doi.org/10.1523/JNEUROSCI.0858-20.2021

Corbetta, M., Patel, G. & Shulman, G.L. (2008). The reorienting system of the human brain: From environment to theory of mind. *Neuron*, 58(3), 306–324. https://doi.org/10.1016/j.neuron.2008.04.017

Crone, E.A. & Fuligni, A.J. (2020). Self and others in adolescence. *Annual Review of Psychology*, 71(1), 447–469. https://doi.org/10.1146/annurev-psych-010419-050937

Curot, J., Roux, F.E., Sol, J.C., Valton, L., Pariente, J. & Barbeau, E.J. (2020). Awake craniotomy and memory induction through electrical stimulation: Why are Penfield's findings not replicated in the modern era? *Neurosurgery*, 87(2), E130–E137. https://doi.org/10.1093/neuros/nyz553

de Haan, W., Mott, K., van Straaten, E.C.W., Scheltens, P. & Stam, C.J. (2012). Activity dependent degeneration explains hub vulnerability in Alzheimer's disease. *PLOS Computational Biology*, 8(8), e1002582. https://doi.org/10.1371/journal.pcbi.1002582

de Lussanet, M.H.E. & Osse, J.W.M. (2012). An ancestral axial twist explains the contralateral forebrain and the optic chiasm in vertebrates. *Animal Biology*, 62(2), 193–216. https://doi.org/10.1163/157075611X617102

DeCasien, A., Williams, S. & Higham, J. (2017). Primate brain size is predicted by diet but not sociality. *Nature Ecology and Evolution*, 1, Article 0112. https://doi.org/10.1038/s41559-017-0112

Dunbar, R.I.M. (1998). The social brain hypothesis. *Evolutionary Anthropology*, 6, 178–190. https://doi.org/10.1002/(SICI)1520-6505(1998)6:5<178::AID-EVAN5>3.0.CO;2-8

Forrester, G.S., Quaresmini, C., Leavens, D.A., Mareschal, D. & Thomas, M.S.C. (2013). Human handedness: An inherited evolutionary trait. *Behavioural Brain Research*, 237, 200–206. http://dx.doi.org/10.1016/j.bbr.2012.09.037

Gabi, M., Neves, K., Masseron, C., Ribeiro, P.F.M., Ventura-Antunes, L., Torres, L., Mota, B., Kaas, J.H. & Herculano-Houzel, S. (2016). Prefrontal neurons not expanded in human evolution. *Proceedings of the National Academy of Sciences*, 113(34), 9617–9622. https://doi.org/10.1073/pnas.1610178113

Greve, A., Cooper, E., Kaula, A., Anderson, M.C. & Henson, R. (2017). Does prediction error drive one-shot declarative learning? *Journal of Memory and Language*, 94, 149–165. https://doi.org/10.1016/j.jml.2016.11.001

Hancock, P.A., Nourbakhsh, I. & Stewart, J. (2019). On the future of transportation in an era of automated and autonomous vehicles. *Proceedings of the National Academy of Sciences*, 116(16), 7684–7691. https://doi.org/10.1073/pnas.1805770115

Hansen, S.J., McMahon, K.L. & de Zubicaray, G.I. (2019). The neurobiology of taboo language processing: fMRI evidence during spoken word production. *Social, Cognitive and Affective Neuroscience*, 14(3), 271–279. https://doi.org/10.1093/scan/nsz009

Hartmann, C., Lazar, A., Nessler, B. & Triesch, J. (2015). Where's the noise? Key features of spontaneous activity and neural variability arise through learning in a deterministic network. *PLoS Computational Biology*, 11(12), e1004640. https://doi.org/10.1371/journal.pcbi.1004640

Jacobs, J., Lega, B. & Anderson, C. (2012). Explaining how brain stimulation can evoke memories. *Journal of Cognitive Neuroscience*, 24(3), 553–563. https://doi.org/10.1162/jocn_a_00170

Jonas, E. & Kording, K.P. (2017). Could a neuroscientist understand a microprocessor? *PLoS Computational Biology*, 13(1), e1005268. https://doi.org/10.1371/journal.pcbi.1005268

Kanner, L. (1943). Autistic disturbances of affective contact. *Nervous Child*, 2, 217–250.

Kesner, R.P. & Rolls, E.T. (2015). A computational theory of hippocampal function, and tests of the theory: New developments. *Neuroscience and Biobehavioral Reviews*, 48, 92–147. https://doi.org/10.1016/j.neubiorev.2014.11.009

Kienast, P., et al. (2021). The prenatal origins of human brain asymmetry: Lessons learned from a cohort of fetuses with body lateralization defects. *Cerebral Cortex*, 31(8), 3713–3722. https://doi.org/10.1093/cercor/bhab042

Kitmura, T., Ogawa, S., Roy, S., Okuyama, T., Morrissey, M.D., Smith, L.D., Redondo, R.L. & Tonegawa, S. (2017). Engrams and circuits crucial for systems consolidation of a memory. *Science*, 356(6333), 73–78. https://doi.org/10.1126/science.aam6808

Kumar, S., Soren, S. & Chaudhury, S. (2009). Hallucinations: Etiology and clinical implications. *Industrial Psychiatry Journal*, 18(2), 119–126. https://doi.org/10.4103/0972-6748.62273

Lamb, M.R., Robertson, L.C. & Knight, R.T. (1990). Component mechanisms underlying the processing of hierarchically organized patterns: Inferences from patients with unilateral cortical lesions. *Journal of Experimental Psychology: Learning, Memory and Cognition*, 16(3), 471–483. https://doi.org/10.1037//0278-7393.16.3.471

Lindenfors, P., Wartel, A. & Lind, J. (2021). 'Dunbar's number' deconstructed. *Biology Letters*, 17(5), 20210158. https://doi.org/10.1098/rsbl.2021.0158

Macknik, S., Martinez-Conde, S. & Blakeslee, S. (2011). *Sleights of Mind: What the Neuroscience of Magic Reveals About Our Brains*. Profile Books.

MacNeilage, P.F., Rogers, L. & Vallortigara, G. (2009). Origins of the left and right brain. *Scientific American*, 301, 160–167.

Menzel, R. & Giurfa, M. (2001). Cognitive architecture of a mini-brain: The honeybee. *Trends in Cognitive Science*, 5(2), 62–71. https://doi.org/10.1016/s1364-6613(00)01601-6

Miller, E.K. & Cohen, J.D. (2001). An integrative theory of prefrontal cortex function. *Annual Review of Neuroscience*, 24, 167–202. https://doi.org/10.1146/annurev.neuro.24.1.167

Molapour, T., Hagan, C.C., Silston, B., Wu, H., Ramstead, M., Friston, K. & Mobbs, D. (2021). Seven computations of the social brain. *Social, Cognitive and Affective Neuroscience*, 16(8), 745–760. https://doi.org/10.1093/scan/nsab024

Nili, U., Goldberg, H., Weizman, A. & Dudai, Y. (2010). Fear thou not: Activity of frontal and temporal circuits in moments of real-life courage. *Neuron*, 66(6), 949–962. https://doi.org/10.1016/j.neuron.2010.06.009

Oldam, S. & Fornito, A. (2019). The development of brain network hubs. *Developmental Cognitive Neuroscience*, 36, Article 100607. https://doi.org/10.1016/j.dcn.2018.12.005

Pellicano, E. & Burr, D. (2012). When the world becomes 'too real': A Bayesian explanation of autistic perception. *Trends in Cognitive Sciences*, 16, 504–510. https://doi.org/10.1016/j.tics.2012.08.009

Reddy, L., Zoefel, B., Possel, J.K., Peters, J., Dijksterhuis, D.E., Poncet, M., van Straaten, E.C.W., Baayen, J.C., Idema, S. & Self, M.W. (2021). Human hippocampal neurons track moments in a sequence of events. *Journal of Neuroscience*, 41(31), 6714–6725. https://doi.org/10.1523/JNEUROSCI.3157-20.2021

Rutledge, R.B., de Berker, A.O., Espenhahn, S., Dayan, P. & Dolan, R.J. (2016). The social contingency of momentary subjective well-being. *Nature Communications*, 13(7), Article 11825. https://doi.org/10.1038/ncomms11825

Schlerf, J., Ivry, R.B. & Diedrichsen, J. (2012). Encoding of sensory prediction errors in the human cerebellum. *Journal of Neuroscience*, 32(14), 4913–4922. https://doi.org/10.1523/JNEUROSCI.4504-11.2012

Singer, W. (2021). Recurrent dynamics in the cerebral cortex: Integration of sensory evidence with stored knowledge. *Proceedings of the National Academy of Sciences USA*, 118(33), e2101043118. https://doi.org/10.1073/pnas.2101043118

Sirois, S., Spratling, M., Thomas, M.S.C., Westermann, G., Mareschal, D. & Johnson, M.H. (2008). Précis of neuroconstructivism: How the brain constructs cognition. *Behavioral and Brain Sciences*, 31(3), 321–331; discussion 331–356. https://doi.org/10.1017/S0140525X0800407X

Skaggs, W.E. & McNaughton, B.L. (1996). Replay of neuronal firing sequences in rat hippocampus during sleep following spatial experience. *Science*, 271(5257), 1870–1873. https://doi.org/10.1126/science.271.5257.1870

Sood, M.R. & Sereno, M.I. (2016). Areas activated during naturalistic reading comprehension overlap topological visual, auditory, and somatotomor maps. *Human Brain Mapping*, 37(8), 2784–2810. https://doi.org/10.1002/hbm.23208

Trauner, D.A. (2003). Hemispatial neglect in young children with early unilateral brain damage. *Developmental Medicine and Child Neurology*, 45(3), 160–166. https://doi.org/10.1017/s0012162203000318

Yang, W. & Sun, Q.Q. (2015). Hierarchical organization of long-range circuits in the olfactory cortices. *Physiological Reports*, 3(9), e12550. https://doi.org/10.14814/phy2.12550

Yu, M., Engels, M.M.A., Hillebrand, A., van Straaten, E.C.W., Gouw, A.A., Teunissen, C., van der Flier, W.M., Scheltens, P. & Stam, C.J. (2017). Selective impairment of hippocampus and posterior hub areas in Alzheimer's disease: An MEG-based multiplex network study. *Brain*, 140(5), 1466–1485. https://doi.org/10.1093/brain/awx050

Yu, M., Sporns, O. & Saykin, A.J. (2021). The human connectome in Alzheimer disease – relationship to biomarkers and genetics. *Nature Reviews of Neurology*, 17, 545–563. https://doi.org/10.1038/s41582-021-00529-1

Zhou, G., Lane, G., Cooper, S.L., Kahnt, T. & Zelano, C. (2019). Characterizing functional pathways of the human olfactory system. *Elife*, 8, e47177. https://doi.org/10.7554/eLife.47177

Chapter 6

Albrecht, U. (2012). Timing to perfection: The biology of central and peripheral circadian clocks. *Neuron*, 74(2), 246–260. https://doi.org/10.1016/j.neuron.2012.04.006

Allen, K. (2003). Are pets a healthy pleasure? The influence of pets on blood pressure. *Current Directions in Psychological Science*, 12(6), 236–239. https://doi.org/10.1046/j.0963-7214.2003.01269.x

Aschoff, J. (1967). Comparative physiology: Diurnal rhythms. *Annual Review of Physiology*, 25, 581–600.

Aserinsky, E. & Kleitman, N. (1953). Regularly occurring periods of eye motility and concomitant phenomena during sleep. *Science*, 118, 273–274. https://doi.org/10.1126/science.118.3062.273

Ashbrook, L.H., Krystal, A.D., Fu, Y-H. & Ptacek, L.J. (2020). Genetics of the human circadian clock and sleep homeostat. *Neuropsychopharmacology*, 45(1), 45–54. https://doi.org/10.1038/s41386-019-0476-7

Aspé-Sánchez, M., Moreno, M., Rivera, M.I., Rossi, A. & Ewer, J. (2016). Oxytocin and vasopressin receptor gene polymorphisms: Role in social and psychiatric traits. *Frontiers in Neuroscience*, 9, Article 510. https://doi.org/10.3389/fnins.2015.00510

Assefa, S.Z., Diaz-Abad, H., Wickwire, E.M. & Seharf, S.M. (2015). The functions of sleep. *Neuroscience*, 3, 155–171. https://doi.org/10.3934/Neuroscience.2015.3.155

Augustine, V., Lee, S. & Oka, Y. (2020). Neural control and modulation of thirst, sodium appetite, and hunger. *Cell*, 180(1), 25–32. https://doi.org/10.1016/j.cell.2019.11.040

Barton, R. & Cappellini, I. (2016). Sleep, evolution and brains. *Brain, Behavior and Evolution*, 87(2), 65–68. http://dx.doi.org/10.1159/000443716

Berendzen, K.M., et al. (2023). Oxytocin receptor is not required for social attachment in prairie voles. *Neuron*, 111(6), 787–796. https://doi.org/10.1016/j.neuron.2022.12.011

Borbely, A.A., Daan, S., Wirz-Justice, A. & DeBoer, T. (2016). The two-process model of sleep regulation: A reappraisal. *Journal of Sleep Research*, 25(2), 131–143. https://10.1111/jsr.12371

British Psychological Society. (2021). *Ethical Guidelines*. www.bps.org.uk/guideline/code-ethics-and-conduct

Callaghan, B.L. & Tottenham, N. (2016). The stress acceleration hypothesis: Effects of early-life adversity on emotion circuits and behavior. *Current Opinions in Behavioral Science*, 7, 76–81. https://10.1016/cobeha.2015.11.018

Cannon, W.B. (1929). Organization for physiological homeostasis. *Physiological Reviews*, 9(3), 399–431.

Carter, C.S., et al. (2020). Is oxytocin 'nature's medicine'? *Pharmacological Review*, 72, 829–861. https://doi.org/10.1124/pr.120.019398

Cho, K. (2001). Chronic jet lag produces temporal lobe atrophy and spatial cognitive deficits. *Nature Neuroscience*, 4, 567–568. https://doi.org/10.1038/88384

Coren, S. (1996). *Sleep Thieves*. Free Press.

Crick, F. & Mitchison, G. (1983). The function of dream sleep. *Nature*, 304, 111–114.

Davis, S., Mirick, D.K. & Stevens, R.G. (2001). Nightshift work, light at night, and risk of breast cancer. *Journal of the National Cancer Institute*, 93, 1557–1662. https://doi.org/10.1093/jnci/93.20.1557

Denver, R.J. (2009). Structural and functional evolution of vertebrate neuroendocrine stress systems. *Trends in Comparative Endocrinology and Neurobiology: Annals of the New York Academy of Sciences*, 1163, 1–16. https://doi.org/10.1111/j.1749-6632.2009.04433.x

Dijk, D-J. (2019). Regulation and functional correlates of slow-wave sleep. *Journal of Clinical and Sleep Medicine*, 5 (Suppl. 2), S6–S15. https://doi.org/10.5664/jcsm.5.2S.S6

Era, V., Carnevali, L., Thayer, J.F., Candidi, M. & Ottaviani, C. (2021). Dissociating cognitive, behavioral and physiological stress-related responses through dorsolateral prefrontal cortex inhibition. *Psychoneuroendocrinology*, 124, Article 10570. https://doi.org/10.1016/psyneuen.2020.10570

Fali, L., et al. (2019). Differentiation of schizophrenia by combining the spatial EEG brain network patterns of rest and task P300. *IEEE Transactions on Neural Systems and Rehabilitation Engineering*, 27(4), 594–602. https://doi.org/10.1109/TNSRE.2019.2900725

Falup-Pecurariu, C., Diaconu, S., Tint, D. & Falup-Pecurariu, O. (2021). Neurobiology of sleep (review). *Experimental and Therapeutic Medicine*, 21, 272–276. https://doi.org/10.3892/etm.2021.9703

Feldman, R. (2012). Oxytocin and social affiliation in humans. *Hormones and Behavior*, 61, 380–391. https://doi.org/10.1016/j.yhbeh.2012.01.008

Girardeau, G. & Lopez-dos-Santos, V. (2021). Brain neural patterns and the memory function of sleep. *Science*, 374, 560–564. https://doi.og/10.1126/science.abi8370

Gompf, H.S. & Anaclet, C. (2020). The neuroanatomy and neurochemistry of sleep-wake control. *Current Opinion in Physiology*, 15, 143–151. https://doi.org/10.1016/j.cophys.2019.12.012

Harrewijn, A., Vidal-Ribas, P., Clore-Gronenborn, K., Jackson, S.M., Pisano, S., Pine, D.S. & Stringaris, A. (2020). Association between brain activity and endogenous and exogenous cortisol – a systematic review. *Psychoneuroendocrinology*, 120, Article 104775. https://doi.org/10.1016/j.psyneuen.2020.104775

Heinrichs, M., von Dawans, B. & Domes, G. (2009). Oxytocin, vasopressin, and human social behaviour. *Frontiers in Neuroendocrinology*, 30, 548–557. https://doi.org/10.1016/j.yfrne.2009.05.005

Hobson, J.A. (2002). *Dreaming: An Introduction to the Science of Sleep*. Oxford University Press.

Holth, J.K., et al. (2019). The sleep-wake cycle regulates brain interstitial fluid tau in mice and cerebrospinal fluid tau in humans. *Science*, 363(6429), 880–884. https://doi.org/10.1126/science.aav2546

Huijgens, P.T., Heijkoop, R., Eelke, M.S. & Snoeren, A. (2021). Silencing and stimulating the medial amygdala impairs ejaculation but not sexual incentive motivation in male rats. *Behavioural Brain Research*, 405, Article 113206. https://doi.org/10.1016/j.bbr.2021.13206

Huttenlocher, P.R., de Courten, C., Garey, L. & Van der Loos, H. (1982). Synaptogenesis in human visual cortex – evidence for synapse elimination during normal development. *Neuroscience Letters*, 33(3), 247–252. https://doi.org/10.1016/0304-3940(82)90379-2

Insel, T.R. & Shapiro, L.E. (1992). Oxytocin receptor distribution reflects social organization in monogamous and polygamous voles. *Proceedings of the National Academy of Sciences USA*, 89, 5981–5985. https://doi.org/10.1073/pnas.89.13.5981

Joels, M., Fernandez, G. & Roozendaal, B. (2011). Stress and emotional memory: A matter of timing. *Trends in Cognitive Sciences*, 15(6), 280–288. https://doi.org/j.tics.2011.04.004

Kaurin, A., Wright, A.G.C. & Kamarck, T.W. (2021). Daily stress reactivity: The unique roles of personality and social support. *Journal of Personality*, 89(5), 1012–1025. https://doi.org/10.1111/jopy.12633

Kim, E.J. & Kim, J.J. (2019). Amygdala, medial prefrontal cortex and glucocorticoid interactions produce stress-like effects on memory. *Frontiers in Behavioral Neuroscience*, 13, Article 210. https://doi.org/10.3389/fnbeh.2019.00210

Kim, S. & Strathearn, L. (2016). Oxytocin and maternal brain plasticity. *New Directions in Child and Adolescent Development*, 153, 59–72. https://doi.org/10.1002/cad.20170

Lazarus, R.S. & Folkman, S. (1984). *Stress, Appraisal, and Coping*. Springer.

Lesku, J.A., Roth II, T.C., Rattenborg, N.C., Amlaner, C.J. & Lima, S.L. (2008). Phylogenetics and the correlates of mammalian sleep: A reappraisal. *Sleep Medicine Reviews*, 12, 229–244. https://doi.org/10.1016/j.smrv.2007.10.003

Lewis, L.D. (2021). The interconnected causes and consequences of sleep in the brain. *Science*, 374, 564–568. https://doi.org/10.1126/science.abi8375

Liblau, R.S., Vassalli, A., Seifinejad, A. & Tafti, M. (2015). Hypocretin (orexin) biology and the pathophysiology of narcolepsy with cataplexy. *Lancet Neurology*, 14, 318–328. https://doi.org/10.1016/S1474-4422(14)70218-2

Loman, M.M. & Gunnar, M.R. (2010). Early experience and the development of stress reactivity and regulation in children. *Neuroscience and Biobehavioral Reviews*, 34(6), 867–876. https://doi.org/10.1016/j.neubiorev.2009.05.007

Lupien, S.J., Juster, R.P., Raymond, C. & Marin, M-F. (2018). The effects of chronic stress on the human brain: From neurotoxicity, to vulnerability, to opportunity. *Frontiers in Neuroendocrinology*, 49, 91–105. https://doi.org/10.1016/j.yfrne.2018.02.001

Marsh, N., Marsh, A.A., Lee, M.R. & Hurlemann, R. (2021). Oxytocin and the neurobiology of prosocial behaviour. *The Neuroscientist*, 27(6), 604–619. https://doi.org/10.1177/1073858420960111

Maslow, A.H. (1943). A theory of human motivation. *Psychological Review*, 50, 370–396.

Monti, M.M., Vanhaudenhuyse, A., Coleman, M.R., Boly, M., Pickard, J.D., Tshibanda, L., Owen, A.M. & Laureys, S. (2010). Willful modulation of brain activity in disorders of consciousness. *New England Journal of Medicine*, 362, 579–589. https://doi.org/10.1056/NEJMoa0905370

Morgan, E. (1995). Measuring time with a biological clock. *Biological Sciences Review*, 7, 2–5.

Moruzzi, G. & Magoun, H.W. (1949). Brain stem reticular formation and activation of the EEG. *Electroencephalography and Clinical Neurophysiology*, 1, 455–473. https://doi.org/10.1016/0013-4694(49)90219-9

Mukhametov, L.M., Supin, A.Y. & Polyakova, I.G. (1977). Interhemispheric asymmetry of the electroencephalographic sleep pattern in dolphins. *Brain Research*, 134, 581–584. https://doi.org/10.1016/0006-8993(77)90835-6

Ohayon, M.M., Carskadon, M.A., Guilleminault, C. & Vitiello, M.V. (2004). Meta-analysis of quantitative sleep parameters from childhood to old age in healthy individuals: Developing normative values across the human lifespan. *Sleep*, 27(7), 1255–1273. https://doi.org/10.1093/sleep/27.7.1255

Onaka, T. & Takayanagi, Y. (2019). Role of oxytocin in the control of stress and food intake. *Journal of Neuroendocrinology*, 31, e12700. https://doi.org/10.1111/jne.12700

Pallasdies, F., Goedeke, S., Braun, W. & Memmesheimer, R.M. (2019). From single neurons to behavior in the jellyfish Aurelia aurita. *Elife*, 8, e50084. https://doi.org/10.7554/eLife.50084

Poe, G.R., Walsh, C.M. & Bjorness, T.E. (2010). Cognitive neuroscience of sleep. *Progress in Brain Research*, 185, 1–19. https://doi.org/10.1016/B978-0-444-53702-7.00001-4

Qi, X.G., Wu, J., Zhao, L., Wang, L., …, & Li, B. (2023). Adaptations to a cold climate promoted social evolution in Asian colobine primates. *Science*, 380(6648), eabl8621. https://doi.org/10.1126/science.abl8621

Rattenborg, N.C., Voirin, B., Vyssotski, A.L., Kays, R.W., Spoelstra, K., Kuemmeth, F., Heidrich, W. & Wikelski, M. (2008). Sleeping outside the box: Electroencephalographic measures of sleeping sloths. *Biology Letters*, 4(4), 402–405. https://doi.org/10.1098/rsbl.2008.0203

Sapolsky, R.M. (2004). *Why Zebras Don't Get Ulcers* (3rd edn). Henry Holt and Company.

Sasidharan, A., Sulekha, S. & Kutty, B. (2014). Current understanding on the neurobiology of sleep and wakefulness. *International Journal of Clinical and Experimental Physiology*, 1(1), 3–8.

Segerstrom, S.C. & Miller, G.E. (2004). Psychological stress and the human immune system: A meta-analytic study of 30 years of inquiry. *Psychological Bulletin*, 130(4), 601–630. https://doi.org/10.1037/0033-2909.130.4.601

Shamay-Tsoory, S.G. & Abu-Akel, A. (2016). The social salience hypothesis of oxytocin. *Biological Psychiatry*, 79, 194–202. https://doi.org/10.1016/j.biopsych.2015.07.020

Shields, G.S., Sazma, M.A., McCullough, A.M. & Yonelinas, A.P. (2017). The effects of acute stress on episodic memory: A meta-analysis and integrative review. *Psychological Bulletin*, 143(6), 636–675. https://doi.org/10.1037/bul0000100

Siegel, J.M. (2022). Sleep function: An evolutionary perspective. *Lancet Neurology*, 21, 937–946. https://doi.org/10.1016/S1474-4422(22)00210-1

Siffre, M. (1975). Six months alone in a cave. *National Geographic*, 147, 426–435.

Stewart, J.D. (2004). Sexual function. In D. Robertson, I. Biaggioni, G. Burnstock & P.A. Low (Eds), *Primer on the Autonomic Nervous System* (2nd edn). Academic Press. https://doi. org/10.1016/B978-012589762-4/50029-3

Trojanowski, N.F. & Raizen, D.M. (2016). Call it worm sleep. *Trends in Neurosciences*, 39(2), 54–62. https://doi.org/10.1016/j.tins.2015.12.005

Vollrath, M. (2001). Personality and stress. *Scandinavian Journal of Psychology*, 42, 335–347. https://doi.org/1467-9450.00245

Walker, M.P. (2009). The role of slow-wave sleep in memory processing. *Journal of Clinical and Sleep Medicine*, 5(2), S20–S26. https://doi.org/10.5664/jcsm.5.2S.S20

Wamsley, E.J. (2014). Dreams and offline memory consolidation. *Current Neurology and Neuroscience Reports*, 14(3), Article 433. https://doi.org/10.1007/s11910-013-0433-5

Wiemers, K.S., Sauvage, M.M., Schoofs, D., Hamacher-Dang, T.C. & Wolf, O.T. (2013). What we remember from a stressful episode. *Psychoneuroendocrinology*, 38, 2268–2277. http://dx. doi.org/10.1016/j.psyneuen.2013.04.015

Young, L.J. (2003). The neural basis of pair bonding in a monogamous species: A model for understanding the biological basis of human behavior. In K.W. Wachter & R.A. Bulatao (Eds), National Research Council (US) *Offspring: Human Fertility Behavior in Biodemographic Perspective*, Panel for the Workshop on the Biodemography of Fertility and Family Behavior. National Academies Press.

Young, L.J. (2009). The neuroendocrinology of the social brain. *Frontiers in Neuroendocrinology*, 30, 425–428. https://doi.org/10.1016/j.yfrne.2009.06.002

Zimmerman, J.E., Naidoo, N., Raizen, D.M. & Pack, A.I. (2008). Conservation of sleep! Insights from non-mammalian model systems. *Trends in Neurosciences*, 31(7), 371–376. https://doi. org/10.1016/j.tins.2008.05.001

Chapter 7

Andoh, J., Milde, C., Tsao, J.W. & Flor, H. (2017). Cortical plasticity as a basis of phantom limb pain: Fact or fiction? *Neuroscience*, 387, 85–91. https://doi.org/10.1016/j.neuroscience. 2017.11.015

Baltes, P.B. & Staudinger, U.M. (2000). Wisdom: A metaheuristic (pragmatic) to orchestrate mind and virtue towards excellence. *American Psychologist*, 55, 122–136. https://doi.org/ 10.1037/0003-066X.55.1.122

Ben-Shahar, Y., Leung, H.T., Pak, W.L., Sokolowski, M.B. & Robinson, G.E. (2003). cGMP-dependent changes in phototaxis: A possible role for the foraging gene in honey bee division of labor. *Journal of Experimental Biology*, 206(Pt 14), 2507–2515. https://doi. org/10.1242/jeb.00442

Ben-Shahar, Y., Robichon, A., Sokolowski, M.B. & Robinson, G.E. (2002). Behavior influenced by gene action across different time scales. *Science*, 296, 742–744. https://doi.org/10.1126/ science.1069911

Bradshaw, J.L. & Sheppard, D.M. (2000). The neurodevelopmental frontostriatal disorders: Evolutionary adaptiveness and anomalous lateralization. *Brain & Language*, 73(2), 297–320. https://doi.org/10.1006/brln.2000.2308

Braga, L.W., Amemiya, E., Tauil, A., Suguieda, D., Lacerda, C., Klein, E., Dehaene-Lambertz, G. & Dehaene, S. (2017). Tracking adult literacy acquisition with functional MRI: A single-case study. *Mind, Brain, and Education*, 11, 121–132. https://doi.org/10.1111/mbe.12143

Budday, S., Steinmann, P. & Kuhl, E. (2015). Physical biology of human brain development. *Frontiers in Cellular Neuroscience*, 9, Article 257. https://doi.org/10.3389/fncel.2015.00257

Cabeza, R., Grady, C.L., Nyberg, L., McIntosh, A.R., Tulving, E., Kapur, S., Jennings, J.M., Houle, S. & Craik, F.I.M. (1997). Age-related differences in neural activity during memory encoding and retrieval: A positron emission tomography study. *Journal of Neuroscience*, 17(1), 391–400. https://doi.org/10.1523/JNEUROSCI.17-01-00391.1997

Crone, E.A. & Dahl, R.E. (2012). Understanding adolescence as a period of social-affective engagement and goal flexibility. *Nature Reviews of Neuroscience*, 13(9), 636–650. https://doi.org/10.1038/nrn3313

Dehaene-Lambertz, G. (2017). The human infant brain: A neural architecture able to learn language. *Psychonomic Bulletin & Review*, 24(1), 48–55. https://doi.org/10.3758/s13423-016-1156-9

Finlay, B.L. & Uchiyama, R. (2015). Developmental mechanisms channeling cortical evolution. *Trends in Neuroscience*, 38(2), 69–76. https://doi.org/10.1016/j.tins.2014.11.004

Grady, C.L., Maisog, J.M., Horwitz, B., Ungerleider, L.G., Mentis, M.J., Salerno, J.A., Pietrini, P., Wagner, E. & Haxby, J.V. (1994). Age-related changes in cortical blood flow activation during visual processing of faces and location. *Journal of Neuroscience*, 14, 1450–1462. https://doi.org/10.1523/JNEUROSCI.14-03-01450.1994

Guo, W. & Polley, D.B. (2019). Nucleus basalis links sensory stimuli with delayed reinforcement to support learning. *Neuron*, 103(6), 1164–1177. https://doi.org/10.1016/j.neuron.2019.06.024

Inzlicht, M. & Marcora, S.M. (2016). The central governor model of exercise regulation teaches us precious little about the nature of mental fatigue and self-control failure. *Frontiers in Psychology*, 7, Article 656. https://doi.org/10.3389/fpsyg.2016.00656

Knowland, V.C.P. & Thomas, M.S.C. (2014). Educating the adult brain: How the neuroscience of learning can inform educational policy. *International Review of Education*, 60, 99–122. https://doi.org/10.1007/s11159-014-9412-6

Kramer, A-W., Huizenga, H.M., Krabbendam, L. & van Duijvenvoorde, A.C.K. (2020). Is it worth it? How your brain decides to make an effort. *Frontiers for Young Minds*, 8, Article 73. https://doi.org/10.3389/frym.2020.00073

Li, K.Z.H., Lindenberger, U., Freund, A.M. & Baltes, P.B. (2001). Walking while memorizing: Age-related differences in compensatory behavior. *Psychological Science*, 12(3), 230–237. https://doi.org/10.1111/1467-9280.00341

Mareschal, D., Johnson, M., Sirios, S., Spratling, M., Thomas, M.S.C. & Westermann, G. (2007). *Neuroconstructivism: How the Brain Constructs Cognition*. Oxford University Press.

Mercer, A.R. (2001). The predictable plasticity of honey bees. In C.A. Shaw & J. McEachern (Eds), *Towards a Theory of Neuroplasticity*. Psychology Press. https://doi.org/10.4324/9780203759790

Nagase, A.M., Onoda, K., Foo, J.C., Haji, T., Akaishi, R., Yamaguchi, S., Sakai, K. & Morita, K. (2018). Neural mechanisms for adaptive learned avoidance of mental effort. *Journal of Neuroscience*, 38(10), 2631–2651. https://doi.org/10.1523/JNEUROSCI.1995-17.2018

Nouvian, M. & Galizia, C.G. (2020). Complexity and plasticity in honey bee phototactic behaviour. *Science Reports*, 10, Article 7872. https://doi.org/10.1038/s41598-020-64782-y

Passingham, R. (2016). *Cognitive Neuroscience: A Very Short Introduction*. Oxford University Press.

Quirk, G.J., Paré, D., Richardson, R., Herry, C., Monfils, M.H., Schiller, D. & Vicentic, A. (2010). Erasing fear memories with extinction training. *Journal of Neuroscience*, 30(45), 14993–14997. https://doi.org/10.1523/JNEUROSCI.4268-10.2010

Resnick, S.M., Pham, D.L., Kraut, M.A., Zonderman, A.B. & Davatzikos, C. (2003). Longitudinal magnetic resonance imaging studies of older adults: A shrinking brain. *Journal of Neuroscience*, 23(8), 3295–3301. https://doi.org/10.1523/JNEUROSCI.23-08-03295.2003

Rogers, C. & Thomas, M.S.C. (2022). *Educational Neuroscience: The Basics*. Routledge.

Saragosa-Harris, N.M., Cohen, A.O., Reneau, T.R., Villano, W.J., Heller, A.S. & Hartley, C.A. (2022). Real-world exploration increases across adolescence and relates to affect, risk taking, and social connectivity. *Psychological Science*, 33(10), 1664–1679. https://doi.org/10.1177/09567976221102070

Seger, C.A. & Spiering, B.J. (2011). A critical review of habit learning and the basal ganglia. *Frontiers in Systems Neuroscience*, 5, Article 66. https://doi.org/10.3389/fnsys.2011.00066

Sekar, A., et al. (2016). Schizophrenia risk from complex variation of complement component 4. *Nature*, 530(7589), 177–183. https://doi.org/10.1038/nature16549. Erratum in: *Nature*, 2022, 601(7892), E4–E5.

Shapira, M., Thompson, C.K., Soreq, H. & Robinson, G.E. (2001). Changes in neuronal acetylcholinesterase gene expression and division of labor in honey bee colonies. *Journal of Molecular Neuroscience*, 17, 1–12. https://doi.org/10.1385/JMN:17:1:1

Simons, D.J. & Chabris, C.F. (1999). Gorillas in our midst: Sustained inattentional blindness for dynamic events. *Perception*, 28(9), 1059–1074. https://doi.org/10.1068/p2952

Sirois, S., Spratling, M., Thomas, M.S., Westermann, G., Mareschal, D. & Johnson, M.H. (2008). Précis of neuroconstructivism: How the brain constructs cognition. *Behavioral Brain Sciences*, 31(3), 321–331; discussion 331–356. https://doi.org/10.1017/S0140525X0800407X

Stiles, J. & Jernigan, T.L. (2010). The basics of brain development. *Neuropsychology Review*, 20(4), 327–348. https://doi.org/10.1007/s11065-010-9148-4

Thomas, M.S.C. (2012). Brain plasticity and education. *British Journal of Educational Psychology – Monograph Series II: Educational Neuroscience*, 8, 142–156. https://doi.org/10.1348/97818543371712X13219598392480

Thomas, M.S.C., Davis, R., Karmiloff-Smith, A., Knowland, V.C. & Charman, T. (2016). The overpruning hypothesis of autism. *Develomental Science*, 19(2), 284–305. https://doi.org/10.1111/desc.12303

Tian, L. & Ma, L. (2017). Microstructural changes of the human brain from early to midadulthood. *Frontiers in Human Neuroscience*, 11, Article 393. https://doi.org/10.3389/fnhum.2017.00393

Toga, A.W., Thompson, P.M. & Sowell, E.R. (2006). Mapping brain maturation. *Trends in Neuroscience*, 29(3), 148–159. https://doi.org/10.1016/j.tins.2006.01.007

van Kesteren, M.T., Rijpkema, M., Ruiter, D.J., Morris, R.G. & Fernández, G. (2014). Building on prior knowledge: Schema-dependent encoding processes relate to academic performance. *Journal of Cognitive Neuroscience*, 26(10), 2250–2261. https://doi.org/10.1162/jocn_a_00630

Weinberger, N.M. (2003). The nucleus basalis and memory codes: Auditory cortical plasticity and the induction of specific, associative behavioral memory. *Neurobiology of Learning and Memory*, 80(3), 268–284. https://doi.org/10.1016/s1074-7427(03)00072-8

Whitfield, C.W., Cziko, A.M. & Robinson, G.E. (2003). Gene expression profiles in the brain predict behavior in individual honey bees. *Science*, 302, 296–299. http://dx.doi.org/10.1126/science.1086807

Wiehler, A., Branzoli, F., Adanyeguh, I., Mochel, F. & Pessiglione, M.A. (2022). Neuro-metabolic account of why daylong cognitive work alters the control of economic decisions. *Current Biology*, 32(16), 3564–3575. https://doi.org/10.1016/j.cub.2022.07.010

Willingham, D.T. (2021). *Why Don't Students Like School? A Cognitive Scientist Answers Questions About How the Mind Works and What It Means for Your Classroom* (2nd edn). Jossey Bass.

Zhang, J. (2003). Evolution of the human ASPM gene, a major determinant of brain size. *Genetics*, 165(4), 2063–2070. https://doi.org/10.1093/genetics/165.4.2063

Chapter 8

Aboitiz, F., Carrasco, X., Schröter, C., Zaidel, D., Zaidel, E. & Lavados, M. (2003). The alien hand syndrome: Classification of forms reported and discussion of a new condition. *Neurological Sciences*, 24(4), 252–257. https://doi.org/10.1007/s10072-003-0149-4

Alm, P.A. (2004). Stuttering and the basal ganglia circuits: A critical review of possible relations. *Journal of Communication Disorders*, 37(4), 325–369. https://doi.org/10.1016/j.jcomdis.2004.03.001

American Psychiatric Association. (2013). *Diagnostic and Statistical Manual of Mental Disorders* (5th edn). APA. https://doi.org/10.1176/appi.books.9780890425596

Barkovich, A.J. (2012). Developmental disorders of the midbrain and hindbrain. *Frontiers in Neuroanatomy*, 6, Article 7. https://doi.org/10.3389/fnana.2012.00007

Bates, E. & Roe, K. (2001). Language development in children with unilateral brain injury. In C.A. Nelson & M. Luciana (Eds), *Handbook of Developmental Cognitive Neuroscience*. MIT Press.

Biotteau, M., Chaix, Y., Blais, M., Tallet, J., Péran, P. & Albaret, J.M. (2016). Neural signature of DCD: A critical review of MRI neuroimaging studies. *Frontiers in Neurology*, 7, Article 227. https://doi.org/10.3389/fneur.2016.00227

Blackford, J.U. & Pine, D.S. (2012). Neural substrates of childhood anxiety disorders: A review of neuroimaging findings. *Child and Adolescent Psychiatric Clinics of North America*, 21(3), 501–525. https://doi.org/10.1016/j.chc.2012.05.002

Brune, M. (2016). *Textbook of Evolutionary Psychiatry and Psychosomatic Medicine* (2nd edn). Oxford University Press.

Caligiore, D., Mannella, F., Arbib, M.A. & Baldassarre, G. (2017). Dysfunctions of the basal ganglia-cerebellar-thalamo-cortical system produce motor tics in Tourette syndrome. *PLoS Computational Biology*, 13(3), e1005395. https://doi.org/10.1371/journal.pcbi.1005395

Chang, S.E. & Guenther, F.H. (2020). Involvement of the cortico-basal ganglia-thalamocortical loop in developmental stuttering. *Frontiers in Psychology*, 28(10), Article 3088. https://doi.org/10.3389/fpsyg.2019.03088

Charvet, C.J., Darlington, R.B. & Finlay, B.L. (2013). Variation in human brains may facilitate evolutionary change toward a limited range of phenotypes. *Brain, Behavior and Evolution*, 81(2), 74–85. https://doi.org/10.1159/000345940

Chen, J. & Yuan, J. (2016). The neural causes of congenital amusia. *Journal of Neuroscience*, 36(30), 7803–7804. https://doi.org/10.1523/jneurosci.1500-16.2016

Chen, J., Tian, C., Zhang, Q., Xiang, H., Wang, R., Hu, X. & Zeng, X. (2022). Changes in volume of subregions within basal ganglia in obsessive-compulsive disorder: A study with atlas-based and VBM methods. *Frontiers in Neuroscience*, 16, Article 890616. https://doi.org/10.3389/fnins.2022.890616

Chugani, H.T., Behen, M.E., Muzik, O., Juhász, C., Nagy, F. & Chugani, D.C. (2001). Local brain functional activity following early deprivation: A study of postinstitutionalized Romanian orphans. *Neuroimage,* 14(6), 1290–1301. https://doi.org/10.1006/nimg.2001.0917

Code, C., Wallesch, C-W., Joanette, Y. & Roch, A. (1996). *Classic Cases in Neuropsychology*. Psychology Press.

Corkin, S. (2014). *Permanent Present Tense: The Man with No Memory, and What He Taught the World*. Penguin Books.

Cowan, P.J. & Browning, M. (2015). What has serotonin to do with depression? *World Psychiatry*, 14(2), 158–160. https://doi.org/10.1002/wps.20229

Crow, T.J. (2008). The 'big bang' theory of the origin of psychosis and the faculty of language. *Schizophrenia Research*, 102, 31–52. https://doi.org/10.1016/j.schres.2008.03.010

Cuijpers, P., Berking, M. & Andersson, G. (2013). A meta-analysis of cognitive-behavioral therapy for adult depression, alone and in comparison with other treatments. *Canadian Journal of Psychiatry*, 58(7), 376–385.

Damasio, H., Grabowski, T., Frank, R., Galaburda, A.M. & Damasio, A.R. (1994). The return of Phineas Gage: Clues about the brain from the skull of a famous patient. *Science*, 264(5162), 1102–1105. https://doi.org/10,1126/science.8178168

Davies, M., Coltheart, M., Langdon, R. & Breen, N. (2001). Monothematic delusions: Towards a two-factor account. *Philosophy, Psychiatry, and Psychology*, 8(2), 133–158. https://doi.org/10.1353/ppp.2001.0007

Deary, I.J., Cox, S.R. & Hill, W.D. (2022). Genetic variation, brain, and intelligence differences. *Molecular Psychiatry*, 27, 335–353. https://doi.org/10.1038/s41380-021-01027-y

DeFries, J.C., Gervais, M.C. & Thomas, E.A. (1978). Response to 30 generations of selection for open-field activity in laboratory mice. *Behavior Genetics*, 8(1), 3–13. https://doi.org/10.1007/BF01067700

Del Giudice, M. (2017). Mating, sexual selection, and the evolution of schizophrenia. *World Psychiatry*, 16(2), 141–142. https://doi.org/10.1002/wps.20409

Delisi, L.E., Szulc, K.U., Bertisch, H.C., Majcher, M., Brown, K., Bappal, A., Branch, C.A. & Ardekani, B.A. (2006). Early detection of schizophrenia by diffusion weighted imaging.

Psychiatry Research: Neuroimaging, 148(1), 61–66. https://doi.org/10.1016/j.pscychresns.2006.04.010

DeYoung, C.G., Hirsh, J.B., Shane, M.S., Papademetris, X., Rajeevan, N. & Gray, J.R. (2010). Testing predictions from personality neuroscience: Brain structure and the big five. *Psychological Sciences*, 21(6), 820–828. https://doi.org/10.1177/0956797610370159

Donkelaar, H.J.T., Lammens, M., Cruysberg, J.R.M. & Cremers, C.W.J.R. (2006). Development and developmental disorders of the brain stem. In H.J. Donkelaar, M. Lammens & A. Hori (Eds), *Clinical Neuroembryology: Development and Developmental Disorders of the Human Central Nervous System*. Springer.

Donovan, A.P. & Basson, M.A. (2017). The neuroanatomy of autism – a developmental perspective. *Journal of Anatomy*, 230(1), 4–15. https://doi.org/10.1111/joa.12542

Eliot, L., Ahmed, A., Khan, H. & Patel, J. (2021). Dump the 'dimorphism': Comprehensive synthesis of human brain studies reveals few male-female differences beyond size. *Neuroscience & Biobehavioral Reviews*, 125, 667–697. https://doi.org/10.1016/j.neubiorev.2021.02.026

Farah, M.J. (2017). The neuroscience of socioeconomic status: Correlates, causes, and consequences. *Neuron*, 96(1), 56–71. https://doi.org/10.1016/j.neuron.2017.08.034

Flynn, J.R. (2007). *What is Intelligence?* Cambridge University Press.

Fournier, J.C., DeRubeis, R.J., Hollon, S.D., Dimidjian, S., Amsterdam, J.D., Shelton, R.C. & Fawcett, J. (2010). Antidepressant drug effects and depression severity: A patient-level meta-analysis. *JAMA*, 303(1), 47–53. https://doi.org/10.1001/jama.2009.1943

Gao, Y., et al. (2020). Gray matter changes in the orbitofrontal-paralimbic cortex in male youths with non-comorbid conduct disorder. *Frontiers in Psychology*, 11, Article 843. https://doi.org/10.3389/fpsyg.2020.00843

Gehricke, J.G., Kruggel, F., Thampipop, T., Alejo, S.D., Tatos, E., Fallon, J. & Muftuler, L.T. (2017). The brain anatomy of attention-deficit/hyperactivity disorder in young adults – a magnetic resonance imaging study. *PLoS One*, 12(4), e0175433. https://doi.org/10.1371/journal.pone.0175433

Goikolea-Vives, A. (2022). *Development and plasticity of structural and functional neural networks in the mouse brain*. Unpublished doctoral thesis, Royal Veterinary College, University of London.

Grasby, K.L., et al. (2020). The genetic architecture of the human cerebral cortex. *Science*, 367(6484), eaay6690. https://doi.org/10.1126/science.aay6690

Gregory, M.D., Eisenberg, D.P., Hamborg, M., Kippenhan, J.S., Kohn, P., Kolachana, B., Dickinson, D. & Berman, K.F. (2021). Neanderthal-derived genetic variation in living humans relates to schizophrenia diagnosis, to psychotic symptom severity, and to dopamine synthesis. *American Journal of Medical Genetics B*, 186(5), 329–338. https://doi.org/10.1002/ajmg.b.32872

Grotzinger, A.D., Cheung, A.K., Patterson, M.W., Harden, K.P. & Tucker-Drob, E.M. (2019). Genetic and environmental links between general factors of psychopathology and cognitive ability in early childhood. *Clinical Psychological Sciences*, 7(3), 430–444. https://doi.org/10.1177/2167702618820018

Hill, W.D., Marioni, R.E., Maghzian, O., Ritchie, S.J., Hagenaars, S.P., McIntosh, A.M., Gale, C.R., Davies, G. & Deary, I.J. (2019). A combined analysis of genetically correlated traits identifies 187 loci and a role for neurogenesis and myelination in intelligence. *Molecular Psychiatry*, 24(2), 169–181. https://doi.org/10.1038/s41380-017-0001-5

Hirnstein, W. (2010). The misidentification syndromes as mindreading disorders. *Cognitive Neuropsychiatry*, 15(1), 233–260. https://doi.org/10.1080/13546800903414891

Ho, K.K.Y., Lui, S.S.Y., Hung, K.S.Y., Wang, Y., Li, Z., Cheung, E.F.C. & Chan, R.C.K. (2015). Theory of mind impairments in patients with first-episode schizophrenia and their unaffected siblings. *Schizophrenia Research*, 166, 1–8. https://doi.org/10.1016/j.schres.2015.05.033

Hoeft, F., Carter, J.C., Lightbody, A.A., Cody, H.H., Piven, J. & Reiss, A.L. (2010). Region-specific alterations in brain development in one- to three-year-old boys with fragile X syndrome. *Proceedings of the National Academy of Sciences USA*, 107(20), 9335–9339. https://doi.org/10.1073/pnas.1002762107

Hopkins, W.D., Russell, J.L. & Schaeffer, J. (2014). Chimpanzee intelligence is heritable. *Current Biology*, 24(14), 1649–1652. https://doi.org/10.1016/j.cub.2014.05.076

Howes, O.D. & Murray, R.M. (2014). Schizophrenia: An integrated sociodevelopmental-cognitive model. *Lancet*, 383, 1677–1687. https://dx.doi.org/10.1016/S0140-6736(13)62036-x

Hu, M-L., Zong, X-F., Mann, J.J., Zheng, J-J., Liao, Y-H., Li, Z-C., He, Y., Chen, X-G. & Tang, J-S. (2017). A review of the functional and anatomical default mode network in schizophrenia. *Neuroscience Bulletin*, 33(1), 73–84. https://10.1007/s12264-016-0090-1

Insel, T.R. & Shapiro, L.E. (1992). Oxytocin receptor distribution reflects social organization in monogamous and polygamous voles. *Proceedings of the National Academy of Sciences USA*, 89(13), 5981–5985. https://doi.org/10.1073/pnas.89.13.5981

Jansen, A.G., Mous, S.E., White, T., Posthuma, D. & Polderman, T.J.C. (2015). What twin studies tell us about the heritability of brain development, morphology, and function: A review. *Neuropsychological Review*, 25, 27–46. https://doi.org/10.1007/s11065-015-9278-9

Jutla, A., et al. (2020). Neurodevelopmental predictors of conversion to schizophrenia and other psychotic disorders in adolescence and young adulthood in clinical high-risk individuals. *Schizophrenia Research*, 224, 170–172. https://doi.org/10.1016/j.schres.2020.10.008

Kafkas, A. & Montaldi, D. (2018). How do memory systems detect and respond to novelty? *Neuroscience Letters*, 680, 60–68. https://doi.org/10.1016/j.neulet.2018.01.053

Karmiloff-Smith, A. (1998). Development itself is the key to understanding developmental disorders. *Trends in Cognitive Sciences*, 2(10), 389–398. https://doi.org/10.1016/s1364-6613(98)01230-3

Kayser, A.S., Sun, F.T. & D'Esposito, M. (2009). A comparison of Granger causality and coherency in fMRI-based analysis of the motor system. *Human Brain Mapping*, 30(11), 3475–3494. https://doi.org/10.1002/hbm.20771

Keil, K.P., Sethi, S., Wilson, M.D., Chen, H. & Lein, P.J. (2017). In vivo and in vitro sex differences in the dendritic morphology of developing murine hippocampal and cortical neurons. *Science Reports*, 7, Article 8486. https://doi.org/10.1038/s41598-017-08459-z

Kenwood, M.M., Kalin, N.H. & Barbas, H. (2022). The prefrontal cortex, pathological anxiety, and anxiety disorders. *Neuropsychopharmacology*, 47, 260–275. https://doi.org/10.1038/s41386-021-01109-z

Kherif, F., Josse, G., Seghier, M.L. & Price, C.J. (2009). The main sources of intersubject variability in neuronal activation for reading aloud. *Journal of Cognitive Neuroscience*, 21(4), 654–668. https://doi.org/10.1162/jocn.2009.21084

Kirkbride, J.B., et al. (2017). Ethnic minority status, age-at-immigration and psychosis risk in rural environments: Evidence from the SEPEA study. *Schizophrenia Bulletin*, 43(6), 1251–1261. https://doi.org/10.1093/schbul/sbx010

Kirsch, I. (2008). Challenging received wisdom: Antidepressants and the placebo effect. *McGill Journal of Medicine*, 11(2), 219–222.

Korzeniewski, S.J., Birbeck, G., DeLano, M.C., Potchen, M.J. & Paneth, N. (2008). A systematic review of neuroimaging for cerebral palsy. *Journal of Child Neurology*, 23(2), 216–227. https://doi.org/10.1177/0883073807307983

Kuhn, T., Blades, R., Gottlieb, L., Knudsen, K., Ashdown, C., Martin-Harris, L., Ghahremani, D., Dang, B.H., Bilder, R.M. & Bookheimer, S.Y. (2021). Neuroanatomical differences in the memory systems of intellectual giftedness and typical development. *Brain and Behavior*, 11(11), e2348. https://doi.org/10.1002/brb3.2348

Latzman, R., Boysen, S. & Schapiro, S. (2018). Neuroanatomical correlates of hierarchical personality traits in chimpanzees: Associations with limbic structures. *Personality Neuroscience*, 1, E4. https://doi.org/10.1017/pen.2018.1

Lee, J.C., Dick, A.S. & Tomblin, J.B. (2020). Altered brain structures in the dorsal and ventral language pathways in individuals with and without developmental language disorder (DLD). *Brain Imaging and Behavior*, 14(6), 2569–2586. https://doi.org/10.1007/s11682-019-00209-1

Lynch, E.D., Lee, M.K., Morrow, J.E., Welcsh, P.L. & King, M-C. (1997). Nonsyndromic deafness DFNA1 associated with mutation of a human homolog of the Drosophila gene diaphanous. *Science*, 278, 1315–1318. https://doi.org/10.1126/science.278.5341.1315

Lyon, A. (2014). Why are normal distributions normal? *The British Journal for the Philosophy of Science*, 65(3), 621–649. https://doi.org/10.1093/bjps/axs046

Macmillan, M. (2002). *An Odd Kind of Fame: Stories of Phineas Gage*. MIT Press.

Matthews, T.J., Williams, D.A. & Schweiger, L. (2013). Social motivation and residential style in prairie and meadow voles. *The Open Behavioral Science Journal*, 7, 16–23. https://doi.org/10.2174/1874230020130925001

McCaskey, U., von Aster, M., O'Gorman, R. & Kucian, K. (2020). Persistent differences in brain structure in developmental dyscalculia: A longitudinal morphometry study. *Frontiers in Human Neuroscience*, 14, Article 272. https://doi.org/10.3389/fnhum.2020.00272

McCutcheon, R.A., Keefe, R.S.E. & McGuire, P.K. (2023). Cognitive impairment in schizophrenia: Aetiology, pathophysiology, and treatment. *Molecular Psychiatry*. https://doi.org/10.1038/s41380-023-01949-9

McCutcheon, R.A., Krystal, J.H. & Howes, O.D. (2020). Dopamine and glutamate in schizophrenia: Biology, symptoms, and treatment. *World Psychiatry*, 16(3), 227–235. https://doi.org/10.1002/wps.20440

Millichap, J.G. (1998). Cerebellar MR spectroscopy in Williams syndrome. *Pediatric Neurology Briefs*, 12(8), 63–64. http://doi.org/10.15844/pedneurbriefs-12-8-11

Moncrieff, J., Cooper, R.E., Stockmann, T., Amendola, S., Hengartner, M.P. & Horowitz, M.A. (2022). The serotonin theory of depression: A systematic umbrella review of the evidence. *Molecular Psychiatry*. https://doi.org/10.1038/s41380-022-01661-0

Moseley, P., Fernyhough, C. & Ellison, A. (2013). Auditory verbal hallucinations as atypical inner speech monitoring, and the potential of neurostimulation as a treatment option. *Neuroscience and Biobehavioral Reviews*, 37(10), 2794–2805. https://doi.org/10.1016/j.neubiorev.2013.10.001

Nettle, D. (2004). Evolutionary origins of depression: A review and reformulation. *Journal of Affective Disorders*, 81, 91–102. https://doi.org/10.1016/j.jad.2003.08.009

Noble, K.G., et al. (2015). Family income, parental education and brain structure in children and adolescents. *Nature Neuroscience*, 18(5), 773–778. https://doi.org/10.1038/nn.3983

Nummenmaa, L., et al. (2021). Brain basis of psychopathy in criminal offenders and general population. *Cerebral Cortex*, 31(9), 4104–4114. https://doi.org/10.1093/cercor/bhab072

Passamonti, L., Fairchild, G., Fornito, A., Goodyer, I.M., Nimmo-Smith, I., Hagan, C.C. & Calder, A.J. (2012). Abnormal anatomical connectivity between the amygdala and orbitofrontal cortex in conduct disorder. *PLoS One*, 7(11), e48789. https://doi.org/10.1371/journal.pone.0048789

Paul, S., Nahar, A., Bhagawati, M. & Kunwar, A.J. (2022). A review on recent advances of cerebral palsy. *Oxidative Medicine and Cell Longevity*, e2622310. https://doi.org/10.1155/2022/2622310

Pinter, J.D., Eliez, S., Schmitt, J.E., Capone, G.T. & Reiss, A.L. (2001). Neuroanatomy of Down's syndrome: A high-resolution MRI study. *American Journal of Psychiatry*, 158(10), 1659–1665. https://doi.org/10.1176/appi.ajp.158.10.1659

Plomin, R., DeFries, J.C., Knopik, V.S. & Neiderhiser, J.M. (2016). Top 10 replicated findings from behavioral genetics. *Perspectives in Psychological Sciences*, 11(1), 3–23. https://doi.org/10.1177/1745691615617439

Polderman, T.J., Benyamin, B., de Leeuw, C.A., Sullivan, P.F., van Bochoven, A., Visscher, P.M. & Posthuma, D. (2015). Meta-analysis of the heritability of human traits based on fifty years of twin studies. *Nature Genetics*, 47(7), 702–709. https://doi.org/10.1038/ng.3285

Polimeni, J., Reiss, J.P. & Sareen, J. (2005). Could obsessive-compulsive disorder have originated as a group-selected adaptive trait in traditional societies? *Medical Hypotheses*, 65, 655–664. https://doi.org/10.1016/j.mehy.2005.05.023

Raschle, N.M., et al. (2017). Callous-unemotional traits and brain structure: Sex-specific effects in anterior insula of typically-developing youths. *Neuroimage Clinical*, 17, 856–864. https://doi.org/10.1016/j.nicl.2017.12.015

Rees, E., O'Donovan, M.C. & Owen, M.J. (2015). Genetics of schizophrenia. *Current Opinion in Behavioral Sciences*, 2, 8–14. https://doi.org/10.1016/j.cobeha.2014.07.001

Reiss, A.L., Eliez, S., Schmitt, J.E., Straus, E., Lai, Z., Jones, W. & Bellugi, U. (2000). Neuroanatomy of Williams syndrome: A high-resolution MRI study. *Journal of Cognitive Neuroscience*, 12 (Suppl. 1), 65–73. https://doi.org/10.1162/089892900561986

Richardson, F.M., Seghier, M.L., Leff, A.P., Thomas, M.S.C. & Price, C.J. (2011). Multiple routes from occipital to temporal cortices during reading. *Journal of Neuroscience*, 31(22), 8239–8247. https://doi.org/10.1523/JNEUROSCI.6519-10.2011

Richlan, F. (2012). Developmental dyslexia: Dysfunction of a left hemisphere reading network. *Frontiers in Human Neuroscience*, 6, Article 120. https://doi.org/10.3389/fnhum.2012.00120

Roelfs, D., Alnaes, D., Frei, O., van der Meer, D., Smeland, O.B., Andreassen, O.A., Westlye, L.T. & Kaufmann, T. (2021). Phenotypically independent profiles relevant to mental health are genetically correlated. *Translational Psychiatry*, 11, Article 202. https://doi.org/10.1038/s41398-021-01313-x

Seghier, M.L., Bagdasaryan, J., Jung, D.E. & Price, C.J. (2014). The importance of premotor cortex for supporting speech production after left capsular-putaminal damage. *Journal of Neuroscience*, 34(43), 14338–14348. https://doi.org/10.1523/JNEUROSCI.1954-14.2014

Seghier, M.L., Lee, H.L., Schofield, T., Ellis, C.L. & Price, C.J. (2008). Inter-subject variability in the use of two different neuronal networks for reading aloud familiar words. *Neuroimage*, 42(3), 1226–1236. https://doi.org/10.1016/j.neuroimage.2008.05.029

Shadrina, M., Bondarenko, E.A. & Slominsky, P.A. (2018). Genetic factors in major depression disease. *Frontiers in Psychiatry*, 9, Article 334. https://doi.org/10.3389/fpsyt.2018.00334

Shin, L.M. & Liberzon, I. (2010). The neurocircuitry of fear, stress, and anxiety disorders. *Neuropsychopharmacology*, 35, 169–191. https://doi.org/10.1038/npp.2009.83

Siever, L.J. (2008). Neurobiology of aggression and violence. *American Journal of Psychiatry*, 165(4), 429–442. https://doi.org/10.1176/appi.ajp.2008.07111774

Squire, L.R. (2009). The legacy of patient H.M. for neuroscience. *Neuron*, 61, 6–9. https://doi.org/10.1016/j.neuron.2008.12.023

Srinivasan, S., et al. (2016). Genetic markers of human evolution are enriched in schizophrenia. *Biological Psychiatry*, 80(4), 284–292. https://doi.org/10.1016%2Fj.biopsych.2015.10.009

Stankov, L. (2018). Low correlations between intelligence and Big Five personality traits: Need to broaden the domain of personality. *Journal of Intelligence*, 6(2), Article 26. https://doi.org/10.3390/jintelligence6020026. www.ncbi.nlm.nih.gov/pmc/articles/PMC6480733/pdf/jintelligence-06-00026.pdf

Stepnicki, P., Kondej, M. & Kaczor, A.A. (2018). Current concepts and treatments of schizophrenia. *Molecules*, 23, 2087–2116. https://doi.org/10.3390/molecules23082087

Stilo, S.A. & Murray, R.M. (2019). Non-genetic factors in schizophrenia. *Current Psychiatry Reports*, 21, Article 100. https://10.1007/s11920-019-1091-3

Surbey, M.K. (2011). Adaptive significance of low levels of self-deception and cooperation in depression. *Evolution and Human Behavior*, 32, 29–40. https://doi.org/10.1016/j.evolhumbehav.2010.08.009

Szasz, T. (2011). The myth of mental illness: 50 years later. *The Psychiatrist*, 35, 179–182. https://doi.org/10.1192/pb.bp.110.031310

Taylor, M.J., Freeman, D., Lundstrom, S., Larsson, H. & Ronald, A. (2022). Heritability of psychotic experiences in adolescents and interaction with environmental risk. *JAMA Psychiatry*. https://doi.org/10.1001/jamapsychiatry.2022.1947

Thind, K.K. & Goldsmith, P.C. (1997). Expression of estrogen and progesterone receptors in glutamate and GABA neurons of the pubertal female monkey hypothalamus. *Neuroendocrinology*, 65(5), 314–324. https://doi.org/10.1159/000127190

Thomas, M.S.C. (2003). Essay review: Limits on plasticity. *Journal of Cognition and Development*, 4(1), 99–125. https://doi.org/10.1080/15248372.2003.9669684

Thomas, M.S.C. (2018). A neurocomputational model of developmental trajectories of gifted children under a polygenic model: When are gifted children held back by poor environments? *Intelligence*, 69, 200–212. https://doi.org/10.1016/j.intell.2018.06.008

Thomas, M.S.C. & Coecke, S. (2023). Associations between socioeconomic status, cognition and brain structure: Evaluating potential causal pathways through mechanistic models of development. *Cognitive Science*. https://doi.org/10.1111/cogs.13217

Uono, Y. & Goyle, J.T. (2019). Glutamate hypothesis in schizophrenia. *Psychiatry and Clinical Neurosciences*, 73(5), 204–215. https://doi.org/10.1016/pcn.12823

van Eijk, L., Zhu, D., Couvy-Duchesne, B., Strike, L.T., Lee, A.J., Hansell, N.K., Thompson, P.M., de Zubicaray, G.I., McMahon, K.L., Wright, M.J. & Zietsch, B.P. (2021). Are sex differences in human brain structure associated with sex differences in behavior? *Psychological Sciences*, 32(8), 1183–1197. https://doi.org/10.1177/0956797621996664

Van Horn, J.D., Irimia, A., Torgerson, C.M., Chambers, M.C., Kikinis, R. & Toga, A.W. (2012). Mapping connectivity damage in the case of Phineas Gage. *PloSONE*, 7(5), e37454. https://doi.org/10.1371/journal.pone.0037454

Vukasović, T. & Bratko, D. (2015). Heritability of personality: A meta-analysis of behavior genetic studies. *Psychological Bulletin*, 141(4), 769–785. https://doi.org/10.1037/bul0000017

Waters, F., et al. (2012). Auditory hallucinations in schizophrenia and non-schizophrenia populations: A review and integrated model of cognitive mechanisms. *Schizophrenia Bulletin*, 38(4), 683–692. https://10.1093/schbul.sbs045

Wood, L., Williams, C., Billings, J. & Johnson, S. (2020). A systematic review and meta-analysis of cognitive behavioural informed psychological interventions for psychiatric patients with psychosis. *Schizophrenia Research*, 222, 133–144. https://doi.org/10.1016/j.schres.2020.03.041

Wright, C.I., Williams, D., Feczko, E., Barrett, L.F., Dickerson, B.C., Schwartz, C.E. & Wedig, M.M. (2006). Neuroanatomical correlates of extraversion and neuroticism. *Cerebral Cortex*, 16(12), 1809–1819. https://doi.org/10.1093/cercor/bhj118

Zhang, F.-F., Peng, W., Sweeney, J.A., Jia, Z.-Y. & Gong, Q.-Y. (2018). Brain structure alterations in depression: Psychoradiological evidence. *CNS Neuroscience & Therapeutics*, 24, 994–1003. https://doi.org/10.1111/cns.12835

Chapter 9

Atkinson, A.P., Thomas, M.S.C. & Cleeremans, A. (2000). Consciousness: Mapping the theoretical landscape. *Trends in Cognitive Sciences*, 4(10), 372–382. https://doi.org/10.1016/S1364-6613(00)01533-3

Balezeau, F., Wilson, B., Gallardo, G., Dick, F., Hopkins, W., Anwander, A., Friederici, A.D., Griffiths, T.D. & Petkov, C.I. (2020). Primate auditory prototype in the evolution of the arcuate fasciculus. *Nature Neuroscience*, 23(5), 611–614. https://doi.org/10.1038/s41593-020-0623-9

Becker, Y., Loh, K.K., Coulon, O. & Meguerditchian, A. (2022). The arcuate fasciculus and language origins: Disentangling existing conceptions that influence evolutionary accounts. *Neuroscience and Biobehavioral Reviews*, 134, Article 104490. https://doi.org/10.1016/j.neubiorev.2021.12.013

British Psychological Society. (2021). *Ethical Guidelines*. www.bps.org.uk/guideline/code-ethics-and-conduct

Brown, R., Lau, H. & LeDoux, J.E. (2019). Understanding the higher-order approach to consciousness. *Trends in Cognitive Sciences*, 23, 754–768. https://doi.org/10.1016/jtics.2019.06.009

Cadete, D. & Longo, M. (2022). The long sixth finger illusion: The representation of the supernumerary finger is not a copy and can be felt with varying lengths. *Cognition*, 218, Article 104948. https://doi.org/10.1016/j.cognition.2021.104948

Chalmers, D. (1995). Facing up to the hard problem of consciousness. *Journal of Consciousness Studies*, 2, 200–219.

Charvet, C.J., Darlington, R.B. & Finlay, B.L. (2013). Variation in human brains may facilitate evolutionary change toward a limited range of phenotypes. *Brain, Behavior and Evolution*, 81(2), 74–85. https://doi.org/10.1159/000345940

Clark, A. (2010). *Supersizing the Mind*. Oxford University Press.

Damasio, A.R. (2008). *Descartes' Error: Emotion, Reason and the Human Brain*. Random House.

Dehaene, S., Pegado, F., Braga, L.W., Ventura, P., Nunes Filho, G., Jobert, A., Dehaene-Lambertz, G., Kolinsky, R., Morais, J. & Cohen, L. (2010). How learning to read changes the cortical networks for vision and language. *Science*, 330(6009), 1359–1364. https://doi.org/10.1126/science.1194140

Dennett, D.C. (2018). Facing up to the hard question of consciousness. *Philosophical Transactions of the Royal Society B*, 373. https://doi.org/10.1098/rstb.2017.0342

DeSilva, J.M., Traniello, J.F.A., Claxton, A.G. & Fannin, L.D. (2021). When and why did human brains decrease in size? A new change-point analysis and insights from brain evolution in ants. *Frontiers in Ecology and Evolution*, 9, Article 742639. https://doi.org/10.3389/fevo.2021.742639

Duñabeitia, J.A., Dimitropoulou, M., Estévez, A. & Carreiras, M. (2013). The influence of reading expertise in mirror-letter perception: Evidence from beginning and expert readers. *Mind, Brain and Education*, 7(2). https://doi.org/10.1111/mbe.12017

Ekert, J.O., Gajardo-Vidal, A., Lorca-Puls, D.L., Hope, T.M.H., Dick, F., Crinion, J.T., Green, D.W. & Price, C.J. (2021). Dissociating the functions of three left posterior superior temporal regions that contribute to speech perception and production. *Neuroimage*, 245, Article 118764. https://doi.org/10.1016/j.neuroimage.2021.118764

Fedorenko, E., Blank, I.A., Siegelman, M. & Mineroff, Z. (2020). Lack of selectivity for syntax relative to word meanings throughout the language network. *Cognition*, 203, Article 104348. https://doi.org/10.1016/j.cognition.2020.104348

Fedorenko, E. & Varley, R. (2016). Language and thought are not the same thing: Evidence from neuroimaging and neurological patients. *Annals of the New York Academy of Sciences*, 1369(1), 132–153. https://doi.org/10.1111/nyas.13046.82

Finlay, B.L. & Uchiyama, R. (2015). Developmental mechanisms channeling cortical evolution. *Trends in Neurosciences*, 38(2), 69–76. https://doi.org/10.1016/j.tins.2014.11.004

Flynn, E.G., Laland, K.N., Kendal, R.L. & Kendal, J.R. (2013). Developmental niche construction. *Developmental Science*, 16, 296–313. https://doi.org/10.1111/desc.12030

Forrester, G.S. & Rodriguez, A. (2015). Slip of the tongue: Implications for evolution and language development. *Cognition*, 141, 103–111. https://doi.org/10.1016/j.cognition.2015.04.012

Greely, H.T., Ramos, K.M. & Grady, C. (2016). Neuroethics in the age of brain projects. *Neuron*, 92(3), 637–641. https://doi.org/10.1016/j.neuron.2016.10.048

Hameroff, S. (2021). 'Orch OR' is the most complete, and most easily falsifiable theory of consciousness. *Cognitive Neuroscience*, 12(2), 74–76. https://doi.org/10.1080/17588928.2020.1839037

Hatemi, P.K., et al. (2014). Genetic influences on political ideologies: Twin analyses of 19 measures of political ideologies from five democracies and genome-wide findings from three populations. *Behaviour Genetics*, 44(3), 282–294. https://doi.org/10.1007/s10519-014-9648-8

Heldstab, S.A., Isler, K., Schuppli, C. & van Schaik, C.P. (2020). When ontogeny recapitulates phylogeny: Fixed neurodevelopmental sequence of manipulative skills among primates. *Science Advances*, 6(30), eabb4685. https://doi.org/10.1126/sciadv.abb4685

Houdé, O. & Borst, G. (2015). Evidence for an inhibitory-control theory of the reasoning brain. *Frontiers in Human Neuroscience*, 9, Article 148. https://doi.org/10.3389/fnhum.2015.00148

Howard-Jones, P.A. (2014). Evolutionary perspectives on mind, brain, and education. *Mind, Brain, and Education*, 8: 21–33. https://doi.org/10.1111/mbe.12041

Immordino-Yang, M.H. (2015). *Emotions, Learning, and the Brain: Exploring the Educational Implications of Affective Neuroscience*. W.W. Norton & Company.

Jefferies, E. & Lambon, R.M.A. (2006). Semantic impairment in stroke aphasia versus semantic dementia: A case-series comparison. *Brain*, 129(8), 2132–2147. https://doi.org/10.1093/brain/awl153

Kim, S.Y. & Kim, Y.Y. (2012). Mirror therapy for phantom limb pain. *The Korean Journal of Pain*, 25(4), 272–274. https://doi.org/10.3344/kjp.2012.25.4.272

Koch, C. (2018). What is consciousness? *Nature*, 557, S8–S12. https://doi.org/10.1038/d41586-018-05097-x

Koch, C., Massimini, M., Boly, M. & Tononi, G. (2016). Neural correlates of consciousness: Progress and problems. *Nature Reviews of Neuroscience*, 17(5), 307–321. https://doi.org/10.1038/nrn.2016.22

Kuhnke, P., Chapman, C.A., Cheung, V.K.M., Turker, S., Graessner, A., Martin, S., Williams, K.A. & Hartwigsen, G. (2023). The role of the angular gyrus in semantic cognition: A synthesis of five functional neuroimaging studies. *Brain Structure & Function*, 228(1), 273–291. https://doi.org/10.1007/s00429-022-02493-y

Kumar, V., Croxson, P.L. & Simonyan, K. (2016). Structural organization of the laryngeal motor cortical network and its implication for evolution of speech production. *Journal of Neuroscience*, 36(15), 4170–4181. https://doi.org/10.1523/JNEUROSCI.3914-15.2016

Ligneul, R. & Dreher, J-C. (2017). Social dominance representations in the human brain. In J-C. Dreher & L. Tremblay (Eds), *Decision Neuroscience: An Integrative Perspective*. Elsevier Academic Press. https://doi.org/10.1016/B978-0-12-805308-9.00017-8

Luria, A.R. (1976). *Cognitive Development: Its Cultural and Social Foundations*. Harvard University Press.

Mareschal, D. (2016). The neuroscience of conceptual learning in science and mathematics. *Current Opinion in Behavioral Sciences*, 10, 114–118. https://doi.org/10.1016/jcobeha.2016.06.001

Mashour, G.A., Roelfsema, P., Changeux, J.P. & Dehaene, S. (2020). Conscious processing and the global neuronal workspace hypothesis. *Neuron*, 105(5), 776–798. https://doi.org/10.1016/j.neuron.2020.01.026

Mazor, M., et al. (2022). The scientific study of consciousness cannot and should not be morally neutral. *Perspectives in Psychological Science*, 28. https://doi.org/10.1177/17456916221110222

Mazur, A.A. (1985). Biosocial model of status in face-to-face primate groups. *Social Forces*, 64, 377–402.

Nishimura, T., et al. (2022). Evolutionary loss of complexity in human vocal anatomy as an adaptation for speech. *Science*, 377(6607), 760–763. https://doi.org/10.1126/science.abm1574

Padilla-Coreano, N., et al. (2022). Cortical ensembles orchestrate social competition through hypothalamic outputs. *Nature*, 603, 667–671. https://doi.org/10.1038/s41586-022-04507-5

Plaut, D.C. & Kello, C T. (1999). The emergence of phonology from the interplay of speech comprehension and production: A distributed connectionist approach. In B. MacWhinney (Ed.), *The Emergence of Language*. Erlbaum.

Price, C.J. (2012). A review and synthesis of the first 20 years of PET and fMRI studies of heard speech, spoken language and reading. *Neuroimage*, 62(2), 816–847. https://doi.org/10.1016/j.neuroimage.2012.04.062

Raleigh, M.J., McGuire, M.T., Brammer, G.L. & Yuwiler, A. (1984). Social and environmental influences on blood serotonin concentrations in monkeys. *Archives of General Psychiatry*, 41, 405–410. https://doi.org/10.1001/archpsyc.1984.01790150095013

Robson, H., Zahn, R., Keidel, J.L., Binney, R.J., Sage, K. & Lambon, R.M.A. (2014). The anterior temporal lobes support residual comprehension in Wernicke's aphasia. *Brain*, 137(Pt 3), 931–943. https://doi.org/10.1093/brain/awt373

Roskies, A. (2021). Neuroethics. In *Stanford Encyclopedia of Philosophy*. Metaphysics Research Laboratory, Stanford University.

Sapolsky, R. (2017). *Behave: The Biology of Humans at Our Best and Worst*. Penguin Random House.

Saur, D., et al. (2008). Ventral and dorsal pathways for language. *Proceedings of the National Academy of Sciences USA*, 105(46), 18035–18040. https://doi.org/10.1073/pnas.0805234105

Shenefelt, M. & White, H. (2013). *If A then B: How the World Discovered Logic*. Columbia University Press.

Stevens, J.R. (2014). Evolutionary pressures on primate intertemporal choice. *Proceedings of Biological Sciences*, 281(1786), Article 20140499. https://doi.org/10.1098/rspb.2014.0499

Svoboda, E. & Richards, B. (2009). Compensating for anterograde amnesia: A new training method that capitalizes on emerging smartphone technologies. *Journal of the International Neuropsychological Society*, 15(4), 629–638. https://doi.org/10.1017/s1355617709090791

Trettenbrein, P.C., Papitto, G., Friederici, A.D. & Zaccarella, E. (2021). Functional neuroanatomy of language without speech: An ALE meta-analysis of sign language. *Human Brain Mapping*, 42(3), 699–712. https://doi.org/10.1002/hbm.25254

Wang, C. (2020). A review of the effects of abacus training on cognitive functions and neural systems in humans. *Frontiers in Neuroscience*, 14, Article 913. https://doi.org/10.3389/fnins.2020.00913

Watanabe, N. & Yamamoto, M. (2015). Neural mechanisms of social dominance. *Frontiers in Neuroscience*, 9, Article 154. https://doi.org/10.3389/fnins.2015.00154

Wemelsfelder, F. (1984). Animal boredom: Is a scientific study of the subjective experiences of animals possible? In M.W. Fox & L.D. Mickley (Eds), *Advances in Animal Welfare Science 1984/85*. The Humane Society of the United States.

Chapter 10

De Las Heras, A. (2014). Evolution of human features driving current unsustainability. In A. De Las Heras (Ed.), *Sustainability Science and Technology*. CRC Press.

Kuiper, T.R. & Parker, D.M. (2014). Elephants in Africa: Big, grey biodiversity thieves? *South African Journal of Science*, 110(3/4), Article a0058. http://dx.doi.org/10.1590/sajs.2014/a0058

Luo, J. (2018). The neural basis of and a common neural circuitry in different types of pro-social behavior. *Frontiers in Psychology*, 9, Article 859. https://doi.org/10.3389/fpsyg.2018.00859

Pascual, L., Rodrigues, P. & Gallardo-Pujol, D. (2013). How does morality work in the brain? A functional and structural perspective of moral behavior. *Frontiers in Integrative Neuroscience*, 7, Article 65. https://doi.org/10.3389/fnint.2013.00065

Piretti, L., Pappaianni, E., Lunardelli, A., Zorzenon, I., Ukmar, M., Pesavento, V., Rumiati, R.I., Job, R. & Grecucci, A. (2020). The role of amygdala in self-conscious emotions in a patient with acquired bilateral damage. *Frontiers in Neuroscience*, 14, Article 677. https://doi.org/10.3389/fnins.2020.00677

Raia, P., et al. (2020). Past extinctions of Homo species coincided with increased vulnerability to climatic change. *One Earth*, 3, 480–490. https://doi.org/10.1016/j.oneear.2020.09.007

Reader, S.M., Hager, Y. & Laland, K.N. (2011). The evolution of primate general and cultural intelligence. *Philosophical Transactions of the Royal Society of London B, Biological Sciences*, 366(1567), 1017–1027. https://doi.org/10.1098/rstb.2010.0342

Reich, D. (2019). *Who We Are and How We Got Here: Ancient DNA and the New Science of the Human Past*. Oxford University Press.

Sawe, N. (2019). Adapting neuroeconomics for environmental and energy policy. *Behavioural Public Policy*, 3(1), 17–36. https://doi.org/10.1017/bpp.2018.2

Tanaka, S.C., Yamada, K., Yoneda, H. & Ohtake, F. (2014). Neural mechanisms of gain-loss asymmetry in temporal discounting. *Journal of Neuroscience*, 34(16), 5595–5602. https://doi.org/10.1523/jneurosci.5169-12.2014

Whittle, S., Liu, K., Bastin, C., Harrison, B.J. & Davey, C.G. (2016). Neurodevelopmental correlates of proneness to guilt and shame in adolescence and early adulthood. *Developmental Cognitive Neuroscience*, 19, 51–57. https://doi.org/10.1016/j.dcn.2016.02.001

Yomogida, Y., Matsumoto, M., Aoki, R., Sugiura, A., Phillips, A.N. & Matsumoto, K. (2017). The neural basis of changing social norms through persuasion. *Science Reports*, 7, Article 16295. https://doi.org/10.1038/s41598-017-16572-2

Zhang, Y-Y., Xu, L., Rao, L-L., Zhou, L., Zhou, Y., Jiang, T., Li, S. & Z-Y Liang (2016). Gain-loss asymmetry in neural correlates of temporal discounting: An approach-avoidance motivation perspective. *Science Reports*, 6, Article 31902. https://doi.org/10.1038/srep31902

INDEX

Page numbers in *italics* refer to figures.